THE TRIVIAL ROUND -

THE COMMON TASK

By

J.R.D. Morten O.B.E.

Best wishes.

Donald Morten.

The photograph on the front was taken at Bakewell Show on August 6th. 1992 by Colin Underwood. My thanks to him for permission to use it and for the copyright.

Also my grateful thanks to Helen Mirtle, without whose persuasion and encouragement I might never have put pen to paper. Helen also corrected, prompted and typed out my handwritten script.

J.R.D.Morten.   April 1994.

Printed in Great Britain

For Church in the Market Place Publications
by
The Gilpin Press
Pottery Yard, Houghton-le-Spring, Tyne & Wear
DH4 4BA

THE TRIVIAL ROUND - THE COMMON TASK

I was born at 6 am. on Sunday morning the 19th. January 1913, at the Creamery on Green Lane in Buxton and it was snowing. Not that I knew, but mother told me. I was the eldest son of John and Sarah Morten and christened John after father and great grandfather; Richard after grandfather and Donald for myself and have been known as 'J.R.D.' ever since.

Mother and father came to live at the Creamery when they were married in 1911. Father came from the Great Rocks Farm where he was born, and which is now a big hole in the ground, quarried away by Buxton Lime Firms - afterwards I.C.I. Mother was born and lived at Pritchard Green, Combs, near Chapel-en-le-Frith. Father loved to tell us the story of going courting on horse back. He would ride one of the milk ponies from the Creamery up Manchester Road, over by Whitehall and down into Combs. He had one or two gates to open, and one night he got off to open the gate, let go of the bridle, and the pony ran back to the stable in West Road. He had to walk back!

I remember sitting between his knees as a very small boy and helping to steer the Model T Ford. Safety people would cringe today!

I started school at the Infant School on Hardwick Square, and on the second day told mother I had been once and did not rate it very highly, so I did not want to go again. I went. By this time I was the eldest of four - two boys and two girls.

We always had plenty of assorted pets. Father was very keen on poultry, amongst other things, and in the fields below Grin Woods where the ponies grazed in summer, he would have pens of Anconas, White Leghorns, Wyandottes and Rhode Island Reds, breeds of hens no longer in general use. There was a small croft behind the Creamery where over the years at different times we kept bantams, pigeons, mice, rabbits, guinea pigs, ferrets and of course always a dog and a cat. We were taught to keep them all clean, fed and watered.

Me, aged 14, with my bloodhound puppy.

I remember when, in my early teens, somebody gave me a bloodhound bitch puppy which had been badly mauled and bitten. Father let me take her to the vets, and I remember how I reared her. She grew into a beautiful dog but she was huge. I have a photograph to prove it. They made me sell her and put the money in Savings Certificates. I never thought much of these things!

At an early age I learned to do little jobs in the retailing of the milk. A customer would ring up to say they had run out of milk, and competition was so keen, with milk at 2d. or 3d. a pint they had to be attended to. I could not have been very old when I was getting up early (it has never been a problem for me) and taking milk to a customer on Green Lane, walking across Temple Fields to the far end of White Knowle Road and then across to Kents Bank Road to oblige another customer with early morning milk. The milk was delivered in small cans before bottles became popular.

We never had enough milk at our farm to supply all our customers, so from as far back as I can remember we took the milk from four other local farms. Three of them were good reliable suppliers, but the fourth was a bit slip shod, and I remember father was always grumbling about him. I shall never forget father sending me on my bike, on a very wet day, because the milk that farmer had brought in the morning was going sour. I was to tell him not to send his milk if it was no better. When I arrived at the farm, the yard was on a slope, and out of one of the buildings on the top side, corn was being washed under the door, and ducks, geese, hens and turkeys were all feasting on it. The farmer came to me and invited me into the house which was on the lower side of the yard, down two steps into a big kitchen. On the opposite side to the door was a big dresser and on the top stood a big stag turkey. Mr. S-took off his bowler hat, which he always wore, and hit the turkey, shouting at it, and it flew towards the door. I have forgotten if it knocked me over, but I remember being very frightened. I believe ones earliest memories are fear, and I have never forgotten that occasion.

*   *   *

My education proceeded from Hardwick Square to Kents Bank and then at eleven years old with a scholarship to the College. I was

Me at the top of Losehill. Castleton.

never very good at school. There were too many other interests, and I joined them all:- choir, orchestra (I learned to play the clarinet), Boy Scouts (I became a Patrol Leader) debating society, field club and all the time looking after pets, and doing other jobs - helping at the dairy and at the farm. I was not very good at sport, except for table tennis, which I enjoyed and was fairly good at, and of course I could play after dark either at London Road School, where we had quite a good club, or at the Y.M.I. club on the Market Place. I still enjoyed a game when I was over 70.

When I became a prefect at College one of the duties was to speak to the assembled school for five minutes. Notes were allowed on one side of a postcard. The headmaster stood beside you and took any more than that away saying, "I know you can read, I want to hear you speak." This has stood me in good stead over the years.

4

In my early teens holidays were spent at home, because these were the depression years of the 1920s. But I know that on several occasions I was allowed to stay with my grandparents in Combs. I used to go on my bicycle round by Dove Holes and Chapel-en-le-Frith. Roads must have been safer then from traffic and hoodlums. I still have a postcard written to mother saying that I had arrived safely and that I got off the bike at Barmoor Clough to make sure my 6d. spending money was safe! I was ten years old at the time.

Another of the pleasures of holiday times was to go with father on his business trips in the car. The earliest one I remember was a Model T Ford. It was black with a canvas hood. There were two foot pedals, one was low gear, the other the brake. The accelerator was on the steering column, and the hand brake had three positions, full off was top gear, half off was neutral, and full on was stationary brake. It was started by swinging the handle. On most Wednesdays father went to Leek market to buy eggs to sell in the shop. If we were short of milk he would go to the cattle market to buy milk cows. These would either be driven, or more often, would come by rail to either Buxton or Hindlow station and be walked down to Cowdale.

*   *   *

We always had a lot of horses. Five milk ponies delivered milk round Buxton every day, another fetched the milk from the farms to the dairy on Green Lane, and usually there were four or five Shire horses to do the farm work. One of these went to work every day in Cowdale quarry, pulling the wagons. This meant that father, who was a good horseman, was often on the look out for replacements. Occasionally he would go to the horse auction at Stockport and it was a great thrill when we were lads to go with him. He used to talk about Ali Baba and the forty horsemen, and from memory they were a rough

Milk round ponies lined up outside the creamery on Green Lane.

lot. I remember standing by the ring side on one occasion watching the auctioneer, when he suddenly said, "Gentlemen, the boys are here, watch your pockets and valuables," and then pointing at men round the ringside ordered them off the premises. One he ordered out was standing near us and I remember being a bit frightened. On the other hand father had some good contacts and was pleased with the horses that he bought there.

*   *   *

Meanwhile my education dragged on. I don't think I had any inclination to do anything except farm, but mother insisted I should stay and take my School Certificate, which I did. I think I had about four passes and I still have the certificate to prove it!

On my fifteenth birthday in 1928 I was given a driving licence as a birthday present. By this time we had a Ford van, so the pony who collected milk morning and evening was made redundant and I began to go to the farm for morning milking and bring the milk to the dairy before breakfast and school.

Roads were still not very grand even in Buxton. Many side roads were still limestone and rutted. I can remember roads like Compton and Spencer Roads being nothing more than rutted lanes. Only the main roads were beginning to be asphalted. On wet days the milk delivery ponies would return to the dairy plastered up their legs with mud and limestone dust. They were all washed down with warm water before returning to the stables in West Road.

*   *   *

One of the extra duties the ponies had to do on Sundays was to take the preachers to the country Chapels at Chelmorten, Flagg and Monyash. We had a small light 'gig' which set off from the front of London Road Methodist Chapel with the men who were 'planned'. Mostly one of them could drive, and the gig would proceed as far as Monyash, where the pony would be stabled until after the evening service, when it would bring them back. Either father or one of the men would then meet it at Buxton and take it back to the stable.

One of the local preachers used to go on his bicycle to take services in the country. He told me the story (which he said was true) of going one winter day to Monyash to take the afternoon and evening service. During the afternoon it started to snow, and it was still snowing at the end of the evening service. Returning to Buxton would have been foolhardy if not impossible, so a local farmer offered him a night's lodging. When it came to bedtime the old man took him to the bedroom where there was a four-poster, and he thought he was in clover. Soon after the bedroom door opened and the old farmer got into the bed, complete with night-gown and night-cap. He still thought he was in clover, until the old man said, "Thou will have to thrutch up, lad, there's the missis yet."

* * *

Roundsmen stayed with us very well, some till they retired, and at least two until they died. It was quite a pleasant job starting at 6.30 am., and by the time booking and cashing up was done it was dinner time. Afternoons had to be spent cleaning the harness and floats, and each man had to look after his own pony. It was well into the 1950s before the ponies were replaced with motors. They were never as good, because they did not know where to stop like the pony did, and, believe it or not, on a wet day you got far wetter jumping in and out of a van than standing on a milk float.

I left school in July 1929 and was absorbed into the dairy staff. We had a good bailiff at the farm who was very capable of the day to day running of the farm. It was the dairy side of the business which was most profitable, and it was growing fast. Not only could we not keep it supplied with enough milk, but we had to supplement the fresh cream, eggs and butter from outside sources. Father began to suffer from back troubles probably caused by working in the steamy atmosphere from the washing up, the pasteuriser and the cream separator.

The dairy at the Creamery, Green Lane, at the early part of the century, before I remember it. On the left the electric motor which drove the shafting. Note the belts with no protective guards. In the centre the cream separator, which I do remember, cream spout on the left, skimmed milk on the right. On the right the pasteuriser, whch functioned for many years and heated the milk to the required temperature before being pumped across to the separator.

John Morten with Chatburn Wellington

When I was in my late teens father was attacked and injured by a bull. I was not there at the time it happened. They were moving the bull, a very good pedigree Shorthorn called Chatburn Wellington, from one side of the farmyard to a loose box, when he suddenly turned round and knocked father on to the floor. Luckily the men heard him shout and drove the bull into his box. Father received some injuries to his thigh, but luckily they were not serious. But the incident did unnerve him.

I was taught how to run a busy dairy, and do all the jobs connected with it, from doing a milk round when any of the men were absent, to all the dairy work, handling the milk, separating it into cream and bottling the milk. It has to be said that the first bottling machine was very crude.

*   *   *

On Mondays father went to Bakewell market to do the buying and selling of the farm stock and we still do this.

Prices in the late 1920s are very interesting. Fat lambs averaged £2 each, calves about £1.15 shillings (1 shilling = 5p.), eggs varied from one shilling to two shillings a dozen, store ewes bought from the Craven Arms cost forty shillings each. Fat pigs were about twelve shillings a score and we were supplying them to Nelson's at Bakewell as early as 1933. Milk cows were bought for under £20 and cull cows were sold from £10 - £14 each. But a good working Shire horse could cost £50 and a milk pony £30.

On Wednesdays father went to Leek market, where there was an egg and butter market. In holiday times, before leaving school, I went with him, and knew the procedure of egg buying and who to buy from. After a year or two I began to go myself. This developed after a time into an egg round. One of the farmers we regularly bought from lived at Sheen and another at Hollinsclough, so I went to Leek first then came back via Sheen, Hollinsclough and Glutton Bridge. The farmer at Glutton Bridge was a great character, and occasionally would give me a couple of trout which had been 'tickled' out of the River Dove which ran through his ground.

Barson's charabanc outside the Sun Inn on High Street. The driver was 'Tidza Jim', and I think the cock horse boy was Frank Webster. The grey mare was 'Shamrock' borrowed for the afternoon and belonging to John Morten. Taken around 1910.

In January 1931 we started to supply the Buxton schools with 1d. bottles of milk. These were one third of a pint bottles and had cardboard caps, with a perforated centre, through which a straw could be pushed. We also supplied the straws. On that first day we sold 720, the novelty did not wear off, and the numbers grew. The following year my brother Maurice started a country round. He supplied Taddington, Ashford, Longstone and Bakewell schools. Maurice was always a fast driver. On one occasion he was going down Taddington Dale in the van, (I think it was a Singer) when a back wheel came off, and the first he knew about it was when he saw the wheel passing his window. On another occasion, this time on a winter's day when the roads were very icy, he went down into Great Longstone too fast and finished up on the village cross in the middle of the Green. One of his pals had asked for a lift to Bakewell, but he never went with Maurice again.

We now had to organise staff in the afternoon to wash bottles and we had a bottle washing machine as well as a bottling machine.

Though we now had two motor vans collecting and delivering, the horses and ponies were still the main means of transport. There were four men with four ponies who did milk rounds 365 days a year in Buxton. I should like to mention three horses in particular. The first was a grey mare and she was before my time. Father thought the world of 'Shamrock'. She took him in the trap from Buxton to be married at Chapel-en-le-Frith and then took mother and father to the reception. In those days, around 1910, there were horse charabancs in Buxton and it was not unusual for the owners to come to borrow a horse for the afternoon trips. I still have a photograph taken outside the Sun Inn of a charabanc belonging to Barsons and one of the lead horses is Shamrock.

The second horse was a bright bay mare called 'Kitty'. She did a milk round day after day for many years, always driven by Tom Edge,

'Lady Andrew' driven by Mr. George Daybell at the Royal Richmond Show. Thank goodness this lovely animal was not condemned to a milk float.

who was a good horseman who worshipped the mare. She was a part bred Hackney and was very showy. Tom took her to several local shows and won a lot of prizes with her. Her only fault was that she was bad tempered. She would kick and bite if the mood took her, but she would never hurt Tom.

The third pony was a thoroughbred Hackney purchased by father on one of his trips to the horse auction at Crewe. Maurice and Philip broke her into harness. (They were better horsemen than me, and father always said Philip was better than Maurice because he was quieter and kinder.) The mare never settled to steady work. She was far too highly strung and could not be trusted with only one man on a milk round. Father sold her to Mr. G. Daybell of Ashford, who bought her on behalf of the Duchess of Devonshire. They christened her 'Lady Andrew' and trained her properly. She won prizes all over the country and became Champion Hackney from very small beginnings.

At the farm the Shire horses were purchased as young ones about two or three years old, they were then broken in and taught to work in shafts. They were kept for about two years and then sold with a 'guarantee'. One of the horse buyers who was a regular was called 'Muggleston'. I can see him now, brown polished leggings and boots and a loud checked waistcoat and jacket. He bought for Liverpool Corporation and Docks. We always kept one or two older horses to do the steady work, as anything could happen with young horses - and occasionally did. I must emphasise that Maurice and Philip were the horsemen and not me.

*   *   *

During the 1930s the dairy business was growing fast, and we were trying to increase the farm production to keep pace. In addition the three of us were now young men and beginning to look around. The opportunity to expand came in 1935 when father purchased the Green Farm, King Sterndale. This included some land which we were already farming - the Park and the Dog Tor field, and the next two meadows. Most of the remainder of the Green Farm was a wilderness. No stock had been on the Cumberland Fields for five years. Although the land is actually called Cumberland Fields, it was such a wilderness, having completely reverted to heath land that we started to call it Abysinnia, after the country which is now Ethiopia, and which at that time was troubled with tribal and internal warfare, and was depicted in the papers as a barren and inhospitable land. One field was still in ridge and furrow.

Father bought a Bedford two ton truck, and we set about carting and spreading lime and pressed sewage sludge on to the ground. Some fields we ploughed and re-seeded, some we harrowed with a pitch pale harrow. It took several years to get it productive. We engaged a bailiff to live in the house at King Sterndale and we took surplus stock from Cowdale. Here is a list of stock on Cowdale on December 30th. 1935, copied from an old diary and before we moved any to King Sterndale:- 97 cattle, 53 ewes, 25 pigs, 6 horses (3 heavy, 3 light), 14 ducks, 130 hens, 2 dogs, 9 cats and one Irishman. He worked for us for several years until he thought there was going to be a war, then he disappeared.

The chance to expand still further did not come until 1940 when Mr. J. Wardle decided to retire and offered us the chance to purchase Highcliffe Farm. This meant that all the land from Staden to Deepdale belonged to us. Father and we three sons were now working flat out, running three farms and an expanding dairy business in Buxton. We had men working for us, though by the late thirties the bailiff had left Cowdale and the house was empty. It became more and more difficult to keep men at the dairy. In addition Maurice and I were beginning to notice that there were girls about.

Two little stories come to mind about this. After tea every night the two of us went into the dairy to bottle the night's milk ready for an early start in the morning. On one occasion I was taking a young lady to a concert and we were late. Father was helping us, and Maurice walked into the dairy, looked at me without seeing father and said in a loud voice, "Aren't you gone yet? B——- off!" Father was conveniently deaf. He never swore himself and did not approve.

On another occasion we had both been to the Pavilion Gardens to a dance. I went home when it was over but I knew Maurice had taken a girl home. When I got in mother was still up. I said I did not know where Maurice was, but when he came in I heard her ask him where he had been and he said that he had been up Fairfield with a girl but he was not going again as it was too far. Mother was flabbergasted. He did go farther though, eventually he went to Peak Forest. Agnes Hadfield lived at Smalldale, Peak Forest, and she and Maurice were married in 1945.

*　　*　　*

In 1939 war broke out and I was wanting to settle down at Cowdale. The house was in much need of renovation and builders were getting very scarce. However by 1940 work of this kind had also become very scarce. The house still had stone flagged floors. The sink in the kitchen was a stone gritstone trough, so worn that the lip edges had nearly disappeared. Cold water came from the pond at the side of the house and hot water from a side boiler to the fire in the living room. There was still the stone cheese press in the kitchen and this can still be seen outside the back door. There were three fireplaces in the kitchen. To the left was a copper to boil clothes, to the right a 'bakestone' on which oatcakes etc. could be made and in the middle was a huge iron open fireplace. There were no cupboards but all along one wall was a pot rack.

In the middle room there was another huge iron fireplace with an oven at one side and on the other a side boiler which ran through the wall so that hot water could be drawn in the kitchen. There was a spit and a hook in the middle of the fire on which to hang a kettle. On the floor just in front of the fire was a grid with a hole underneath, on to which you raked the ashes and threw the unburned ones back on the fire. Once a week a wheelbarrow was brought in and the pit emptied. The front room had an earth floor and was used to store harness etc. The ground floor rooms all had wooden shutters to the windows, and those in the middle room are still intact. The larder was used as a dairy at an earlier date. It still has the flagged floor, stone benches, a salting trough and a 'still' trough.

Our wedding day 12th. September 1940.

In 1940 we employed Fred Alcock, a local builder and handyman, who installed a bathroom, replaced the middle fireplace with a modern one, the front room fireplace with a modern lounge fire, and concreted the floors in both the middle room and the front room.

*   *   *

On September 12th. 1940, Kathleen Helen Thompson and I were married at London Road Methodist Church by Rev. R.W. Callin. In my diary of that date all it says is, "Morag calved a bull calf." I

18

don't know whether my priorities were at fault or not! Kathleen came to Buxton from Stockport with her parents in 1935. Mr. Thompson was a civil engineer and came to work for Ryan and Somerville Quarries at Hindlow. He was a great help to us, making cupboards and doing repairs to the house. He was great at D.I.Y. which put me to shame.

* * *

The war years are best forgotten. Sometimes I was on my own, with help from Philip and quarrymen. One or two would come and do an hour or so before they went to work and at week-ends. Then we had that dreadful double summer time. We always started work at 6 am., winter and summer, so that when the clocks were moved two hours forward in summer it meant we were actually starting at 4 am. Nights were light and labour scarce so we were managing on four or five hours sleep at night In addition the war time summers were non-starters. We had land girls during the early war years, who were not very successful I am afraid, except for one, and she did not stay very long. Then at the end of the war we had two German P.O.W. and they were much better. One of them was a peasant farmer from Bohemia, the other came from Hamburg and, though a bit queer tempered, was a good worker.

Our transport was a Ford Popular which cost me £18. It ran on a mixture of petrol and paraffin, but even then we could use it very little. Kathleen used to walk to Buxton for shopping once a week. Richard arrived in 1941 and Stephen in 1943, and she used to load them in the pram and leave them at her mother's on Dale Road, do her shopping and then walk back. Kathleen walked back down Ashwood Dale, and she used to say Richard would always fall asleep in the pram at the bottom of Cowdale Hollow, so she had to push them both back up that very steep hill. A young lad out of the village used to go down the hollow and give her a pull up.

Opposite the back door at the farm was an old building which we used to call the wash house. At one end was the outside earth closet, a two seater, and very draughty it was! The wash house had a big copper boiler at one end and we kept wood for burning at the other end. There was a beam across the building with pulley blocks on it for pig killing, and a trestle bench for scalding. The building has now been pulled down but it stood on part of the site where the garage is now.

In 1946 I cracked up and had to go into hospital for an operation and then to Christie's for three weeks treatment. I am one of the lucky people and have never had a recurrence of the trouble.

1947 remains in my memory as the worst winter I have experienced. It snowed and blew a gale for weeks. The car never left the garage for nine weeks. The Germans made a sledge and took the milk on it down the hollow, where Philip met them at the bottom with a truck. They fixed the sledge with a brake because it over ran the horse going down the hollow. Gangs of P.O.W. came and dug the road out, and each time they did it the wind filled it again. It was April before we were able to get about again. The summer was very late and, contrary to the weather wise people, it was not good after a bad winter.

Although we lived fairly well through the war and after, the little extras were absent. Kathleen's father kept the boys in home made toys. He could conjure up toy wheelbarrows, cars and even miniature arm chairs out of bits of scrap wood. When they started school they caught the bus at the bottom of the hollow until they were big enough to have bikes.

It was about this time that I began to take an interest in the politics of farming. I began to attend N.F.U. meetings and advisory meetings on agriculture organised by the 'War Ag.' Department. I was never a silent member of any organisation and so it was not very long before

I was made chairman of the local N.F.U. branch, and started to attend the county committees.

*   *   *

Meanwhile on the farm I continued father's policy of breeding better cows. The aim was to have a pedigree herd of high milk producing Shorthorns. Grandfather had started this and one of father's cows won a cup in the early 1920s for the highest yield in Derbyshire. I believe she gave 1500 gallons (just under 7000 litres) in the year. Derbyshire Y.F.C. still have the cup she won and we have a photograph of her. Father had always purchased pedigree Shorthorn bulls and he became keen to purchase a few pedigree cows, so we made several trips to the sales at Penrith. Gradually the herd improved and it is interesting that one of the families of cows can be traced back to

John Morten and R.B. Morten with Red Rose. I think she won a milk record cup.

grandfather's time. Although the herd never became fully pedigree and the economies of milk production made us change to black and whites, the foundation animals were Shorthorns and the herd was no worse for this. The change over did not take place until the 1970s and we had blue cows for generations as a result of crossing the Shorthorn cows with Friesian bulls.

*   *   *

In 1953 I became chairman of the County N.F.U., and the following year was appointed to the executive committee of the Ministry of Agriculture at Derby. This was the old 'War Ag.' which was now not only enforcing restrictions still in existence from war time, such as food restrictions (cattle as well as humans) but petrol rationing and the price fixing on cattle, sheep and pigs. I found it very rewarding work, and within a year or two was made chairman of its milk committee. At this time many of the herds were still not tubercular free, testing for brucellosis had not started and milk was still being produced under conditions which I shall certainly not describe. It became my job as chairman to visit problem farms with the ministry milk officers to persuade, and occasionally to order farmers to make improvements in hygiene and conditions of milk production, or to find some alternative means of farming. I can honestly say I never fell out with anybody. Our own herd had been tubercular free since 1935, and had been machine milked since 1929.

The Agricultural Executive Committee was a government appointed body, responsible for the agriculture and administration of the county to the Minister of Agriculture. The main A.E.C. was now, through its officials, taking on a much more advisory role as well as dealing with all regulations and subsidies. One of the things we did was to stage advisory exhibitions at the two shows in the county - Derby and

Bakewell. Although I had been to Bakewell Show with father nearly every year I can remember, the earliest mention I can find in a diary is 1927. I began to take an interest in the show management and I still do this.

I was chairman of Derby's N.F.U. in 1953 and 1954, and was then appointed to represent the county on the main council in London. I did this for ten years but was never very happy in the job. It entailed a lot of running about, not only to London (which I was always glad to see the back of) but reporting back to different committees in the county. I had to travel by train from Miller's Dale Station, and never left the farm until the last minute. Kathleen would drive me to Miller's Dale whilst I got dressed in the car. I have been known to shave on the train! Many a time the station porter would hold up the train if he saw the car coming down the road. I always went by the 6.30 pm. on a Monday night. On one occasion when I arrived at the station he told me that my train had been cancelled and the only other train was an express which did not stop at Miller's Dale. He persuaded the signal man to put the signals against it, and though the train did not actually stop, I managed to jump aboard. Normally it took five station people to put me on that train and many a time I was the only person to get on.

By the mid 1950s we were all finding the dairy in Buxton too much. The daily through-put was nearly 700 gallons and though we now had a good dairy man, one of us went everyday. Maurice married Agnes Hadfield in 1945 and farmed the King Sterndale farm, while Philip married Molly Andrews in 1947 and moved into Highcliffe. Father's health was not very good. I had now developed my other interests as well as the farm so we decided to sell the dairy business. It continued to trade as Morten's Dairy for many years and our milk still went there. But it was a relief not to have the additional work load.

*   *   *

I think before I go any farther I should recall the town of Buxton as I knew it as a boy. The changes in the twentieth century are incredible. As I have said before the roads were very rough. All side roads were still stone tracks, and men were employed to fill in the ruts with small stones which, by the way, were broken down by men with hammers. In the lay-by down Ashwood Dale, a few hundred yards past Lovers Leap, was a stone-breaker's hut where loads of stone were brought which were broken up to repair the road. For many years this was done by a man called John Swan, always known as Stallion Jack. There were three Shire stud farms in the vicinity, one at Pictor Hall, one at Hargate Hall and one at the Orient Lodge. There was a Peak Shire Horse Society which would hire a stallion for the three month breeding season, March to May. A man was hired to walk the stallion round from farm to farm each week during the three months. He had a fixed itinerary and the man I remember was 'Stallion Jack'. It was not an easy job, some stallions are not the friendliest of creatures, but John Swan was a very fit man and he always took a pride in his job.

I remember High Street from the Swan Hotel to the Market Place being quite a narrow road, with a row of trees on the left hand side, and grass between the trees and the shops. Similarly on the Market Place between Scarsdale Place and the road there was grass, and a horse trough where the turning for Market Street leaves the main road. At the bottom of Terrace Road on the left hand side was the cab rank, and just off the road on the slopes was the shelter for the cabbies. Terrace Road up to the early part of the century was called Yeomans Lane, and my grandfather always called it 'Yeomans Lane'.

In the middle of the space at the bottom of Terrace Road was Turner's Memorial, until a bus demolished it. Just round the corner on the left was where the bath chair men lined up. In summer on the other side, by the Thermal Baths, were the horse drawn charabancs waiting to do their afternoon trips. There were very few motors indeed, and all food shops had their ponies and floats to deliver their goods. There were stables all over the town, and I remember those on Byron Street, Market Street, Heath Street and Torr Street. Our own stables were at the back of West Road. The council stables were in the corporation yard, and the railway had stables on Bridge Street. There were more stables at the back of Spring Gardens. There are still one or two archways between the shops and scrapes on the sides where drivers have hit the walls with their vehicles. There were blacksmiths on Church Street, South Avenue and Fairfield.

On May 1st. there was a parade of horses on the Market Place, with prizes for the best turned out horses. Corporation and railway horses always turned out but anyone could enter providing the horse was working in the town.

The river ran open behind Spring Gardens on the other side, and still does of course, but at the bottom end it crossed under the road from Bridge Street to Spring Gardens' end of Sylvan Park and then ran open until it crossed under the road into Ashwood Park. There was a band stand in Ashwood Park where any band could play, and I remember there was nearly always one at week-ends. Street musicians were common, and I remember we had a regular who came to the corner of Compton Road and played 'The Last Rose of Summer'. Father said that was the only tune he knew, but he always sent us with a copper or two for him.

I can just remember the Town Crier with his bell standing in the middle of the cross roads at the bottom of High Street.

What was the coal yard on Hardwick Square had previously been Higher Buxton Station. The Ashbourne trains stopped there and a lot of quarry staff used them to go to all the quarries as far as Alsop. I often stand and wonder at the cost of building the viaduct from Bridge Street to Sylvan Cliff, then the cutting through solid rock to Higher Buxton, and the bridge over Dale Road, and last but not least the huge, long viaduct over Dukes Drive.

Higher Buxton Station also had a cattle dock and we had to drive any cattle or sheep that father had purchased from there to Cowdale.

Also in the station yard was a big cattle feed storage building, where firms like Bibbys, Silcocks, Lever Brothers and many others would have stocks of feed which farmers could draw on as needed, or the railway company could deliver. Some of the feed came in two hundredweight sacks, and one and a half hundredweight was common. No wonder farmers were bow legged and suffered with bad backs!

On Spring Gardens opposite the Royal Exchange building - and by the way this was originally called Winster Place as can still be seen in the stone work at the end of the building - was the big fish and fruit shop of Sydney Oram. This later became MacFisheries. The front was double sided, and on each side was a big flat tiled slab, open to the footpath and covered with fish. I can remember the live lobsters crawling about on them. There was a similar shop on the Market Place, where the chemist is now, belonging to Simpsons, and next to it was Billy Bills the butcher, and on the other side Holme and Ash who sold everything in the hardware line, from a kettle to farm machinery.

One other old building which has recently disappeared was where the new cottages are at the corner of London Road and Heath Grove. Through the archway from London Road into the yard was the wheelwright. He was called Jim Beswick, and he sang and whistled all day. I have never heard such a loud voice as he had. On one side of the yard were the joiners shops where he made the wheels. He did it with all the old fashioned tools. As far as I can remember there was no machinery. On the right hand side of the yard was a building with a big blacksmith's hearth, where he heated the iron rims for the wheels until they were nearly red hot. It was a pleasure to watch a real craftsman at work and all the time he sang or whistled and drank. I think he must have been a good customer at the pub just below, which was called the Blazing Rag, and it was a standing joke that none of the tradesmen's ponies would pass the 'Rag' without stopping.

I can just remember the horse drawn fire engine which was stationed on Market Street just below the corporation yard. They did not have their own horses, I believe there were hired horses on standby. I can just remember going on my bike to watch a fire at the top of Temple Road.

The cattle market was held on Saturdays, and there were special 'Fair' days throughout the year. Neither the cattle market at Buxton nor the one at Chapel-en-le-Frith, which was on Thursdays, have survived. I still have some old photographs of father and grandfather at Buxton cattle market.

Buxton Cattle Market.
Father, with hands on hips, in the centre of the photograph.

I only know of one farm building in the town itself which still survives. This is the newspaper shop at the top of Terrace Road. It must be one of the oldest buildings in the town, and, if you look up at the side, you can still see the round holes for pitching the hay into the loft. There was a small field until fairly recently where Otter Controls new factory is built.

On the left of the passage way leading to the Slopes, to the right of the Town Hall, in fact in part of the Town Hall building, was 'Daddy' Rain's bath chair and bicycle repair shop. There were three saddlers in the town, one on High Street (who rejoiced in the name of Handley Ashworth), one on Spring Gardens, and one at the top of Fairfield Road. There were several farms at the top of Fairfield but only one, 'Hawthorn Farm', still remains in the same family, though not now a farm.

*   *   *

In the mid 1950s I was looking for ways of increasing the output of the farm. We could only milk 52 cows, with two shippens for six at the top of the yard, and 40 in the big building. I was fond of poultry and pigs as well as the cows, and decided to increase both. The stable building was not now used for horses, so we altered this to make fattening pens, as well as part of the crew yard buildings. 'Crew yard' was the old name for the cattle or stock yard. I found a farmer at Whaley Bridge who could supply a steady flow of weaners, and set about finding regular butcher customers who would take fat pigs every week. On the poultry side I got in touch with a hatchery at Prestbury, who were looking for supplies of hatching eggs. They supplied the breeding stock, we put up the sheds and bought the feed and they purchased the eggs. It worked for many years and was quite a good source of extra income.

Richard was now getting close to leaving school and had no doubts about wanting to come into farming. I would have liked him to go to Agricultural College but he was not at all keen. I thought it would be a good idea to gain new ideas instead of getting into a rut at home. In the end he went for twelve months to a progressive dairy farm at Alderly. I missed him very much, but he came back with different ideas and telling me what should be done. Over the years we have argued, but never fallen out.

On 11th. March 1959 father died. He had not had very good health for several years. He was always very popular in the town, generous and friendly, and had worked hard and successfully all his life. The church was packed for his funeral service. I think he would have been amazed at the number of people from all walks of life who were there, because he was so unassuming.

Stephen left school in 1960 and did as Richard had done. He went to work on a dairy farm at Siddington near Holmes Chapel. In June 1961 he had an accident on his bike, skidded on some loose gravel and had bad gravel rash on his arm. They took him to the hospital where it was treated. They gave him an anti-tetanus injection, to which he was allergic and we lost him. Kathleen and I were shattered. It was a long time before we recovered from the shock.

*   *   *

The 1960s saw a lot of changes at Cowdale. Richard was not keen on poultry, and when the hatchery at Prestbury closed down, we went out of poultry. We were both keen on increasing cow numbers, but were tied to a maximum of 52 as that was as many as we could accommodate. Eventually we decided to build a completely new outfit, with silage pit, cubicle shed, collecting yard and herring bone milking parlour. We also started to breed black and white cows from the Shorthorns.

My son Richard and I talking to Stuart Percy, the British Oil and Cake Mills Advisory Officer.

In October 1963 Richard was married to Mary Elliott, the daughter of our very good friends Arthur and Eva Elliott of Hope. They moved into Dale View, the cottage at the farm gate.

By the mid 1960s I had been representing Derbyshire on the main N.F.U. Council in London for ten years and I had had enough. I always did my best, but never thought I fitted in with the big barley barons from the east, or the large dairy men from the south and west. I was still the chairman of the Ministry Advisory and Executive Committee in the county and retained the position until it was disbanded.

There were two very enjoyable spin-offs from this. On one occasion Kathleen and I were invited to a garden party at Buckingham Palace. It was a lovely day and it was nice to mix with the 'nobs'. The food was not very satisfying. I think we probably went for fish and chips afterwards but I cannot remember for sure.

The second occasion was in the Palace itself. I was awarded the O.B.E. for services rendered, and it was a truly memorable occasion. Kathleen and Mary went with me. We went through the main entrance and up the marble staircase flanked by pike men in ceremonial costume and then Kathleen and Mary went into the ceremonial hall, with the minstrel gallery at one end, where the band was playing. At the other end was the raised platform with officials and guards waiting for Her Majesty to enter. She pinned the medal on my jacket, we talked briefly and it was all over. Kathleen bought me a miniature to wear on special occasions, but we had burglars in November 1982, whilst we were out at a show dinner and they took the lot. I have still got the signed citation, but that is all. Kathleen wanted to buy me a replacement but I said, "No. The Queen gave me the medal and neither money nor a new medal would replace it." We both have treasured memories of the day. It certainly was a highlight.

I must say a little about Methodism. The family have been Methodists for generations. Great grandfather Morten and grandfather were local preachers, but neither father nor I, nor any of my brothers ever aspired to the idea. We were brought up in a strict Methodist household, church twice on a Sunday, no swearing at home and strictly teetotal. I am afraid I have strayed a bit from these ideals, though I am still very temperate on all counts. I was a Society Steward at London Road Church when quite young, and became a Steward of the Buxton Circuit, following in the footsteps of father, grandfather and great grandfather.

I am a non-conformist at heart, and all the gimmicks and ritual of the established church leave me cold, and in fact irritate me. I love to sing those old traditional hymns and listen to the readings and a sermon (if it's not good I find my mind wandering). But most of all I like the quiet, the still small voice of calm. I think I could have been a Quaker. I have taken part in all church activities, including taking part in the service itself. I was sitting next to grandfather in church one Sunday as a boy, when the preacher said something he did not agree with. In a loud voice he said, "Nowt of the sort." I have never done that, although sometimes I have felt like objecting. There is a lesson in that event; grandfather was involved in the service. All churches need a leader. Not for me someone on a pedestal clothed in gorgeous robes and with a crown and mitre, but someone on my own level, whom I can meet man to man. The church should not be aloof, but should be so attractive that everybody wants to take part and enjoy and learn of the wonders, seen and unseen.

*   *   *

Once the cows moved into the yard and parlour we had to decide what to do with the old buildings. I had always been fond of pigs as well as cows and Richard was keen to start breeding our own. We altered the main building into a breeding section for the sows. Ten crates in each shippen, plus three spare crates in the small shippen across the yard. The idea was to farrow five sows each week and wean at three weeks old. New sheds were built to house the boars and a separate one for dry sows. We also purchased an expensive, but efficient, fattening shed which housed the little pigs at three weeks old in heated rooms and carried them on to finished pork and bacon pigs. I think now with hind sight this building was too capital intensive and was expensive to run with electric heaters and fans, though easy to manage in terms of labour.

*   *   *

In 1968 mother died after a long and painful illness. She was a marvellous woman. She had looked after the business side of the dairy, as well as raising six children and taking part in outside activities, mainly connected with the church. She was a good singer and played the piano well. She was something of a martinet, but with six children, four of them boys, I do not think this was a bad thing, even if we did not live up to all her high principles and strict morals. She had a very dominant personality, loved her church and took a leading role in many of its activities. I am sure some of her has rubbed off on all of us, and we must be better people because of it.

In 1971 Richard and Mary had a little girl Helen Jayne, and we became proud grandparents. Their second daughter Patricia Mary was born in 1975.

*   *   *

33

One of my outside interests which I have mentioned briefly is Bakewell Show, although I have never been an exhibitor and am not a showman in that sense. Grandfather and father were always interested and as far as I remember usually went. The earliest memory I have was going with father and I think the show was then on the recreation ground. The first time I took part was when I was connected with the Ministry of Agriculture. We put on quite a large advisory stand at the end of the war when farmers and food were badly needed. Quantity came first, quality followed later. Artificial insemination was in its infancy, tuberculin testing of cattle was being encouraged, contagious abortion elimination was only being thought about, hybrid pigs and poultry were still a pipe dream for the future. Milk hygiene was in the front line and a large proportion of cows were still hand milked.

It was about this time I first came into contact with Mr. L.M. Waud, who was for many years the Ministry Advisory Officer for North Derbyshire. He was a farmer's man, friendly and knowledgeable, and he persuaded and encouraged farmers to change their habits and methods and improve production. He always talked as a farmer's son and from personal knowledge. He was a good bass singer and very much sought after as a speaker at all sorts of occasions. He used to boast that he had been on every farm in north Derbyshire and in most of the fields.

It wasn't long after I became involved in the Show that I was invited early in the 1960s on to the Show committee and then to be a steward on the Dairy Shorthorn section of the cattle. When Mr. Eddie Caudwell retired as chief cattle steward in the early 1970s I was asked to take his place as Chief Livestock Steward (cattle, sheep and goats) and I still retain this post in 1993 with a lot of assistance on Show days from some very good helpers. I should have said that between Mr. Caudwell finishing and me taking over, my very good friend Arthur Elliott was Chief Steward. Unfortunately he was not very well although he did it in 1977 when I was Show President. I am glad to say he was Show President himself in 1979

As I have just said, I was Show President in 1977, the first year it became a full two day show. We had two marvellous days. The weather was kind to us, not as hot as 1976 and certainly not as hot as 1991, when we had to let some of the cattle and sheep go home suffering from sunburn.

*   *   *

On the subject of weather, when I think over my lifetime, I have seen extreme seasons of all kinds, from hot to cold and wet, and certainly in 1947 the winter of the most extreme falls of snow. It had been cold all through the January then towards the end it started to snow. It lasted weeks and it was April before we became mobile again. The winter of 1963 was notable for the extreme cold. Again it started towards the end of January and although there was a fair depth of snow, it was the intense cold which was dominant. I have notes in my diary of the temperature hovering round nought degrees Fahrenheit for several weeks. The lowest seems to have been minus eight degrees Fahrenheit on the 8th. February. It froze the rising main up the yard and to the house, and we had to run a moveable pipe from the village water tank to our tanks for several days. Luckily we managed to keep the cows' and pigs' supply running.

The 1969 winter was not very pleasant either, not so much because of snow and frost (though there were several heavy falls in February and March), but because it continued to be very cold and wet through April and May. The cows did not go out until May 18th. and the note in my diary says it was still cold and wet and the cows were very unsettled.

Cowdale in the snow.

Another freak year was 1975 when it snowed on the 2nd. June, and the cricket match on the Park between Derbyshire and Lancashire was cancelled. The amazing thing was that by the 6th. June we were silaging in blazing hot weather with shirts off, and it stayed dry and hot all summer.

The hottest summer I have ever known was 1991. It had been a very mild winter, we never had more than a cover of snow and it never settled. I believe June that year was wet but by the middle of July it really was hot. Water was scarce and the reservoirs were very low. I think I have already said that at Bakewell Show that year we had to let cattle and sheep go home because of sunburn and distress and the attendance was down, because it was just too hot. In places down south the temperature got very close to 100 degrees Fahrenheit.

I think the dryest year I have known was 1959. The River Wye down Ashwood Dale dried up. The only water going into it was from the filter beds and some from the springs at the Devonshire Pub and the Cresswell Spring at the bottom of Cowdale Hollow, which at that time was still supplying Cowdale with water. It is a marvellous spring water supply, bubbling up out of the ground and never failing. The authorities used to test it once a month for purity and it never failed. It sparkled clear and never smelt of chlorine or fluoride, but it was very hard and needed a lot of soap. It still runs to waste into the river, because the boffins said it was too expensive to use. We were therefore put on the main water supply whether we liked it or not. The old name for the spring was Cresswell Spring and you can still gather water cress from it in the springtime, although between the road and where it runs into the river it suffers from oil off the road.

The first pump to push it up to Cowdale was a water ram driven by the river and you can still see the remains of the building next to the remains of the old toll bar cottage just below the railway bridge. On the opposite side of the road were four cottages, now demolished, but how people lived in them I do not know. It does not have to be very wet weather before the road at that point becomes a river and the front doors of the cottages nearly opened on to the road.

We often say that if Buxton is flooded with water there must be a lot lower down. I have known floods on two occasions. The first occasion was the first week in December 1964. It had been a wet November with a snow in the last week. Then came a quick thaw, and it poured with rain. Ashwood Park was like a lake. Down the Dale the road was flooded and it was deep and running like a torrent, closed to

37

all traffic. Richard had gone to Smithfield Show in London by train with Stuart Elliott and Victor Wilkson. In the middle of the night the phone rang. It was Mary to say that Richard had not arrived back. The train had been down to a walking pace all through the Midlands, as the track was under water. When they got to Derby the train was diverted to Sheffield and then across to Manchester via Hope Valley. They managed to persuade the guard to slow the train down at Hope Station and then to jump for it. He arrived back next morning in the Elliott's Land Rover!

The other flood was not quite as bad. It was in 1969. It had been quite a wet spring, with some snow and cold. I have forgotten exactly what happened to the small reservoir at Lightwood but it began to empty down the valley and flooded the narrow neck at the bottom of Hogshaw, completely destroying the bridge and flooding the bottom of Lightwood. The culvert under the road which also continues under the Charles Street houses and under the railway line which has crossed Fairfield Road, could not cope with the flood. Once again Ashwood Park was flooded, but not the Dale.

*   *   *

In 1973 we decided to move out of the farm house. Richard was keen to move in so we began to look round for alternatives. One idea was to build a bungalow at the top of the village, approximately on the site of Rose Cottage, which had been demolished many years ago after 'Granny Chapman' died. She was an incredible old lady. There was only a cold water tap on the kitchen sink. There was an old copper in the kitchen and a side boiler to the living room fireplace, which had to be filled by buckets. She used to take in washing and the small larder room at the back of the house had a hole in the stone slate roof which she would not have repaired as she said she could dry the clothes better on wet days. She was as hard as nails. She cleaned the school at King

Sterndale and lit the fire, walking over every morning through the wood and up the park, then walked over every afternoon after school to tidy up and lock up.

We abandoned the idea of re-building on a site nearby. It was not ideal. The access to the road was not easy and by the time the powers in authority had put all their restrictions and building regulations on it the cost was too high. Eventually we decided to move to Buxton. Allcock was building sixteen houses on part of the Empire Hotel site. We purchased 6 Carlisle Grove and moved in on 12th. November 1973. It was a dreadful day, gales and rain in torrents. It blew in the big doors to the silage barn and one of the big skylights out. I don't know where it went. We flitted ourselves and finished up wet through and bruised, trying to hold furniture down. But it was a lovely house in a nice situation, with a garden on three sides. It seemed to get bigger every year!

Kathleen's mother came with us, and continued to spoil me. It was Kathleen who had mother trouble, not me who had mother-in-law trouble! She was a marvellous old lady, active until the day before she died at the age of ninety-two, and lived with us for twenty years after Mr. Thompson died. We stayed at Carlisle Grove for 13 years and enjoyed it. The only black spot was the burglary we had on November 5th. 1982. We had gone to a Show dinner and when we came back the double glazed window in the lounge had been forced open. We lost all our family silver and valuables. Some of the silver was old family heirlooms which are not replaceable.

*   *   *

About this time I started to suffer from the farmer's occupational hazard, bad back and rheumatism. I had all sorts of treatment at the Devonshire Hospital, massage, heat and electrical treatment, until eventually in 1989 the surgeons suggested that I had an operation on my right hip to replace the joint. By this time I was very lame and the pain was with me night and day. I went into the Devonshire on April 5th. 1990 and had the operation. Although not 100% successful (I still cannot help limping) the operation has made a wonderful difference. All the pain has gone and I feel much better for that. I must confess I quite enjoyed the experience after the first day or two. When I woke up the morning after the operation in the small recovery ward with the nurse taking my blood pressure, I said, "Good morning, nurse", and a female voice on the other side said, "Good morning." I told the nurse that that was the first time for fifty years I had shared a bedroom with a different woman. I found it very interesting learning to walk again, with the help of the physiotherapists and nurses and I have nothing but praise for the N.H.S. and the Devonshire Hospital in particular.

When I began to suffer with back problems and especially the arthritis in my right leg I realised that living at Carlisle Grove was going to be more and more of a burden. The garden was not easy, all of it on a slope, and although a large part of it was lawn, it needed cutting and trimming. I had a rose bed in the front and it certainly could grow roses. There were steps to the front door and to the back door and from the garage into the house. I was now over seventy and Kathleen was not far off, so we started looking at flats. In 1986 we sold the house and moved into a ground floor flat on Hardwick Square. It is very convenient and we are very happy there.

*   *   *

In the mid 1980s we decided to change the farm policy and get rid of the dairy herd. Staff to milk cows twice a day 365 days a year were very scarce, and although the herd was highly productive, averaging 7200 litres per cow one year, costs were also very high. We had a nucleus of Hereford cross Friesian heifers and young females coming

40

on to form the basis of a suckler herd. Over a period of twelve months the Friesian cows were sold, some into local herds privately and some at Uttoxeter Mart. We purchased a very good Limousin bull to serve the heifers and the result was a disaster. We had endless trouble calving the heifers and the bull himself thought he was qualified for Aintree. Walls were no barrier to him, he visited all the neighbours in turn. His reign was short. We now use a Charolais bull and the result is much better.

We also increased the sheep flock to 280 ewes and we are using Texel rams for the lamb production. Mary is invaluable to the smooth running of the flock and I am sure Richard would agree that, without her help, the job would be twice as hard.

The pigs are still on the farm though out of our control. The improvement in quality of pigs with the advent of the hybrid is amazing. When I think back to the days of Large Whites, Middle Whites, Saddlebacks and Large Blacks and compare this fat pork and bacon with the lean and tender meat that is now on sale, I am amazed. This doesn't just apply to pigs, but to lamb, mainly due to the arrival of the Texels and to beef, again due to the continental breeds, mainly Limousin and Charolais.

*   *   *

During the 1960s we took several holidays abroad. We visited Denmark, Spain on three occasions, Yugoslavia and Portugal. I am glad we went when we did, as on all the trips we toured and saw as much as possible. I am not much for lounging on beaches. Yugoslavia in particular was very spectacular and primitive. I am glad we went when we did as the country can never be the same again after the events of 1993. Mostar and Sarajevo were particularly spectacular and the walled city of Dubrovnik must be unique. The scenery in Denmark was very ordinary and flat, and Spain was just hot and mainly barren. I found the most interesting places were the old cities of Cordoba, Seville, Granada, Toledo and of course Madrid. We found that Portugal was still medieval in the country areas and even the towns of Oporto, Santarem and Lisbon were still a bit backward, but the people were very friendly and helpful.

After these several tours in foreign countries we lost all interest and desire to go to any other places abroad. This is unlike Kathleen's mother who at the age of 82 decided she would fly to America to visit her relations, and thoroughly enjoyed herself. We have received many invitations to visit my American relations, but have never plucked up the courage or the enthusiasm to go.

*　　　*　　　*

Characters I remember as a boy were many. Father seemed to attract them.

Father's best man when he was married in 1910 was Will Morten of Beeley Hill Top. He was a second cousin of father's and was a great character. He was one of the family of Beeley Hill Top Mortens which included triplets, Ernest, Albert and Mortimer. I remember going to their fiftieth birthday celebration at Beeley. Will Morten was a bachelor and very eccentric. He would ramble through the woods of the old park at Chatsworth. I remember him taking me and pointing out birds' nests and young animals, especially the young deer in late spring. He would recite poetry which he had written himself, mostly about local flora and fauna. He was immensely strong and I have a photograph of him standing with a cow's front legs on his shoulders. He took part in one or two radio programmes from Manchester, before the days of television.

Matthew Nall had a small flat cart and used to come round selling 'briquettes'. They were blocks of coal dust, about the size of a brick, which we could burn on the boiler at the creamery. This was when coal and fuel were very scarce at the end of the first world war. He used to buy old hens and he would pluck and dress them at his stable on Newmarket Street. He was also a go-between dealer in ponies. He certainly was a character and called all us boys 'little jiggers'.

Also on Newmarket Street were the stables of Websters, who ran horse charabancs and broughams for hire. On the same side were stables of Bainbridges, who were 'cabbies'.

On the other side of the road were the big stables of Jimmie Kirkland and these had an outlet on to Byron Street. Mr. Kirkland was quite a big man in the top drawer of the hunter and race horse world. He was very much the old fashioned jockey type, brown leggings, boots and check waistcoats. He had a shop at the corner of High Street and West Road where he sold all sorts of animal food (the old equivalent of a pet shop). There were always a lot of horses at his stables, which he hired out to the 'gentry'. He had two daughters who were very 'horsey' and they rode and hunted regularly. Between Bennett Street and Crowstones were two fields which they used for exercising, I don't remember anyone grazing them, but I do remember them being used by the circuses, when they visited the town.

Another of the regular callers at the dairy was a chap called Ted Bunting. I never knew him do any work, and he lived with his sister who was a teacher. He was always well dressed and would arrive at the dairy mid-morning and just stand about and talk to anybody who would talk to him. Father never ordered him off, but I don't think he had much time for him and seemed just to ignore him, but if mother appeared, he went!

Back on Newmarket Street was the vets, and of course the surgery is still there, while round the back are the stables and coach house. The first vet I remember was George Howe. He was a big bluff character, very much a horse vet, for whom the other farm animals came a very poor second. Somewhere there is a bill which mother kept which just said, "To iles and cummin." In English he meant to say, "To embrocation oil and coming out to visit." Unfortunately it seems to be lost, like the letter which mother had from a milk customer, who said she was pleased to hear a roundsman so cheerful whistling and singing, but not at 7 o'clock on a Sunday morning. Or the note from a customer who wanted a pint of 'Grey day' milk.

A real character from my boyhood was Sam Hooper. He was a fishmonger by trade and a game poulterer, but his hobbies were many and varied. He was an amateur boxer and promoted bouts. He was a raconteur and his stock of stories was endless. He was always involved in any event in the town and generous to many of the youth organisations.

Isaac Brunt was a cattle dealer in the 1920s. He came from the Leek area, but I am not sure where. He was a big bluff character with a red neckerchief who would arrive 'on spec.' in a pony and trap and enquire if we had anything in the cattle line to sell. He would barter in the old fashioned way, and a slap of the hands concluded the deal. Sometimes he had his drover and his dog or dogs with him, but from memory he would arrange to collect his purchases on a certain day. It did not matter whether his purchases were bulls, cows or young stock, they were driven from farms in the area to a certain point and then driven by his drovers to Leek. He came to a sad end. He always paid on the spot in notes and cash, and I remember seeing him pull great wads of notes from his pockets. But in the end he was mugged and robbed, and he never recovered from the shock. We never saw him again.

Eric Fox was a builder, a one man outfit. There are a number of cattle sheds and barns in North Derbyshire which are a memorial to him. He built us the silage barn, cubicle shed, collecting yard and parlour. He would arrive between nine and ten o'clock in an old van, loaded inside and on top with the requisites for the day. One day he had not fastened his load securely and shed part of the load off the top in Matlock. He ate pencils. He always carried his pencil between his teeth and one a day was about his ration. But as a builder he was brilliant. He made the concrete stanchions for our buildings in situ, with wooden shuttering and then poured the concrete in from the top, with bolt holes for the purlins at the top of each. When he had three or more stanchions erected he would look through the holes to make sure they were in line. They always were. He made the timber roof trusses on the floor and drilled the holes at each end to bolt them to the stanchions. He hoisted them into position with an old tractor which had an ancient hoist elevator attached, and he would then push the bolts through at each end, and I never knew one not in line. The roof was covered with 'big six' asbestos sheets which again he hoisted up with his tractor. He would walk about on the purlins, singing or whistling with a complete disregard for safety, and it was twenty feet high at the eaves. He had two hobbies, motor bikes (he disappeared for the fortnight of the T.T. races on the Isle of Man) and later he took his wife on their annual fishing trip to Ullapool. I thought it was an awful long way to go fishing.

George Mycock was always known as 'Bunny'. He lived at a cottage which is now part of the Devonshire Arms down Ashwood Dale. He always carried his ancient 12 bore hammer gun. The stock was wrapped with string, and the hammers had rubber bands to make them fire. He would not let anybody else use it. He did not smoke but chewed twist, and his lips and tongue were as black as his hands, and black juice leaked from the side of his mouth. All the work I ever knew him do was mole trapping for local farmers, but it was common knowledge that moles were only an excuse for poaching, and rabbits were his main target. Every sentence he spoke concluded with the word 'definite' and he would punctuate anything that was said to him as being 'definite'.

*   *   *

On May 1st. on the Market Place was held the annual working horse show. I think it continued until the late 1930s. All the horses on show had to be working in Buxton. There were classes for the best turned out heavy horse, (pedigree did not come into consideration) and several of the corporation and railway horses would compete as well as coalmen's horses and haulage people's horses. There were also classes for tradesmen's turnout and I remember that as well as our milk ponies, there were the butchers', greengrocers', fishmongers', and many others. One of the judges was always George Howe, the vet.

There was also a Buxton Agricultural Show, held in September either on the Silverlands where the football field, Police Station and Army buildings are now, or it was held on Cote Heath. Unfortunately it was never run very successfully, and father had no good opinion of the man who was secretary-treasurer so I will not mention his name.

The Pavilion Gardens was the centre of entertainment in the town until the late 1930s. A season ticket was a guinea and this entitled you to most week-end concerts. I have heard renowned soloists sing there on Sunday evenings, including Denis Noble, Paul Robeson, Isabell Baillie, Peter Dawson and many others whose names don't spring to mind. On Saturday nights there would be a dance, and I don't mean a shuffling, bottom wriggling smoochy affair, I mean a proper dance. There were at least two local dance bands which were very good. Eddie Smith's 'Black Cat' dance band and Fred Alcock's Dance Band. They were both very popular.

In August there was a tennis tournament and bowls and croquet were also very popular. I have known the lake frozen over and skating taking place on it in winter.

Tobogganing was also a popular winter sport (there must have been an ice age when I was young) and the popular places were Temple Fields, Cavendish golf links and Manchester Road, which even when we were lads was very dangerous and there were accidents. Eventually someone was killed and it was stopped.

*   *   *

We used to rent the field at the bottom of Dale Road and Dukes Drive for the milk ponies. At the bottom of the field on Dukes Drive side was a spring, which never went dry. Someone has built a bungalow on it. It ran into a stone trough and then into another stone trough on Dukes Drive. The overflow was piped into stone troughs on the main road just below. They have all gone now, but when it is very wet there is always a lot of water on the main road where the troughs were.

Further down Ashwood Dale at the bottom of Conning Dale is the remains of the old saw mill. Conning Dale is the dry dale which starts behind the golf club house on Fairfield Common and winds its way down to Ashwood Dale joining the river at the old saw mill. Driven by a water wheel, with water from the river, the mill was in daily use until the 1940s when both sons were called up for war service.

A little farther down the Dale and just under the next railway bridge was, on the left, a toll keeper's cottage, which I don't remember, but I have a photograph of it, and, on the right, four cottages which I do remember and have mentioned before, because of the effect of the flooding.

If you look up at the next bend in the road, at the bottom of Cowdale hollow, you will see on both sides some very sheer rock 'tors' which have interesting names, Pig Tor, Kid Tor, Dog Tor and Cuckoo Rock. Locals know them as Pictor, Kitty and Doctor.

On the road to Chapel-en-le-Frith, at Barmoor Clough was a bone crushing mill, driven by a water wheel. The mill leat was on the left of Barmoor Clough corner, between the road and the railway. It was fed by the ebbing and flowing well, which was a little higher up the Dove Holes road. Unfortunately the well no longer flows and the site of the leat is grown over with weeds. The site of the mill was a little further down on the right hand side, as the road turns down the Clough. You can still see the gritstone back wall of the mill, and I can remember it working and the smell. I still have old sale notes of bone meal purchased there for spreading on the land as fertiliser.

There were two slaughter-houses in Buxton, one at the back of Heath Street, used by the Whites, the Simpsons and the Bills, although all these families have now gone. One of them is still a butcher's shop. The other slaughterhouse was in Charles Street, and there is very little of this left. It was used by Joules, Rushworth and others, and again none of these families remain under those names.

*   *   *

Following the River Wye to Bakewell there were several water driven mills and most of them I remember working. At Miller's Dale there was Dakin's Corn Mill, where you could take your own corn and have it ground.

Then there were the big cotton mills at Cressbrook and Litton Mill. Lower down, before you came to Ashford were the Bobbin mills, and the buildings and the water wheels are still standing a little past the

48

'sough' from the Magpie Mine. They made the wooden bobbins for the cotton mills at Litton and Matlock.

At Ashford was Flewitt's Corn Mill just on the left at the end of the by-pass. This was a family firm which as far as I know has completely died out. Just as you come into Bakewell was the 'D.P.' battery works which were completely driven by water wheels. A little further on was Bailey's Corn Mill, and there you can still see the remains of the water wheel just behind the building. The next mill is the corn mill at Rowsley, until fairly recently run by the Caudwell family. This mill, which is driven by the river, is still working. It is open to the public and is well worth a visit. One thing that interested me at the mill, is that when they are milling fine flour, the whole building shakes, and I understand it is designed to do this, because if it were rigid something would break.

*   *   *

At King Sterndale Hall lived the Pickford family, related to the haulage firm. In the 1920s the family consisted of Lord Sterndale, who, when he was younger, had been Master of the Rolls, and his two daughters who never married. The staff were more than interesting. They consisted of William (I never knew his surname) who was known locally as Sweet William. He seemed to be general factotum, gardener, handyman, butler, etc. Under him was Joe Gibbs, and his son-in-law John Thomson, who was general dogsbody. Every morning you could see them sweeping the track which led from the house across to the church, and another which led from the house to the gate at the top of 'Kitty' Dale, and down to the lodge at the bottom, by the A6. This has now been pulled down. I remember they had an old donkey, whose duty was to cart water from the spring by the A6 before there was a piped supply from the same spring. There was a large kitchen garden at the rear of the house with a high wall round it. There were all kinds of fruit trees trained up the wall all the way round. There was a large

49

heated greenhouse in which, besides exotic flowers like camellias and orchids, there were oranges, lemons, nectarines and vines. Unfortunately all these have gone, under the modern syndrome of making it easier to manage.

The King Sterndale church is lovely inside and I should think is well endowed. I can only remember three vicars who lived at the vicarage, which is bigger than the church. Their names were Trotman, Sloman and Maine. Someone had a sense of humour.

*   *   *

Cowdale quarry when I first remember it was part of Buxton Lime Firms and most of the people in the village worked there. Indeed the houses were really 'tied' cottages. The eight at the top were built at the end of the 19th. century, and the ten at the bottom in the 1930s. The quarrymen were variously known as 'getters', 'poppers' and 'fillers'. The 'getters' had to keep the face safe by climbing up and crow-barring loose rocks down. Then there were the 'poppers' whose job was to drill holes in the large rocks and with a charge of dynamite blow them into manageable sizes for the 'fillers', who loaded into 'Jubilee' trucks, holding about 30 hundredweight, by hand. The trucks ran on lines down to the weigh bridge and then on to the top of the kilns, where they were tipped. I think it was four trucks of stone and one of coal. They were kept burning continuously. At the bottom of the kilns were the lime drawers, whose job was to sort out unburned stone and wheel the pure lime from the bottom of the kiln in wheelbarrows and tip it into railway wagons. Can you imagine anyone doing this job today? It was dreadful. Thankfully, it is now mechanised.

We always had a horse employed by the quarry. One of the quarrymen fetched it each morning and brought it back at night. Its job was to pull the empty Jubilee trucks back from the kiln to the quarry face. The full ones ran on their own. The horse also had to pull the empty railway wagons into position at the bottom of the kiln. I remember on Friday nights the quarryman who brought the horse back also brought its wage packet, and grumbled because the horse's wage was greater than his own. I remember on one April Fool's day we moved the horse out of the stable and tied a cow up in its place! The best horse we ever had for this quarry job was a mare called Dinah. She was a part bred Clydesdale. She was a bit slow and steady which suited the job of moving wagons, as she learnt that just by leaning forward the wagons started rolling, instead of snatching at them.

The pony that used to take the milk to Buxton before the motor vans was called Rose. She was white and was of Welsh cob type, though father used to say she was part bred Percheron. When she was young she was like a bottle of pop, and only the horsemen were allowed to drive her. I remember we used to bring the float across to the dairy by hand and load the milk churns on to it, before we brought Rose from the stable to harness her to the float. One man held her head whilst someone harnessed her to the float, and whoever was taking her had to be ready to jump because as soon as her head was released she was off. As she got older she calmed down of course and was a very good farm horse and lived to a good age.

One story about her which I was told recently, was that on a Saturday night several of the quarrymen from the village and some of our farm men always went down to the Devonshire Arms in Ashwood Dale. One Saturday night one of the quarrymen had over celebrated. The others managed to carry him to the bottom of Cowdale Hollow, where our horseman suggested he waited with the others and he would fetch Rose, who was in the stable, which he did. They loaded him on her back and carted him home. She must have been older when this happened, otherwise she would have tipped him off.

A load of hay from the farm for the milk ponies, on its way to the stables in West Road. Taken outside the Creamery on Green Lane. The shaft horse was Gilbert and the chain horse was Prince. John Morten, with his hand on Gilbert's rump, and Percy Rains (father's cousin) is standing on the shaft rail. Taken in the late 1920s

As well as the regular work horses on the farm we always had one or two young horses being broken in. Both brothers Maurice and Philip were good horsemen, who took after father. They had to be careful not to let young horses learn bad habits. Some developed habits which were incurable such as biting or kicking, and these were scrapped, especially ones that kicked, because they were dangerous. I remember one horse had a very Roman nose. He seemed to be working well and was left with a youth rolling one of the fields up the lane. When he had finished he decided to bring the roller down the lane into the yard. When the roller rattled on the old lane the horse took off, with the lad sitting on the roller, but when it arrived in the yard there was no driver. The men found him sitting on the lane at a corner, unharmed, muttering "Bloody hell," which was all he could say.

Of the regular work horses which I remember most were black. There were at least three which worked for years on the farm. All were black and in order of age they were Gilbert, Prince and Tiny. I have a photograph of the first two with a load of hay outside the Creamery on Green Lane, which they had brought from the farm for the milk ponies. Their stables were at the back of West Road, halfway up a very steep hill on the left. Tiny was so called because he was huge. I think he was eighteen hands (six feet) at the shoulder, but he was a real old slave and was very popular with the men. In addition to these father bought pedigree Shire mares at different times with the idea of breeding our own. I cannot remember that we had any success with this. In fact I remember one very good looking mare, I think she was called Chilcote Pearl, who slipped on the concrete with a load of manure, displaced her hip joint, and was never any good again.

*   *   *

We must have employed many scores of men and women over the years to run the farms and the dairy in Buxton. I remember going with father to Longnor 'statutes', held in the market place at Longnor, on Boxing Day. Men, women, girls and boys stood around looking for employers. Employment was offered from New Years Day to Christmas Eve. When you agreed terms with a suitable employee, you gave him a shilling (5p.) and that was binding. We employed many very good men in this way.

Left to right - Moses Sigley, John Morten and Charlie Slack with brother David looking over the wall.

My earliest memory of a farm man was Moses Sigley. He came from a big family who lived in the village. His father was one of the original quarrymen who started Cowdale Quarry. When I knew him he was a crippled old man, injured in the quarry as so many of those early quarrymen were. Moses was a very good farm worker and father thought a lot of him. I have a photograph of him dipping sheep with father and Charlie Slack in the old dip by the stable. David is standing on the wall watching them. Charlie Slack was a very good cowman and a good hand milker. Again, he came from a big family who farmed at Wildboarclough. Over the years we relied very heavily on quarrymen for casual help. They would come at night for hay making, walling, harvesting of corn and potatoes and for singling and hoeing of root crops in season. One or two would even come early in the morning and 'muck out' in winter time before they went to work in the quarry. It was no problem getting them to come especially in war time and after, when 'perks' such as milk and eggs and other products were scarce.

I have briefly mentioned the cattle market held in Buxton on Saturdays on the cattle market, with special 'fair days' in May, September and October. The auctioneers were Hampsons, and I can just remember Mr. Thomas Hampson, the founder of the firm. He was a big man and like a lot of men of that time he always wore a top hat. I still have a photograph of him in the cattle market together with father and grandfather (who also wears a top hat and I have still got the hat with his initials inside the rim). Also in the photograph is Mr. John Slack who farmed at Countess Cliff. He was a seventh son and also had seven sons, the youngest was also called John, but I never noticed he had any peculiar talents.

The market was used by local farmers who walked their cattle and sheep to and from the market, but when transport became available it very quickly faded in favour of Bakewell, Leek and Ashbourne. In addition of course, when war time came all livestock for slaughter was, in theory, purchased, marked by the government and rationed, and Buxton was not big enough to warrant an official 'grader'.

*　　*　　*

Buxton Cattle Market. Sheep Sale.
Grandfather Morten (R.B.) is in the middle at the back. You can just see
his top hat and white beard.

If I have not said anything interesting in these ramblings of an octogenarian, then I shall blame my family and friends for badgering me to write it down. I do not believe in the good old days totally. There have been good times, but many that were not so good. I lost my father, a brother and a son all in twelve months and that was a very traumatic experience. Fate sometimes kicks you when you are down. However, I have had marvellous good health for most of my life, except for one or two lapses, but thanks to a wonderful N.H.S., my own doctors and the Devonshire Hospital I am still fairly active. Last but not least I have been pampered at home by a succession of women,- mother, sisters and of course for the last 53 years by Kathleen, who still more than mothers me, and waits on me hand and foot.

I don't think I have ever had any startling achievements, though I have always tried to, "Fill the unforgiving minute with 60 seconds worth of distance run." I am very proud of my family past and present, and if pride goes before a fall I had better shut up - at least for the time being!

Becoming Atheist

Becoming Atheist

Humanism and the Secular West

CALLUM G. BROWN

Bloomsbury Academic
An imprint of Bloomsbury Publishing Plc

B L O O M S B U R Y
LONDON · OXFORD · NEW YORK · NEW DELHI · SYDNEY

Bloomsbury Academic

An imprint of Bloomsbury Publishing Plc

50 Bedford Square
London
WC1B 3DP
UK

1385 Broadway
New York
NY 10018
USA

www.bloomsbury.com

BLOOMSBURY and the Diana logo are trademarks of Bloomsbury Publishing Plc

First published 2017

British Library Cataloguing-in-Publication Data
A catalogue record for this book is available from the British Library.

ISBN: HB: 978-1-4742-2449-9
PB: 978-1-4742-2452-9
ePDF: 978-1-4742-2454-3
ePub: 978-1-4742-2455-0

Library of Congress Cataloging-in-Publication Data
Names: Brown, Callum G., 1953- author.
Title: Becoming atheist : humanism and the secular West / Callum G. Brown.
Description: London ; New York, NY : Bloomsbury Academic, an imprint of Bloomsbury Publishing, Plc, [2017] | Includes bibliographical references and index.
Identifiers: LCCN 2016023284 (print) | LCCN 2016036286 (ebook) |
ISBN 9781474224499 (hardback) | ISBN 9781474224529 (pbk.) |
ISBN 9781474224543 (ePDF) | ISBN 9781474224550 (ePub)
Subjects: LCSH: Secularism–History–20th century. | Atheism–History–
20th century. | Secularization (Theology)–History–20th century.
Classification: LCC BL2747.8 .B758 2017 (print) |
LCC BL2747.8 (ebook) | DDC211/.809045–dc23 LC record available
at https://lccn.loc.gov/2016023284

Cover design: Sharon Mah
Cover image: (front) Happy Humanist symbol,
© British Humanist Association, (background) Getty Images.

Typeset by Integra Software Services Pvt. Ltd.
Printed and bound in India

CONTENTS

LIST OF TABLES

PREFACE

This is the last part of my trilogy of books on the secular revolution of the 1960s and the working out of its legacy, in each of which secularization has been written about in different ways. *The Death of Christian Britain* (2001) deployed a cultural-theory approach to secularization, exploring the means of success for the hegemonic religious discourse from 1800 to 1960 and then its spectacular collapse in the cultural and sexual revolutions of the 1960s. *Religion and the Demographic Revolution* (2013) used a quantitative approach, showing how, in the United Kingdom, Canada, the United States and Ireland, secularization since 1960 has been acutely correlated with women's changing sexual activity, fertility, education and economic lives. *Becoming Atheist* brings the story of secularization home to individuals, to women and men born in eighteen nations and now living in the United States, Canada, the United Kingdom, India, France and Estonia, who came in complex ways from the mid-twentieth century onwards to have no religious faith.

Secular historians, like secular people generally, are usually the least interested in secularity, leaving this particular historical narrative to be compiled largely by those writing from a faith position. The result has been a tendency for the literature to approach the issue as a negative story about the decline of religion, morality and even civilization in the West. This volume seeks to expose a positive story of the social history of blossoming atheism. It seems a natural progression, then, to move from culture and statistics to personal testimonies that can swing around the leviathan secularization story of the late twentieth and early twenty-first centuries from one of subtraction to one of addition – to the millions of people of a new ethical Western world who have discovered themselves to be good without god.

The themes raised in this book are expanded upon at the blogsite I host and moderate, and contributions would be welcomed. Visit http://humanisthistory.academicblogs.co.uk/

ACKNOWLEDGEMENTS

Rarely is a book on the social history of religion so indebted to those who spoke about its loss. I hope I do them justice. In the last six years I have met many people – humanists, atheists, agnostics, skeptics, secularists, rationalists, freethinkers – who have entrusted me with their memories. These respondents each showed me generosity of time and spirit, taking me to their homes, feeding me and, in some cases, becoming tour guides (Glenn and Lorraine showing me Vancouver on two visits, and Caroline Nalbankian proudly driving me round her patch in South Boston). In several cities, respondents placed enough trust in this stranger to consent to being interviewed in my hotel room. I recruited volunteers after giving talks in Vancouver, Toronto, Boston, London, Perth, Inverness, Edinburgh, Dundee, Glasgow, Preston and Birmingham, and additionally I met leaders and followers of non-belief associations in Victoria, Birmingham, San Francisco and Berkeley. And it all started at my kitchen table where in 2009 I conducted the first interview with Mary Wallace, the Humanist celebrant who married my wife and I.

I know of five respondents who have died since they gave me their testimonies: Pat Duffy Hutcheon, Ernest Poser and his wife Jutta Cahn, James Machin (pseud.) and Peter Barton. They each gave me especially thoughtful and reflective accounts, which feature prominently here. Thanks to those who helped me reach respondents: my research partners in Humanist Society Scotland (HSS), British Humanist Association (BHA), BC Humanists, the Humanist Association of Toronto, the Bay Area Atheists, the Ethical Society of Boston, Atko Remmel of the University of Tartu in Estonia and the Black American Humanist Association in Washington DC. My transcribers worked very hard: Jenni Ross, Shivani Gupta, Charlie Lynch, Deborah Hackett, Victoria Stepien and Benjamin Huskinson. Four of them – Jenni, Shivani, Charlie and Benjamin – were also students I supervised, conducting research which extended my understandings of religion, whilst Rachel Cheng helped my archival research. Academic colleagues have informed this study, notably John Arnold (University of Cambridge), Tina Block (Thompson Rivers University, BC), Sarah Browne (Scottish Women's Aid), Matthew Engelke (London School of Economics), Steve Kelly (Strathclyde), Sonya Luehrmann (Simon Fraser), Lynne Marks (Victoria, BC), David Nash (Oxford Brookes), Tony Pinn (Rice), Steve Sutcliffe (Edinburgh) and, at the University of Glasgow,

Jane Mair, Stuart Airlie, Stephen Marritt, Andrew Roach and Marilyn Dunn. Special thanks go to the anonymous reviewer who helped me bolster my argument. Lastly, key individuals who helped my understanding of atheist and humanist movements are Andrew Copson and Ian Scott of BHA, Gary McLelland of HSS, Conrad Hadland of BC Humanists, Larry Hicok of Bay Area Atheists and Charlie Lynch and Douglas McLellan of the Scottish Secular Society.

Logistical support came from the following: for travel to Canada in 2009 from the Carnegie Trust for the Universities of Scotland Research Fund; for transcription costs from the University of Dundee School of Humanities research fund and a University of Glasgow professorial dowry; and, for accommodation during interview visits from Dean (Professor) David and Louanne Hempton, Harvard University, and Ed and Linda Jay, Comox, BC. Thanks to each.

I am grateful to the following for granting consent to use copyright oral-history testimony in Chapter 2: Dorothy Allison, dorothyallison.net; the Sophia Smith Collection at Smith College, Northampton, MA; the Center for Digital Scholarship at Brown University, Rhode Island; the David and Barbara Pryor Center for Arkansas Oral and Visual History, University of Arkansas; the UCLA Center for Oral History Research, California; the Southern Oral History Program at the Center for the Study of the American South, University of North Carolina at Chapel Hill; the Rutgers Oral History Archives, New Jersey; the UK Data Service, Colchester; and David J. Wood of oralhistory.co.uk.

Thanks go to Andrew Copson, CEO of the British Humanist Association, for granting copyright permission to use the Happy Humanist motif as the book's cover image.

Most of all, my partnership with Lynn Abrams is deep-rooted, not merely in a Humanist marriage but in her scholarship on women's and feminist history, and oral history theory and practice, each of which features hugely in the text that follows. She read and saved me from error. What remains is my responsibility.

CHAPTER ONE

Introduction

One by one

Millions of people in the West in the last sixty years have become atheists. One by one, without significant rancour or obstacle, and without coercion by governments or an invading political ideology, individuals have come to live their lives as if there is no god.[1] No central source for this is immediately apparent; with no atheist religion, mass movement, schema or charismatic leader, people have come to a decision pretty much for themselves. The process has been fuzzy and hard to discern, yet the evidence for its astounding scale is rather difficult in the 2010s to overlook: the statistical data of declining churches, falling belief in a god and rising secular values are profuse. Atheists are walking tall, and in enlarging numbers. Scholarship is showing us the antiquity of atheism and its medieval variant,[2] but mass unbelief is very recent, commencing in a brief moment of dramatic cultural change between the late 1950s and mid-1970s. We know quite a lot now about this religious revolution of the 'long sixties', narrowed down in much literature to 1957–74, what one religious historian described as 'a rupture as great as that of the Reformation'.[3] We have statistical studies and cultural studies to show how the contemporary secular West was moulded in those times. But we don't know how the process took place, nor where it led, for the individuals who walked out on churches and forsook religious marriage and the baptism of their children.

To find out, this book asks people how they came to lose religion, or to not adopt a religion in the first place. What were the special circumstances for the sixties generation, the triggers to losing god? What role did family and work play? How did the experience vary between men and women, between people of different races and religious backgrounds? What manner of ethical position replaced religion? Listening to individuals' stories is really the only sure way to discover how the rush from faith worked in the Western world. Its end result, as we shall see, is a brand of secularity described by respondents as a positive moral outlook distinct from a traditional religious one. They proudly described their values to me: justice, equality and the rights of all humans, regardless of race, gender or disability; recognition of all sexualities, freedom to control fertility and to cohabit or marry free from church and religious values; the right to life and to a dignified death at a time of one's own choosing; the power of evolution and the right to education free from irrational beliefs and religious censorship; and a citizen's right to freedom from religion as much as freedom of religion. They spoke to me movingly of the dignity yet the smallness of human life; many dwelt on the awe they felt on beholding the night sky and its billions of stars, and their sensation of humankind's fragility as just another animal, but an animal with special responsibilities on our planet. Uniformly, they spoke of how they held to these beliefs and values for decades before discovering a name – humanism (often known in North America as secular humanism). In this way, they adhered to the values that mark Western secularity *before* the realization that they were, as some noted to me, 'Good without God'.[4]

I recruited eighty-five volunteers to study this great modern transition. They were mostly between 40 and 90 years of age, born in eighteen different countries from Canada in the West to India in the East, contributing through migration to the kaleidoscopic composition of Western society, and all were interviewed by me in the United Kingdom, Canada, the United States, France or Estonia. I sought as wide a spectrum of atheism as possible. I recruited humanists, agnostics, atheists, rationalists, skeptics and secularists, many of them members of non-belief societies or ethical societies, with additional respondents unattached to any group. Various patterns emerged – ranging from those who claimed to have become atheists in childhood, through those who drifted indifferent to religion for decades, to those who, from young adulthood to senior years, underwent dramatic turns from faith. The heady years from 1960 to 1980 were especially difficult, notably for women seeking to break from domesticity and to contrive an autonomous self. By the 1990s, the liberalization of Western culture allowed the individual in most countries to be comfortably alienated from church and faith without fear of censure or social stigma, releasing my younger respondents – those born after 1975 – to espouse humanism and atheism from their teens and twenties. A few had it tougher, coming from evangelical or cult groups where the individual found it hard to nurture religious doubt, fearing systematic 'shunning' for leaving their religion. Many felt they had been trained to be their own gaolers, indoctrinated or, as some described it, brainwashed to ponder faith alone. 'I was still thoroughly indoctrinated; it took years before I gradually ---' was a typical, broken narration. 'It's these tiny little needles that they put into your brain', said another, whilst the politest expressions were 'early socialization' to a 'supernatural mindset'.[5] The word 'indoctrinated' occurred thirty-one times in my testimonies, 'brainwashed' fourteen times and 'thought control' twice.[6] Some laughed and some cried at the remembrance of their own credulity.

The cultural rupture centred on the 1960s took decades to be resolved. Different nations, regions and ethnic groups experienced at staggered dates the opening of access to a life without god; for Blacks and Asians, access came later if it came at all. Such disparity applied, too, to the sexes. Since the eighteenth century, religious scholars have noted that men and women have had different routes into religion and to conversion as born-again evangelicals. Likewise, this book shows that men and women had starkly different routes *out* from religion, and it was females who had to make by far the most difficult negotiation of family and societal opposition to become atheists. And it remains the case that women of ethnic minorities in the West, especially of non-Christian minorities, encounter difficulties in being accepted as devoid of religious faith.

This volume is a work of oral history, in which individual narratives let us see how cultural change works in free societies. Sometimes, those societies are the hardest in which to escape religious culture – as in Ireland, Northern Ireland and many parts of the United States – and we shall see examples of the problems budding atheists had in those parts. But shining throughout is the agency of the individuals to change themselves and, in the process, to change the culture around them. The historian can too easily be engrossed with the wider mechanisms of cultural assimilation and dissemination of normative beliefs, and see the individual as the victim of untameable cultural forces. But if the researcher focuses on individuals' narratives of re-crafting personal beliefs without a god, the statistics and cultural processes become seen correctly as the measures of what men, women and – most surprising of all – children achieved for themselves.

Imagining secularization

Secularization is a concept with a troubled history. It came into its own in Britain in the middle of the twentieth century as a 'pessimist' school, when social historians and sociologists broadly united in seeing religion as having fared poorly during industrialization and urbanization from the 1750s to the 1950s. That outlook was challenged in the 1980s and 1990s by a revisionist or 'optimist' school of historians drawing upon existing American scholarly sanguinity that city growth had gone hand-in-hand with religious diversity, vibrancy and church growth over the same period of history. This optimist interpretation turned in the 2000s into a side-revolt against secularization: one group of religious sociologists started to maintain that the world was 'de-secularizing' – a wild idea not borne out by any credible evidence – whilst another group, influential in Europe, started to see secularization as a 'master narrative' of ideological secularism. Taking a shine to this revolt, religious studies scholars, confronting the withering evidence of year-on-year decline of European religiosity, started to reinterpret secularization as a new stage in Christianity – a stage beyond old paradigms of churches, parishes and forms of worship, evident in newly venting individualized faith, mega churches, house churches, spiritual seeking of one type or another and an autonomous secularity – what Charles Taylor dubbed a 'buffered self'.[7] This trend detects some *change* in religion into a new idiom in which people no longer go to church but still have a faith – hailed by many as 'believing without belonging'.[8] Other optimistic explanations persist. One American argument is that declining Western religiosity has simply been miscounted – that numbers of adherents and god-believers stand largely where they have always been.[9] Another approach blames the Christian church for failing God's purpose – the 'bad management' argument.[10] Collectively, these various optimist arguments amount to 'secularization denial' – a repudiation of the magnitude of contemporary religious decline and, for some researchers, a rejection of the very concept that humans can be born without, or can lose, religion. Some Christian scholarship seems intent on rejecting the idea of religious decline, or statistically *secular* secularization, in modern Western society.[11]

Meanwhile, an 'old school' of secularization scholars has held out, untempted by re-imaginings of divine intentions. It is to that old school that this volume adheres, convinced beyond peradventure that secularization remains as Bryan Wilson defined it in 1966 – the declining social significance of religion – and as he narrated its burgeoning in the modern societies of England and America.[12] He may have got some of the historical dimensions awry, and we know the nature of secularization in much more sophisticated terms now, but the concept remains a measureable, demonstrable historical process as much as any other cultural change. Though confessionalist scholars are influential in religious history, the rest of the academy, comprising the secular cultural historian and social scientist, as well as scientists of various hues, are, by and large, happy to acknowledge, mainly silently, that secularization has been self-evident in the late-modern Western world.

This invites the question, what is the secular? Anthropologists and sociologists of religion, to their credit, try to imagine and analyse 'the secular', 'the secular being' and secular society. Historians have really not done this at all, being more interested in process than outcome, and remaining wary of social absolutes. The historian's concept of secularization has been around since the eighteenth century, but has diversified into secularization of the state, mind, society and individual.[13] But historical consensus, quite widespread between the 1970s and 1990s, has in recent years been abruptly challenged by those, led by Jeff Cox, who dispute secularization as a process and work towards its elimination from scholarship.[14] This joins the wider religious scholarship that tends to diminish, or rename, secularization as a Christian evolution, not its collapse. Of course, this might seem to challenge the integrity of those very large numbers of people who say they have lost religion. It might also seem to compromise the social scientific study of religion.

So, academic interest in the issue of losing religion has been barrelling around both sides of the Atlantic for several decades. But it has left clear deficiencies. The first is that little focus has fallen upon *permanent* loss of religion. Greater emphasis has fallen recently on the fuzzification of religiosity – on the spectrum between religion and non-religion rather than the capacity to create atheists. The second deficiency is that the historic scale of what has been happening is not in sharp focus: Christendom is sliding from most Western nations, including in heartlands like parts of the United States where, in recent estimations, religious decline is a key element in a foundational cultural and political shift underway towards liberalism.[15] Third, much of the research is encased in negativity – about loss of religion, collapsing churches and moral deterioration – and fails to conceptualize the positive story of freedom from religion fostering a new comprehensive moral outlook and a blossoming of the autonomous self.[16] This book considers the oral evidence for secularization as a positive human development.

Of numbers and cultures

In trying to understand secularization, I have been inclined as much as any other academic to turn first to cultural history and statistics. This book is preceded by two other volumes devoted one each to these approaches.

In *The Death of Christian Britain*, published in 2001, I promulgated from modern cultural theory the idea that the mark of a Christian country is not narrated by a social history of religious practice (which never attains a uniformity anyway). Instead, it is to be beheld in the power of *discursive Christianity*, by which a nation's culture is dominated by religious discourse which, in the case of the 1800–1950 period, overwhelmed citizens to accede to strongly gendered modes of religious behaviour. It was in ways of being suborned by religious discourse into personal cultural submission, rather than any compulsion to attend church (which never operated), that the Western nation was united in Christianity. As a result, the perennial attempts of historians to gauge the religiosity of a society purely by the proportion of churchgoers or religious adherents, or by the voting for religious politicians and religious policies, were doomed to not so much fail as to miss the point. The historian who thinks because only 40–50 per cent or so of Britons went to church on census Sunday, 30 March 1851, that the nation was secularized doesn't grasp the significance of the popular culture beyond the churches – in the streets, the mines and factories, and in the public houses too – where hymns were sung and devotional tracts and pictures were stuck to the walls. The culture *beyond* the church is where the measure of a society's piety is to be made, the non-churchgoer more than the churchgoer making a nation Christian. In like manner, in the United States in the 1990s, the Christian character of the nation was not to be found in the 22.1 per cent of people attending church, chapel, synagogue or mosque each week, as measured by a careful and very difficult enumeration project by scholars there, but more impressively in the *further* 20 per cent of people who had *lied* to Gallup pollsters that they had been to church.[17] Secularization can be better timed from when the factory hymns and deceit about religious practice fade. In that regard, my book told a history of the religious culture of Britain remaining strong from 1800 to the 1950s, even if churchgoing was falling; popular culture, including magazines, songs and biographies, sustained religious discourse, telling men and women how, separately, they should deport themselves to uphold Christian ideals. But I identified a huge change occurring in the 1960s, when discursive Christianity collapsed as a monopoly moral position in British culture. I identified this as a change wrought overwhelmingly by the declining acceptance by young women of the traditional restrictive Christian ideal of marriage, motherhood and domesticity.

That narrative of change in the 1960s was also the story I told in a second book in 2013, *Religion and the Demographic Revolution: Women and Secularisation in Canada, Ireland, UK and the USA since the 1960s*. In that, I used demography and the tools of statistical analysis of population from censuses and opinion polls to demonstrate the strength of the link between changes in religion, sexual activity and sexuality, education levels and the economy. On the face of it, this was a sharp change of methodology, but it was not a rejection of the cultural approach. Far from it. I argued that the greatest problem for the cultural historian is not to explain how culture survives, but how it changes, and that never occurs in isolation. I compiled and analysed the data on church decline and falling patterns of churchgoing, praying and religious identity in the four nations, and showed how secularization picked up speed fast in many places in the sixties, notably mainland Britain and parts of Canada, but came much later in others – in Ireland, the rest of Canada and the United States. And in using statistical measures, I was able to show that women were central to these processes. The change to women's religious ideals in the sixties was located in women's demographic lives – the declining fertility ratios, later marriage, rising singlehood, married women's increasing labour participation rate and the new power of higher education (which I showed was strongly correlated to diminishing religious identity). In all of these, the collapse of women's acceptance of (in the jargon, *reflexivity to*) traditional religious discourse on marriage, motherhood and, above all, domesticity was to be beheld. The book showed how the measures of religiosity turned a sharp corner in many parts of the West in the late 1960s and early 1970s, and how in all places the changing demographics of women's lives interacted with religious behaviour.

Statistics also, of course, demonstrate the scale of what has been taking place. Losing religion has become a very important phenomenon of our times. The people of no religion represented less than 2 per cent of the population of most Western nations in 1960, but numbers started to rise in the late 1960s and continued to do so. In Canada, people with no religion made up a mere 0.14 per cent of the population in 1871 and in 1961 still only 0.5 per cent; the figures then rose sharply to 4.3 per cent in 1971 and 23.9 per cent in 2011.[18] In 2001, 14.6 per cent of English people, 18.5 per cent of the Welsh, 27.6 of the Scots but only 1 per cent of those in Northern Ireland ticked 'no religion'; by 2011, the figures had reached 24.7 per cent for England, 32.1 per cent for Wales and 37.5 per cent of Scots and over 5 per cent of those in Northern Ireland.[19] In the United States, Gallup measured those without religion at 1 per cent in 1950, 2 per cent in 1960, 5 per cent in 1972, 9 per cent in 1987, 14 per cent in 2010, then accelerating to 19 per cent in 2014.[20] Statistics on belief in god produce quite widely differing results depending on the precise wording of the question. In Canada in 2012, belief in god was affirmed by 71 per cent of women and 64 per cent of men.[21] In Britain as a whole, the failure rate to respond affirmatively to the question 'Do you believe in God?' scored between 23 and 27 per cent between 1968 and 1990, but in 2001 reached 39 per cent.[22] In 2005, 18 per cent of the population of the European Union responded negatively to the question 'Do you believe in God?'.[23] In the United States, Gallup in 2011 found 92 per cent of Americans believed in god, down only a little from 98 per cent in the 1960s.[24] Where research has explored the beliefs of no religionists especially, it tends to show very low levels of belief in god. In England and Wales, of the 25 per cent of the population who didn't hold a religion in 2011, research by Linda Woodhead in 2013 suggests only 16 per cent (i.e. 4 per cent of the population) believe in a god.[25] Increasing evidence also shows that religious belief and practice is becoming confined to the older sections of the population, with a speed of change that is terrifying some church leaders.[26] Atheism is thus a highly appropriate academic label. There are complexities as to why there has been reluctance to self-describe as 'atheist', and we shall explore these later in this chapter and in Chapters 4 and 8. But the term is all the more apposite when used more broadly to cover those who live their lives as if there is no god.

Statistics can thus be a very good way of illuminating cultural history. They show how recent is the mass rise of disbelief, how fast it has grown since the 1990s and how it has started to spread out from Western Europe to the West generally. Discourse analysis and demographic analysis can be coupled together quite effectively to identify when the big changes in religious history occurred. But, the historian needs to always assert that the people are the agents of such change in a free society. Western secularization has been a sweeping transformation *of* the individual, and not something that has happened *to* him and her. People secularize themselves and, thereby, society is changed too. Secularization transforms the individual at all levels: from the interiority where the individual thinks about one's self, via their eyes which 'read' the world, through to the presentation of the self as an exteriority and on to the body's demographic life of sexual relationships, family formation and children, as well as work and educational life. The individual changes from what he or she was like before, and from what one's parents and forbears were like. It has been rare to depict secularization in this manner as a one-by-one process of individual loss of religion. It has been even rarer to depict it as a process that ends with millions of people living life as if there is no god. Methodologically, that is the next step after culture analysis and statistical analysis. It is time to turn to the people who lose religion.

What is the secular?

Central to the analysis of this, as of my two earlier books, are women. Helen Boyd was one of five cousins raised in northern England in the 1940s and 1950s. It was a rigid Christian extended family which Helen described as enveloped in a status-defined 'religion of respectability' that went by the title of Methodism. For a woman, her place was to be in marriage and the home. Though the brightest of the cousins, she was given the least prospect for career or qualifications. Yet, defying expectations, she trained as a nurse, emigrated to Canada and became a head nurse. After marriage, motherhood and widowhood whilst still a young woman, she retrained as a librarian where she again reached a senior role in the government libraries' service. On arrival in Canada in the sixties, she joined the Unitarian Universalists in their ethical intellectual phase in which, later, she found also a role for spirituality. How did the four cousins get on?

> Well, it's worked out. My brother was an out and out atheist; he wasn't that keen on royalty either you know, sell the crown jewels and settle the national debt. My next cousin, next to me, fell in love with a Jewish girl and converted to Judaism, and, you know, has been the President of the Synagogue and many things. The next cousin he is a lay Baptist preacher. And the youngest, she became a fundamentalist very much, but possibly the sweetest fundamentalist I know. She doesn't push anything on, or tell everybody she knows she is right, and, you know, every sentence she writes to you is the Lord be praised or so and so. But that's fine – it's her realm.[27]

This one family of five cousins displays important characteristics of modern Western religion and society. First to note is the rising gender equality and the possibility for married women's career achievements. Second, it shows the breakdown of religion as the definer of the extended family's culture. Third, there is the blossoming of the West's multifaith society, involving the breaking of the rigidities of inherited denominationalism, and the rising social freedom of religion and freedom from religion. Fourth, the cousins illustrate the opening up of loss of traditional religion. Two cousins broadly lost their religious heritage, and instead adopted positions between the atheistic and the spiritualistic, whilst three others converted to other religious stances. Consequently, one can say that there has been a rising diversity not just *of religion* but *of no religion.*

Despite this diversity, the West is being drawn together by a new story embedded in this remembrance. Until the mid-twentieth century, it was an axiom of the historian that the Western world was Christian and the rest of the world was, broadly speaking, not. But not any longer. With the benefit of hindsight, we can see that, from the late 1950s, parts of Western Europe started to secularize with barely credible rapidity, marked by decline in popular religiosity (adult churchgoing, younger children's Sunday-school attendance, rates of confirmation and first communion), and bewildering the churches as they confronted sexual revolutions and massive moral shifts in state and society. Behind this lay the rise of people without religion from a tiny minority to become, by the end of the century, between 15 and 25 per cent, and now in the 2010s from 25 to 52 per cent of the people of the most secular nations in Europe, Australia, New Zealand and Canada.[28] But even nations long thought immune to significant growth of people without religion – like the United States, Brazil, Malta, Cyprus, Poland and Ireland – have since the mid-2000s shown clear evidence that people are losing attachment to churches and faith.[29] There is now no nation in the Western world, including former Eastern Europe and Central and South America, in which measures of religiosity *per capita* are not in decline. In some of these nations the religiosity rate is still high and the rates of decline slow, but the ubiquity of change is significant and the pace has quickened. This loss of religiosity over the last seventy years has outstripped rates of religious conversion or religious switching, leaving the religious community in relative decline in the West. Elsewhere in the world, faith remains high and broadly static in most other zones (in Africa, the Middle East and South East Asia). Within that religious community, there are shifting allegiances – between the major religious traditions and between groups within them (such as the growth in some nations of Pentecostalism at the expense of Catholicism). Some sociologists and other academics have argued that a de-secularization, or re-enchantment of the whole world, has been going on.[30] The evidence in the West is overwhelming that they are wrong: the rate of losing religion *per capita* far exceeds any contrary trend.[31]

This makes understanding how people come to lose religion of huge importance. It raises issues immediately of defining the nature of what people are adopting *in lieu* of religion.

There is rarely a formal status for an individual losing religion. In Norway, individuals have historically been automatically registered as adherents of the Lutheran state church, to which a portion of taxes is earmarked, but, if wishing to de-register from that and not register for another church, the citizen can register for the Norwegian Humanist Association. Similarly, Icelanders are required to register their religion for tax purposes. That formal state-recognized status is limited amongst nations. Few people in censuses, usually less than 1 or 2 per cent, even today, have chosen to refer to themselves by a positive non-religious moniker – such as atheist, agnostic, humanist, rationalist or secularist – in large part because they were not offered such categories by census enumerators. So, the identity of the person with no religion is rarely described well. But this does not mean that it is an uncommon condition. Quite the reverse. The condition has become *so common* in the West since the 1960s that the individual's sense of necessity to have a moniker has weakened. This is a marked outcome of recent secularization: most without a religion do not adopt a substitute identity, and the majority, when pressed, still prefer not to. So, there is a huge category of Western people, growing rapidly, composed of those who have abandoned church connection but only a small proportion of whom have adopted, or think they have a need to accept, an identity.

This poses an issue about the public profile and the self-regard of those who lose religion. These are people who tend not to join an organization representing their non-religious position; they tend not to adopt a label and may positively conceal it. They may be consumed by doubt and uncertainty; they may not have a thought-through idea of what their non-religious position actually is; or, they may not care. This series of positions is likely not a complete inventory of the possibilities, and part of the research of this book is to explore the diversity more fully. But taken together, these positions tend to make the non-religious person illusive. Despite being in their tens of millions, real methodological problems attend researching the people of no religion.

The way in which scholars have approached no religionists has varied, and has suffered from its small-scale, limited disciplinary interest, poor methodological design and problems in conception. Of these limitations, that of conception is by far the most troublesome. Frequently, confessionalist linkage (of researchers or in recruitment of respondents) has weighted the understanding of what has been going on in a number of ways. One dominant assumption has been that the loss of church connection is overwhelmingly a temporary phenomenon, one affecting either specific generations (of the young mainly) – the sixties baby boomers, Generation X or Generation Y; this has been an idea rampant in American religious sociology since the 1970s.[32] It is clear in retrospect that it has been a false assumption, and misses the huge growth of those who have permanently lost church and faith. A second assumption has been that loss of church membership has been caused *by* the churches – by poor management, failure to attract and hold young people and lack of innovation; the latter issue in particular is an approach that has diverted American Christian churches since the 1960s.[33] A third problem is that because there is a church-driven concern with stopping the loss of people, the best way to study this subject is *either* by looking at those, mainly children, who show signs of *declining* religious attitude but have not left (and indeed are often recruited for study through churches or church schools) *or* by studying those who have lost and then *regained* their religion.[34] This practice of recruitment (often through churches) has meant that empirical research has rarely been reaching the significant group, those who have lost religion permanently. A fourth limitation has been the rise, and then the decline, of the Putnam thesis. This is the idea put forward first in 2000 that the decline of the churches in the United States (extended by some scholars to Britain and elsewhere) has been part of the wider collapse of the institutions of civil society as people allegedly have been withdrawing from participation in all forms of civil affairs – ranging from community action and leisure through political voting to communal pursuits like attending sports events and churches.[35] This thesis has been adopted by many in the churches as a sort of relief from the concept of religion declining alone, but has been attacked by other scholars as unfounded[36] and seemed to be singularly watered down by a second Putnam volume in 2010.[37] In these ways, joined by some others, research has been deflected from the glaringly obvious: organized religion, mainly Christianity and to an extent Judaism, has experienced severe and unremitting decline in popular adherence in all its forms in the West, specifically measurable since the 1960s.

The research methods described above have had certain consequences upon the results. Christian researchers have tended to find that the depth of no religionists' secularity is shallow because they have invariably restricted their research to those who have found their faith again;[38] such 'returners' are the least likely to have developed comprehensive secular selves, including atheism, during their lives. In addition, much of the research has been conducted by evangelical researchers examining those who have left evangelical churches; these are again the least likely to have become atheists – a group fed most by defection from mainline and liberal churches.[39] The development of scholarly doubt about loss of religion actually being a loss of religion at all has a long pedigree. It is quintessentially part of much Christian sociology to think that nobody truly loses a religion, whether because they were baptized in infancy (and thus have a changed state in the eyes of God and church) or because they will always retain a spiritual dimension to their self (even if they don't wish to or acknowledge it). But in the academic field of religious sociology, it was amongst North Americans of the late twentieth century that impermanency of losing religion became, for a period, axiomatic. Reginald Bibby in Canada argued in 1993 that 'most reaffiliate, typically identifying with the religion of their parents', and a decade later: 'The *Religious None* Category is characterized by a very high level of switching in and switching out. The category is more like a hotel than a home for many people.'[40] Meanwhile in the United States, Rodney Stark suggested that of the 11 per cent of Americans in 2005/7 who professed 'no religion', only one third were atheists 'who would reject anything beyond the physical world'.[41] In like manner, Stark with two co-researchers concluded that 'the apparent irreligiousness of many people in the United States, Sweden, and Japan is an illusion caused by a failure to define religion with sufficient breadth and nuance'.[42] This has given rise to debate about the 'fuzzy fidelity' of most who claim no religion. One study by Lim, Macgregor and Putnam split 'nones' almost equally into secular and 'liminal', and raised doubts as to whether the latter might return to a religion.[43]

A more plausible reading of the experience of the majority of those who self-describe as of 'no religion' is that it has been the underlying driver of the trajectory of secularization.[44] The proportion of this category that can be regarded as religious returners has been higher in the United States than in Britain, but it also seems likely that the proportion is declining as the overall numbers of those losing religion rise. So, as the normativity of holding to a religion is broken in a region, country or nation, so the possibility of *proclaiming* permanent loss of religion seems to rise. There is a new generation, those born in the late twentieth century, who agonize less over leaving religion, and commit for atheism young, quickly and more determinedly. In this regard, then, liminality or fuzzy fidelity might be seen as itself a *temporary category* – a transition condition of the late twentieth and early twentieth centuries arising from the sixties generation, providing a staging post for people in societies which were *en route* to deeper secularization. Certainly, the results of the research in this book suggest that there was a generational group, born in the second and third quarters of the twentieth century, who were once fuzzy in their doubt, but who have since faded to certainty.

Researching the little imagined atheist

How does the person without religion imagine himself or herself? Helen Boyd, quoted at the start of the previous section, made the point eloquently that part of the condition which she entered has a space for something she was happy to call 'spirituality'. Just as the term 'Christian' covers a huge spectrum of belief and belonging (and includes a minority identified by researchers as agnostics or even atheists), so those without religion cover a spectrum. There are issues in singling out a term to cover this spectrum. The most appropriate in my view is 'atheist'.

'Atheist' is not the most common term used by non-believers. Most by far – almost 99 per cent in most cases – merely accept 'non-religion' or 'none' as a category offered on a census form, with just over 1 per cent offering written-in descriptions. In the England census of 2011, written-in identification came, in order of popularity, as agnostic, atheist, humanist. In Canada in the same year, written-in identification came in the order atheist, agnostic, humanist, collectively making up 1.1 per cent of those without religion.[45] But whether the term is used in self-identity or not, it is the comprehensive loss of religion by millions of individuals that marks out the dominant historical trend in Western religion since the 1960s. It is this that obliges our focus. And atheism is the best description of the end product of losing religion. Historically, the atheist is actually a person most commonly branded by those who dislike him or her. It has been so since ancient Greece, when the term 'the *atheos*' came to apply when, after a long period of general freedom of religion and non-religion, trials started of 'the godforsaken' in the fifth century BCE.[46] The term was common from the Middle Ages to the nineteenth century (and led Thomas Huxley to coin the term 'agnostic' in 1869 as a more acceptable alternative that met the circumstances of science and reason), and became a moniker of ideological terror in the second half of the twentieth century as part of the Western right-wing prosecution of the Cold War.[47] Not surprisingly, then, the bulk of atheists haven't called themselves atheists. Mostly, they don't call themselves *anything*. This is different from being 'fuzzy' about their 'fidelity'. It is about a deep and historically new disinterest in having religion or any moniker whatsoever concerning religion (including atheism) in their lives.

The typical atheist of the period since 1960 is hidden, self-concealed, inarticulate, difficult to locate because he or she rarely volunteers for the role and, in most cases, is too disinterested to put a hand up to be counted. In part, the problem is epistemological. The terms which are available for the respondent to use are various, but their popularity in interview discourse varies hugely. The tabulation in Table 1.1 cannot be used to directly divide the interviewees into categories, and this is almost impossible, and undesirable, since each used different terms – for instance, to describe their position at different points in their lives or, in some cases, to describe their multiple self-descriptions at any one point in time. The words were sometimes spoken by me, sometimes in a prompt (for which see my discussion below). But the table reflects the vocabulary of discussion of my interviewees and the words they use in articulating their non-religious self.

If the table represents a guide to solving the issue of labelling the non-religious person, the biggest problem is that there is a reluctance to come upon – to approach – any of these. Even amongst those I have interviewed who are members of an organization with a word like 'Secular' or 'Atheist' or 'Humanist' in its title, there can be a reluctance to self-describe using these terms. Sometimes, the respondent describes having gone through different stages – from agnostic to atheist is common, though, occasionally, it stops at agnostic or the reverse happens. To get some respondents to self-

Table 1.1 How respondents discussed the non-religion in their lives

Terms used in conversation with 77 interviewees: Rank order of usage	Incidence of use
Humanist/humanism	1,266/602
Atheist/atheism	622/165
Agnostic/agnosticism	131/19
Spiritual/spirituality/spiritualist	98/41/7
Skeptic/skepticism*	81/7
Rationalist/rationality/rationalism	39/15/14
Secularist/secularism/ secular**	28/21/218
Freethinker/freethinking/freethought	20/6/3
Ethical society	19
Non-believer/unbeliever	10/0
Apostate/apostasy	1/1
Unaffiliated	1

*Including sceptic and scepticism.
**Secular was used both as a self-describer and as a description of society.

describe at all, I occasionally had to offer terms. I would characteristically say towards the end of an interview where a respondent had not made clear how they described themselves: 'So, how would you describe yourself: atheist, agnostic, humanist, or what?' I look more closely in Chapter 8 at the terms and their usage by respondents.

Does this make the growing magnitude of the modern Western atheism unresearchable? Overall, sociological attempts to explore the *causes* of the rise of no religionism have been rather basic. They have tended to focus on the influence of non-religious parents to produce non-religious children, of non-religious peers to associate and the greater propensity of liberal Christians to lose religion.[48] But these findings miss the central issue that secularization, as a major historical shift, requires explanation of change – of how people who have a religion then lose it. Some have explored the particular position of religious doubt and decline amongst school children, but this has suffered from three main flaws: first, they have almost entirely been conducted in schools which are either managed by churches or have a strong religious ethos; second, they have been mostly conducted within a strong framework of religious understanding; and third, they did not follow up the children in the long term to see whether they actually lost religion or not.[49] There have also been thoughtful and well-informed studies by individuals who have lost religion.[50] But the growing collections of atheist narratives rarely address issues of historical causation.[51] Oral history may be able to assist in filling this gap. What is actually going on when somebody loses their religion? What are the triggers, the processes and the contexts?

It is important to explain something of the methodology of this study. Oral history is now a well-known and much-used tool of the cultural historian, as it is of scholars of many disciplines. It is a technique that once was framed by social-science methodologies of the 1960s and 1970s – of mass interviewing, representative national samples, fixed and lengthy questionnaires seeking standardized and quantifiable answers and hired interviewers trained to only ask the questions listed. Those approaches withered in the 1980s and 1990s, being replaced by semi-structured interviews with trained interviewers providing flexible space in which respondents may develop the narration of their lives, with latitude to contextualize as they think fit. Through the 1990s and 2000s, more attention fell upon the narrator, the manner of narration, the interaction with the interviewer and what might be learned from these. This makes the manner as much as the content of narration important to analysis, and elevates the interviewer as an unavoidable element in a process that generates non-standardized testimony that is oftentimes idiosyncratic and always revealing. National representative samples are now widely recognized as impracticable. It is not representativeness that is important, but discerning the diversity of experience and narration. The aim is to project the spectrum from which emerge typologies and paradigms. Academic oral history practitioners typically suggest that when an oral historian keeps hearing the same stories, often at around twenty to thirty interviews, then he or she has interviewed enough people to have plausibly exhausted the typologies.[52] This project has eighty-five respondents so that sub-groups are better explored.

From this, the conceptual framework for the oral history analysis is dominated by two different but parallel approaches. On the one side, there is the 'empirical-historical' information gleaned from respondents about the circumstances of their loss of religion and what they became as a result – the age, timing, triggers and descriptions of their post-religious self. The result is an informed review of the demographic circumstances dominating individual religion loss. But on the other side is oral history theory. Here, the focus is not on the 'surface information' of an interview, but rather on a series of conceptual tools deployed by oral historians.[53] The first of these is a regard for *the self*, in which the nature of selfhood becomes explored through people's own words, and how changes to the nature of selfhood during the narrator's lifetime may be perceived through changes in, for example, language, emotion (both recalled emotion and emotion evident in the interview) and in the form of narration evident in the testimony. The second conceptual tool is *composure*, in which (the theory argues) each narrator is composing and seeking composure – or creating a story *and* a contented acceptability of their life. Dis-composure, including emotional narrative, is a useful tool for analysing the problematic, traumatic ways in which loss of religion occurred for some narrators. The third tool is *memory*, in which the interest is not in the *reliability* of memory over particular incidents or dates, but over the way in which a narrator links the present (the time of the interview) with the past in the construction of a story. Memory takes verbal shape in the interaction between the time of telling with the time recalled. This includes examination of the influence upon the construction of an individual's memories of 'collective memory' of nation, community or family, and the place of religion within that – a hegemonic popular memory, or absence of one. Fourth, there is *narrative* – the examination of the ways in which people place religion in their interpretation of the world, which features prominently in some chapters ahead. Fifth, there is intersubjectivity, the interaction of interviewer with interviewee, and what can be learned from this creative encounter. Additionally, we will come upon other theoretical issues, some of them new, as we go through the evidence.

Life stories are an especially important method for the historian of the second half of the twentieth century. The idea of doing oral history has been around for some time amongst Christian scholars interested in allowing churches and religious organizations to better understand the targets for evangelization. Christian researchers who use life story or oral history research tend to have explicit acceptance of the normativity of religious adherence, the teleology of rescue of the 'lapsed' and a seeming incomprehension at the failure of individuals to accept the Christian message.[54] Some studies have been sensationalist, usually the product of writing for church audiences, intended to shock by making the loss of religion seem dramatic and even catastrophic, and tend to presume that every human has 'spiritual needs', and that those losing god can readily find him or her again.[55] But even in historical scholarship on the early-modern period, the idea of the shallowness of conversion *out of a* religious culture is common.[56] In contemporary history too, scholars seem overly convinced that such conversion might be transient or vulnerable.[57]

Psychology is one discipline in which value judgements like these seem to be unavoidable. Certainly, much of psychologists' research has used normative religious concepts, especially in relation to children (which we examine in Chapter 3); this was most famously evident in Hardy's 1979 study of spirituality which only sought recruits with spiritual experiences, but even a recent major textbook, whilst acknowledging the limited extent of research, seems to understate the quality of unbelief and exaggerate the evils of atheism.[58] But things have been changing. In 2004, Altemeyer recognized the significance of the sharp rise of non-belief in Western nations, though creating a non-religious-based secularity score is still only in its infancy.[59] Luke Galen leads in his research on well-being in showing that non-believers have not got lower well-being scores than religious believers, and can have higher scores;[60] he has also shown that atheists have high scores for seeking to do good for others (prosociality).[61] Yet, the discipline seems to have a long way to go to recognize the importance of becoming atheist as a research priority. Meanwhile, an anthropologist, Matthew Engelke, has initiated research into the nature of organized humanism in England, and this is surely an area where research will expand.[62]

Value judgement on belief and unbelief may for some disciplines be unavoidable. But the oral historian's judgement can and, I would argue from an ethical research viewpoint, can only be legitimately based on the respondents' judgements upon themselves. So, unlike Galen, I am not measuring nor judging for myself the well-being of the individual atheist in contrast to the religionist; apart from anything else, as a social historian, I am not equipped with the skills to do this. But the *sine qua non* of this study is that becoming atheist has all the potential of being a life-enhancing transformation. To do that, I accept the judgement, explicit or implicit, of the respondent himself or herself in their narrative. There is no other ethical position for an historian without means of empirical testing to adopt. In contrast to faith-informed studies, this book studies atheism in itself, doesn't regard the loss of religion as a catastrophe for either the individual or for society and takes the word of my respondents on the absence of faith in their lives at face value. It also approaches atheism as capable of being a positivity, as an enhancement of the individuals' sense of their self if expressed in interview. But it is not my place as a historian to measure this.

So, the emphasis here is on ways of narrating and what is narrated. The study starts in Chapter 2 by locating the narrative of losing religion beside the other main narratives about religion to be found in existing oral history archives. Then, Chapters 3–8 examine the circumstances of losing religion and coming upon humanist and atheist identity. Seventy-eight people were interviewed face to face, six by email; one failed to sign off 'consent to use' after interview and transcription.[63] Reaching atheists in different nations posed problems. I initiated the project in 2009 by creating a website containing my question schedule of twenty topics which I wished to raise with volunteers, along with details of the project's aims and expected outputs, an informed consent form and the copyright clearance form. I instigated volunteering by joining atheist, ethical and humanist organizations both at home in Britain and abroad in Canada and the United States; this posed no ethical problem for the author, as I am a humanist and atheist. Volunteers were each referred to the website, generally weeks before I actually met them, and, when I did, I answered any questions they might have.[64] This system ensured that my volunteers were well aware of the project's aims and were often rehearsed and certainly committed to giving me their stories. This resulted in a lack of unresponsiveness (though some hesitancy did arise, of which more later in the book) and a proliferation of rather well thought-through accounts, some of them deeply affective. British respondents were almost all recruited after I gave lectures to humanist or secularist groups –

in London, Preston, Glasgow, Edinburgh, Perth, Dundee and Inverness –
whilst some were recruited in the Birmingham, Bristol and London areas
through emailing the leaders of such groups asking for volunteers. Those
from Canada and the United States were mostly recruited after I joined
local online MeetUp[65] groups and posted invitations to volunteers, but then
following up with a visiting lecture at which the recruits came forward.
I would then spend three to five days in a city interviewing, the cities
being Berkeley and San Francisco in California (visited in 2009); Boston
in Massachusetts (2013); Washington DC (2014); Vancouver (2009, 2012,
2014) and Victoria (2012) in British Columbia; and Toronto (2009) and
Hamilton (2009) in Ontario. I interviewed further Americans whom I met
whilst they were visiting in Canada and the United Kingdom, and a few
by email. Other individuals were recruited by recommendation in France
and Estonia, by chain recruitment, by chance readers of my website and by
being referred to me. All the interviews were conducted in English, and one
to one, except for one woman whose elderly husband sat in silently at the
back of the room. One additional interview I cite was undertaken by my
colleague, Lynn Abrams. The interviews were conducted in respondents'
homes, my hotel room, my university office or a borrowed university
room whilst abroad, and one by telephone. They characteristically lasted
between one and two hours, usually in one go, though two interviews were
conducted over two sessions. They were digitally recorded,[66] transcribed
by paid transcribers and then checked by me against the recording. A small
number of respondents requested anonymity and were asked to select or
were assigned pseudonyms. Testimonies quoted are straight transcriptions
with minor infelicities (such as routine verbal tics and repeated words)
removed; in some cases, infelicities have been left to truthfully convey the
intensity of discourse, whilst incomplete sentences or phrases are marked
thus '---'.[67] For analytical purposes in this volume, the oral testimonies have
been aggregated in chronological order of interview in a *Compendium
of Oral Testimonies* (COT, totalling 1,124 pages and 649,000 words in
pdf format) and a *Compendium of Written Testimonies* (CWT, totalling
86 pages), which will be deposited with the audio files and transcripts at
the conclusion of the project in the Freethought and Humanism Collection
at the Bishopsgate Archive, London. The footnotes refer to these two
Compendia.

The routes from religion to no religion the eighty-five told me were
diverse. The stories are personal and well-remembered aspects of the
individuals' lives. Compressing their stories into a book such as this will
necessarily tend to denude detail, complexity and autonomy. In the words
of the postcolonial historian Ranajit Guha, to seek to explain something is
to seek to control it, and to start the movement away from the individual
as an agent of history. The causes identified in analysis lift the historian's
narrative one step above the place of the individual: 'To know the cause of a
phenomenon is already a step taken in the direction of controlling it.' This,

then, becomes a power exerted by the scholar, employing the categories of the historian, the debates and intellectual contexts in which he or she moves, and brings an alien series of structures to the individual's life narrative. The danger is that the historian becomes 'a prisoner of empty abstractions'.[68] This is unavoidable, yet also necessary. For the purpose is to seek out the reasons why a unique demographic phenomenon of mass evacuation of religious self-identity occurred in the Western world between the end of the Second World War and the early twenty-first century. It is important to seek out the trends, reasons and outcomes.

The dimensions of losing religion and coming to atheism and humanism are not exhausted in this book; the testimony I have obtained is rich and capable of much further analysis. One topic, the denominational origins of those who lost religion, I have started to examine elsewhere,[69] whilst certain characteristics of becoming atheist which I touch upon here are also left for further study – the influence of spirituality, sixties radicalism and death. Here I concentrate on the six most striking dimensions: childhood, indifference, women's narratives, men's narratives, ethnicity and the humanist condition which emerged for so many of them. These fit in with my writings since 2001 that secularization links culture, demography and the individual's life changes, and never more violently as in the 'long 1960s'. This book completes my trilogy on that pivotal moment. Discourse, demography and testimony are three very different but connectable ways of imagining secularization, fused in the theoretical ideas I entertained in an earlier book on postmodern theory.[70] Through life-story analysis, I adhere to the viewpoint that culture is not something merely endured by the individual, but is something that is changed by the individual. This is especially the case in relation to religious decline in the 1960s when there was, broadly, no detectable policy by any sizeable institution to weaken religious culture but, on the contrary, was something driven (traditionally expressed, though perhaps sometimes with a disrespectful disdain, as 'from below') by people. Discourse was slow to change in the 1960s: the people moved faster. What they were seeking and how they were challenging the existing cultures of a dominant religious culture have not been properly explored before. This is what I am doing in this book.

CHAPTER TWO

Narratives of Belief and Unbelief

Oral history and religion

People with a faith tend to find an easy rhetoric to express it. In the United States, oral evidence is central to much scholarship on the religious culture of the nation, as it is also to modern congregational, denominational and ethnic identities.[1] In Britain, oral history has moulded recent writing on the history of religiosity and its decay.[2] By contrast, oral history has played much less role in the exploration of *loss* of religion. Why? First, it is conceptually difficult to approach the decline of religion within an individual's life story. A narrative of diminishing religiosity may be an unappealing attribute of a life story; it is negative, perhaps feared as diminishing of morality, and conceived as hollowing the self. Second, there are major cultural consequences to admitting absence of faith. In nations with strong religious cultures, like Ireland, Poland and the United States, alienation from religion has conventionally dented the appearance of conformity, patriotism and citizenship. Third, a narrative of personal loss of religion has not been long available in some cultures, rendering difficulty in articulating it. As we shall see, there is little atheist heritage – discourse or collective memory – to draw upon.

This chapter explores the place of 'becoming atheist' narratives within the spectrum of oral life stories of religion since the 1950s. Here, I read in detail over 200 oral history interview transcripts, from over a thousand reviewed in existing archives of life stories, to draw lessons about the chronicling of religion and secular change within life narratives. These interviews come from archives in the United Kingdom, the United States and Canada, chosen because they comprise 'whole life' interviews from projects with no special interest in the loss of religion but, instead, other interests – radicalism, black consciousness, feminism, social class, working-class history, community history or music. It cannot be said that oral history is ever without a purpose, so there is no 'neutral' in that sense (even if that were desirable, let alone feasible). Still, the rest of this book concerns those who have lost religion and were recruited for that reason; the interviews analysed in this chapter constitute a 'control' set. Just how does the story of losing faith intrude into individual and collective life narratives? These 'general' life testimonies come from oral history collections where, first, the narrators discuss, or were offered the opportunity to discuss, religion in their lives; second, the collections collectively provide a range of respondents by gender and ethnicity; third, the interviewees come from a cross section of American, British and Canadian society. Fourth and last, the interviews have been transcribed, open to researchers; and consent to use extracts in publication has been allowed. The collections, and numbers of transcripts, consulted are listed in the Sources. We start with normative narratives – how religion was placed as a standardized, accepted and acceptable feature in the life story. From there, we move to the emergence of normative-breaking life narratives – including from socialists and feminists.

The Christian self

There is a long-standing argument that oral testimony is reflexive to discourse. As Penny Summerfield put it in 1998, an individual draws upon 'the generalized subject available in discourse to construct the personal subject'.[3] There has, however, been a recent critique, led by Michael Roper in the study of gender, of the way historians stack reliance upon cultural discourses to deliver satisfactory understanding of the self.[4] This would be translated in the present research to ask if the religious self is that greatly dependent on the cultural environment. I will return to the case and its critique at later points. But in this section, I want to draw attention to the continued applicability of cultural reflexivity of the individual as a useful approach in societies with potent discourses. I suggested this in an earlier book, studying Britain between 1800 and 1960, in which what I termed 'discursive Christianity' was a powerful cultural normativity few could resist, evident in oral history with individuals reflecting back to the interviewer – often in deeply committed and hybridized personal ways – the acceptable religious narrative of their culture. But I noted its decaying power in secularizing Britain from the 1960s.[5] Contrastingly, in the present study we include a society like the United States in which Christian culture has remained from the 1960s to the 2010s exceptionally strong and largely normative. Does oral history reflect this divide between post-1960 America and Britain?

There has possibly never been a nation as religiously diverse as
the United States. Even by 1890, 143 denominations and numerous
independent congregations were listed in the census.[6] This did not
weaken, but strengthened, the salience of religious normativity, tending to
render outlandish those narratives that were non-religious or secularist.
Paradoxically, modernity's ecclesiastical fractures could grant security
against the erosion of the religious narrative; a multitude of churches assured
adaptability, and the relevance, of the *idea* of the normative. This is plain
to see in late twentieth-century American oral history archives which play
back to the researcher the multiplicity of the normative narratives. Take the
testimony of Anne Thomas, born in 1930 and brought up in Flemington,
New Jersey, interviewed in 2007. About one third in, the interviewer asked:

Interviewer: You had mentioned that you and your friend were
                 at Sunday school. I wanted to ask you about the role
                 of religion in the town or in your family; was there a
                 prominent denomination within the town?
Thomas: We were Presbyterians. There was a Baptist church, a very
                 active Baptist church, a very active Methodist church, a
                 small Episcopal church. There was a very small Jewish
                 synagogue and a Catholic church.
Interviewer: That sounds pretty diverse, for a small town.
Thomas: Yes, it was, it was. My father was chair of the board of
                 trustees, or whatever it was called in those days, of our
                 church, and we went to church, we went to Sunday school,
                 every Sunday. [laughter][7]

And that, broadly, was the only direct mention of religion in a 43-page life
testimony. But it stands as an expressive token of the place of religion in
the life. For those born before the 1960s, it is a common, almost totemic,
insertion into the oral narrative, signalling the strength of church affiliation,
weekly attendance and managerial support for a congregation in the story of
an archetypal American family, whether Protestant, Catholic or Jew. Indeed,
it describes a community, common to much of the Western world from the
late eighteenth century, in which religious identity was nearly universally
standard, with favours divided between major denominations with names
like these. Religious belonging was thus fractured but common, and its
narratives normative.[8]
   But within the normativity lay important variation. One concerned
gender. In oral history archives, life stories of women born early in
the twentieth century and interviewed in their senior years sparkle
with reference to religion and its role in youthful femininity. Women's
testimonies very often revolve around effervescent recollection of
childhood churchgoing in Sunday-best clothing, with stories of special
dresses, coats and gloves, and the purchase of these. Monica Strack, born

into a German Catholic community in 1905 in Minnesota, Oklahoma and Arkansas, recalled with tenderness in 2002 the day she dressed up for first communion:

> I made my first communion in Oklahoma. That was called a private communion. It was very nice. They made a special day out of it. We had a big breakfast. When I was about thirteen. They called it a solemn communion at that time. We dressed like a little bride and the boys were dressed up in suits. That would have a bigger crowd. They were both highlights in my life.[9]

From Scotland comes near identical testimony from 1990:

> Oh, you always had something good to wear on a Sunday, and it was kept for the Sunday, and your Sunday boots or shoes…Oh, I thought I was a princess. I can mind [remember] one of them was cream and the other was blue, and they were full from the yoke down, and I used to burl out and there was a pair of boots and oh, they came practically almost up to my knee and they were all tooled. Oh they were beautiful. Oh I was a toff![10]

British female respondents recall also the time spent in church. Here's Mrs Annie Snow, born 1885 in Hinckley in Leicestershire, England, speaking in 1984:

> The Holy Trinity…That was my church, it was lovely. But of course it was the old Trinity Hall, did you know that? It's down now. The Leisure Centre's there, that was our church. I was brought up there. I went to the day school at the side of it. You know, all our lives were spent in church 'do's'. There was nowhere else to go: I was married in the old church in 1906; the new church was dedicated in 1910. Anyway, as I was saying, our lives were spent at church. You had Band of Hope on Monday nights; Bible Class on Tuesday nights; Church values to go on Wednesday night; Thursday night, you had a social in the upper room. I mean, Fridays was bath night and about the only night you was away. The church on Sunday, you was there all day. Sunday School in the early morning, then out of there into church, 'cause it was next door then. We spent all our lives at church and loved it.[11]

For all that early twentieth-century churches might have been patriarchal institutions active in recirculating discourses of female subordination, women's testimonies ooze with a gratified sense of the church service as a feminine space, of 'chumming' with friends and daring to be saved on a regular basis: '[Y]ou would look along the line to see who wanted to be saved and if you thought you were safe you would put your hand up and you'd

Laughter

go forward...I must have been ten or eleven or something by that time. Oh yes, it was all religion.' As this respondent recalled: 'I don't know why we didnae sprout wings [laughs].'[12] Sunday was special, a day of restraint from pleasure and all but work of necessity or mercy, but paradoxically it was also 'everyday' – a regular day for a devotional spectacle that risked deviancy for those failing to submit.[13]

Such comments are standard fare in Western oral history testimony of elderly women interviewed late in the twentieth century. Narrators often ended their description of Sunday churchgoing and special dresses with laughter. This was an emotional distancing between the self of the present and the self of the past, a record of change and bemusement – as when Anne Thomas the elder is recalling Thomas the younger. But the distancing was more acute in British oral history, the 'sprouting wings' remark a clear estrangement of the British adult from her childhood self. Interviewer and interviewee shared a significantly more secularized perspective on the religious past – the laughter is more frequent, its jovial self-mockery sharper, a signal that cultural transition has occurred. In the density of that laughter, the researcher may detect a symptom of secularization.

Other emotions come into play with male respondents who, much less given to light-hearted or tender religious recollections, bring a gravity to their narratives. In the American South, commentary in the oral history archive had both white and black oral history respondents referencing the Ku Klux Klan; one white respondent recalled: 'They were primarily against Catholics and Jews and the blacks...you know that back in the 1870s, if it hadn't been for the Klan in the South, that was the only home rule that we had any semblance of.'[14] In Britain, men recollected their detestation of the stiff little suits they were forced to don for church. Ronald Walker, born in 1902 in Leeds in northern England, was exasperated in 1970 recalling childhood:

> I was dressed, Heaven help me, in sailor suits, dark blue in winter, white on summer days, so you haven't to sit down anywhere for fear you'd dirty your backside, until I got – I don't now, 8 or 9, and then I was into, of all things, an Eton suit for Sundays. And these were very much our Sunday clothes.[15]

Here is one normative British narrative showing change between the time remembered and the time of remembering, expressed with male derision rather than female celebration. Like the laughter, the displays of infuriation signal secularization between the past and present.

By contrast, American oral history projects seem less able to winkle out *altered* normativities – the result either of reticence to chronicle lower religious devotion or, as many testimonies indicate, because men's religiosity was largely unchanged in its intensity since youth. Also, American oral history interviewers present more religious discourse in their questions.

Quite apart from numerous religious-based oral history projects in US archives,[16] general life history interviews often contain explicit invitations to mark the religious content of home and community life. When one interviewee in a 2008 university project spoke of the type of songs sung around the family piano as a child, the interviewer said, 'Sounds all secular. Was there any hymnal?' The outcome was that the interviewee was spurred into recollection of religious songs.[17] Compared to most British researchers, American oral historians demonstrate a greater facility with religious issues, and a readiness to invite evidence of their respondents' religiosity. This 'sympathetic' religious intersubjectivity is much rarer in the United Kingdom, where interviewees and interviewers tend to be more secular and seemingly more sensitized to the possibility of offence being taken. More than that, the American cultural narrative visualizes religion within the overall life story, bearing an unquestioned prominence and burden of meaning in citizenship and patriotic dreams, whilst in white British culture – more secularized than black and Asian immigrant culture – religion becomes subordinate, broken off from the life, reduced to a question about Sundays 'in those days' rather than religion in the life.

This difference is mirrored between British and American politicians. In the United States, though several early leading US politicians were either deists or agnostics, by the twentieth century it was difficult for politicians to fail to discuss their religiosity. This became, and to a great extent remains, the case in the American South and in the black community. It is evident in the interview of Thomas Bradley, born to a family of African American sharecroppers in Texas in 1917 that moved to Los Angeles when he was seven. Serving as a police officer for twenty-one years, he became five-time mayor of Los Angeles from 1973 to 1993, and, like many American politicians, his oral history life story told in 1978 discusses religion a great deal. He spoke especially of his mother's influence: 'She was a woman who was deeply religious.' He described how on Sundays she gathered all the children and took them on a streetcar to spend the whole day at Baptist Sunday school, including for church and dinner, and often staying too for an evening service:

> I suppose that without any preaching, without any great detail about what she expected and wanted of her children in terms of their moral and ethical values, without calling it the Golden Rule, she lived that kind of life, and she always spelled out for us that she expected us to do the same thing: to treat our friends and fellows with respect, to do unto them as we would have them do unto us.[18]

By contrast, outwith Northern Ireland, British politicians have rarely spoken of their personal religiosity like this, and a general convention has long prevailed for it to not be a subject for discussion by either press or political opponents. So much so that when in 2003 Tony Blair, the British prime minister, started talking on television of his religious faith, he restrained himself, saying, 'Best not to take it too far', whilst his spokesman said pointedly, 'We don't do God.'[19]

A distance emerges between American and British oral history of religion – a cultural distance. Despite remembrance of near identical facets of church life, the manner of recollection by the last quarter of the twentieth century came with different inflections – in Britain, medleys of laughter, derision, fading faith, some silences about religion and diverging intersubjectivity dynamics, exposing the decay of religion in popular culture.

The fortified religious self

These divergences flourish on turning to the distinctive American narrative of *strengthening* religious activity in adulthood compared to youth. This was almost wholly absent in British oral history archives. This was shared by two groups who might customarily be categorized as religious opposites – the evangelical and liberal Christian.

Here is the narrative of the growing religiosity of the *liberal* Christian self. Mary Lou Norton Busch, born 1923 in St Louis, Missouri, was brought up Presbyterian and sent to Sunday school even when her parents didn't go, and on marriage her husband 'became a Christian'. The couple moved a great deal, and with time Mary Lou increased her church voluntary work. Strongly liberal in politics and moral issues, she recalled how, when they lived in Cleveland, Ohio, in 1964–6, her Presbyterian church minister pronounced to the local presbytery (for which she was preparing the dinner) that 'Ministers have no business marching for Civil Rights'. She remembered:

> That's the first time I think I had ever questioned a minister and would have left a church, because of it. I believed you put up with whatever ministers believed, but that statement, to me, was heretical. How in the world, if you believe in Jesus Christ, or don't, at least know anything about His teachings, you could possibly say that? … So, that's what I believe in and I tried to write what I believe in, and it's very hard.

When her husband died in 1989, she was already very active in international women's organizations at home and overseas, including Women's World Banking to extend financial training to poorer women. She became a devoted volunteer for a wide variety of Presbyterian church projects in California, emerging in the 1990s as a volunteer friend to HIV/AIDS victims in the gay community, a helper in a food pantry for the poor and an assistant in a sanctuary movement for undocumented immigrants. Her church activity became effectively full time, including attending

Presbyterian church retreats: 'I call it my "spiritual fix" for the year.' Her adult religious activity was markedly more frenetic compared to her youth, but she carefully described herself as being far from strong in her faith:

> I'm really not very religious. I am a poor person for that, but I do believe in social justice … I can't live that life, with the wealthy. I just can't live the culture. I'm wealthy, I guess, but I can't be comfortable with people who are not worried about the poor people and injustice. I was getting to the point where; well, I have to say that, unfortunately, I think, with religion, the more older you get and the more educated you get, the more [of a] problem you have with religion, organized religion.[20]

Yet, Mary Lou located her social activism on poverty and homosexuality in a religious environment, making for a paradoxical, but perhaps not uncommon, rising intensity to her church belonging. Though she maintained that she was not 'very religious', her testimony came alive as she talked uninterrupted for an extended period on a church life comprising a truly impressive, almost daunting, range of charitable and social action deeds.

This narrative is not uncommon in American oral history, but is much harder to locate in British archives. Liberal Christian activism was an important feature of the 1950s and 1960s, especially in relation to the Church of England's part in fighting for decriminalization of homosexuality, the Campaign for Nuclear Disarmament, the anti-apartheid movement and for Labour and Liberal activists opposing wars and fighting racism.[21] But two things are different. First, each of these movements in the United Kingdom was by no means dominated by Christian-led organizations, but included a very large contingent of secular people, gay men and women, left-wingers and communists (including Trotskyists), and Afro-Caribbean and Asian organizations. Second, American oral history archives include the liberal Christian activist much more frequently than British archives do. A not untypical example is Mary Robinson, born in about 1921 in New Jersey, brought up by Quaker parents, who remained inspired by Quakerism, leading her to play a significant role during the 1940s in objecting to racial segregation in church services of the Women's Army Corps.[22] The national narrative of radical social action in the mid-twentieth century is strikingly more Christian-based in the United States than in the United Kingdom, reflecting the much greater involvement of voluntary organizations in welfare activity, even in the least 'churched' states like Washington.

A feature that arises, perhaps in part explaining this, is the different connection between religion and the Second World War that emerges between UK and US oral history. The war emerges in US oral history interviews as both vital to family formation and to the location of religion in this process.

Here are three examples. First, Bertha Bell, born 1922 in Indianapolis, Indiana, had a Jewish mother and father who had met via a 'matchmaker' in New York; her father was a tailor who wanted a Jewish woman who could cook. Her mother kept a kosher household, and Bertha and her family observed all the Jewish holidays, and when she was at the University of Indianapolis she continued to attend a conservative synagogue. She narrated how it was during military training in 1942 that she met her husband, the third man she had dated, and straight away knew she would marry him. But they had to wait until he returned from service in 1946, and thereafter they sustained a Jewish connection during their marriage and the bringing up of their children.[23] Second, Marie Griffin, born in 1919 in New York City, noted how much dating went on in the war years, and how many young couples got married. She too got engaged, recalling, 'And so one October day, we became engaged. There was an engagement party. I got a brown velveteen suit in honor of the occasion.' But she became concerned with the mania for marriage during the war years, and decided she would delay her own, and met another man, Wes. She referred in interview to the correspondence between her husband and herself in 1944 as he underwent military training. He wrote as follows:

> God and my country have been good to me. Under my church and the stars and stripes I have been able to choose my own profession, work for an education, and love the girl of my choice. In none of the axis nations is this possible. I need not fear a knock on the door, what I may say in public, or what I may do consciously or unconsciously. In this country my home is my castle, my God my fortress. Everything a free people believe in, live for, and desire is at stake.[24]

On marrying they had five children, becoming a typical churchgoing family of the 1950s and 1960s. And third, Ruth Moncrief, born 1921 in Bridgeton, New Jersey, was raised in a Methodist church but during her life moved around a variety of Protestant churches – all of them, she reported, were 'good'. Her testimony comes alive recalling in great detail her wartime church wedding with a wedding dress and a reception organized despite war privations.[25]

In the United Kingdom, there was a similar boost to marriage and the birth rate as a result of the Second World War. But though there is evidence there and in some other European nations of Christian resurgence after 1945,[26] it is markedly less prominent in general oral history archives. In recollection, religious experience of the 1950s and 1960s, which are in general UK oral history collections, tends to dwell upon church activity rather than religious commitment: the routines of Sunday worship, and even Billy Graham's crusades as novelty, rather than as part of a spiritual history of the individual.

The most striking, malleable and resilient normative narrative of religious growth was that of the evangelical – a story with staggering influence from the 1790s, with its distinctive emphasis on oppositional polarities of good and evil, sober and drunk, born again and heathen, and female piety and masculine temptation. This generated a narrative structure for most occasions, strikingly prominent in children's literature and teenage girls' magazines as late as the 1950s and early 1960s.[27] Oral history archives demonstrate how commonly interviewees spoke in evangelical ways, being reflexive to the discourse structure of either/or. One example is Jim Blair, born 1935 in Arkansas, who was taken to church by relatives who rarely attended themselves. He spoke of gaining ideas at the Baptist Church Sunday school, recalling a song there that undergirded his strong integrationist views in adult life: 'Red and yellow, black and white/They are equal in His sight/Jesus loves the little children of the world.' At the age of 12 in 1947 he was part of what he termed a 'youth revival', inspired by a charismatic, 'very hypnotic' preacher at Baptist Wednesday night meetings when he experienced 'my big conversion' and was baptized. The youth revival became regular, occurring the following year too, and in the midst of an acrimonious business night meeting he heard God:

> And God speaks to me, and God says, 'Go up there and take the microphone and tell those people to shape up', which I did. I mean – and do I now believe that God speaks to thirteen-year-old boys? No, I don't. I suspect it was some kind of autohypnosis. I have no idea. But I'm telling you, the voice was very real. The command was very real. And so I did exactly that. And as a consequence of that, I got marked in the church as being maybe more religious than I actually was. But they began to lean on me to do things, and as I got older, I got sent to fill in as a religious speaker for some occasions where there wasn't an appropriate speaker.[28]

Such revivalist experience was not uncommon amongst American teenagers in the late 1940s and 1950s, but in British oral history it seems markedly more regionally confined – such as to the Western Isles of Scotland – or was the output of specific religious-history projects.[29]

But in Britain, the reflexivity to the evangelical narrative also generated confused and embittered remembrance, manifest in Ronald Walker's testimony above, given in interview as early as 1970, which drifted into and out of evangelical concern with good and evil, drunkenness and sobriety, religious respectability and hypocrisy, and sin and redemption. Evangelicalism injected a sustained bitterness scattered throughout his life-story interview.[30] Such a phenomenon, and even religious doubt itself, is much harder to trace in American oral history testimony, even after 2000.

Race and ethnicity

The survival of religious narrative is strong on both sides of the Atlantic in the testimony of ethnic minorities. Life stories, notably autobiographies, often exploit religious identity in the accounts of African Americans, British Afro-Caribbeans and Africans, and in the lives of Jews, Muslims, Hindus and Sikh peoples in all Western nations. Yet, the story is far from even.

On the one hand, for many minority ethnic groups, religion is mixed with racial identity. Alice Archibald, born in New Brunswick in New Jersey and raised in the Mount Zion African Methodist Episcopal Church – her grandfather a pastor – grew up in the 1900s and 1910s in a city district of mixed races and religions: 'The whole people on that city block knew us, we were the only Afro-American family there, but we didn't know we were Afro-Americans, they didn't know they were Italians, Jews, Irish, Hungarians. We all grew up together, we ate together if company came.' But her narrative reveals the wider urban environment to be racially segregated. She recalls city institutions were segregated, especially cinemas, where in one the people of colour were confined to 'the peanut gallery', and some schools refused blacks. After gaining a number of college degrees, including at Howard University, she worked as a teacher in schools of the American Missionary Association in North Carolina, in a community with strict segregation of toilets and other facilities. Reference to church inflected much of her life story, but she related it habitually to segregation. She attended a black church, noting the effective ghettoization in American religion, but sought integration in other realms: 'there's a tendency for likes to go with likes because they feel that they have more in common, which is no way to integrate, because you'll never integrate if you always go with your own group'. She added, 'I mean there's too much of, we have too many segregated churches and what not. They say Sunday morning is the most segregated time in the country, you have your separate churches. But more churches are integrating and getting away from, you know, one idea.' Alice, in her narrative, took the church to be the backdrop, but not really the focus, of her life story. At the end she said of her black congregation: 'I grew up there, was in the cradle roll, so I'll be there from the cradle roll to the grave, so.'[31]

Such pride in faith suffuses testimonies from ethnic groups. Naomi Craig, a black woman living in Rhode Island, provided a typical conjoining of church with moral worth in her interview:

> And I always taught Sunday School. I always was in church, so I could teach Sunday School and love other people's children and be kind to them. That bitterness and meanness, people didn't want me to do this, I said, that's okay, I'll be the best I can at whatever I do, and whatever I did, I was the best. Then finally, when things opened up, I did get a job, I

took an exam, I was a court steno, no not a court stenographer, but just a stenographer, and I got a job, and I worked for the state and I had a good life doing that.[32]

She made it her practise to always attend racially mixed churches. Migration disturbed, but rarely dented, the faith of people of colour. Bruce McLeod, brought up in Jamaica in the 1940s in a mixture of Catholic kindergarten, Anglican public schools, Scots Presbyterian Boys' Brigade and Episcopalian church, joined in American gospel churches on coming to the United States in 1965.[33] Sometimes, though, African American interviewees placed religion less centrally in their life recollections. Walter Alexander II, born in 1922 in Petersburg, Virginia, trained in the early 1940s first as an engineer at Rutgers University, then as a USAF fighter pilot and after the war as a dentist; he recalled mandatory chapel attendance at university, but as 'less religious' and more of an information event, and the rest of his testimony was devoid of any reference to church or religion.[34] For other testimonies, there is recollection of social divisions; Mary Pinsdorf from Teaneck, New Jersey, spoke on the sharp religious-ethnic divisions exacerbated by anti-German feeling in the 1940s.[35] In such ways, a range of emotions and experiences fasten faith in the memories of interviewees from ethnic minorities.

In the United Kingdom, the centrality of religion is very evident from the testimony of black Christians, Asian Muslims and Hindus who were raised overseas. Esme Lancaster (1917–2009) was born in Wilmington, Jamaica, and raised in the Church of England, but on coming to England in 1950 she was repeatedly rebuffed by the racist vicar of a white congregation who said: 'I'm asking if you could find another church to worship because I don't want to lose my parishioners.' For this treatment, she rejected the Church of England, more in sorrow than in anger, and she and many like her turned to the blossoming independent black churches, and proclaimed, 'I am a Pentecostal; and I'm very glad I am.'[36] In the midst of sharp secularization amongst the overwhelmingly white population of mainland Britain, ethnic minority testimony into the twenty-first century has remained pretty firmly in the faith.

The feminist liberation narrative

Feminist life stories of the third and fourth quarters of the twentieth century exhibit strong aspects of secularizing narratives. In the United States, they mark a very full spectrum of religious orientations, much more so than the equivalent European community. Certainly, there is markedly lower loss of religion amongst US feminists compared to those in Britain. But a useful and in many ways representative case study across both nations comes from Katherine Acey.

Katherine, like most American oral history interviewees, invariably locates her origins in childhood neighbourhoods defined acutely by race and religion. Born 1950 in Utica, New York, she was raised in a Lebanese extended family living on the edge of an Italian neighbourhood. Her testimony acknowledges a strong awareness of race and religion – of Lebanese, Syrians and Italians – in her community: 'So I always felt it as both a religious and a cultural experience growing up.'[37] Her family was Maronite Catholic, the church of high importance to her parents who sent her first to a parish Catholic grade school and then to an all-girls Catholic high school. Though sad at not having learned more of her mother's Arabic language, she was surrounded by an invigorated patriotism in the 1940s and 1950s: 'Everything was very pro-American. Everything was anticommunist. Everything was, you know, it's great to be an American, freedom.'[38] Katherine then provides a lengthy racial description of her community, yet noting with every generation a little more intermarriage with new nationalities – European, African American, Puerto Rican, native American – creating an increasing variation to the extended family. In the midst of this, there is a sense that the diversity has actually a strong common core of family loyalty and the place of marriage and children, exuding the notion of a common narrative that bound the diversity, defining nationhood and citizenship. In similar vein, Katherine describes her parents in a typical rhetorical form, often lacking verbs and objects: 'So there was that adherence…So they – Church and religion, faith. So they weren't like fundamentalists in that sense, but faith and church and those laws.'[39] Church and faith take up a central, dominating place in her life narrative. The word 'Catholic' and 'Catholicism' appear twenty-nine times in her testimony, 'church' twenty-one times, 'religion' five times, 'faith' three times, almost entirely in the first third.

These roots form the backdrop for her second-stage story – of political radicalization and emergence as a lesbian and feminist. Katherine recalled her father's double strictness with his children and his religion, keeping old Catholic regulation even as the pope and the church modernized in Vatican II. This sets the narrative structure for her early radicalization as a teenager. Her father was very proud of his daughter going off to college: 'But I think in some ways, as my politics became more and more defined, and more radical in his eyes – and they were radical – I really came to believe that he saw it as somewhat a rejection of him.'[40] They would 'lock horns', she reports. But the relationship between what she became and her roots was symbiotic:

I also feel that some of my politics come from my parents and my Catholic upbringing. Let me explain that, because it's complicated. I feel what I learned – Well, you know, the three tenets of Catholicism are faith, hope, and charity, and I really believed those things and in a way I still do. Also, it was about taking care of people. You know, it was certainly loving God and being a good person, but it was also very much about caring about other people. And I do feel I got that from the priests and the nuns and my family. So I got a very, very strong value that was about, you just don't think about yourself. So a sense of family, a sense of community that was even bigger. So I'm grateful for that, because I rejected Catholicism and the church. I came back around in later years to feeling like that's what gave me this core sense of values about people.[41]

Radicalization started as her neighbourhood became slowly more racially integrated, and she, like some other girls, dated a black guy. She could never bring him home, so the nuns at the school allowed the couples to be brought there. When 18 in the heady years of 1968–9, the nuns helped resolve a tension over whether she and her boyfriend should have sex. She and her friends went to an all-girls Catholic college in Buffalo where she became a student leader right away, and joined the struggle to end compulsory skirt-wearing to dinner. Katherine was for two years president of the student body, and a variety of radicalisms were in the air, transforming student and national life. In the midst of joining a Black Awareness group, and all the strikes and demonstrations of socialist and anti-war groups, she recounts her weakening ties of religion: at first going to Mass; having a radical chaplain, who left the priesthood and later got married; having two socialist professors directing her to read Marx; and then getting involved in solidarity work and fighting racist attacks.[42] She looked askance at the burning bras of feminism: 'I wouldn't even think of going anyplace without a bra. I was not at all connected to the women's movement. I didn't get it'.[43] But she identified strongly with the civil rights movement and black culture, wearing her hair in 'very big bushy Afros'.[44]

Katherine Acey's narrative then moves into a period of feminist radicalization after college in which she was drawn to crisis intervention work, campaigning against rape and sterilization and for abortion, and starting in her late twenties to come out as a lesbian. Her narrative is one of a complex radicalization and change for herself: 'it was a big struggle then, because here I was, I was dealing with sexual identity, racial politics and identity, and also kind of just figuring out that transition. In a way, I was coming into my own, but I didn't belong anyplace. It was being in that place of confusion and just a lot of turmoil.' She describes herself as coming out at the age of 30 and developing a new position in a feminist organization. She reports in the late 1970s and early 1980s of being in turmoil politically and personally, with her mother dying and she starting a job with a New York radical community fund, and then her coming out in 1980 and starting her first long-term relationship with a woman.[45] From then, her testimony is absorbed in professional campaigning work in human rights for women, queers and transpeople, and in Palestinian rights, and in her being the executive director of Astraea Lesbian Foundation for Justice for twenty-three years from 1987 to 2010.

The radical life which this represents is, in the American context, one of enormous excitements and massive change, notably in the ferment of ideas on race and human rights. In the narrative, though, religion appears not so much as rethought out as repositioned by other things, almost 'lost' in the story of new moral modalities, political ideologies and activity. The intersubjectivity with the questioner is clearly strongly concerned with lesbianism, student radicalism as well as interest in personal issues in family and sexual life, but very much less to do with religion. Reading her testimony, by this stage it becomes clear that religion has been repositioned in her life.

Such repositioning was common amongst feminists. In studying British women's autobiographies, I found radical women commonly spoke of this, whilst later in this book we shall hear of the next stage for those women whose feminism interacted with loss of religion entirely.[46] Some American feminists, too, were quite blunt about the extent of their secular revolution. Sara Gould (b. 1951), raised in Grand Haven, Michigan, noted how by the early twenty-first century a family member challenged her on the evident religious disaffiliation she had undergone: 'And so, recently, I think one of my sisters said to me, "But Sara, you've never been affiliated – you know, since you grew up – you haven't been affiliated with a religious institution." And I said, "You know, actually, feminism is my religion." And I mean that.'[47] In Gould's testimony, as in many others, this slide from faith goes unrecorded, the intersubjectivity of the interview tending to be directed towards the feminist movement, rendering religious change seemingly infrequently conceptualized as part of this. For some American feminist respondents, too, there is no proffering of a religious component to their life story. Dolores Alexander (1931–2008, Newark, New Jersey) does not use the words 'faith' or 'religion' at all, and 'church' only once in quoting somebody else.[48] The novelist Dorothy Allison, born 1949, doesn't feature religion in her narrative beyond a few casual references relating to the impact of a Baptist upbringing upon her character: 'Take me as I am, I'll get better'; 'I know how to be destructive; I was raised in the Baptist church'; 'Oy, Baptist church is a pain in the ass. It gives you a lot of resources, but it can fuck you up.' She acknowledged her debt to religion in talking about spirituality and how 'the doorway is sex' to much of revelation: 'There isn't any other way to talk about it without using the language of my childhood, the Baptist church [laughs], but it's true.'[49]

Most American feminist radicals generally portrayed a slide from religion in their lives, but oftentimes there was a limit to secularization. Virginia Apuzzo, born 1941 in New York, reflected on sexual reassignment even at the age of 11 or 12, and recalled this in her interview with reference to her religion:

I'm Italian Catholic. So the issue of redemption is very, very significant to me, and particularly when I was younger. My question was, 'What am

I?' and 'Is it OK? Is this something that – will I go to hell for this? Is this what falls under the category of bad thoughts when I go to confession? Am I going to live a sin for the rest of my live?' And if I do – remember, I come out of the Baltimore catechism.[50] Why did God make you? God made you to know Him, love Him, serve Him in this life and be happy with Him forever in heaven. Am I going to get there?[51]

She entered a Catholic convent in 1966 at 26 and studied theology as a route to her radicalism.

Faith and unbelief. I was reading redemptive politics. Think of this time. This time in the church was activist. It was an activist time. It was a lot of situation ethics, a lot of relative-relativism, a lot of sense of place and circumstance, and a church that was willing to open itself up to people. It was opening up. It was recognizing that oppression in any form is not a good thing. It cramps the soul. And the people who were getting visibility in the church were people who were resisting and protesting and asserting and-and I was totally persuaded that that is a sanctified pursuit. That protest is necessary for change. That resistance is a good and decent thing. And so I did.[52]

The church in the late 1960s was the way she found a route towards radicalization, reading in radical theology. She stayed three years and left to pursue radical politics, coming out as a lesbian, and spent twenty years in high-ranking positions in political administrations (including that of Bill Clinton).

High religiosity was clearly more prevalent amongst feminists of colour. Dázon Dixon Diallo, an African American woman, born 1965 in Fort Valley, Georgia, grew up in an integrated Episcopal church, her parents both with doctorates and a strong social commitment, leading her at college to become active in anti-apartheid and women's health issues; by the age of 19 she was the only lay health worker of colour at the Feminist Women's Health Center in Atlanta.[53] Dázon placed her sense of justice firmly in a Christian context: 'But my own belief system…means you believe in Jesus Christ as the Son of God and the Trinity, and those types of things. That's a root that I have and that exists in my family and my parents. My parents were both raised Baptists, who became Episcopal – Episcopalian. So there is a deep-rooted sense and knowledge of Christianity.' She spoke in interview of how these Christian roots mixed with her own New Age explorations of 'some kind of energy that has power to make things happen'. She spoke of the 'eternal, infinite connectivity into existence in any text, whether it's the Bible, the Qur'an – anywhere'. She went on: 'And if that is an energy that comes from a God, so be it; that's what people can call it. If it's a spiritual energy – whatever that is. I think that life is intertwined, it has its purpose, it has its purpose for good. And that where it isn't, we're supposed to be working to make it better.' Dázon added 'because womanism follows behind that'.[54] If dogmatism is taken as one form of irrationalism, then one might regard such non-dogmatic irrationalism as a league or two from conventional religionism, and a prelude to rationalism.

So, a full spectrum of religiosity was evident amongst American feminists. Compared to British feminists, the Christian orientation of most American feminists' personal life experiences is quite pronounced. Two pieces of research by Kirstin Aune show, firstly, that British feminists are mostly atheists, humanists or agnostics, and, secondly, that evangelicalism failed to resist secularization in England. On the contrary, 'while evangelical religiosity continues among women occupying more traditional social positions (as wives and mothers), adherence is declining among those whose lives do not fit the older pattern of marriage and full-time motherhood'.[55] This research underlines the much more secular orientation of British feminist discourse. This is a topic to which we return in Chapter 5 when contemplating the place of feminism in atheist lives.

Secularization narratives

Secularization comes into general oral history narratives in different forms and stages, some mere repositioning of religion in the life, but often entwined with other liberation narratives. In the aggregate, there is an erosion of churchianity and an opening of intergenerational loss of faith. The way this operated was varied, including between Britain and the United States.

As with Dázon, whom we have just encountered, the sixties threw up a concept of the religious seeker. Starting from the North American tradition of switching churches and religions, from the sixties 'new age' spirituality gave it a new edge, much of it relating to eastern mysticism and Buddhism. This was manifest in a life narrative that exuded a 'liberation' dimension, which for many made church and faith more vulnerable. Regina Jones, an African American woman born in 1942 in Los Angeles, recalled as a child being 'very curious about God' and joined her mother in first a Methodist then a Baptist church: 'I remember – this is definitely out of line, but I remember watching the preacher there, Reverend AB, preach, and people would get all excited, and I thought that was ridiculous. I didn't like that, and I'd sit there and pray that whatever happened to them never happened to me in public.' She recalls being a questioning child – for instance, challenging Sabbath rules applied against a child but not an adult. Around the fourth or sixth grade she approached the Catholic Church, though her religious orientation became confused and changeable, followed by radicalization in civil rights in the 1960s and single motherhood at the age of 16. Her interviewer asked, 'What, if any, role did any sort of spiritual expression play into your awareness and your life at that time? I mention this partly because I noticed that when you went through this very stressful challenging period, you didn't say anything about seeking solace in religion or anything like that.' Despite the interviewer's injection of a normative Christian narrative, Regina explained in detail how she lost her respect for the Catholic Church when her priest said her son was a bastard because she hadn't been married in church. As worshippers would 'wiggle in the pews' in discomfort at her proximity, so, she said, 'I started to lean more and more towards agnostic, because if these are churchgoing, God-fearing people, please protect me from ever being one of them'. Her personal religion, she said, was integrity and spirituality, and she sought this in the late 1960s and early 1970s, through yoga and various New Age and other organizations. As an older woman, she found it difficult to find a church in which she was comfortable.[56] This is an example of the religious 'seeking' story that is common amongst Americans and Canadians recalling the 1960s and 1970s, that disturbs faith connection and causes the worshipper dissatisfaction with traditional churches – an example we will come across in later chapters amongst those who transited from the New Age to humanism and atheism.

More transparent secularization narratives came from some for whom the 1960s was transformative – radicalizing, sexually liberating and freeing of former faith. Patricia Donnelly (pseud.) was born in 1950 in Providence, Rhode Island, to an Irish-Catholic family. She told an interviewer in 1998:

> 1968, you have to understand, is a very different year than 1958, or 1964. 1964 the Beatles come to America, okay. By 1968 it's like *Sergeant Pepper's* time, we're all, we all have long hair and have altered consciousness. A lot of things happened between '64 and '68. If you'd asked me in 1958, I would have told you I wanted to be a missionary nun. If you'd asked me in 1964, I may have wanted to have been a scientist or a teacher. If you'd asked me in 1968 [laughs], I didn't have a clue. What did I want to be in 1968? I wanted to be a poet or a photographer in 1968, you know. I was getting out of high school, and I didn't have any plans to go to college … [B]y 1968 I thought 'College! Who wants to go to college? There's too much fun to be had out there'. So, I did not have plans to go to college immediately after high school, which upset my college advisors to no end. So, I didn't know what I wanted to do, I wanted to go away and lead an exciting life somewhere, and make a new world [laughs]. I wanted to make the revolution.[57]

Patricia centres her life's narrative on the events of the 1960s. She sets up a classic contrast in her chronicle between her mother's life in the 1950s and her own in the 1960s: 'My mother when I was born was not employed; she was a homemaker; it was the fifties; that's the way it worked then … she was a very capable woman, but in the fifties that was, when you had little babies you were home.' From this introduction, she started to construct a comprehensive and detailed liberation narrative beginning with disaffection from Catholic schooling:

> I went to Classical High School. Instead of going to St. Xavier's, which was where my family planned for me to go. But I had reached rebellious puberty before then and decided I had quite enough, thank you very much, of Catholic education and refused. So the only public high school that they would even consider allowing me to go to was Classical. So I went to Classical High School and was very much in a minority. Most of the kids there were from another part of the city, most of them were not Irish-Catholic. So I met a lot of different kids and started to have a number of different experiences.[58]

Even this non-Catholic high school proved too restrictive for her emerging adult self. She reported, 'And a lot of it, again, was me pushing against them, they were this repressive force that I was fighting against constantly. I mean, the world was blowing up and they wanted me to learn Latin!' She then opens up a wide-ranging narrative of involvement in sixties radical causes on and off-campus, ranging from civil rights to opposing the Vietnam War. She notes the attraction of the Kennedy brothers Jack and Bobby to those like her from a poor family in a poor neighbourhood, but then turns to her involvement in black activism and her own dating of an African American.

At the heart of her narrative, though, is a long exposition about sexual liberation. She devotes over a thousand words to this. 'You probably won't find a more sexually adventurous group of humans', she starts. 'The generation right before me were terrified of sex, for fear of unwanted pregnancies.' But not for her generation. Sex in her poor neighbourhood she likened to the sports recreation of richer neighbourhoods: they played rich people's sports, and the poor kids had sex. She was sexually active in both high school and college: 'By 1968, pretty much everybody was active. We did not fear unwanted pregnancy because we had this sense of, not always well-founded, sense of security in birth control.' Sexually transmitted diseases she recalled were fixed by 'three shots of penicillin and it was over'.

> Our view of sex was a very healthy, all-inclusive kind of thing. It was sort of like, oh, we really saw it as a natural outgrowth of your affection for somebody. It wasn't tied to lifelong commitment, it wasn't a tool you used to get attention or give attention or maintain control. The sexually, quote 'sexually liberated' women or girls that I ran around with, felt for the first time in generations that they had control of their own body and they were gonna use it any damn way they pleased and they didn't use sex as a way to manipulate men, you know.

She said that 'in 1968 the last thing on my mind was "find a husband and raise a family"'. In that year, she and her friends 'weren't playing hard to get, we were making the decisions, if we slept with someone it was 'cause we wanted to not because they wanted us to'. She describes it as 'a very proactive, almost aggressive sexuality, but we were comfortable, I mean we were just busting out of a closet, you know, we were'.[59] Patricia put the sixties revolution at the heart of her generation and changing America:

> I wish I could say the sixties affected the United States more. It affected me personally; it affected the people in my life who mean the most to me, my longest standing dearest friends. I checked the things they do for a living. They all in some way or another are involved in things that require personal commitment to make the world a better place. They're involved in politics in the best possible way. They are lawyers who do a lot of free pro-bono work, are anti-poverty lawyers, or they run veterans' centers. I have a lot of friends who work in veterans' centers working with the guys who were destroyed by Vietnam. I deal with the people that have nowhere else to go. Most of the people that I care about are people who have a shared value system and it is not this 'family values' thing. For me the values were of social justice and fighting to end bigotry. I had no tolerance for any kind of bigotry. Bigotry against people of different colors, cultures, experiences, or sexual orientations. You stand on who you are and who you are is based on what you have done in this world. I see it as what kind of integrity you have, not in what you say, but in what you do.[60]

Patricia Donnelly provides a narrative exemplary of the cultural revolution's impact on the individual young woman in the sixties, combining sexual, lifestyle, attitudinal and left-leaning liberal change, as well as demographic and religious change. She fits pretty precisely a paradigm I drew in a recent book on women, religion and the sixties demographic revolution.[61] There is a paradox to be faced. On the one hand, religious liberation narratives are much stronger in the United States and Canada than in Britain, depicting the sixties as prominent pivots of change in the popular, feminist and academic remembrance of the decade.[62] On the other hand, in a story ably told by Hugh McLeod, the challenge to religion down to about 1972 was much stronger in Britain (though more delayed in Canada) compared to its weaker and more temporary impact in the United States, leading afterwards to a divergence for some decades in American and European paths.[63] This explains why Patricia Donnelly's narrative can be representative of a much wider American remembrance of the sixties.

Those who lose religion are hard to find in the American oral history archive, but, as in Britain, they exhibit diverse triggers and routes from faith. Jim Blair from Arkansas was a born-again Baptist by his teens in the late 1940s, and gave extensive testimony on his conversion and church life. But he reported three factors that led him from the church. First, he was dismayed at local congregations failing to adequately back integration in the late 1950s, to which he became a key legal figure and later participant in Bill Clinton's cause in the Democratic Party. Second, he said that he became 'too intellectual', partly influenced by studying philosophy at university. And third, critically, when his seven-year-old daughter became obsessed with hell, getting to the point where she was incapacitated by fear she would go there, he 'absolutely left the Church'.[64] That child's fear of hell we will encounter later amongst several atheist respondents. But for Jim Blair, his narrative of losing religion is rather different from those of women in the oral history archive, tending to come later in life, and being centred on a rejection of the church.

Certain common features emerged of the incidence of secularization narratives in oral history archive collections on both sides of the Atlantic. First, the membership of atheist, ethical and humanist organizations was very small, and though there are many recent publications by and about atheists in the Western world, very few people interviewed concerning the mid-twentieth century in academic oral history archives were members of such organizations.[65] In my entire review of over a thousand transcripts in three nations, I only found one respondent reporting to be a member of a non-belief organization – Miriam Null, born 1926 in Brooklyn, New York, who joined in civil rights and anti-Vietnam marches when she and her husband were members of Ethical Culture – the Ethical Society movement of humanists.[66] Second, members of ethnic minority groups in both Britain and the United States rarely exhibited complete loss of religion. African American collections of oral history show exceptionally little evidence of this, though Afro-Caribbean male respondents in British collections give greater hints of religious alienation.[67] Third, on the other hand, the numbers of white interviewees who claimed to be alienated from the churches was quite high in the United Kingdom, mirroring findings by Hugh McLeod's survey of three major oral history collections in the 1980s that only 40–50 per cent of respondents were brought up in households in the early twentieth century in which at least one parent was a regular churchgoer.[68] Those figures for religious alienation soared for those raised after the 1950s, and more especially after the 1980s.[69] But one of the surprising facets of recent oral history in the United States is the extent to which even politicians talk about having little connection to organized religion. Mike Beebe (born 1946), governor of Arkansas since 2007, when asked if there was much religion and church involvement in his family replied, 'We didn't have any. No, we didn't.' However, he spoke of the undue influence of the normative family portrayed in the television programmes of the 1950s and early 1960s, and the isolation suffered by the single-parent family in viewing such programmes as *Leave It to Beaver* and *Ozzie and Harriet*:

> Yeah, there's a mom and a dad and a boy and a girl and whatever in the neighborhood and one car. And you went to church, and you went to the drive-in, and you did all those things that – and that was the culture of the time, at least in a kid's mind. If you weren't that, then there's somethin' wrong.[70]

Here was an American politician pushing back in 2008 against 1950s religious discourse about happy nuclear families and churchgoing.

We can perceive such resistance build-up in the oral history landscape of both Britain and America as signs of latent secularization: laughter or anger at recollecting of religious youth, challenge to normative visions and reasons for dissent. As Roper has suggested in relation to gender, individuals were re-constructing identities without reflecting discourse.[71] In religion, they were challenging discursive Christianity in various ways and with various outcomes for their faith position. Voluble anti-church rhetoric is discernible, though anti-religious rhetoric is rare, but growing disinterest did emerge from the 1960s to the 1980s in British testimony. Three generations of families, all interviewed, displayed declining interest in religion, culminating in the last generation of the 1980s showing stunted replies to questions on religion, like 'I was never interested in religion.'[72] British oral history testimony stands out for its marked evidence of a secularizing self which discharged the relevance of discursive Christianity. In the United States and Canada, by contrast, the oral history archives showed all respondents volunteering a commentary on religion, either unprompted or when asked. But challenges can be found building in testimonies from the 1990s and 2000s.

Conclusion

Testimonies from the life-story archives of oral history demonstrate a divide notable between the United States and Britain. On the British mainland, oral history projects have tended to focus on religion as a cultural artefact centred on a fading concept of religious Sunday (including the Jewish Shabbat). In the United States, encouraged to greater or lesser extents by their interviewers, narrators bring to their stories three religious-based hubs: personal faith, religious-based ethnic and community solidarities, and civil and patriotic religiosities. On both sides of the Atlantic, we find faith readily intertwined in the life story, and secularization entering with difficulty. Yet, there is evidence of a distinctive, post-religious ethical culture emerging around homosexual equality and human rights.

We can see how discursive Christianity offered a ready vocabulary of association and also of critique in which people find things to say about where religion has fitted into their lives, accompanied by anecdotes, touchstones and sketches of family and faith rituals. Religion offers a complex brickwork by which individuality is built in to the past, in tradition, but that richness to life's architecture is rarely blemished by any graffiti resembling a substitute rhetoric of unbelief and atheism. Coming from a different angle, David Nash has recently argued that Christian narratives survive in low-religiosity peoples to blend with the secular, to become useful to men and women of belief and non-belief alike.[73] More striking, I think, is that there is no strong heritage of atheist narratives, no suitable collective memory and a skimpy cultural language or discourse upon which the early secular mass culture of the sixties generation can draw. This leaves cultural space for Christian and other religionist narrative types to survive for a generation or two in everyday rhetoric and aphorism and, to an extent, in life narrative too. In a remembrance of religious loss, the warp and weft is thin at best, and most often absent. For a small number of people in the general oral history archive, what can be there, instead, is a story of pain and struggle, often prolonged, and also possibly told at length. But for most, it is a short and stunted story about a religious change, and little remarked upon. In this way, we come upon the evidence of an inability to speak of having no religion – either of having nothing to say or of not wishing to comment, a desire for silence commented upon by sociologists in the United States.[74] Atheists have long been reticent or discreet, keeping secret their absence of faith and life without god, by drawing upon the language of religion, and upon performance of religious rites, attending church and even saying prayers. For the religiously indifferent, it will apply even more.

But we have spied ethnic and gender differences, and these will expand in our vision in three later chapters. Likewise, we have heard the impact of the sixties in some of the testimony, of new identities emerging from sex, the New Age, radicalism and protest. To march against the Vietnam War and segregation involved many people of faith, but it tended to break down barriers of respectability around all sorts of change. The lived experiences of religion diverged increasingly from norms; religion itself was cracking codes of conformity in the sixties, with the very notion of normativity in religion being corrupted. In feminist narratives we see quite clearly the re-chiselling of identity. An absence of available cultural discourse in the public sphere or collective memory might hold up, but could not completely thwart, the budding atheist. To find that person, we turn now to interviews with those who lost their faith, or found they never had one, and whose subjectivities were starting to be rampantly creative in the 1950s, 1960s and 1970s surrounding a life lived as if there is no god.

CHAPTER THREE

The Atheist Child

Religion and child development

David Pollock, born in Beckenham in south London in 1942, commenced his interview with me with a stark recollection:

> The first time I encountered religion was when I went to school at the age of five, and went into a morning assembly where all the kids went down on their knees and put their hands together and started muttering. And I thought, 'what the hell is this?' And I decided right from the start that it was nothing to do with me, but I'd better conform.

He then recalled two other episodes. The first was at the age of 12 when he decided that he should at least investigate Christianity: 'I thought I'd read the Bible. And I got halfway through Exodus before I lost patience with it! [Laughs] It was nonsense! And so that was that.' And then in his final year at school in the late 1950s, he confronted a friend who was taking Anglican confirmation classes with three hours of questioning: 'What the duce do you think you're doing? Why are you doing this? What's it mean to you?'[1]

Childhood as a turning point towards atheism is something little considered in academic literature. Whilst churches since the eighteenth century have held fears that puberty heralded the danger of declining success for religion, psychologists' interest in children as religious agents has been minimal, a point noted in 2010 by Paula M. Cooey.[2] Ideas on childhood learning and on the diversity in religion were both strongly influenced by William James between the 1890s and 1910s, and then in the 1970s with James Fowler's theory of faith development, based on six stages starting in early childhood and instigated by cognitive and affective development.[3] Adopted widely in religious education and religious studies,[4] Fowler's approach takes faith and transcendence as universalized and normative

Christian, and strongly Protestant, in conception. Meanwhile, research into loss of religion in psychology has until recently been described as descriptive rather than analytical, and producing at best fragmented ideas of why people 'de-convert'.[5] Church concern continues in more recent studies using interviews and surveys of young people, such as in the United States, where, with little religious education in most schools, attention falls upon the church and the home as the locus of de-religionization.[6] Though some studies stress adulthood in church leaving,[7] British church concern is almost always directed at teenagers, pointing to failures in religious education at day schools, most of them funded by the state, emphasizing falling youth religiosity but not the acquisition of atheism.[8] Before the later twentieth century, the perception was that, with religious education in British state schools and strong levels of Sunday school attendance, younger children had little likelihood of not religiously believing, or of avoiding participation in religious ritual. Additionally, many cultures inhibited knowledge of the *possibility* of not believing in a god. An atheist and humanist whom I interviewed, Khushi Ram, who was born in 1923 in the Punjab in the lowest caste (he described it as 'outcast') and later moved to Canada, reported that even after his university education he was not fully certain of the position of not believing in God: 'I had some *inkling* that some people don't believe in God. But I never worried about God.'[9] Few people grew up with the reverse religious understanding – not knowing of faith. But, from the middle of the twentieth century in the West especially, knowledge of unbelief grew – first in the hostile Cold War context of the 1950s, and increasingly as a possibility for personal adoption.

The most sustained research has been stimulated by Leslie Francis, who, since the mid-1970s, has generated many studies in Britain of declining Christian-ness (and also of other religions) amongst school pupils – mostly students in church schools (ranging from Methodist to Catholic).[10] At the outset of this research, he developed a Francis Scale of Attitude towards Christianity to assign individual youngsters a numerical strength of religion; subsequently he collaborated on scales of attitude to Judaism, Islam, Hinduism and theistic faith as a whole.[11] Methodologically, there are significant issues with this work. The studies are located in highly confessional environments where the scale of religious loss might be expected to be lower than in the child population at large in non-church schools. The nature of the scores is infused with confessional ideas, and implicitly accepts that children losing faith is a 'problem' and one that can and should be ameliorated. And the research stops in the mid- to late teens (and doesn't use longitudinal research to trace the young into adulthood), meaning that there is no real idea as to whether the loss in childhood links to a sustained loss (that lasts into adulthood and is permanent, however that is to be defined), nor the degree of loss in youth compared to adulthood. Advising the churches about haemorrhage of their support, the Francis researchers study children who have *declining* religiosity but not those who may have none. Actually allowing for the possibility of child atheism may be the far greater hurdle.

One of my respondents, Julia Stuart from Scotland, perceptively told me,

> What I wonder about now is how children, really me, how can you believe this indoctrination god thing, and yet at the same time, one of my uncles was a great *Marvel Comics* fan? And I loved all that. The Superman, the heroes, loved it all. But how do we decide that the god thing is 'real', but we know that Superman ain't? So I wondered how you decided that as a child – why you kept on believing in the dogma but you knew that Superman stuff was play?[12]

In recent years, their children's acquisition of religious belief has been exercising the conscience of atheistical parents, with a sizeable market for books and websites that deal with this.[13] More broadly, non-religious organizations in many nations address the nature, extent and suitability of religious education in state-funded schools. Understanding of non-belief in this mix is clearly in its infancy.

Religious childhoods

Nearly all the respondents I interviewed, excluding those from Belgium, Sweden and Estonia, were brought up before the 1970s in religious ways. Invariably, parents were at least nominal religionists, mostly Christians, and usually attended church regularly, and packed their children off to Sunday schools. Even children of parents with little active church connection went to church or Sunday school, sometimes at their own behest, though again sometimes because they were sent. The particular church to which they went depended on various factors. In Europe, denominational heritage was powerful in families, but in Britain religious experimentation was common amongst the young, with the Church of England being attended for participation in its choir or bell-ringing, and Nonconformist and Pentecostal congregations for pursuit of drama, variety or romantic connection.[14] In some other European nations, state day schools also imposed religious education and enforced religious worship, characteristically at the start of the school day. But in the United States, and to a degree Canada, outside of Catholic and Jewish families, there was incredible flexibility, and with so many independent church groups, as Robert Sanford from Portland, Oregon, told me, the child's ecclesiastical destination 'was more geography, I think, than theology'. It was a question of which church was nearest, as Leslie O'Hagan told me of Texas, where she buddied a girlfriend to the nearby Methodist church and its summer camp.[15]

About a fifth of my respondents experienced what might legitimately be described as very religious childhoods. In Dundee in Scotland, Ann Auchterlonie's father was a Church of Scotland elder, the beadle of two congregations (one Church of Scotland and the other United Free Church) and a stalwart of a local mission, and Ann frequently accompanied him on mission work in the city. Every day of the week except Monday and Tuesday there was a religious event for the family to conduct or assist. On holidays Ann went to a Faith Mission or mission halls with her father, and had to abide by a strict moral code (saying 'Good Heavens' was swearing). In the mid-1950s, she heard visiting evangelical missionaries and American preachers. At one of these in Dundee's Caird Hall in 1956 she recalled the following:

> [W]hen they ask for people to come forward and all the rest of it, and we were actually quite near the front, I did go forward, you know, I was definitely affected by it. It certainly made me, afterwards, after I went forward, I was ashamed I had. I was very unhappy with myself that I had done that…I just, I can remember feeling very, very uncomfortable that I had gone forward because I had been --- I had begun to question, and I felt I had let myself down and I felt I had been swept up by --- I mean, I did at that time feel I had been swept up by the emotion, and I was there with another two friends and they wanted to continue following it up, and we had been given contacts and things to follow it up, and I wouldn't.[16]

This was the first sign in her life narrative of a rebellion against her religion, recalled in some emotional detail. Around the age of 11 and 12 years, she had started questioning things such as the Catholic–Protestant divide and missionary work (even though she won an evangelism award), and challenged the minister at a Congregational Church Bible Class. At home she felt unable to contest Bible stories, such as Adam and Eve, and Noah and the Ark, with her parents, so she questioned them repeatedly in church groups. 'By the time I was 16, I would have said I wasn't a believer in the way that I had been accepting. You know, there's a difference between acceptance and belief. And I think if there was a time when I believed, it was a very short time, because I got to that questioning stage by about 15, 16.' Though she had an uncle who was an atheist, she said it would never have occurred to her at that age to say she was an atheist. But she was being prompted by her uncle: 'Yes, but who made God, Ann, you know, because that's the unanswerable question.' Things were stirring: 'You begin to recognise that that's an unsatisfactory answer. So, I was conscious of atheism.'[17]

Ann was distinctive, though not unique, amongst my respondents born before 1960 for the active evangelism she undertook whilst questions were emerging in her mind. But the vast majority, born in whichever of the eighteen nations whence my respondents came, had a close familiarity with religion in childhood. They went to church or Sunday school, learned hymns and prayers and, in the United Kingdom and Ireland, at least got religious lessons in school. They recalled all this readily, even when it was over seventy years ago. Doctrine and theology, and the rhythms of the religious life and the fellowship community were each well understood. Maria Berger, raised a Catholic in Switzerland, reported the idea of eternal punishment both attractive and traumatic, and, by childhood questioning of faith, became drawn first to Protestantism and subsequently to Evangelicalism.[18] Respondents were aware of the goldfish bowl experience of being watched and tested regarding faith; this reached a higher point in certain denominations, notably for two respondents raised in the Jehovah's Witnesses who were alert to the punishment – the 'shunning' or separation from family – which transgression entailed. All grasped the seriousness of religion: how it could define morality and personal decision making, govern various aspects of behaviour from swearing to sexual encounters and, in some cases, determined who could be friends. They knew how the totalizing experience of religion trumped all else in the mid-twentieth century.

Growing up faithless

A minority of my respondents grew up with more limited experience of religion. One of the earliest cultures of faithlessness, and still one of the strongest, is that of secular Jewry. Many post-war secular Jews inherited their secularity from parents brought up before the war. This didn't inevitably mean that the child became atheist. Moses Klein, born in Oakland, California, grew to adulthood largely in a Toronto household split between the kosher domesticity of his mother on the one hand and the secular humanism of his father (which led amongst other things to being non-kosher outwith the home). His extended family was equally a balancing act between religious and cultural Jewishness. The family frequently visited his maternal grandmother on Rhode Island, who was orthodox Jewish and spoke a great deal to the children on religious matters. As with most Jews of the twentieth century, Moses took bar mitzvah. This contributed to his being rather diffident about religion in his youth:

> I was pretty much agnostic, and if you'd asked me if I believed in God, I think over the years I would've given answers ranging from maybe to probably not. But you know, if man invented God, at the time it didn't seem a bad thing to me, but I didn't have a problem at least with a metaphorical God at the time.[19]

If the short-term consequence for Moses was religious diffidence, the longer term result was to be atheist and humanist. It is worth noting that amongst some Jews, Marxist upbringing was defining. Harris Sussman, whom I

interviewed in Massachusetts, referred to the 'red diaper babies' – those
of the baby-boom generation whose parents were communist and initially
sympathetic to the Soviet Union. But he also noted that many Jews were
atheist but wouldn't utter the word.[20]

Prior to 1939, European respondents who had rejected religion were
frequently raised socialist. In Belgium, Claudine Raulier belonged to a
family of atheists, a not uncommon condition for upper-middle-class male
civil servants like her father. But it was her grandfather's generation in the
late nineteenth century, she reported, who had undergone the 'conversion'
from Catholicism to atheism, whilst her father, who worked for Liege
municipality, said of himself, 'I am a humanist. I like to know everything.'
He was, she reported, 'a very, very keen observer, ... he read a lot, ... he spoke
three or four languages, he knew a lot more. Well, he could read Spanish.
He could read, he was always trying to learn something'. Her mother,
unusually for her generation, had obtained a *science ménagère* degree to
teach in secondary school. 'I lived in a very protected atmosphere from that
point of view. My parents were not married in Church, I wasn't baptised,
and that sort of thing seems to be very straightforward to me, so there
was no drama, religious drama.' Claudine felt part of a civic intellectual
elite driven by knowledge, observation and service, and she joined it with
a chemistry degree that led to a decade of research at Liege University. She
was accepting of, rather than stridently supporting, religious non-belief:
'I worked for people who were obviously atheists as well, so the question
has never been urgent for me.' Yet, if the elite class determined her atheism,
she nevertheless had to make a social and gender decision at the age of 15:
'It was so, for those girls, it was so obvious that they had to go to Mass,
they had to have their *premiere communion*, said, you know, that; so that I
said, "No, I am not".'[21]

The socialist atheists did not always form a social elite. Ann
Auchterlonie's working-class background in Dundee and her socialist
uncle tempted her to see Christianity as a socialist theology, and then to
view the church's problems with socialism and communism as wrong.[22]
Robin Wood recalled when, at the age of 34 in 1974, he joined the
Glasgow Humanist Group, he was the youngest of the forty members,
the others being a pre-war generation of radicals combining socialism
with humanism in an act of twin ideological rebellion. In the early 1980s
the majority of non-religious funerals were for communists and trades
unionists where a fellow comrade would act as celebrant.[23] The socialist
connections of atheism were strongest amongst those I interviewed from
Scotland, and it was only after 2000 according to Robin that conservative
humanists became more numerous.

In the respondent set, many reported parents in the interwar period who
didn't go to church due to a variety of atheistical outlooks. Some were socially
or geographically isolated. Pat Duffy Hutcheon's father was a freethinker
in rural south-east Alberta, having broken away from a strong Catholic

family. 'When he was a young schoolteacher he had started reading, he said a lot of things and he had made a decision that these religions weren't for him.' Her mother was brought up Methodist, and though she couldn't be described as 'non-religious', she was, Pat reported, quite content to live with somebody who wasn't religious. Pat said, 'she was happy to be free of her Methodist upbringing because of the rules and the social regulations, and that's really all that mattered to her.' This resulted in Pat being what she described as 'an unusual child in that way', being advised by her father not to tell other children at school that she was a non-believer, nor to tell them there are no gods: 'It's just like telling them there's no Santa Claus when they're little. He said you'll hurt them and there's no need to.' Pat went by that rule as she got older, steering clear of talking about religion until considerably later in life.[24]

The respondents' narratives about religious upbringing exhibit a degree of cultural malleability. Kathleen Dillon, raised in a Presbyterian household in Belfast in the 1930s and 1940s, reported, '[As a child] I used to occasionally go to the church. I mean I quite like singing hymns and things, but I never had any religious background really.'[25] This comment reveals a number of things. First, to the modern eye, going to church even 'occasionally' would be likely to denote a religious identity of some kind, certainly religious practice and one affirming the religious alignment of the family. Second, Kathleen is describing religion as the unavoidable cultural wallpaper of the mid-twentieth century. This was especially the case in Northern Ireland, which then, as now, has been one of the most religious parts of Western Europe; fewer than 1 per cent of the people responded 'no religion' in the 2001 census.[26] This cultural wallpaper lasted different periods for interviewees. Kathleen Dillon and her husband reported that when they moved to London, Ontario,

> we joined the Unitarians there because our daughter went to kindergarten and the first week she came back home and he said, 'Why don't we go to church? The teacher this morning (Sunday morning) asked us why we weren't at Sunday school?'. So I thought 'Right!', well, we thought we better do something about this, so we went to the Unitarians to bring the children.[27]

In British Columbia, Conrad Hadland felt the same when he left the Jehovah's Witnesses and joined the Unitarians. There was an urge to belong to a church, even if he didn't believe in god: 'there is a vacuum in many people's lives, we have to have a place where they can share their joys and sorrows, and that's what offering good services to a group can be'.[28]

So, the child of unbelieving parents could have quite intimate connections with church, but still recall having little sense of religion in the home. Mary Wallace grew up in a rural village near Northwich in England where her socialist parents were not churchgoers (though her father started going late in his life). She was recruited when she was 12–14 years of age as a bell ringer in the Church of England, describing this as 'a fascinating little thing to do, a little part-time job at the weekend because you got paid for ringing the bells for weddings, but entirely unconnected with the religious side of the church'. She loved this job, 'absolutely loved it', but it had no impact on her religious beliefs. Religion, she reported, 'was just *there*'.[29] Religion was something unavoidable, a childhood practice drawn by friendships, interesting activities on Sundays (when other activities were restricted) and rarely a conversion or theological decision. Indeed, for Mary as for so many others, it was to be two decades of mainly indifference to religion before she, too, made a sudden and decisive step towards humanism.

Research from the United States has stressed the significance of non-religious parents (and peers) to the non-religion of late-twentieth-century 'nones',[30] but this was much more common in Europe. The professional baritone Anders Östberg grew up in Sweden in the 1980s in what he describes as 'a very strongly atheist family' of professional people who had been atheists over several generations. It was a society by the second half of the twentieth century in which religiosity was very weak (arguably the weakest in the free world). His family were mostly medical professionals, and this he links to their religious position. He reported, 'I think they all knew they were atheist, I think they would be happy to say that we were atheist, not that they would act in any way.' People in Sweden, he recollected, 'sort of, they just knew that they were atheist', and it was not an issue. Because it's such a strongly non-religious country, Swedes, he felt, 'sort of think that people who will go to church often are slightly weird'. Ironically, citizens there were until 1996 automatically enrolled after birth in the state Lutheran Church (partly to secure wedding and funeral rites),[31] and the individual had to make the decision to leave, which Anders did when he was 16.[32] Though he wasn't wholly certain where his atheism grew from, he recalled reading widely from the age of 10 or 11, and it was discussed in school. By 15 years of age, he was convinced and settled in his atheism, and this was, from his perspective, by far the norm for Swedes, and by early adulthood he knew that he would not have a religious marriage or funeral: 'a church funeral would be blasphemy to me'.[33] Though another Swede I interviewed said she was unaware in childhood of atheism as a concept, she recalled categorizing Bible stories as fairy stories, regarding them as fantastical and devoid of connection with reality.[34]

By the last two decades of the twentieth century, being without religion was becoming more of a norm in European households. Those born in the 1980s and 1990s could enter second- or even third-generation religiously indifferent or atheist families. One woman recalled to me her mother's fury in the 1970s and 1980s against the church (for unspecified wrongs) which she made plain to her own children in the 1990s, who, in their turn, grew up with no religious contact or interest, and remained that way into adulthood. Grant Hill noted that in Dundee in the 1980s and early 1990s it was 'uncool' for a child to talk about god or religion.[35] A religiously antagonistic generation might lead to an indifferent one, evident to the oral history researcher in the latter's increased inarticulacy about religion. I have described this in previous research as a 'stunting' of the conception of religion, where an absence of training at home, church or school in the nature of religion restricts the respondent's ability to express either religious or non-religious views.[36] It becomes difficult to speak even of agnosticism or atheism. Atheism can be clandestine to the atheist, a hidden condition. To this condition we shall return.

Converting the family

But first, a rarely thought of model of childhood religious experience is of a different stamp altogether. This is the instance of a child who, raised between the 1930s and 1950s of parents with no interest in religion, became intensely religious – sometimes evangelical, Pentecostal or fundamentalist – and converted their parents. Time and again, the context was the strong evangelical movement of the time, epitomized by the crusades of Dr Billy Graham. The child was usually a girl in her teens. Amongst twenty-eight female interviewees, I had eight who were subject to strong religious influence in their youth, self-describing as experiencing a conversion, amongst whom four were the instigator of converting their parents and other family members, whilst other women fostered a more general heightening of family religiosity.

In the mid-twentieth century (and perhaps before, though I doubt the evidence can now be found), many young children developed childhood dreams of becoming religious in some way or other. As we noted in Chapter 2, this included girls nurturing a pious femininity in churchgoing fine dresses. But young boys might dream of becoming a priest or minister. Ken Matthews, raised in Glasgow, recalled the following:

> When I was younger obviously when you are going to Sunday school as a child, I wanted to become a missionary. I think every child wants to go and help 'the wee black babies, and I'll go to Africa'; and yes, you know, because you believed what you were told, and there were no questions and they were nice wee stories of Jesus making folk better, you know suffer the little children.[37]

David Lambourn presented in interview a far more complex story of childhood clerical aspiration. Raised in a well-to-do south of England family headed by an authoritarian and 'very anti-church' father, David as a schoolboy escaped his influence almost nightly at the swimming baths and the library, learning bookishness there, and built up a life around the Anglican Church by joining youth organizations. 'I had to become who I wanted to be, so to speak, partly at school and in the youth club and Scouts.' Whilst a chorister, he constructed an alternative image of fatherhood based on the life of Christ: 'I was beginning to form an image of a possible father.' Sent by his father against his wishes to industrial training in Scotland, he escaped first by volunteering early for National Service, then brief university training and finally training at an Anglican theological college. His father was enraged when David was ordained in the Church of England, and 'did the usual thing of cutting me off without a penny'.[38] This unsettling childhood narrative opened the door to this young man seeking a solace and an identity in Christianity in a way largely forbidden in the parental home.[39]

It is surprising how many children were enveloped in religious culture when their parents were to varying degrees religiously indifferent, negligent or even hostile. Raised in households in mid-century that had little faith connection, by various routes the children became religiously active, thus impacting the parents. Joan Gibson grew up in Malaya in the 1950s, where she was placed with other British girls in two Catholic schools: the first had no proselytising, but the second multiracial school exposed non-Catholic children to what she described as indoctrination. Yet though describing herself as 'a Christian probably', her parents were alienated and resentful of the churches because her mother was divorced and no church would marry them at that time.[40] An even more telling example is that of Ruth Majors, who, born in 1941 in London into a working-class family, half Catholic, half Protestant, but 'not really churchgoers' as she described them, went in 1950 to North Africa when her father was posted by the British Army. There, she attended an American Baptist church; her parents hated it and took her away, but back in Britain in 1952 when she was 11 years old, she became interested in an evangelical church across the road from her grandparents' home. And she became a born-again evangelical, attracted by a charismatic husband-and-wife preaching team. 'I marched my parents off to Billy Graham rallies, and they got converted.' So, she said, 'we became an evangelical family'. Her brother became the church organist, and Ruth recalls chiding her mother for wearing lipstick to church and vacuuming on Sundays, saying she was an embarrassment.[41] She adopted one 1950s model of femininity, the puritanical one. However, Ruth's evangelicalism didn't last long, losing her faith whilst a university student a few years later. In such ways, parental religious habits could move in symmetry with those of their offspring. Lorraine Hardie, born in 1939 and raised in Vancouver, reported that her parents went to church less frequently because they sent her and her siblings to the neighbourhood Anglican Church Sunday school. But in their older teenage years, their interest in weekly attendance waned: 'and the interesting thing was that they sort of relaxed too and started doing other things on Sundays. Maybe that was just how the culture was evolving anyway, you know, was so things started to be more relaxed'.[42]

The same context often produced opposite results in high religious cultures. In rural Armagh in Northern Ireland in the 1930s and 1940s, the Protestant Sabbath was rigidly observed in James Machin's household, enforced by his father, which prevented harvesting or polishing of shoes on Sabbaths, but required him to count the cattle and check the sheep. Yet, his mother only went to church twice a year, for the children's service and harvest thanksgiving, whilst his father 'got the job' of accompanying up to six of the children to Sunday school and then to church where, invariably, he fell asleep during the sermon, inflicting shame on the children. Like many respondents, throughout his testimony James uses the language of 'being sent' to Sunday church, his parents 'sending them' to Sunday school, being 'sent' to summer evangelical tent missions and 'sent' to a Brethren portable tin hut. His narrative showed how, little-by-little, his resistance grew, passive but significant.[43] A significant number of respondents spoke this rhetoric, sometimes referring to 'a guilt trip' by their parents. Three respondents, Dick Hewetson (born 1930 in Minnesota), David Fowler (born 1947 in Ontario) and Dave Kong (born 1962 in Iowa), each spoke of a relative or family friend inquiring of the parent why their child or children didn't go to church, and being persuaded to allow their offspring to be picked up on Sunday mornings. Dave Kong said that his mother 'had us go just out of being polite' to a Bible class conducted by a neighbour for a week during the summer. Dick Hewetson's mother sent him to Sunday school: 'I think it was some part of a guilt thing with her, you know, she wasn't being a proper parent because we weren't going to church, and so we went to a Baptist church.'[44]

Respondents who attended Sunday school and church when their parents did not have a propensity to drift from religion. In British Columbia, Grace Daniels' mother had been brought up a Seventh Day Adventist, but gave this up and raised her children largely without religion. But Grace opted at age 4 or 5 to go to Sunday school because 'it sounded kind of cool', but left at age 9 after the pastor changed church, undermining her sense of steadfastness, and because of being offered candy at the end of each service as a bribe to return the following week. An underlying driver of reason and reasonableness came out, leading her to leave church of her own volition. She reported that she retained 'a belief in something', in a God not to be found in a church, noting that 'a little bit' of this attitude was a rebellion against her mother's atheism.[45]

Though others might not have converted the family, quite a number became during their childhood distinctly more religious than their parents. One such was Mary Wallace, who joined a Pentecostal group, an Assembly of God, in her early teens and said she was 'completely hooked' for six months, absorbed by the really passionate gathering, with lots of young people, and attracted by the drama of worship, including the speaking in tongues. 'It was *ridiculous*, but it was fascinating', Mary said, describing herself as an impressionable 13-year-old who was 'completely taken in'. 'But there was a very, very nice sense of belonging in that group…And that was really quite nice you know. But I just worked out that the whole thing was absolute gobbledegook.'[46] For those like Mary not raised within firm faith families, the childhood appeal of religious groups was expressed in diverse forms of attraction and fellowship. Dick Hewetson was reminded that in Minneapolis in the 1930s and 1940s his mother led him first to a Baptist Church and then to an Episcopal Church where the atmosphere was beguiling: 'I was just really, really impressed with this church we went to, you know, the pomp and circumstance and all, and got quite caught up in it. We dressed up to go to church.'[47] He became successively a choir boy and an altar boy, from which he entered seminary and became a priest. In these various ways, the church might act for a child as a focus for excitement, grandeur and belonging.

Several of those I interviewed decided in childhood to train for the priesthood or ministry. Maternal encouragement was common, as in the case of Ernest Parker in Washington DC, whose mother took him aged eight to the Jehovah's Witnesses, where he became a member of the ministry team and was teaching others from age 9.[48] Similarly with Conrad Hadland in British Columbia, whose family led him into the Jehovah's Witnesses at around 8 years of age, and it was noted that he got very good at answering questions in Jehovah's Witnesses magazines: 'that sort of gave me a certain amount of status', leading to him being asked to conduct meetings at the age of maybe 11 or 12.[49] Others referred to this process too – of childhood proficiency leading to family and group status, and thence on a track to ministry. Even those like Dick Hewetson in Minneapolis, who followed his grandfather's example into an Episcopalian seminary and then priesthood until the age of 42, implicitly seemed to emphasize momentum rather than faith as keeping him in the church; in interview at the age of 79, he told me, 'I didn't have any belief because nobody gave me any belief as a kid.'[50] Though two respondents who intended for ministry gave up before commencing, most of those I interviewed who were heading for priesthood from their tender years stayed on this pathway until adulthood when abandonment of faith occurred between their thirties and sixties.

Childhood disaffection

Larger by far than the previous groups of respondents was the group who, whatever the parental attitude to religion, encountered their own religious doubts, ecclesiastical disaffection and what some described as considered atheism. It is a remarkable finding of this project that a considerable proportion of respondents reported that their loss of faith happened between the ages of 7 and 13.

Childhood atheism is startling. For those grounded in a world of losing religion in an act of coming of age or adult education, or mature philosophical reflection, it is something of a surprise to discover just how important early upbringing is to loss of religion. Interestingly, there are two major tropes offered by interviewees. The first is that of losing religion in younger years, often between 7 and 13 years of age, leading to many decades of an indifference to religion in which there can be varying degrees of hardening of sentiment against the churches, religious ritual and the religious intrusions of the state. The second trope presented is that of the respondent who claims in later interview (in adulthood) to have become from 7 to 13 years a decided speculative agnostic or atheist, then maturing by about 16 to 17 years as atheists or, in three or four cases, as humanists.

The first trope, of religious alienation before age 14 leading to extended religious indifference, is by far the most common route to becoming atheist amongst all those interviewed. This is the creation of a space in the sense of a self that is vacated by religion and which remained unfilled until a later decisive change. During this period typically, the respondent notes in older age that there has been no specific identity – such as atheist, skeptic, rationalist or speculative agnostic – adopted. There is, in a very strict sense, no religion and no no-religious position chosen. Gillian Stewart from Fife in Scotland said of religion in her early teens: 'You know, so it just became something that was there but not really thought about.'[51] In another example, David Lord, born in southwest London in 1942, felt his first inklings of alienation from religion at the age of 13. It started very mundanely, and moved swiftly to a matter of principle. He found the Church of England service boring, and only found the Scout parade interesting. But he does remember not saying the Creed – 'I believe in God the father' and so on – because he was taught not to lie: 'the words didn't mean anything so I didn't say it'.[52] The child's sense of principle was hardened when he was later excluded from his local Anglican Scout troop because he had attended a Methodist Sunday School. Thereafter, from the age of 15 to 60 years of age, David was an archetypal British no-religionist:

DL: I never knew what to call myself. I never liked the word atheist and I would have not called myself an atheist, because I didn't know really what the definition was. Okay, I knew what the dictionary definition was, you know as compared with agnostic and so on … Let's say from the age of 15 I knew that I didn't really have a belief in religion.

CB: Okay, what about in God?

DL: No, I would say I didn't have, I wasn't brought up to believe in a god, I was bought up to say godly things at the appropriate times, so say 'amens' and so on and sing hymns in school. But that was mechanistic, and my feelings were totally neutral, that is I wasn't against – I wasn't for, totally neutral, it was mechanistic. It was something that I was taught like time tables and so on, it was just something that was there. As I say 15 to 60.[53]

It was only in his mid-sixties, after a career in electronic engineering and technology marketing, that Lord began to read in skeptic, atheist and rationalist literature, and came to redefine a specific atheist identity.

In yet another example, Alicja Stettin was born in Eastern Europe in 1947 and brought up a Roman Catholic. But as she said, '[I] cut my ties to religion' at the age of 8. 'I would sit in the pew beside my mother and listen to what the priest was saying, really concentrate on what he was saying and think to myself this makes no sense whatsoever.' The specific turning point occurred when she went to her first confession, and was probed by the priest if she had sinned. When asked if she had ever argued with her mother, she said yes, an incident in which her mother had hit her for failing to take some garlic medicine for a cold; Alicja refused to speak to her for a week until her mother apologized. The priest told her to say Hail Marys, but during her recitation she came to a halt: 'I stopped right in the middle of the second one and I said to myself: what am I doing, this is ridiculous? And I got up and walked away and went home, told my mother that's it, I'm never going to church again, this is --- This is --- It all doesn't make any sense. It's illogical [laughs].' But her mother bribed her – with going to the cinema on a Sunday after worship – to attend church and catechism training for first communion. There, she fought with the priest weekly in the hope of being ejected: 'all I did was argue. I mean, whatever reading we had, whatever lesson we had, I would go through it and point out all the absurdities and all the illogical things in there'. But the priest apparently enjoyed the verbal fight, and she ended up around ten years of age at communion where she felt a hypocrite: 'I thought if you have any shred of self respect you're gonna get up and walk out of here. You don't believe in any of this.' But then, she said, 'I looked at my mother sitting beside me. I couldn't do that to her, so I stayed I had my communion', and in her communion photographs on the church steps she said she looked a most miserable child.[54]

This pattern is extremely common amongst my respondents born in the 1940s and 1950s. They led lives from their teens to their later middle age, or even old age, in which an absence of concern for religion, church or philosophical consideration of any real consequence dominated their narrative. The things being shed were, as David Lord puts it, the 'mechanistic' effects of religion in childhood lives. Initially, he was not hostile to the churches, though this attitude did change: 'I was neutral, benign to them. They had no relevance in my life, and perhaps going through the decades very slowly it was more, I would say I had more antipathy towards them, and would now, yes I would now campaign against their influence, and certainly argue against their influence.' Lord represents many of those from the later 1950s onwards who, characteristically leading professional lives in science, engineering, medicine or applied-scientific occupations (such as public health), relegated questions of religion and no religion to the 'back of their minds'. In great part, this seems to have been because for the decades during which they 'came out' from organized religion there was very little public debate about alternative positions to being religious or being church active. David recalled, 'I was quite comfortable because again in the groups in which I mixed it was never a subject, it was never a topic of conversation, and I am not a person who sort of spends long evenings in the pub to get into that kind of discussion.' For those beyond the confines of high intellectualism, socialism or ardent secularism, there was no common and attainable articulation of atheism in the 1950s and 1960s, no discourse readymade for absorption. Few atheists were honoured in public discourse: one of note was Bertrand (Lord) Russell, who inherited an earldom and was much acclaimed, even by the right-wing Christian press. But for most other atheists and humanists, notably socialists and women, an entirely different and hostile discourse of opprobrium awaited them if they raised their heads above the parapet.

Accordingly, the unfilled space was a common experience. As an active Trotskyist and Marxist from the age of 15 onwards, Terry Martin, born in London in 1941, was *de facto* an atheist and engaged in various forms of action in pursuit of the class revolution. But as he put it, 'I think it's safe to say, Callum, that religion was bracketed in those years, aside, while I was busy doing other things.'[55] In an American example, Robert Sanford, born in 1941 in Seattle, attended Sunday school until the age of 12, and the revelation of mythologies – Viking and Christian – led him to abandoning churchgoing. When in the US Army and required to state his 'church preference', he avoided Sunday services by carefully selecting 'Gothic', which, with no church, conferred free time.[56] These were small victories, the everyday resistances, which might sustain the religious void.

This trope – of childhood ecclesiastical breach, followed by decades of indifference – is far less common amongst those I interviewed who were born after 1980. As younger people in their teens or twenties, they came to a decided non-belief position, part of the distinctive growth of atheist, secularist and humanist movements in the 2000s and 2010s. This suggests that what we are looking at is less an age-contingent loss of religion than an historically contingent one – when the age of the respondent is less important than the period at which he or she came to lose religion. It seems to be that that *loss of religion* at 7–15 years of age was common amongst those born in various decades; but, what happened in those tender years differed, with those born before 1980 tending to merely lose their church-religion, and those born after that date tending to both lose church-religion and become atheists or agnostics.

The child atheist

Robin Russell was an atheist by ten years of age. He recounts it as a process of precocious logic. He says of religion, 'By the time I was about 10 years old I was pretty much set in. I remember about grade 4 thinking this is all a crock, like just on purely logical grounds. This doesn't make any sense to me.' He told me, 'I was 12 years old, had just turned 12 years old, and we were leaving school and there was a crowd of 5 or 6 little kids and I just announced to the group: "You know what, there is no God".' He was overheard by the daughter of the Baptist minister, whom he described as someone who 'bought into the whole thing hook, line and sinker. She gasped, she looked at me, and said "you're going to hell". She never spoke to me again as long as the two of us lived in the same town [laughs]'.[57]

The testimony of the childhood atheist has key characteristics. The first is to refer to the great determination and often anger he or she felt in childhood coming out from the shadow of religion. For Robin Russell, born in the mid-1950s into a strict evangelical extended family in Yorkton, Saskatchewan, religion had been a practice drilled into him. But he built up a resistance and scepticism which, he says, extended from a very young age when his doubt prevented him from getting his prize Bible, stars and tick marks at Sunday school. He couldn't kick against this regime because his mother had a real temper, 'so this was obviously extremely important to her and it was just part of the package'. But the episode of announcing there was no God when leaving school one day was an indication, reported Robin, that logic was kicking in:

> It was a purely, as I recall it, intellectual decision. There was no 'no God has done this' and 'no God would allow this to happen' kind of reasoning at all. It just was very simple – it's irrational. It doesn't make sense. I learned … how the cosmos can affect you … Where I grew up [in] the prairies in Saskatchewan and its small town, when you looked up from your backyard at night, there was no little city light. You literally saw a million stars and galaxies out there. And I can recall as a young kid looking up in the awe and beauty and wonder of it, and thinking it's just not possible with all those thousands and thousands of stars out there that there aren't some planets with some life on them … As later I heard Carl Sagan put it more eloquently than me, do you think there's life out there? He said, well it'd be a terrible waste if there isn't. Again just pure logic. And having that backdrop helped in coming to that conclusion.

The intellectual decision had familial consequences. He reported that his mother was 'devastated': 'you could see it destroyed a part of her being as a human being that I would believe that. But it was just at the point I just couldn't hide it anymore'.[58] From that point he had no hesitation in repeating his atheist position to everyone.

Robin became atheist so young that he couldn't remember the process in detail. But the power of logic and reason as the driver is a main cause offered in interview. Kirsten Bulmer is perhaps common of the respondents in this group. Brought up in Livingston in Scotland in the 1970s and 1980s, she had doubt from early in primary school:

> I remember being deeply sceptical as a child and I've always been should I say anti-religious, organised religion. I've always been sceptical, even would say cynical about it as a child. I remember thinking 'what's this about, this isn't right, how can this how can this be, how can people, how can men assume that they have understood the message?' To me it was obvious it was entirely manmade as a child.[59]

By her twenties she was a firm atheist, and felt able, in the rapidly secularizing environment of the east of Scotland, to be explicit about her position. The childhood loss of belief in god was not confined to the West. I interviewed Nanendra Nayak, who was born in 1951 in Mangalore in Karnataka state, India, and lost his belief in God – and became by his own description anti-god – when, at the age of 8, he prayed hard and deeply for his father, a pharmacist, to stop socially unacceptable behaviour. When his prayer went unheeded, he started, as he put it, 'experimenting with God'. Every time he had a school examination, his mother told him to pray; one day, he only pretended to pray and got full marks. For the next examination, he dared, 'God, fail me in this examination if you are there.' Once again he scored well. 'So next time it came for an examination my mother said, "pray to God and go" and I said, "God is useless, there is no God". You know her reaction was something which I think of even now, she said, "Oh you realised the truth at a very young age", she said.' From this, Nanendra started to lose his faith 'in all these things, God, religion', including rejecting the 'thread ceremony' initiation into Brahmanism and refusing his secret Gayatri Mantra.[60] He recalled this with clarity as a defining series of linked episodes – his experimentation with God through to his rejections of religion. Interestingly, his narrative brought the science of his father's occupation, which had initiated his prayer challenges, to his own reasoning for atheism.

The mixture of morality and science in Nanendra's explanation featured also in Ellen Ramsay's account of departure from religion during her primary school years in Vancouver and London. In Vancouver, she noted that the attendees at Sunday school were 'problem children' and she felt uncomfortable there, and her mother gave her permission to withdraw. At primary school in Bedford in England, she made a similar association: 'There was the school assembly in the morning which had both prayers and songs followed by, at that time, strappings. I found it most disconcerting to have the principal of the school, I believe it was, saying about peace and love and good things followed by strapping of some students in the school.' Ellen relates how this firmed up into a rejection of religion:

> I very much followed what the science teachers were doing. My parents would ask me questions about what happens when we die. 'Have you learned at school what happens when people die?' So I said to them that I had learned in science class that they simply return to nature. Something of that nature, you know. I tried to put it in simple terms that I understood. I was only about 8 or 9 when they were asking me.[61]

Recoil from unreason, irrationality and immorality was reportedly widespread amongst my respondents. Dave Kong, born in 1962 in a small town in Iowa, obtained at between 8 and 10 years of age a copy of *Chariots of the Gods* by Eric Von Daniken – which, as Dave described it, 'is of course complete pseudo science'. But critically, the *science* in the pseudo was important. It made him cultivate a demand for evidence, as Daniken claimed to have: 'And even as a kid I was going: "Well, I dunno if I'm buying this whole thing about aliens coming down and all that stuff". But at the same time as a kid what he's trying to say is that "if all these things in the Bible actually happened there is some scientific basis for these stories".' This logic led him to conclude that 'there's obviously no miracle producing God'. Having not heard of atheism in 1970s Iowa, he reacted privately to himself: 'Oh wow! This is a completely mind-blowing new idea.' His mom told him he was wrong, though five years later, when he was 13 or 14, he reported her saying, 'You know, I've been thinking about it and you're right'.[62]

It is not surprising, perhaps, that parents feature as the foil of child atheism. But a second strand of child atheist testimony is a context of distress. Dennis Duncan, born in Edinburgh in Scotland in 1929, left the Catholic Church at the age of 14. He had already had a series of traumatic experiences with what he describes as 'a few bad tempered nasty young Irish priests'. At the age of 8, as a war evacuee child, staying with his grandparents at Pittenweem in Fife, he had barely served a couple of weeks as an altar boy at the local Catholic church when he was forced to stand-in for an absent older lad. But, wearing an oversize cassock, he tripped walking down the altar steps, dropping one of the Mass vessels. In 'quite a traumatic experience', the priest threw him off the altar in great rage, making him feel disgraced. A year or so later, he tried again at a Catholic church in Edinburgh where he was asked to read the Benediction, but then the priest rejected him, causing more grief and what he felt was a 'schlimazel'.[63] Finally, after emigrating to Canada, he attended a Catholic church in Ottawa where he lined up with other men for confession.

> One Saturday night age 14, I guess, I went to confession and knelt there near the back of the church. You wait around like in a barber shop, and

only nobody paid any attention to me. And so after about 4–5 times of being cut off by some eager adult to say his confession, this hit me – the hell with this thing. Just got up and walked out, never went back.

Dennis' narrative of religious alienation runs from one childhood insult to another, amounting to a narrative of extended hurt. He felt abandoned: 'I had no nurturing in any way to keep me going, and I just copped out, as it were.'[64]

Another narrative trope came from those atheists born into families in which one or both parents were highly religious. Recoil at parental, or occasionally grandparental, religiosity was regularly a revolt against both religion and authority, notable, like Dave Kong's experience, in rural or small town communities. Pietistic or evangelical rural religion conflicted with more liberal urban upbringings. Kai Kristensen spent some of his childhood in Copenhagen's relaxed social atmosphere of the 1930s, but he was sent to his paternal grandfather's rural community on the coast of Jutland, where he had to kneel on the floor to pray before meals, and he resented those experiences.[65] In Albany, Oregon, when Larry Hicok told his strongly religious mother in the 1950s he was an atheist, she was very upset, but he said he very much clung to the positive values she gave him and developed. He 'came out' as an atheist to his school friends, with long-lasting repercussions:

> I came out to my schoolmates and the reaction was generally negative. I became a bookworm. I subscribed to tons of magazines, read them. I read a lot of books. I became a strong bookworm. That's what I did. My social life in my adolescent years was pretty bad. You know, things got much better when I went to college, and then after that they got much better and much better.

Larry said that it was when he graduated from high school in 1968 that he became more accepted for his atheist standpoint.[66]

As with Kristensen and Hicok, a sense of injustice oozes into recollection of those becoming, by their own accounts, atheists in childhood. Part of this was directed at family, but churches were common targets for criticism. Unfairness, excesses, hypocrisies and sheer bloody-mindedness of churches – these are catalogued as triggers to loss of faith. Children were terrified by tales of hell, as James Machin (1931–2012) was, both as a young child and later when he was seriously ill in his mid-teens in the 1950s, when an evangelical minister in Belfast sought to convert him on what might have turned out to be his death bed. James reported, '[T]hat really turned me. That was one of the things that influenced my thinking, you know when you are the most vulnerable, you come in for the prey.'[67] At the other end of the emotional spectrum, there is reference in some testimonies of a less distressing nature concerning Santa Claus – about being fooled when young by tales of Santa, leading to a widespread angst amongst respondents as to how to handle the 'Santa issue' with their own children and grandchildren.[68]

A few acknowledged substitute religions. Terry Martin attended a Dominican school in north London in the 1940s and 1950s where, he reported at the age of 12 and 13, 'I was overcome with a longing to be with God and the whole Catholic panoply of discipline and faith and belonging to the church.' His mother proudly encouraged him, but his father, an ex-communist, stopped his ambitions, telling him, ' "My advice is don't. Never mind what your mother says, never mind what the priests say, I don't want you to".' From there Terry in his mid-teens met a girl who took him to a meeting where he met a charismatic radical Marxist and almost instantly Terry became an ardent Trotskyist, involved in political campaigning. In his narration of his life, his interview moves from the world of Catholicism and Dominican theology to that of Trotskyism and Marxism, Althusserian structuralism and Foucauldian postmodernism of the 1960s and 1970s and what he called his 'early awareness of bourgeois humanism'. As he spoke to me, he spotted that he was sliding in and out of different total worldviews, with the linguistic change from theological to Marxist terminology in his manner of speaking, noting, 'I mean, even the terminology I'm using --- can you not see it all coming back, can you not hear it?' From signing seminary papers at the age of 13, by the age of 16 years, he was thoroughly radicalized as a Marxist and a *de facto* atheist, and remained dedicated to the cause in various ways for decades until the late 1980s.[69]

Final breaks with church and faith during early to mid-teens were often through the plain flowering of adolescent logic. Alienation from church, faith and religious rites instigated various emotional states – including anger, depression and fear. Losing god at 15 years of age, Grant Hill recalled becoming depressed at the loss of the 'comfort net'.[70] Despite the variety of experience, reactions to unreason and immoralities of one kind or another vein through many narratives. The injustices corroded religion, blending with a propitious rationality. They also involved in some instances alienation from their childhood peers – some with pride and bravado, others with a terror that might last into adulthood. But shining through much of the recollection of childhood alienation from religion is an emerging state of moral consciousness, one balking at injustices, inconsistences or hypocrisies committed in the name of religion.

'What colour is life?' The youthful maturation of atheism

After the age of 13, religious alienation matured. Jutta Cahn was born in Berlin in 1925 of an assimilated Jewish father and Lutheran mother, and brought up in a household with very little religion, though she described learning it at Protestant school. But on moving to England at age 11, she took herself to the Church of England.

> The war was on and I was inquisitive at the time and took confirmation classes and got myself confirmed. My parents had no say in the matter, I decided on that. But within a year I left [laughs]. And had had quite enough of the religious teachings that I had taken as a result of becoming confirmed in the Church of England.

The trigger for her about-turn was having family in both Germany and Britain during the war: 'On the German side the Christians I suppose were asking for their God, so to speak, to smite the enemy, namely the Brits. Where did that leave me? In a state of confusion. And it was enough for me to quit, and I quit for the rest of my life in terms of being a religious person.'[71]

This sense of deciding for oneself as a youth is strong amongst my respondents – both for religion, and in walking away from it. But if oral history might foster claims to autonomous choices, the outcomes were little known about by the respondents in mid-century. The start to atheism was often narrated as a 'drift' – a word that appeared thirty-four times in the testimonies. Respondents were able to identify, in most cases, very specific triggers to their drift, even at quite young ages. In Wales, Cerys Davies (born in 1939) told me, 'At school studying evolution, anatomy and physiology in science gave me a sound basis for developing a naturalistic, as opposed to a supernaturalistic, worldview.' She put immense effort into writing an essay on her idea of god for a school competition, in which she described such ideas 'as a means of social organisation and control and the centre of a system of belief that lends authority to those who seek to exercise power and influence over others'. The head teacher tore up the essay in front of her; the distress she felt instigated anti-religious debating in sixth form that annoyed the teachers but led her mates to elect her class captain. In the midst of a strongly Jewish upbringing, she reported, 'Although I was by natural disposition a secular, non-religious person I had, unfortunately, no knowledge of Secularism, Humanism or Rationalism since no one I knew mentioned this way of thinking.'[72]

Three respondents joined humanist groups at the age of 16 in the 1960s, but lack of knowledge of such choices was widespread amongst the young in those decades. In a different social milieu at an English 'public' (private fee-paying) boarding school, Peter Barton reported to me that most boys found religious services and confirmation classes 'a boring compulsory routine', and in the Christian Union 'the atmosphere of Jesus and good clean fun was not at all to my taste'. Already dissatisfied with the intellectual integrity that socially surrounded religious faith, he reported, 'I would say that matters religious were of little interest to me during my schooldays'.[73] Some openly, some silently, rejected the religious message

"God punished his son" - effect on child

in youth. Alistair McBay in Scotland recalled being in Sunday school at a very young age, listening to what was being preached at him, and thinking: 'I don't believe this, this doesn't sound right to me.' He went on to say that

> I remember one episode where we were being told that God had sacrificed his son because of the sins of others and it had a cruel death visited on him and blah blah blah, and I remember thinking, 'Gosh I better behave when I go back in case my dad does that to me'. This is what goes through childish minds, but I still thought at the time that this seems odd to me. This all happened thousands of years ago; why [are] they telling me this?[74]

Childhood questioning, widely reported, often started at Sunday school or youth fellowship, where Gillian Stewart, raised in Scotland in the 1960s, recalled thus: 'I remember thinking what is this all about? I don't get it, you know, I don't quite understand what all the fuss is about, if you like.'[75]

The high frequency of childhood doubt amongst those who came after 1960 to live their lives without god gives comfort as to the reliability of their remembering, and attests to its social significance. This is given even more credence when we alight on the respondents of that generation who were destined to a religious life prior to losing religion in later adulthood. They comment in precisely the same manner, of the same ages, about the issues which framed their journeys to God. Bill Kennedy in Winnipeg was immersed in his growing up years in the 1930s and 1940s in religious ideas and sensibilities. As the last of his mother's brood of eight, he recalled the constant adult conversation in the house: 'there was always a little boy listening and puzzled by all these strange stories that were coming back from people going out'. When he asked questions, he was told like this:

> 'Billy you can't understand that'. And that one got me and I said 'why? Why can't I --- I understood the other things why can't I understand?' 'Because you haven't seen life' [laughs]. And...I would lie in bed and ask myself what this life was. What colour was it? It can't be green because green is all around...I've seen green trees, grass. I wonder what colour life is. I don't think I spent a lot of time on that but that memory is sharp that I had to figure out what life was, what it looked like, smelled like [and] so on.[76]

His question what colour was life, and the answer he got, he says in a thoughtful recollection of childhood understanding of epistemology. It led to fifteen years of training to be a Jesuit. By the same trigger that pushed him on a trajectory of priestly religious training, others were pushed on a trajectory towards atheism.

Puberty and the proximity of adulthood brought religion and sex into close quarters. Respondents of all kinds recall churchgoing as a means of observing, and seeking dates with, the opposite sex. Some boys recall going to many churches of different denominations in pursuit of girls. When he was 15–16 years of age in about 1956–7, Robin Wood in Sussex tried out the services of various denominations: of the Church of England, the Baptists and the Methodists: 'And I even went to a Catholic one once cause I knew a girl who was a Catholic and I thought I'd just go along [to] see what all that's about. And I thought oh this is a load of hokum you know, this is just --- By that time I'd decided no, no, no, this is silly.' And Robin narrated that as the moment of his breach from organized religion and the possibility of religious faith.[77] Leaving the grasp of faith came more easily on the threshold of adulthood.

CHAPTER FOUR

The Silent and
Indifferent Atheist

Approaching indifference

Must the budding atheist or humanist repudiate God? Prevailing approaches in histories of atheism and humanism tend to expect clear affirmation of non-belief, and many philosophers and others follow the scale and nature of repudiation in demonstration of this.[1] But what is true for philosophers and writers is rarely true for others. The social experience of losing religion shows that for very many people, at least initially, atheism is founded upon either *forgetting* God or *never knowing of* God. This fosters a state of indifference that is a practical atheism – a *disinterest* in any god being equivalent to *not asserting* his or her existence. That equivalence extends the reach of secularization into a large demographic group, perhaps the largest religious group in Western Europe, and one growing fast elsewhere in the West. Whilst in other parts of this book we tackle rejection of religion and god by deeds, statement or confession to self by the sixties generation, in this chapter we approach a fairly common period in atheists' lives, invariably following childhood or youth, that continues characteristically for several decades. This is a period of general silence upon religion – one produced by diffidence, indifference or rational choice.

Before approaching the testimonies which illuminate the period of indifference, we need to reflect upon the analytical and methodological difficulties. This part of a person's life might be accompanied by closure of interest in church and religious activities, an abandonment of attending worship or participating in religious ritual, and will likely have no other discernible private religious activity (such as prayer or religious reading). This might be described as a thoughtless or non-speculative atheism, one unlikely to give rise to religious descriptions we might recognize – atheist, secularist or humanist – though 'atheist' or 'agnostic' might be used as a handy moniker in social situations in which an individual feels compelled to offer some term. This numerous category is important, but it poses difficulties.

First, many researchers have in recent years been exploring the religiosity of those without firm faith or religious identity; we noted this research in Chapter 1, and the variety of terms – *apostates, unaffiliated, liminals, secular Christians, lapsed* and *fuzzy fidelity* – has sprung up amongst researchers of various hues. The group I am discussing here includes those who, at the start of their indifference, may have lingering religious or ecclesiastical attachments, partly the result of family pressures, and partly through their own indecision. But for them, as we shall see from the testimony, there is an evident trajectory to atheism – a long-term journey, sometimes of several decades, but a journey characteristically without much sustained intensity of reflection. There can be a lightness of touch to their discarding of religiosity and to the atheism they *de facto* enter. But some people are firmer in their indifference, accompanied by a disdain for religion or for the churches. Yet, the foremost feature is an indifference which amounts to boredom, weariness and a mental lethargy concerning questions of faith and religious practice.

Second, this group is not well recognized, let alone well covered, in existing historical research. Though some psychologists have noted indifference as one form of atheism,[2] the indifferentists are given little independent existence. Churches are prone to claim indifferent persons to their own by dint of having baptized them as infants; *vide* the Church of England, which is still referred to today as claiming 26 million people in the Anglican communion in England – a fantasy figure more than ten times higher than active Anglican adherents.[3] Meanwhile, historians and philosophers of atheism and humanism tend to presume that the act of *losing religion* and not merely lapsing from it must be a conscious one, and especially in a society of high belief and worship, and with a culture immersed in religion. They conform to the idea put forward by Proust and by Nietzsche that the atheist must renounce God and, as the latter put it, 'vanquish his shadow, too'.[4] Leaving religion is thus perceived as something deliberate and pre-meditated, an act of conscious abandonment of faith, however that is triggered or accomplished.

The evidence presented here points to something rather different in highly secular environments and in societies of low religiosity since the 1960s. Here, the bulk of people who have been leaving religion have done so, *not* because they became at the point of losing an atheist or humanist, but for reasons characterized by diminishing consciousness or premeditation. They are rarely hostile to religion in any organized way, though they can be on a casual basis when, for instance, they find church influence an irritant in their lives. But, in nearly all contemporary European nations, the loss of religion has developed, over many decades now, to be a silent leaving of religion – an act often attended initially by little or no conscious decision or deep deliberation. These will be people who say that they never did believe in god; they may say they attended church or Sunday school, but never believed. They may have held to a religion and worshipped in church (with or without a belief in god), but lost all of this religious orientation through boredom or finding competing preoccupations. God may have slunk off. More than this. This group may include those who are so disengaged from religious issues that they are not really aware of holding any position at all. They may be living their lives as if there is no god, but constituting atheists without knowing it.

For a period of his life, John Edwards was one such. Brought up in the Baptist and Methodist churches in Mossley in Liverpool, he found himself still attending church, though poorly, during his teenage and university years. But having married in church in 1972, he reported that by the time their son was born in 1981 'something had happened in the meantime because we never dreamt of having him christened. We thought "No, we don't want to bring him up in a religion, why should we? We don't believe it, so why should we?"' If their son picked religion in life, that was going to be his affair, but the couple decided not to create a Christian environment for him.[5] The transition from faith to unbelief for John and his wife, as he reported it, had been obscured. This was an unclassifiable period in one sense, but *de facto* was a period when God left their lives.

Whatever manner these people may be tussled over by researchers pushing them into one category or another, they make for a distinctive research problem. How does the oral historian, keen to hear the memories articulated by those who have lost religion, set about acquiring testimony from a group characterized by a process such as this? How does the person who never had god, or who forgot God, and has been long-term disinterested in religion, get enticed to speak about it to a researcher? There is a methodological difficulty, one which may involve an invitation to the respondent to institute a transformation of their position *vis-à-vis* their religious stance – a transformation comprising the attempt to awaken their forgetfulness. This process has dangers, clearly, in altering the atheist condition. It is asking the respondent to come up with an historical narration which they may never have attempted or felt the need for; it may require a re-remembrance of god or faith in their life; and it may at the extreme invite them to imagine themselves, not as apathetic, but as reasoned in their atheism. The oral history respondent does not wish to be seen to be inarticulate about themselves. So, the intrusive oral historian may, perhaps certainly will, destroy the indifference previously felt if he or she is successful in eliciting a considered response. In this way, success in the research of the disinterested would be self-defeating. This lies on top of the problem of actually identifying and recruiting volunteers of the disinterested; again, to be successful is to render null the disinterest. Such an invitation by an oral historian is an invitation to become a *cultured atheist* – not in the sense of being artistic or mannered, but in the sense of having a culture of atheism comprising a personal history of a marked loss of religion (a moment, a process, perhaps a place and context), a recoverable progression and a rational testimony. The purpose is not well served if we tempt the respondent into recalling being a garrulous atheist.

There is a way round this, though. This is to interview those who developed a considered position on religion – including atheists – in later life, and ask them to reflect back on their years or sometimes decades of indifference. In this way, it is possible to have a volunteer group who can acknowledge their indifference at an earlier point in their lives, but can legitimately be asked to comment upon it without jeopardizing that indifference. This is not a perfect solution, of course. The intervening years may distort recollection of what it was like to have had no interest in religious issues when younger. Those who transited through indifference to a more thoughtful position may not be wholly representative of all the indifferent. Yet, for the period of their indifference, they offer a window into that state of affairs.

In previous research, I have signposted evidence of the silent atheist that I found in British oral history archives. In 1999, I sat for a week reading oral history transcripts from the 1960s, 1970s and 1980s at the Qualidata Archive (now part of UK Data) at the University of Essex in England, and I was struck by how the interviews conducted amongst respondents in their teens and early twenties generated answers on religious questions markedly different from those of older respondents. What I found was that a young respondent, asked to comment on the role of religion in their present or past life in the 1970s or 1980s, was often close to inarticulate on the matter. He or she might offer answers of curt brevity – 'I was never interested in religion', or 'I never went to church', or a bare 'I don't know'. This answer closed off the questioning on religion, shut it down, and usually the interviewer then moved on to the next topic on the schedule. This phenomenon I called 'stunting', meaning restricted answers.[6] Stunting is a condition in which, firstly, there is apparently a shortage of memories to recall, and, secondly, a shortage of words with which to articulate an attitude to religion. Stunting is a condition of short, inarticulate, abrupt answers to questions, in this case about religion. The respondent has a resistance to answering, and the very abruptness of their response is an invitation to not probe any further. They are reluctant to speak on this topic. Now, of course, the sceptic might legitimately consider that there are other possible explanations for this phenomenon. One might be a respondent's desire to protect their privacy on religious matters. In an another possibility, Stephen Parker, in oral history interviews for his social history of religion in England during the Second World War, found 'stunting' as something temporary and brought on by wariness. Parker commented, 'Characteristically, in order to uncover the religious reality forming the backcloth of the social world of interviewees, it was sometimes necessary to overcome the initial discomfort of admitted religious belief or upbringing, and then relief of finding, in the interviewer, someone sympathetic towards this world view.'[7] So initial embarrassment, desire for privacy or shyness are important characteristics in interview, but are the product of initial or temporarily deliberate concealment of a religious view, rather than stunting as a condition in which the respondent is to be found. In research in the late 1990s, Susan Wiltshire found young people in Edinburgh rather unresponsive to questions on 'religion', though much more responsive to issues put to them as dealing with 'spirituality'.[8] This is instructive. But, I reassert that stunting was a distinct phenomenon to be observed in 1980s interviews, and stands apart amongst respondents who, as far as we can tell, genuinely had nothing to say on religion. This was most common amongst the young, as those who were older in that decade had been brought up in a British society in which church involvement was much harder to avoid. For the young of that decade, as I reported in my findings, the stunted answers of many young people often involved some abrupt dismissal of the notion that they had at any time a developed interest in religion; this would tend to suggest immediately that the respondent is not against talking *per se*, as the answers on other topics were fulsome, but rather had, broadly, specifically nothing to say on religion. In Chapter 2, I reported that in the United States a variety of factors might produce evasive or short answers on losing religion; but the phenomenon of stunting was far more pronounced and, I would aver, genuinely reflecting disinterest in religion in the British interviews I have examined. In the oral history archives I examined from the United States and Canada, I found, largely, every respondent when prompted said something on the topic of religion. This is an interesting cultural difference.

The silence of non-belief

People are apt to speak little about an absence of faith. Atheism and indifference both tend to be very quiet. The latter, as we have seen, may be unrecognized as significant for the indifferent person; questioning may end the indifference. A few of the former, by contrast, a very few, shout loudly about their atheism, secularity and campaign in various ways for causes. But demographically, this is highly unusual. Silence grips 90 per cent of atheists. They don't speak of being without god, they don't argue with religionists at parties, they don't campaign in the streets and they don't join an organization which expresses their position. For centuries, they have been pretty noiseless or inaudible. And in the second half of the twentieth century at least, silent atheists have not all been silent merely because they are indifferent to issues of religion and belief. This makes them interesting yet difficult to study.

Many reasons can be adduced for this. One is a simple mechanical one, if you will: people without an express faith have less to talk about – not a church of unbelief, little or no ritual of unbelief (with the attendant artefacts and photographs one finds with religious ritual), and, because it is a negative or absent category, no theology, little history and, for the first-generation atheist and indifferentist, rarely any family traditions or recollections of unbelief to recall. This leaves oral history of unbelief immediately bereft of much narrative substance. A second is that atheists are seldom made in a single process or act of conversion. They go through stages which are often personal, quite subdued affairs, perhaps lacking key signs – even to the individual. Atheists speaking about how they got to that state of being find difficulty in identifying dates or stages, or even processes. The atheist may not be aware of when he or she became one. As Gordon Lynch has observed in his book on his own loss of evangelical Christian faith, people losing faith have a tendency to deny that it is going on – especially to themselves.[9] A third reason is that the majority of practical atheists do not describe themselves as such, and the indifferentist has no term realistically to hand. The atheist may choose other terms or a mixture of terms, given that 'atheist' is often seen as too negative for an identity, and they may prefer 'humanist' or 'agnostic' – the latter often because it is deemed as more rationally accurate. Fourth, atheists in many nations have found difficulty in articulating their atheism, sometimes because it is, or recently has been, illegal; or that it implies some associated potential illegality; or that it is socially or politically unacceptable; or that it may endanger their employment; or it may not describe themselves. Within the most advanced secular nations, fear of 'coming out' is falling. But the staged process is an important issue in personal narratives of becoming a person of no religion.

So, self-defining as an atheist has not been exactly hugely popular. Most people who don't believe in God don't describe themselves as 'atheist', nor volunteer even as an indifferentist. We can go further: we can say that many people who don't believe in a god don't *think of themselves* as not believing in God. Proving this might be difficult, indeed almost impossible. Once you ask for people to come forward who don't believe in god, they are not able to *not* define themselves that way; it's a self-defeating research strategy. A way of understanding this problem is as follows. Social science research presumes that the answer precedes the question: that the respondent holds a view (atheism) prior to being asked about it (are you an atheist?). But what if the answer does not precede the question? What if the question cultivates the answer? People who have no faith don't necessarily think of that as a primary or significant source of their identity. Yes, some do, but even amongst those who are members of atheist organizations, they rarely bring this up as at the forefront of their sense of self. Indeed, amongst many committed and energetic campaigning 'atheists', there are those who detest the word. One of the interviewees for this book, David Lord, is a campaigning secularist; but in recalling his developing non-religious attitude during his later teens and twenties, he reported, 'I never liked the word atheist and I would have not called myself atheist.'[10] This further complicates oral-history silences on unbelief.

This is the first reason why adoption of the label 'atheist' is rare in even the most secular of societies. There are other reasons, which we shall come to in a moment. But sticking with self-defining of the non-religious self for a moment, we then must confront methodological problems in researching this. As an historian informed by social scientific method, I am concerned that statements that I make are composed of evidence-based argument. Getting that evidence on non-belief is hard. Notwithstanding this, we need to think of atheism as a large category that characterizes the Western world, and one that constitutes the underlying dynamic of secularization. These are the people who leave churches, stop religious ritual and come to live their lives as if there is no god.

There are some important characteristics of this group. First, the level at which people will expressly say they do not believe in God – by answering 'no' to the question 'Do you believe in God?' – is higher than the proportion who will self-describe as 'atheist' or, even, 'atheist' plus 'agnostic'. A simple negative to the simplest belief question scores higher than any question which complicates the expected response from the individual. Second, one reason for low scoring for self-identifying atheists is that, unlike questions on religion answered positively by respondents, to select a term signifying a negative position (such as 'atheist' or one of the others) is known by survey specialists to be unpopular. People rarely find a negative position attractive or useful for personal identity. Individuals want to seek identity in a positivity, in answering 'yes' to a question rather than 'no'. A very small number of people tend to adopt 'atheist' as their primary identity, some perhaps in a curmudgeonly mood of resistance to social norms. Though the number of no religionists has risen very significantly since the 1960s, for most of that period 'atheist' has not fully shared that growth in popularity. Yet, it is important to look upon 'atheist' as a definition for the social history of losing religion. For many it is the last of as many as ten stages of disengagement from religion; for others it may be an early stage, socially concealed by sustained churchgoing and outward signs of prayer and faith. Either way, people who arrive *de facto* at non-belief in god are *de facto* atheists.

Third, the atheist is typically undemonstrative. He or she is someone who rarely proclaims their position, by word or deed, in the manner of the religionist. To hold to no religious belief is to vacate a whole realm of personal behaviour. There is an underlying logic to the undemonstrative atheist. For one thing, they often regard those who do hold a religion as doing something unnecessary for the modern world. For those people who don't think about god in their self-definition, having a god-centred definition seems slightly socially awkward and perhaps bizarre. Faith definition by other people may seem peculiar, perhaps anachronistic. In Western European countries notably, holding to a religion has become by the early twenty-first century, as one of my oral history respondents put it, 'slightly weird'.[11] The attitude might be hypothesized as 'Why do we need a faith in the secular environment in which we live? We have other well-crafted moral stances, we don't need to bow to an irrationality in order to maintain personal or national identity, or the social or moral order.' Though I emphasize that this is a fictional remark, it theorizes what may be a position both articulated and non-articulated amongst a very significant proportion of the population.

Fourth, there is a more constructive reason why individuals don't use the term 'atheist', even if they don't believe in god. Self-describing as atheist is rare in modern society, influenced by the social and ideological complications of articulating being seen to be without a religion. Until comparatively recently, the framework for defining one's religious self was set in virtually every nation by religious authorities (in the West by the Christian and Jewish churches) and even by the state. Every church in every age has feared heresy, and prosecuted it as late as the nineteenth century. But churches feared the collapse of Christianity even more. They routinely lambasted the faithful and the negligent alike for 'backsliding', for falling from religious ordinances, not reading the Bible and poor attendance at church. To lose faith, to be a professed unbeliever, has been surrounded at some time in virtually every world culture with criticism, offence and anger. Belief is normal – a normative position from which few have historically found freedom to deviate. And this shaped ways in which unbelief was (and in perhaps a fifth of nations remains) criminalized.[12] A human self without religion was deviant and in most nations blasphemy was illegal, with offences ranging in severity.[13] The last to be executed for blasphemy in Britain was Thomas Aikenhead, a divinity student at Edinburgh University, who, whilst walking past the Tron Church in the High Street in August 1696, chatted to a fellow student of his doubts concerning the miracles, the trinity and other key Christian doctrines. His companion informed on him to church authorities, who passed it to the judicial authorities, leading to Aikenhead being tried, hanged and burnt the following year.[14] Trials for blasphemy continued into the twentieth century. The last Briton to be imprisoned for this offence was John W. Gott in London in 1922.[15]

In such an atmosphere, a benign narrative of being an atheist, or even just a person without a religion, was very difficult. In the 1960s, Robin Wood, then working in a national government office in Glasgow colloquially known as 'little Vatican' because of its concentration of Catholics, was being driven by a trade-union colleague to a conference in Lancashire when Robin said he was an atheist; the man went white in the face, clearly petrified, said he had never met an atheist before, and, yes, he was concerned that the car might be struck by a thunderbolt from God.[16] Going to church was the norm in the United States, Canada and in many places in Britain and Europe. In Ontario, David Fowler found at both school and university religious observance was the norm; at school, teachers asked if pupils had been to church on Sunday, whilst at McMaster University, when he went there in 1966 to study engineering, religion was built into the curriculum:

'McMaster sprung from a Baptist college and still had its roots. We had chapel break every morning, we had lectures from I think 8–9 and 9–10 and 10–10.30 was chapel break, and then 10.30 classes start again.' He reported that he never knew anybody who went to chapel; he himself used it to get a half hour sleep in mid-morning. He also recalled that in the common room was a lot of religious discussion; David recalled one 'very, very rigid Baptist' who said, 'if you do not have Jesus Christ you don't go to heaven, Period!'[17] As late as 1966, Pierre Berton noted of the religious revival in North America: 'statistically it is impressive'. The fact that, he said, 94 per cent of people believe in God was a paradox in a society of evident growing youth alienation from religion and rising general apathy, but could only be explained by being skin-deep. He argued that it was part of a world in which status and conformity were worshipped.[18] In 2013, Harris Sussman in Cambridge, Massachusetts, told me that he knew many Jews who were *de facto* non-believers, what are often described as 'cultural Jews', atheists who wouldn't dare to call themselves that.[19]

The conformity demanded in the 1940s, 1950s and into the 1960s made 'atheist' a hugely difficult identity to broadcast most everyplace in the West. It was cast as a slur to besmirch an opponent rather than a soubriquet of self-identity. A benign narrative seemed impossible in the West during the era of the USSR between 1917 and 1991. In the era of the Cold War after 1945, 'atheist' was an equivalent to 'communist'. As a result, broadcasting non-religious views was difficult. In the United States, Clifford Durr (1899–1975) was an Alabama lawyer in the Federal Communications Commission during 1941–8 who supported a legal submission from an atheist in San Francisco, who was refused access by three radio stations to broadcast his views; Durr reports in an oral history interview that he argued for the balancing of educational and commercial interests in broadcasting, and for the upholding of an existing but unenforced condition of radio stations' licenses to give airtime to all views. The upshot was government attention falling upon Durr and his wife, a supporter of black enfranchisement, including from the House Un-American Activities Committee and surveillance by the FBI.[20] Meanwhile in Britain in 1955, press and public vilification fell upon a university lecturer, Margaret Knight, for giving two lectures on BBC radio advocating the teaching of secular humanism to children – an offence exacerbated in the eyes of the right-wing press for being committed by a childless woman.[21] To say that not believing in God was unpopular in 1950s British culture is an understatement: a girl who proclaimed her unbelief in the school playground later recalled being taunted and called 'a heathen' by her classmates.[22] Into the 1980s, American intelligence sources, provided to Canadian military intelligence services as background on the Soviet people, stressed the USSR's hostility to Christianity; one of my respondents concluded that 'more than half of military people in Canada were probably atheists', but not military personnel in the United States, where, he noted, 'it can be harmful to career progression, at least during the Cold War, to be labelled anything other than Christian'.[23] This toxicity of 'atheist' in the United States lingered into the twenty-first century; it was harder in 2006, three sociologists demonstrated, for an American to 'come out' as an atheist than to come out as gay.[24] And ironically, as Martin Vallik told me, 'atheist' has been a word which in Estonia has connoted agreement to communist rule, despite the country having the lowest level of god-belief in the world.[25]

Tarnished by communist Eastern Europe down to the 1990s, 'atheism' has remained a difficult term for popular adoption. This extends to those who, for social reasons, concealed their lack of faith. Ann Auchterlonie had questioned the deep religious faith of her upbringing in Dundee during her teenage years, but she did not totally reject religion in early adulthood. She had various incidents over two decades of religious doubt and unease. One was her marriage in her late thirties in a Congregational church; the pressure from her mother for this was too great to ignore. She then joined her husband in being an active Christian attending church:

> at that time I did go thinking 'well, this will be a test because let's see if going to church is about going to church, or if it's about going to church because that's where all my friends go, and it's a social occasion.' So I went to church in Glenrothes and thought 'this is a farce', there was nothing about the service that I enjoyed other than the singalong at the hymns, which I still enjoy at Christmas, but there was nothing else I enjoyed about it at all.

Then, moving to a new city and with a young child, she thought it was good to go to church to meet friends and ended up teaching in the toddler class of the Sunday school. 'And I was secretary of the Young Wives before I knew it.' Her disenchantment grew as she found the basic Christian principle, with which she could agree, being subverted – such as holding the Christmas Eventide service at 9 o'clock so the drunks wouldn't come in. Moving to a new district and yet another new church she continued to go along with churchgoing to give her children structure whilst growing up, but her disenchantment was slowly eating away her resolve to masquerade. When asked to participate once more in the youth work of the church, she responded,

> 'No, I'm sorry, you know, I have played along with it' and I had this feeling that I had played along with it for years because of pressure from the family, in as much as that it meant so much to my mother, my father died when I was 34, by then I didn't honestly believe that he believed, you know, despite all his preaching and everything…It was a gradual process.

It is in the looking back she decides that, though she continued to be connected with the church well into her late thirties, she thinks she wasn't a Christian for a lot before that: 'I mean I would have said that from when we came back from Glenrothes, I would not have described myself as a Christian and I would have been, at that stage, 27, 28. I would not have described myself as a Christian.'[26]

Growing up in Chile and then living from his twenties in Texas, Cecil Bannister likewise found openly denying his faith difficult for a long time. He said,

> I wasn't participating on the religious activities with the church and all that, I felt the, I would say that I was, I had to believe in God, you know I had to. It was a wrong thing to do, not to, you know. And if I don't, then I would be a bad person, my principle would not be there. Atheists, if you were to say that you were an atheist, you know, it was something really bad, you know, something really bad. I mean it's like a sin, so being in margins, sort of not participating was my comfort zone, but still I felt the pressure obliged to conform, to believe at least in that, to be safe. From there slowly I started, as I say, questioning and then maybe moving more into agnostic, right, and then even at that point, it's so strong the influence of the conscience, the religious aspects of it.[27]

Social pressure and a lingering religious conscience made atheism largely silent in many countries in the twentieth century, and the atheist highly illusive. The person without a belief in god was, and remains, most often an indifferentist, without claims on a religious identity, not given to social expressions of unbelief and very often, it might be speculated, not given to real discussion with herself or himself regarding the precise condition of unbelief the person is in. They do not volunteer their indifference. One young American I interviewed in the Bay Area of California said he called 'atheism as a path, like it's not a place to be; it's not a position that you take, like, "Oh I'm an atheist". It's where you are on a journey'.[28] This means that finding him and, until recently, especially her, was really quite difficult. This is where the people I interviewed become so important. For, a majority of my eighty-five respondents reported having lengthy periods of indifference to religion before subsequently, in middle age or senior years, becoming more affirming of an atheist position. Asking them about this episode in their lives provides a rare insight into the nature of being an indifferentist.

The character of indifference

Perhaps half of my European respondents recall a long period in their lives dominated by indifference to religion, and around a third of those from the United States and Canada. They characteristically lost belief in God, or support for a religion, or any faith, by the age of 15 or thereabouts, and then spent years or decades – not infrequently, most of a lifetime – with no interest in religion, no connection with it and no active belief in god. The character of the religious indifference varied, as we shall explore.

The first thing to observe is that respondents often found it difficult to say very much about indifference. Even as I pressed some of them about this, they found it challenging to go beyond the bald statement that they had no religious activity or interest during this lengthy episode. In Vancouver, Lorraine Hardie represented a characteristic drift from religion when she was 16 and 17 years of age in the mid-1950s. The cause of her drift she put down to: 'Just that there were more interesting things to do…When you are a teenager there is other things that start tugging at your desires and I thought there were just other things to do, and so I stopped going to church, at that point I won't be going to Sunday School.'[29] Paul Bulmer, born in Halifax in the north of England in 1957, lost his interest in church slightly younger, in his early teens. He reported being alienated from Christianity by the persistent indoctrination he experienced in school. But asked about any developing constructive non-religious views thereafter, Paul expresses surprise: 'It's amazing, Callum. It's quite hard to kind of think back really to my state of mind. I mean, I feel quite strongly now. I feel quite anti-religion at the moment and I can't believe I was kind of neutral about it, but I think genuinely it was just something that I didn't really, didn't really think about.'[30] The reason for an empty indifference to religion was similar for David Lord, who from 15 to 60 years of age was indifferent to faith, in a state of being 'totally neutral' about religion for 45 years.[31] This was a period which for some respondents seemed inexplicable; it was something that just happened. Respondents in interview don't dwell upon this period in their lives, with the indifference they allude to being, in a sense, matched in their manner of speaking of it. The memory provides little in the way of substantial material for them to compose a narrative.

The duration of the period of religious indifference, and the extent to which religion remained a feature of everyday life during it, varied considerably. Sometimes, the period was very long. Ron McLaren told me that 'for the first thirty-five [to] forty years of my humanist view I didn't know that's what it was called'. He noted that when people attended weddings and funerals where he was the celebrant, many reported to him that they had now discovered the term that applied to them.[32] For others it was much shorter. Frank Brown, living in Vancouver in the 1950s and 1960s, reported on disinterest in religion during at least twenty years of being busy 'earning a living, raising a family and so on'.[33] Frank O'Hara, born in 1926 in Toronto, was a faithful Catholic in his youth, but in his later teens and twenties he became 'a not faithful Catholic for some years', gradually edging away from faith; he recalled reading Albert Schweitzer's *The Quest of the Historical Jesus* as a turning point moment. But he had a period of drift for a number of years before developing a firm loyalty for humanism and for active philanthropic work for humanist endeavour overseas.[34] In a different generation, Gillian Ferris, born in 1977 in Dundee, stopped going to church at around the age of 16.

> [W]hen I was younger, to me [Christianity] made sense as a moral code, and it was something I thought, 'yes, you know, that in terms of living my life, this is an approach that I think is good'. And because I saw it in positive terms, I didn't see it in negative terms at all, and so I did, you know, regard myself, I think, as a Christian, but then, as I got into my teens, sort of middle teens around 16 or so I was kind of getting through school, thinking about life ahead and I just stopped going to church. I just lost the interest and I think that's --- Yes, I'm not clear as to why I did that, because my recollection is going to church, but I don't have clear memories as to why I just suddenly stopped. Maybe it was a lazy teenager thing, I don't know. It was maybe because I was going out on a Saturday night, I was managing to get into the local nightclub, you know, or interest in guys or whatever, or discovering drink or whatever I think took over. I think that meant that I was kind of happy to drop that time with the grandparents, the Sunday, the kind of ritual, I was sort of growing up and this is what I was doing, I was having these experiences.[35]

Gillian's commentary here exposes the general absence of hostility to religion for those experiencing this episode of indifference: there is rarely any bitterness towards religion. There is a general equanimity on the matter, leading in many instances to respondents recalling that religious rituals were sustained. This was the case for Mary Wallace, who, after attending Church of England and an Assembly of God in her younger teens, drifted from religion during secondary school and study for a degree in geography at university. She reported,

> I think as an adult, I mean I think I was probably in the back of my mind an atheist from my late teens I would say, onwards, middle to late teens, but not in an acknowledged way, if you know what I mean. And I think that carried on through my twenties because there was no point at which I needed to address it or needed to stand up and say I was an atheist or needed to be challenged on it or to debate it or anything. It was just there.

She follows this up by recalling that she had a Christian wedding because her husband's family had a connection to a particular village church. She laughs at the remembrance of their religious ceremony, saying wryly, 'I'm impressed [laughs].' Given that both she and her husband were to emerge within a few years as firm atheists and humanists, she surprises herself in her recollection: '1989, yeah and I kind of --- I don't think either of us really sat down and said "what kind of wedding ceremony do we want?" There weren't options at that time --- you could get married in the registrar's office or you got married in a church.'[36]

In recalling this period of indifference, respondents pointed to an absence of resolve to iron out the inconsistencies, the hypocrisies, the embarrassments and the weakness of tenacity in their approach to religion. The period even afflicted those who, in youth, had developed a reputation as something of an atheist. Alistair McBay had been directed by a school teacher to read in atheist authors, but lost this interest.

> I've got to say when I went to University, for the next 4–5 years, and certainly in my twenties and thirties, religion wasn't an issue at all. I didn't give a blind bit of attention to it or noticed, it was something other people did, as long as it didn't affect me and I didn't think it did affect me, I didn't care.[37]

Respondents fell into routinized rituals rehearsed in the societies to which they belonged. In Canada and the United States, there was a route to follow that was much rehearsed and seemingly more popular and well known than in Britain – Unitarian Universalism. Eight of my respondents – just under 10 per cent – aligned with Unitarians at least for a while, most in the period between the 1960s and 1980s when they reported local congregations of the group were markedly undemanding in terms of expecting faith in god. Ena Sparks, born in 1954 in Vancouver, had grown up attending Sunday school, and at 17 became a born-again Christian. But her first husband was killed in a car accident when she was 22, and she seems to have drifted for a period, and it was only at the age of 30 when she remarried that she came to the conclusion, accepted by her new husband, that she had lost her faith. 'And I think by then I was kind of saying that I don't believe in God, but so a friend of mine had said, well you should go to the Unitarian Church then.' They used to take their children to give them something, as Ena put it: a direction, a meeting group and experience of a fellowship community. After close on twenty years, at the age of 48 she joined a humanist group, and was able to more fully admit to herself that she was living without a religion or belief in god.[38] In a similar vein, Pat Duffy Hutcheon became in the later decades of her life one of the best-known writers on humanism in Canada. But she came to it late. She had a struggling life as a child and in her first marriage, escaping to enter university late to do a master's degree and then a doctorate. There too she had some difficulties in regard to obtaining a full-time position, but she wrote sociology of education books and was very active in her profession. And after recounting this at great length, she reported, 'I did have an interesting life doing various jobs, but so that was my experience in academia. And university --- You know the religion didn't really come into --- My life was too busy.'[39] Like Ena, her route out from indifference was via Unitarian Universalism. This fulfilled a variety of functions, according to my respondents. It provided fellowship, politically liberal campaigning opportunities, community activism (especially in relation to racial and poverty equalities) and a place for free discussion and thought for them and for their children.

There was even a level, sometimes a high level, of apathy amongst those who stayed in a religion. Those who were active might spend decades of their adulthood attending church, getting married in church, ensuring their children were raised in the church's tradition, but all along they entertained varying degrees of disinterest in, scepticism about and even disregard for the religion to which they were attached. John Manuel was born in 1940 in Liverpool, and emigrated to Canada at the age of 13. He was raised in a mingling of Anglican and Catholic traditions, staying in the Anglican Church and, from 30 years of age, the United Church of Canada until he was about 60 years of age:

> I took religion very seriously until about 20 years ago. In fact I was church organist for a while in Canada and I was Sunday school superintendent. I took it quite seriously. But inside I always had the feeling it was sort of like play acting, like it was make believe. I always had the feeling it was make believe. But a good role to cast somebody into. A role that was *fulfilling* in many ways and I think religion *fulfils* a lot of people today. Even though I'm now a complete atheist, I recognise that religion fulfils a lot, an important role in many people.[40]

John Manuel describes his slipping from faith as taken place between 55 and 70 years of age. Having been a serious Christian until then, he entered a period hovering between faith and non-faith:

> Well, the actual acceptance would've taken place within the last 15 years. The actual commitment to the --- And acceptance of the belief or non-belief. It's hard to put a date on it because it was a gradual process. And I gradually began to more and more and more become --- Like it was a wide corridor that I moved from one side of the corridor to the other side of the corridor kind of thing. It wasn't like stepping over a line or something like that. And there was a corridor that led me to the other side and once I reached the wall on the other side as it were I reached through you know the nearest opening and I was away. But there's still there's still an acceptance that religion can be good for people. It gives them hope. It gives them security where very often it's hard to find elsewhere. And so I don't challenge that. I understand that. I just know that it's make believe.[41]

This is one of the few respondents who had a developed metaphor to describe the nature of the loss of belief. In ways similar to how some religious converts express that experience, it's a description of physical movement from one state to another.

One of the paradoxes that Manuel's testimony throws up is that apathy need not be neutral, need not be something devoid of a personal commitment, only lacking in organizational commitment. Kris Kristensen never really stopped attending church – partly for his children, and partly because he and his wife had been attracted to Orthodox services in California. But in this 'trying various things', he reported, 'I ended up getting pissed [off], actively pissed, you know, going to, having to go to a church ceremony of any sort'. And he did stop going, and had quite clear ideas, based on medical science training, about the nature of life and the absence of an afterlife. But he said he wasn't really a joiner of things.[42] This is a common sentiment; twelve out of the eighty-five respondents used the phrase 'not a joiner'. Larry Hicok, leader of Bay Area Atheists, told me that 'the biggest problem is that atheists are not joiners'. He reported that Madalyn Murray O'Hair (1919–95), founder in 1963 of American Atheists,

> used to say it's like herding cats. And it's true, you know, I mean they just hate it. Even establishing rules and meetings that we --- you know, we wait to be called on and we always let someone who hasn't spoken talk before somebody who has spoken before. Even those things, it's like 'you've brought me here to tell me what to do'.[43]

However, there were others I interviewed who were very frequent joiners; Dick Hewetson in San Francisco told me how he joined American Atheists, Freedom from Religion, Secular Humanists – 'I belong to all of them', he said.[44]

So, the researcher can be perplexed. In the slide of Western society from thinking about god in a structure of religious understanding of this world and a next one, to thinking about this world without god and not thinking about the next world at all, atheism is an untidy category in epistemology and behaviours. As the literature specialist Michael Lackey has suggested, 'Genuine atheism does not occur in a single moment; it is a process in which the culture eliminates from its consciousness the ontotheological assumptions that continue to inform its intellectual systems despite the apparent absence of the God concept.'[45] Huge research complexities attend attempting to identify and interview those who might be categorized as atheists due to indifference. But, this may only apply to those who were born into a religious culture; once the culture has changed, the generations that follow may well be unafflicted by a religious legacy. Furthermore, indifference can be replaced.

Leaving indifference

For those of my respondents transiting indifference to religion, a thread common to their narratives is one of discovery of who they were. They iterate with unfailing agreement that when they moved beyond indifference, when their minds came into focus on the religious question, nothing changed in their mindset, in their attitude to religion or in their self-identity. It is a narrative of self-realization, not of transformation, of a new alertness, not of conversion.

The processing from indifference to a realization of a non-religious identity is not one to which oral history interviewees suggest any precedents. There is no particular discourse about what the nature of this process should be, no really widely admired blueprint in the literature of atheists and humanists. Indifference, first of all, hardly appears in possible reading; autobiographies and biographies of well-known atheists and humanists hardly ever speak of indifference, focussing on damascene moments of what the French philosopher Théodore Simon Jouffroy (1796–1842) called 'counter-conversion' and what atheists like Bertrand Russell had more commonly recounted like a de-conversion.[46] The only similarity that comes to conversion is that it is often sudden, a realization that comes upon the indifferent. It generally involves no new ideas, principles or orientation of outlook. There is rarely high emotion involved, and certainly no particular sadness. It is a 'dawned on me' type of event, a new clarity. It is sometimes accompanied by a 'coming out' in a group or in family, trying out a word like 'atheist' or 'humanist' for the first time. The word might be described as filling a missing part in an identity by giving a name to the condition in which the interviewee had been, sometimes for decades. But that would not, I think, be fair or accurate. More commonly, I feel, the name is dispelling the miasma of indifference, allowing the self to be revealed to the narrator. It is sometimes in private, sometimes reading a book or a simple pamphlet, or even a bare advertisement. It is routinely recalled in happiness, though not in a high emotional state.

Writers and speakers were influential in drawing the indifferent to an assertion of atheism. Dennis Duncan lost his connection with the Catholic Church at the age of 14, but though his experience of the church as a child he described as traumatic, his adult years were spent mostly in an apathetic standoff from religion. He reports that when he retired in 1993 at the age of 64 from a long career as a research and development chemical engineer, he became interested in Darwin and 'deeper subjects':

> That was where my heart was with things like that, and I gradually began to realise that I didn't have any faith. I would have to say I would be agnostic at this point and not at all upset by going to church or going to religious service. There was no hatred or tension, throw rocks on religions or anything like that. I just reached a certain point in my own thinking.

Finally, in 2001, on reading an article by Canadian Pat Duffy Hutcheon talking about how she was a humanist, he grasped his position: 'I didn't know what a humanist was, and how she didn't believe in the life hereafter and mythical gods or anything like that, but how she felt that humans should try to make some good in the world, and be fairly ethical and so on.' In consequence, he realized how this described him, and he and his wife started going to humanist meetings: 'I don't know, just realised that here was somebody that wasn't a bad old atheist that everybody else thinks badly of, but felt very much like I do; that there isn't any life hereafter and that [we] must make the best of what you have got here, do the best to your fellow man sort of thing.'[47]

Triggers to ending indifference came to include late in the twentieth century the growth of humanist weddings, which for some has been an experimentation and a means to loss of indifference to religion. Several of my respondents volunteered for interview for this project because they had been married by humanist celebrants. Humanist weddings must be counted as the single most important trigger to coming out as an atheist, humanist or speculative agnostic in those nations where it is widely available. The Scottish evidence suggests that something in the region of 1,000 to 1,500 couples per year since 2005 have joined the main humanist organization there, many of whom, one imagines in the absence of research, becoming more consciously humanists without religious belief.

I interviewed separately one couple who were drawn to reflect upon their no-religious belief as a result of undergoing a quite lengthy process of thinking about the type of ceremony they wished, and the values to be engrossed within it. Sheralee Hayes-Fry was somebody who fits comfortably into the large group in society that spent most of their teenage and young adult lives without firm, or even any, religious conviction. She was educated at a comprehensive school in the east of England, where there was no enforcement of religious views or practice, attending Sunday school around the age of 9–10 for a while until she became unhappy with not being allowed to ask questions of the 'tales' she was being told. She reported leaving home at 18:

> How would I have described myself? Probably not having given it much thought, to be quite honest. Too busy doing other things to really think about it very much. I mean if I said that I was, at that point agnostic, I think I wouldn't even be entirely sure what the definition of agnostic is. I would say I was more sort of muddling through somewhere in the middle having some idea that there might be some big plan, but certainly I can't ever remember in believing things like Jesus as a concept. That never really rang true for me, never convinced by that. So, but not in any deep way to be quite honest, it wasn't at that point in my life. I wasn't thinking deeply about anything really apart from going out and having a good time.[48]

Almost a decade and a half followed before, reflecting about marriage, some confrontation with issues concerning the nature of celebration arose. For both her and partner Ian in the mid-1990s, a religious marriage was out of the question.

> We started over the course of the years to drift towards the idea that maybe we would get married at some point if we ever found a formula that appealed to us. And over the course of that time, you know, we talked quite a bit about how there is no way we would get married in church either of us, because how could you possibly take vows and swear allegiance to something that you don't believe in. For us it would make the marriage completely meaningless to be getting married and saying something that you know, making oaths to something that we didn't believe in.[49]

Being able to say things to each other, rather than to God, was what emerged as the important ceremony they wished to construct. They discovered the British Humanist Association (BHA) and its wedding:

> [We] looked at that and thought that's it, that's exactly what we are looking for, we are looking for a way of having some ceremony and meaning to what we are doing without it being false. And it was fantastic. I looked at how they handled funerals and christenings [sic], and just thought this is, this is for me, the beliefs that were written down.

Sheralee obtained the leaflets from the BHA and found that they 'just seemed massive common sense really'. The liberal variety gave them scope and choice: in her words, 'It's, dare I say, it's a broad church?' Like many wed by humanist celebrants, Sheralee found the experience 'a wonderful time, was really meaningful': 'I honestly do think that we probably thought an awful lot more about the vows we were making to each other than most people that get married in church.' She reported that 'we did *think* about every single word we were going to say to each other and whether we felt we could say that truly and mean it. It was a really good process to go through and that was the start really, of me starting to seriously think about what I believe'. And in the ten years since her ceremony, Sheralee thought an awful lot more about what she did believe. 'And I think I still, I am still not entirely dismissing the existence of God, but I think I am dismissing any existence of God that follows any religion I have come across have viewed him/her.'[50] Sheralee's husband Ian had similar experience of emerging from religious indifference, having his last contact with organized religion at the age of 11, when he left a Church of England primary school. He can't put his finger on any specific reason, merely a change of environment, change of interests and exploration of left-wing politics. Religion opposed any kind of enjoyment: 'life-denying is how I feel about religion', Ian said. This lasted for more than a decade, and it was whilst preparing for his wedding to Sheralee that his mind became more focussed on what he did believe:

> there wasn't a prescription for what makes marriage, what makes a couple, how the husband should, as so many religions have, how a husband should act and respect his wife, what wife's obligations are. All of those things that in so many religions are so rigidly laid down or seem to be.[51]

A second couple underwent a not dissimilar process whereby the desire for a humanist wedding brought them to the atheist movement.[52] Other triggers to losing disinterest, or simply bypassing it, have no doubt been in place, especially since 2000 in Britain, Canada and, though to a lesser extent, in the United States. One trend hints at this: the rise since 2007 of atheist, secularist and humanist groups at universities and colleges, and the development of the Skeptics in the Pub movement, which is dominated by the young. This has raised the number of the young involved in active secularism quite markedly, and brought new blood to a movement that has been characterized since the 1960s as middle-aged to elderly.

It is clear, however, that amongst my older respondents the mere fact of ageing is introducing them to a loss of indifference to religion. So many respondents spoke of emerging from indifference and silence to activism, and finding a voice of unbelief, that it seems to be a major trend amongst those born on both sides of the Atlantic between 1945 and 1975. Alistair McBay recalled that his outlook changed when he became a house husband and active father to young children. The internet was in its infancy too, and this gave him the opportunity to explore online: 'you start reading stories and for some reason the religious stuff interested me and intrigued me, and it went from there really'.[53] This led him to become a leading activist in Scotland for the National Secular Society. In Canada, Peter Scales reported himself as indifferent and apathetic to issues of religion through secondary school, until he went as an exchange school student to Belgium where his three host families had various levels of religious observance, which aroused interest and critique. He joined the Canadian Air Force in the 1980s, where, despite church parade, the dominant culture was one of religious indifference: 'they tended to see gray in everything', was how Peter put it. But in Intelligence training he learned of the atheism of the Warsaw Pact countries, and read US Intelligence materials where this and the Christian basis of the NATO nations were emphasized. This alerted Peter to religious issues, and when he demobbed he subsequently became involved with Unitarian Universalism, which, he described, 'as almost the same thing' as humanism.[54]

Just as my older respondents left indifference behind, some reported that they had children who were indifferent to religion, giving them succour as to the succession of reason and virtue, but sometimes frustrating them that the young didn't take the matter seriously.[55] One woman I interviewed,

Ann Auchterlonie from Fife in Scotland, feared the apathy of the secular, dreading that a challenge to British society was emerging from churchgoers who had become much more vociferous in their faith: 'Those who don't go [to church] have become the apathetic majority, so you know, this apathy rules okay. And I think we have a very apathetic, secular society who are asleep and are not seeing that increasingly we are moving towards changes in our legislation which will become faith-based again.'[56]

Indifference, as a major episode in the life narratives of late-age humanists and atheists, may be a particular trend of the recent past – of the sixties' generation. It may have been a distinctive feature of those born in the mid-twentieth century and growing up in a society of the 1960s and 1970s that *allowed* indifference to religion in a way that was less feasible before and since. The cultural revolution of those decades granted leave to ignore institutions of authority, and that is what the young did in huge numbers in some countries and, in the case of the United States, had strong regional impact. Certainly, it is clear that the alienation of the young in their teens and twenties was demographically the mainstay of secularization in Western Europe and Canada in those years, and were the main challengers to the hegemony of faith in the United States. Indifference has been eroded, too, by the rise of higher education. The proportion of young people attending university and college in the West has risen dramatically in the last sixty years, and it seems inescapable that this has been a major agent in rising desertion of the churches, religious alienation and decline of faith. I showed in a previous book the very strong correlation in Canada during the 1970s to 1990s between rising higher education (especially the proportion of women with degrees) and proportion of religious 'nones'.[57] In such ways, religious indifference may well have been the victim of advancing education and changing social mores. For those born late in the twentieth century, certainly in Britain and Canada, having no religion became vastly more acceptable. Routes to atheism, humanism and allied positions opened up.

CHAPTER FIVE

Women, Feminism and Becoming Faithless

Narrating the gendered non-religious self

There is good cause to believe that the ways in which men and women lose religion are subject to differences. At least four reasons inform this. First, there is ample evidence that men and women experience religion, including conversion, differently.[1] Second, we already know that people of no religion were until the 1950s overwhelmingly men; the pressures imposed upon women in public discourse made it extremely difficult for them to contemplate disclaiming faith.[2] Third, whilst men were proportionately much more common amongst the people of no religion before the 1960s, this difference diminished thereafter, approaching equality in many Western nations (with the United States lagging some way behind), which indicated that something distinctive has been happening to female loss of faith.[3] Moreover, it is clear from autobiographical accounts that there have been distinctive factors playing on the female experience of religious loss.[4] Meanwhile, male clergy have been diminishing in many Protestant churches: in the Church of England, the proportion of men amongst ordinations fell from 100 per cent in 1992 to 62 per cent in 2010.[5] Fourth and last, I have argued for many years for the instrumentality of women in instigating the rapid secularization that commenced in Britain (and elsewhere) since 1960.[6] This raises the possibility that it was women coming to atheism and humanism that has been of such significance to secularization amongst the sixties' generation, and to those emerging without faith in the West in the generations that followed.

Of my eighty-five respondents, twenty-eight were women. This was not a planned imbalance, but arose out of who volunteered, and slightly under-represents the gender imbalances against women amongst self-identifying 'nones' and in atheist, humanist and secularist organizations.[7] But, the imbalance in my interview set seems due to another factor: the greater willingness of men to speak in relation to loss of religion. Women seemed more reluctant to volunteer – perhaps because of deeper feelings about expressing atheist identity, perhaps because as a male interviewer I may trigger an anticipation of intersubjective friction or perhaps, as we shall explore, some women may regard the way they narrate their story as not conforming to my expectations and feel less worthy to speak. More practicably, the circumstances of my research, notably in the six North American cities I visited, may have meant that the choice between interviewing in the respondent's home or in my hotel room was too off-putting.[8] There is a significant literature about women's greater reserve in oral history speaking.[9] They certainly tend to give shorter testimony: my interviews with men averaged 67 minutes, those with women 54 minutes, though, again, this may be due to the subjectivity I wielded. Scholars of gender history and oral history theory have noted women's and men's distinctive ways of narrating, and they mirror my findings over narrating loss of religion.[10] This difference relates in part to the influence of feminism, but partly because women's narratives placed family, relationships and everyday life centre stage. Men's narratives of losing religion were much less located in family, and instead were centred strongly on education, intellectual development and entanglement with religious authority. So, there seem to be gender-specific conceptions of secularization.[11] For women, it adopts a 'family narrative' which I will discuss here before looking at the evidence.

When I opened an interview with a man or a woman, I explored the context of family, neighbourhood and schooling, before moving onto education and work in adulthood. In each life context, I asked whether they had a settled religious view, and from this my interviewees opened up narratives about that period or focus of their lives. For women, this often led to narratives that related to family history, to faith and relations and to the familial moulding of their religious outlooks. Responses were thus deeply contextualized – I would say rooted – in a narrative of family. This might be a very positive narrative, one that they recall with affection, or it might be very troubled, and, in a significant proportion, perhaps a quarter, what they described as traumatic. Journeys from conventional religious faith and belonging towards no religionism and atheism became, in female testimony, voyages through the intimate networks of life. Their birth families, marriages or partnerships, children and extended family emerged as the landscape locating progression from faith. Explanation of their experience – the triggers to loss of faith and the intellectual journeys too – were described in experiential terms. This is especially marked in relation to the one ideology that was distinctive to the age group I was exploring – second wave feminism. Shortly, I will introduce various sub-narrative types for women's testimony of losing religion, each featuring the parental or marital family as a common location for their religious loss.

Women who turned their backs to religion were by no means new to the post-1950 period, but I found my interviewees rarely referred to predecessors. In the Victorian and Edwardian period, the secularist movement in England incorporated an important atheist feminist contribution in which, as Laura Schwartz has shown, there was lively intellectual debate over women's participation in secularist circles. In the 1890s, Annie Besant personified the merger of the feminist, secularist and socialist, nowhere more controversially than in the birth-control debates that raged from the 1880s to the 1960s.[12] But notwithstanding such debate, these were relatively rare women, for the culture of the Victorian period on both sides of the Atlantic was dominated by a Christianity embedded in everyday life and rhetoric. Tellingly, references to famous female models of secularism came only from my male respondents: Margaret Knight (referred to by six British male respondents), Madalyn Murray O'Hair (referred to by three American male respondents) and Marie Stopes (two references by British male respondents, even though she self-identified as Quaker); there was only one reference to Annie Besant, by a Muslim man born in the Middle East. With the tradition of female freethinking seemingly so little impacting on today's older generation of female non-believers, how did the post-1945 woman imagine a route to atheism or humanism?

In 1992 the sociologist Danièle Hervieu-Léger theorized secularization as triggered by the post-1960 collapse of the nuclear family. Speaking of France, modernity sustained a 'chain of memory' of religious ritual, but not of religious beliefs, caused in her account by the 'religious crisis' that came in the 1960s and 1970s with ultra-low fertility, rising divorce, cohabitation, births outside marriage and the end of what she called 'the traditional family'. 'Individual well-being and fulfilment take precedence', she remarked.[13] This account shares a great deal in common with demographer Ron Lesthaeghe's hypothesis of the Second Demographic Transition, timed for the same period, which was triggering fundamental population change in Western nations from the 1960s onwards, and which correlated closely with secularization.[14] I took this argument further in a 2012 quantitative analysis of the links between secularization, the sexual revolution, changing family formation and women's economic role in the United States, Canada, the United Kingdom and Ireland. I concluded that particularly strong positive connections existed between, on the one hand, the rise of no religionism and, on the other, an interconnected torrent of life change for women: rising non-marital heterosexual activity, ultra-low fertility, delayed women's marriage and steeply rising women's penetration of the labour market and of university education.[15] This theme of family change also features in Kirsten Aune's recent case study of evangelical women in England which postulated that 'evangelicalism does not seem to have succeeded in resisting secularization', noting how women's sustained religiosity suffered where traditional positions as full-time wives and mothers were eroded.[16] Likewise, Lynn Abrams, exploring from the position of a gender historian of the emerging self-hood of sixties women, has demonstrated the limited manner in which religion featured in the narratives of British women she interviewed: 'religion ceased to provide a framework for the way one chose to live a life'.[17]

Against the background of this important body of work, the interviews examined in this chapter demonstrate that women invariably use the family motif or frame to narrate the story of their loss of religion. Women locate meanings about life within the family, positioning both the religious self they are leaving and the non-religious self which they embraced within narratives about family belonging. As in all oral history, their communication strategies differ from men's in being located in stories about family networks and their breach, whereas men's stories focus much more on their already autonomous self.[18] Additionally, women have been theorized as doing 'narrative labour' within the family. If the male self is theorized as literally *self*-centred (on achievement and worldliness), a woman curates family history, memories and heirlooms, and ensures rites of passage are observed, making her own identity spun in a familial web of belonging, moral respectability and, traditionally, religiosity.[19]

One trend in recent scholarship, both in oral history (notably of trauma, of which more later) and in the study of loss of religion, has been to suggest that the individual uses, and perhaps requires, a commonly acknowledged and accepted narrative to explain their move from faith to atheism. In oral history theory, the emphasis has been upon acknowledging the reliance of narrators upon cultural stories – familiar narratives upon which they draw to construct their own narrative and to gain legitimacy for it.[20] Laura Schwartz has shown how well-known Victorian feminist freethinkers provided a highly publicized literature drawn upon by women of that period who lost religion; they felt compelled to draw upon it in order to demonstrate the 'authenticity' of their own de-conversion.[21] But the circumstances were different in the mid-twentieth century, when few female secularist autobiographies seem to have attracted attention or entered public discourse as attractive narratives for ordinary women to admire and mine for a new self. As we shall see shortly, an atheist woman of the 1950s was likely to be derided and humiliated, rendering her narrative template unreachable by the ordinary woman, whilst men frequently cited atheist memoirs of men or women.

This is striking, and has implications. It means that women, in constructing narratives with no template pattern, have been relying very strongly on assembling their own narratives. When asked for the trigger to their loss of faith, many provide a lengthy disquisition on their place in a birth family, their marriage or partnership and their relationships with church people (most often ministers, priests or nuns). Personal relationships become the setting for telling their story in a way much, much rarer amongst men, and usually without recourse to an established pattern of faith loss to be found in literature or popular culture. This implies something about the speed of religious change. The concept of the tipping point or pivotal moment, when there is a breakthrough in thinking and understanding, is often raised in relation to conversion to religion – including evangelical rebirth – and is equally raised in many quarters regarding 'de-conversion' or 'counter-conversion' from religion.[22] Though Abrams has recently identified 'the epiphanic moment' in women's oral narratives of life change in the 1950s and 1960s, she isolated religious change as different, observing that women's talk on 'loss of religion' is located in a context of family and relationships but devoid of a tipping point.[23] My own results, as we shall see below, suggest that there is greater variability to this amongst female respondents than Abrams allows. Some women speak of stark moments of religious de-conversion – sudden self-realization, revelation, a thunderbolt, often as severe and melodramatic as male respondents. However, the nature of the trigger to secularity, identified by respondents in oral history interviews, does quite sharply distinguish women from men. Nowhere is this more apparent than in relation to distress and trauma.

'It's really rotten being a woman sometimes': Trauma and the family

The oral history of trauma is now a well-known area of study. A key theory that has developed is that trauma is only enunciated by victims when their narrative has been rehearsed by others and is in the public arena already, and they are consequently assured of a sympathetic reception.[24] The current project suggests something different. Before proceeding, it must be noted that, unlike in most 'trauma studies' in oral history, the trauma itself is not the object of study in this book and has not been prefigured in the research design; thus, there was no deliberate canvassing for volunteers who have experienced it. Instead, recall of distress arises unprompted in interview as part of some respondents' explanations for loss of religion. So, trauma rests beside other explanatory factors for the emergence of a life without god.

Three conceptual issues arise immediately: first, defining trauma; second, the incidence of respondents referring to trauma in their explanation of religion loss; and third, the gendered nature of the trauma being experienced and described by respondents. In relation to the first of these, trauma is a psychologically difficult response to an event, and in this the historian needs to be wary of dictating the impact upon individuals – both because it becomes impossible to measure the impact scientifically and because it is disrespectful to volunteer participants in a history project. As a researcher, I am not going to 'test' for, nor calibrate a hierarchy of, trauma. If a respondent tells me he or she experienced trauma, or uses terms and emotional narratives that imply this, I accept his or her judgement; to do otherwise would create analytical impossibilities for a historian; would, in my view, be unethical; and would breach my relationship of 'good faith' with the volunteers. As to incidence in losing religion, trauma is discussed by around a fifth of respondents, with a higher proportion of women reporting traumatic experiences than men. But, most importantly, this leads to the third issue: the gendered nature of the traumas described. I will look at men's narratives of trauma in the next chapter.

In relation to women, when referring to the 1950s and 1960s, many found the rapid and far-reaching cultural changes deeply affecting their expected place in society – in terms of equalities of opportunity and treatment. These were years fraught for women in the West with a peculiar difficulty to negotiate as their expectations – ranging from work and education through to sexual life and recreation – were changing more radically than for men. This is manifest in oral history narratives characterized by tension between the ordinariness, restraint and conventionalities of the 1950s and the burgeoning excitement, freedoms and radicalisms of the 1960s and later. And the main locus of this tension for women was the family. We will explore this through a few case studies.

Julia Stuart was born in 1952 and brought up by her Catholic grandmother in Dundee, a city she described as 'still a grey place'. Julia attended Mass every Sunday even before she reached school age. From the age of 5 to 15, she went to church as much as her family wanted her; she estimated a quarter of her school life was in one way or another spent with religion, with never-ending religious instruction classes, saints days, benedictions and attendance at chapel. Not being involved was not an option, as she was attended by intense fear and a recurring nightmare: if she was naughty it was 'the big bad fire', and limbo, where she was concerned that her mother, who had died young, was located. Leaving this religious condition was difficult, but it started with Julia's teenage rebellion of skiving chapel by hanging around an ice-cream shop with her friends. But, Julia reported, it was just impossible to disbelieve in the Catholic faith until she left home and Dundee. Equally, she narrates the difficulty in making any career advancement: men in her household exclaimed that there was no point in her getting education as she would just marry. Yet events elsewhere beckoned. Julia recalled that in 1967 she listened to Radio Luxembourg to learn of the 'summer of love' in Haight Ashbury in San Francisco, and read *Watchtower* for its lurid deprecation of the times. Everything from jeans to flower power, she reported, 'it just went past us'. So, it was only after she left school that she questioned enough to conclude that 'the god thing' wasn't true. Julia Stuart established in interview that she lost her religion by the time she left school a week before her fifteenth birthday and, working as a book-keeper, she also left home, thus escaping Mass and the 'brain washing'. She remarked, 'I mean, I was quite a teenager, a late teenager, before I realised that they have been feeding me full on nonsense.' Within two years, her life changed when she became pregnant at 17, leading her to depart for London, where her child was adopted through a Catholic agency. There, she at last found the sixties, getting into drugs and rock 'n' roll: 'I suppose you maybe even consider the Stones has been part of my anti-Christ kind of things, cause of course they were my favourite band.'[25]

Young women in the 1950s and early 1960s paid a high price for sexual transgressions. Like Julia, Liz Currie also had a strongly religious upbringing (partly Roman Catholic, partly Exclusive Brethren), but her father eventually removed the family from this influence, and on joining the Women's Royal Air Force (WRAF) in the early 1960s, she drifted away from religion. She was rudely dragged back when she became pregnant. Her father disowned her for two years, and she was forced to leave the WRAF when the service arranged her entry to a Church of England home for unmarried mothers in Wiltshire. She described it as very strict:

> They used to get us up at about half five, six o'clock in the morning. It was Church of England, mother and baby home, and they'd have us scrubbing floors. I mean it was, it was this sort of thing you think 'this sort of thing didn't happen', and it did! We'd all be scrubbing the floors, you know, cleansing our souls of our sins and what have you, but it was something you had to get on with, you couldn't fight it, it was happening to you. And so you sort of blamed yourself because it was only through your own weakness that you got yourself into that situation anyway. You weren't strong enough to say 'NO' and that was it. And then once you'd had the baby you ---- Most of the babies went up for adoption, and that was sad. There was one girl, we were having a meal and the Matron, she was quite a hard woman, she came in and she said 'Alright Margaret, the new parents are here now; if you'd just like to come and say cheerio to your baby.' [Pause as respondent sounds upset]. Sad. [Recording is stopped and restarted.] I was lucky because I knew I was going to get married anyway or I had somebody who cared for me enough to want to get married, but it was just this poor girl, and these babies were so beautiful, and she was giving it away. It wasn't because she wanted to, it was because society said well, this was what you had to do because nobody would accept you if you were, you know, if you were an unmarried mother, so that's what used to happen. I should be writing a book, I think [chuckling].[26]

In the home, Liz recalled that 'I didn't really think of religion at that point because I was wrapped up in this baby, all other thoughts were out of my mind'. But in the next breath comes the memory that they said grace, morning and evening prayers, and a 'severe' local minister came visiting twice a week, whose 'booming authoritative voice' blared out in the home's small chapel. The women were all confirmed a second time in what Liz took to be a form of cleansing of sin. For Liz, as for many women in the same predicament, the clash with religion instigated a drift from it, but not an immediate breach.

Episodes of sexual transgression and its consequences appear as preludes in the narratives of several women's journeys from conventional faith. The churches' claims to control the female body have a long pedigree, but the continued attempts to sustain religious systems of control were starting to fail in the 1960s and 1970s.[27] Unimpeded access to reliable contraception and medical terminations of pregnancy were part of the story, but more fundamental was women's growing unwillingness to submit to this regime. I found trauma relating to sexual issues to be a recurrent theme amongst several women humanists and atheists. In Devon in the 1950s, Annette Horton recollected her Catholic childhood as 'a very conflicted mess' for her grandmother and herself in relation to men's sexual abuse and demands. Unusually amongst my interviewees, she joined a humanist organization in the 1960s at the age of 16, and then spent a lifetime in service as a doctor in England, the United States and Canada. In between, her narrative contained a plethora of ordeals, one of which occurred when she became pregnant at medical school, threatening her with ejection – what she describes as 'a very great trauma to me'. She tormented herself over this, but survived in college, commenting, 'Anyway, but you know, this added to my sense of right, you know --- It's really rotten being a woman sometimes, and so this is sort of a theme [laughs].' With so many issues to do with sex and abuse in her family, she told me at one point, 'I think I became a psychiatrist to sort this whole mess out.'[28]

In their narrative of losing religion, women respondents' sexual trauma was joined by episodes of wider distress in relationships. Joan Gibson, born 1943 in Cheltenham, became a born-again Anglican evangelical at around the age of 20, after which she wedded a Church of Scotland minister in 1965. But then in the early 1980s she developed a strong feminism at the same time as her marriage broke up. She says, 'I mean, I had all these sort of marital personal problems and my father had died of cancer of the oesophagus, which had been horrible, and I think I was just realising that religion didn't have any answers.'[29] From this Joan moved over a number of years to a humanist standpoint, becoming a leading figure in the Scottish movement. In another example, Maria Berger, born in 1976 in Switzerland and later living in Britain, reported an intensifying focus upon religion from 9 years of age, becoming traumatized from her teens to late twenties by a concept of hell that interacted adversely through a marriage and divorce, and then in her thirties moving from being an evangelical churchgoer to becoming agnostic and then atheist in her later thirties; on coming out, she regarded herself as having emerged from very subtle 'religious child abuse' and brainwashing.[30]

Many of those who became atheists in mid-century during their teens or twenties faced distress from their parents and extended family members who put extreme pressure upon them to get married in church. In Eastern Europe in the post-war decades, one father told his daughter, Alicja Stettin, that if she did not get married in church, he would ever after regard her as a whore. After three years her marriage crumbled, and her husband shifted blame to her, declaring that her atheism was a contributory cause.[31] Religious trauma concerned family especially in the case of two Jehovah's Witnesses I interviewed where the threat was of 'shunning' instigated by the church, which could lead to estrangement from the family.

The vast majority of those who lost their religion, denied their belief in god and became atheists or agnostics were customarily very firm and determined about the change in their attitude. Few expressed doubts in an intellectual sense, and once a corner was turned away from faith, there was little upset. But their determination to withstand family pressures created a family trauma that was almost entirely unique to women humanists and atheists. In many ways, women's struggle for autonomy in the third quarter of the twentieth century was an assault on patriarchy in the home and the church, and discursive Christianity – the religious culture which surrounded their everyday lives – was inevitably going to be a victim. But they acknowledged that they had to renegotiate that narrative because it had framed their mothers' public respectability; this explains why daughters, when asked questions about religion, often referred in their answers to their parents' and sometimes their grandparents' generation, and their own girlhoods.[32] In this way, many women losing religion between 1950 and 1980 had to contemplate making a double rejection – of religion *and* family. This prospect diminished for the next generation that I interviewed, those born since 1960, for whom living without god grew decreasingly debilitating for family relations.[33]

Narratives arising from death and bereavement came mainly from female respondents. They speak of grief as a trigger to questioning faith and to exploring the alternatives. Two women referred to the death of their children as bringing realization of atheist and humanist values, leading both to become humanist celebrants. One was Mary Wallace, who, within days of her child's Christian funeral, was discovering the ways to hold humanist funerals, and soon became a full-time celebrant and for many years a celebrant trainer. The other was Gillian Stewart, who described becoming a humanist as a process of stages of disbelief, arising mainly from a succession of Christian funerals over two decades. Each religious ceremony raised more doubts: her grandfather's funeral, her father's, her mother's and then lastly – the decisive one – her son's death when he was 4 years of age in 1991. Some years after the church funeral for her son, a family celebration of his life was restorative emotionally, exposing how good it was to speak of the dead without religion 'as people as when they were alive and not about where they've gone or anything like that'.[34] These deaths were deeply felt by Mary and Gillian, who each embarked upon stark changes to their outlook and lives. Mary gave up her university post and with her husband downsized to country living, whilst Gillian worked in a children's hospice, first as a volunteer, then trained in counselling, joining the care team a few years' later and became a humanist celebrant. Two men also mentioned death in the family as influential in their route to disbelief, but, perhaps strikingly, they tended to do so in the context of working out a rationalist worldview rather than in terms of the grief itself. For men, death was a stimulus to decide that atheism expressed their standpoint.

Distress features distinctly more in women's stories of losing religion. Men may be more reticent generally about speaking about such things, but, as we see in the next chapter, are quite frank about the intellectual trauma they suffered in leaving religion.

'To be a person': Living feminism and the loss of religion

The place of atheism within modern feminism has rarely been considered in its own right. For women's historians, attention rests on the diminishing power of religion in shaping women's lives,[35] whilst an influential strand of religious history has diverted attention to the growth of Christian feminism from the later 1970s.[36] Partly, feminism relates to the ideology. But partly, and in many regards more importantly, it relates to how women have *lived their feminism*. Many women came to feminism in the 1960s and 1970s, not through reading and learning in feminist tracts or attending consciousness-raising groups of the classic feminist historical narrative,[37] but rather through a determination to affirm their autonomy from prescribed conventional norms for women's careers, ambitions and family destinies. It is in this context, in this lived feminism, that a life without a god emerges – a freedom from patriarchy leading to a freedom from religion. There is, thus, a 'double liberation' narrative in this feminist route from religion.

Joyce Murphy found northern England in the 1950s an oppressive society in which to reach adulthood. She explained,

> My mother's family were very strong Methodists, and I would now say that my grandmother's religion was really, 'Respectability and what the outsiders would think'. But 'Methodists' was the title. So nothing was ever explained or said, it was very confusing. I was sent to the Church of England, every child went to Sunday school. And this [one] was the closest and it was also the more sociably acceptable, you know. Baptists and Methodists were kind of [a] little lower on the social scale. So it was a very --- nothing was ever discussed, nothing was done. But I had little germs of ideas that, now I knew about Jews (but I didn't know about Muslims), but it seemed to me that if the Jews were right and the Catholics were right and the Methodists were right and the Church of

England were right, either they were all right or they were all wrong. And it just seemed a format that you went through. I loved the ceremony in the church, the beautiful music and it was beautiful – I loved it. But I felt that I didn't fit in … It just wasn't the right thing for me.

In this atmosphere, religious experience was linked to social status: 'expect God and the Bible could be used when it was to your advantage'. Her grandmother was a great one for opening the Bible at random and her interpretation was always exactly what she was looking for. Running in parallel, but not directly connected, Joyce says, was the 'stifling' life prospect stretching ahead of her. The expectation that she would marry and have no career made her unhappy. The family saw no point in higher education: 'What was the point?', she recalls the sentiment, 'Because, as one of my uncles put it: "not only is she not good looking but she is too bloody bright. Who is gonna want to marry her?"' This stifling mood discouraged her, with learning to drive being impressed upon her as pointless because, she was told, she wouldn't cope. Joyce remembers that she did want to get married, but in the English industrial society of the 1950s it was a choice of either marriage or career, not both. So, she went into nursing – 'very much against the grain', she adds as an aside – where women who married had to give up the career. This, she said, was made very clear as part of 'one's behaviour outside and what was expected of one'.[38] Though she became highly successful as a midwife and paediatric nurse, eventually becoming a head nurse, she had to let go at that time of her dream of a library technician's degree. This was 'something that I would really have wanted to do'. The situation was bleak for Joyce in the mid-1950s:

> You were this person in the social strata and this was what was expected of you, you know. My mother was an invalid, and therefore I would be looking after her for the rest of her life. You know, there was no --- one didn't even go to secondary school because all you learned there was French where, as you know, you could just finish school and [be] gone. So, yes, very much so that [you] didn't have your own personality. And what was outside the home were very important, you now. Things were kept inside but certainly the appearances, that's what [was] said [by] my grandmother, appearances was the absolute.

Joyce came to realize this: '[If] I was going to be happy or be a person I would have to get away.' At the age of 22, freedom came via emigration to Western Canada, and there she felt that she started to develop a self-identity. 'I was no longer surrounded and part of, you know, what was expected of me, and what one should [be]. So, I mean it was a very stifling existence.'[39] There, in 1958, she discovered Unitarian Universalism, which for her, like for many North American humanists and atheists, was a route out of conventional religion in the mid-twentieth century. There she found

888888

8888888888

fellowship and acceptance in what she calls its 'academic intellectual phase – in many ways nothing spiritual at all'. She was drawn to its ethical sermons and its community and its debates. With a marriage to a man who wanted nothing to do with being part of any religious community, she found both the career and the space inside and outside the home to become 'a person'. Gaining a degree in librarianship, she ran the British Columbia government's ministry libraries, whilst in 2008 becoming a lay chaplain (or celebrant) of the Unitarian Universalist group, working for gay and lesbian rights, including their marriage rights.

This is a narrative driven by a self-developed feminist discourse, and it is incredibly common, and one seemingly underrated in feminist historiography. Underlying her life story is a feminist impulse not encased in an intellectual tradition or scholarly reading, but in a drive for selfhood that led from traditional religion to a new ethical creed. This narrative was to be found amongst women respondents raised in the middle decades of the twentieth century. The historian Sarah Browne has come to a similar conclusion, commenting upon her study of autobiographies and interviews with Women's Liberation Movement activists in Britain in the 1970s that 'it became clear that girlhood experiences, particularly, the role of religion were of critical importance, leading to their politicization'.[40] This drive was lifelong and evident in the feminist framework of their interview stories in which the life story itself becomes the source of self-identity in late modern Western society. As the sociolinguist Charlotte Linde has argued, for 'a comfortable sense of being a good, socially proper, and stable person, an individual needs to have a coherent, acceptable and constantly revised life story'.[41] In this project, I am suggesting that young women of the mid-twentieth century embarked on crafting an autonomous self, and the narrative of a lived as much as a theoretical feminism may be seen as a narrative device to establish this required coherence of the life story. Renegotiating the religious self emerges as a critical part of this process.

The selected narrative playing field, if you will, is the family. Astonishingly frequently, when I posed a question concerning religion in childhood, the narrative response was an interweaving of a feminist narrative around other issues. As an example, Lorraine Lavoie was born in 1944 in Newport, Vermont. I asked her about her religious experience as a child, and after explaining how she was raised by strong Catholic parents and attended a nuns' school, her narrative turned, unsolicited, to how her life destiny seemed to be in her father's hands. Her father told her he would help her financially if she became a nurse, a teacher or a secretary, to which she said she wouldn't be any good at those, and threatened to leave home, earn money and go to college on her own terms. Her mother described her as immature, and specifically banned her from losing her religion, and sent her to live with an aunt and uncle. There, Lorraine scrimped to get to college to study as a medical laboratory technician. This changed her place in the family: 'And when I graduated…my father was so proud he called me "his daughter the doctor" [chuckle].' When her father became unwell, she persuaded him to get tests, which diagnosed him with Parkinson's disease. 'So then', she said of her mother and father, 'I think they started to realise that I was a little bit different than what they had given me credit for.' For the first time, at the age of 40, she was allowed to drive her father's car. At this juncture, I turned the interview back to religious issues:

LL: I was about 40 then! So it's like when it suited them, I could do certain things.

CB: So, can I turn you back to younger years, would you have described yourself in your teens as a Christian? Did you believe in God?

LL: I didn't question it at that time. Um, I do know that I started doubting certain other things before I started doubting religion. There were things I didn't like at home, and I decided there's got to be a better way to do things, and I wanted to do things differently. My father was very critical, there wasn't much of anything I could do right. However, my mother was ill and could not do everything she was expected to do around the house. I was given a choice of doing housework or cooking. 'Housework?' I says 'I clean my room and it's a mess as soon as I turn around' [chuckling]. So I started being the family baker and my father never criticised anything I made, so that was a safe area for me to be in. The Women's Movement comes along about the time I am in High School and they say 'get out of the kitchen'. And I say 'no way, I will do both. I will pursue a career and I will enjoy what I enjoy in the kitchen!' So later on, it's when, you know, I wasn't --- My mother was ill and she wasn't able to be the typical nurturing type of mother, my father was not well educated, he wasn't very nurturing, he did provide for us but it was different. I was allowed to grow in ways that weren't restricted by them.

Here, Lorraine links the emergence of her questioning of religion with her questioning of 'other things' – how her critiques of domestic roles and career choices came to provide the templates for developing a critique of religion.

CB: So you had some freedom.

LL: I had some freedom, and at one point I had friends who were trying to tell: 'Oh if you're not going to the Catholic church, pick another church'. And I'd say 'well, gee, you know, pick another Christian religion, or go to the Jewish religion, you know, what's going to be the big difference?' Then somebody was telling me about the Ethical Society [of Boston] and I decided to go, and slowly started going there more and more.

Through dating men of different faiths and none,

> it was like I was drifting away further and further from the church, and
> since I wasn't living at home there was no need for me to go to church,
> so the only times I went was when there was a funeral or a wedding, or
> something like that, and then eventually I decided that I didn't even want
> to go to church when they had the family reunions.

Over a period of sixty years she moved from religious belonging to joining
Boston's oldest humanist group.[42]

A woman vigorously aware of how such lived feminism could lead
from Christian faith to humanism and atheism was Tanya Long, born in
1944 in an isolated mining town in Ontario in Canada. As a teenager in
the 1960s, she identified with liberal causes and what she described as
religious fervour, marrying a man training for the ministry. Together, 'we
had this vision of the two of us kind of sailing our ship and he was gonna
be the captain and I was gonna be the helmsman, and we were gonna go
out there and do all these wonderful good deeds [laughs]. Well, that lasted
about 6 months [laughs]'. As the marriage deteriorated, both lost their
religious fervour, he apparently finding her fervour to be ridiculous. But she
remained an active Anglican, attached to one of the most liberal and pro-
gay rights congregations in North America, and in the 1970s she became
deeply affected by the women's movement, leading her to careers in teaching
and publishing. Gradually, she came to realize that she couldn't handle the
sermons at church because she lacked a belief in God, and she turned first
to Buddhism, and then in the 1990s to atheism and humanism.[43] For Tanya,
the search for professional success and loss of religion shaped a new sense
of selfhood. Her testimony comes alive with memories of the radical liberal
Christianity that so energized herself and her husband in the late 1960s and
early 1970s; she spoke of tears coming to her eyes on hearing of her church's
acceptance of a gay minister. Framing her journey was her feminism – both
as a lived experience of discovering her autonomous and educated self, and
as an ideology of change for women.

> The women's movement affected me profoundly. And I became involved
> in first of all for myself the Toronto's women's movement, which was
> very Marxist. And I actually quit them when they said you couldn't
> read Doris Lessing because Doris Lessing had the gall to criticise Stalin,
> so no way you could read Doris Lessing. I thought 'okay this is not
> the organisation for me'. But one of the things I did at Scarborough
> [College] was I started a women's group. I guess it was a kind of support
> group…a conscious-raising group…but there were some other staff
> members and students…We met in a classroom so we actually did it
> on campus. And it was mainly students. As I said, there were a couple
> of other faculty members, but it was mainly students. I think we talked

about what it meant to be a young woman, how did women feel about getting married or about their careers, or what were the issues that they were dealing.[44]

Tanya's journey from a firm faith coincided with her flirtation with radicalism and the impact of the women's movement. She read in feminist literature, and Germaine Greer became an idol. She said,

As the marriage kind of fell apart, I think feminism probably played a bigger role than I realised, because I think it was very tied in with the deterioration of my marriage. Because I did still continue to have some involvement with the church on my own even after our marriage split up. But sort of the more I got involved in feminism and thought about it and looked at the attitudes that the church held and saw the fights that gay people were going through and the abortion issue and those things [that] are still issues, I think the angrier and angrier I got.[45]

Feminism and loss of religion were for Tanya related:

I would say that my involvement in feminism did contribute to my moving further and further away from any kind of organised religion, and any kind of personalised image of God, because when you are raised a Christian it's very hard to separate out God from God the father. Now I have a friend who's a United Church minister and he's a very liberal minister and has this sort of ethereal 'God is the ground of all being'. I think that's Paul Tillich who coined that phrase. It tries to move away from the idea of God as any kind of personalised image into some sort of life force that moves life forward. But it's very hard to make that shift, and in my view it doesn't solve anything. To me if you say, 'well, okay, if you don't believe in God, then how did the world get started, how did things happen, how did they develop the way they did?' Well, to say God did it doesn't answer anything at all, it just raises more questions. So in the end the whole concept of God seemed to me not only irrelevant but damaging – damaging to women, damaging to people generally, when it gets into factionalism and tribalism and one group saying 'well our God is better than your God', and all the horrendous things that come out of that.[46]

Tanya came to identify herself as an atheist only later in her life, and discovered what she described as her courage to make this declaration after being a member of a community of atheists, the Humanist Association of Toronto. When challenged by a work colleague, she said, '"I'm making a choice. I'm an atheist. I don't believe there is a God." And I thought I would never have done that [laughs]. And that was the first time that I remember stating so clearly what my world view was in that sense.'[47]

One of the most searing accounts I obtained was from a Canadian interviewee, Pat Duffy Hutcheon (1926–2010). She survived a poverty-stricken upbringing and abusive marriage in the dust bowl of rural Alberta of the 1930s and 1940s, and her life story was dominated by the struggles to stay warm, to find food, raise her son, obtain university education and then to find positions in university research and teaching. Displaying a sense of duty in keeping two families from starvation, her mode of narration brings to mind Carolyn Steedman's study of the economic self-conception of women of the past.[48] My questions to her were on diverse matters, but Pat's testimony returned relentlessly to the theme of economic survival. Here is a short sample from a very long interview:

CB   Did you have a settled view of religious matters in your teens?
PH   Oh yes. Yes, much before my teens I had a very settled view. I had to go after working --- Our family had to split up and I had to try to find a job from grade 9 on, try to find a job. Worked my way through high school by keeping working as a house helper, home helper and then getting to school and getting my board and room that way. So that's how I tried to get my high school, and I didn't have much time to worry about other issues [laughs] other than getting fed.[49]

This becomes a feminist narrative of survival, of finding an identity within that and then, after ten years of marriage, of leaving her husband with her son to start a university degree as a single mother. From there, her feminism developed ideological and professional elements, becoming a teacher and writer on social-science method. She confronted sexism and abusive sexual advances seemingly at every stage, including on arrival at an American Ivy League university when her doctoral supervisor demanded that she sleep with him. Immediately, she abandoned that dream. But she progressed in her field, obtaining university posts in Australia and Canada, and all the while her atheism and humanism grew beside her feminism. In her narrative, her liberation from religion becomes a story of economic struggle, social science and an advocacy of enlightenment rationalism in research. Her story entwines the fleeing from faith inside a narrative of herculean effort, patriarchy and sexual abuse of women. Pat's struggle for autonomy and freedom from religion is a torrid survival story against egregious obstacles.[50]

The narratives told me by Joyce Murphy, Lorraine Lavoie, Tanya Long and Pat Duffy Hutcheon were impressive accounts of an assertive feminist individualism at the heart of rejection of religion. Amongst fifteen women I interviewed with strong feminist narratives in their interviews, there were shocking episodes of wife-beating, struggles with poverty, domestic and sexual abuse, insulting treatment and discrimination in jobs and divorce from the marriages, as much as from husbands, that suppressed their autonomous selves. In a sense, in even the most distressing of accounts from the mid-twentieth century, there is a claim to independence, to a personal sovereignty that demanded departure from family and community expectations for a young woman's life. Other women gave me similar, though less fearful, accounts. Carolyn Nalbandian from Boston, Massachusetts, brought up in the interwar period in an Irish-origin Catholic family, gave an excited and explosive narrative about her life, studying philosophy, social work and psychotherapy, and her professional ambition. Nietzsche and Sartre featured prominently in her thoughts, but it was when her son was born that she 'ended up going' to the Unitarian Universalist Church and later joining the Ethical Society of Boston – her ethical outlook sharpened by the radical causes of the 1960s and 1970s.[51] These were women changing themselves and women's history at the same time.

I turn lastly in this section to how my interviews revealed feminism and atheism as linked ideologies of the 1950s, 1960s and 1970s. Despite its blossoming in the movement of Victorian women freethinkers, female atheism in the mid-twentieth century possessed a cruel toxicity for those who found it shaping their sense of selfhood. Women had a desolate struggle against the inherited expectations, heightened in the 1950s by the Cold War and fear of godless communism, that a woman was a bulwark of not just the family but of patriotism and 'normalcy' – as experienced in January 1955, when Margaret Knight advocated humanism on BBC radio.[52] But atheism was an important adjunct to feminism for many women on both sides of the Atlantic. Some I interviewed were key feminist activists. Joan Gibson recalled the inspiration given by the UN Decade for Women 1976–85 and her own predicament as the wife of a Protestant clergyman working in an isolated private boarding school. But on travelling to meet a prominent feminist campaigner, she came to find a 'natural instinct' for feminism. After marriage, she restarted work as a nurse, where the Christian outlook on death brought her to see the virtue of assisted dying and 'helping people to have as comfortable a death as possible'.[53] Joan agreed all the seven points in the feminist charter and drifted inexorably towards humanism. Yet, she was quite clear that, at the time, she made no connection between her feminism and her humanism. But by the 1990s, she emerged as a leading member of the Humanist Society of Scotland and a founding member of Engender, one of Scotland's leading feminist organizations.[54]

It is a common theme amongst female oral history respondents that, though they may have been effectively alienated from church and religious activity in childhood, their feminist impulse predated a turn towards recognition of their atheism and humanism. Ellen Ramsay raised feminism as a defining ideology which guided her life, starting at university in Canada, where, driven by campaigning against poverty, she constructed a sense of achievement with fellow feminists on her master's program, and in England, where she spoke of imbibing socialist radicalism and alienation from Christianity.[55] In a different context, Ena Sparks from British Columbia likewise records that the expression of no religionism as a key part of her identity came later in life than her feminism; it was into her fifties that she read about atheism and humanism, and found a new understanding of feminist issues like abortion, whilst placing her role in business in the context of feminist thinking about discrimination.[56] This drift from feminism as human rights to humanism as human rights is a vein detectable in many women respondents' interviews. Having suffered a degree of alienation from organized religion, a settled and conscious self-ideology of atheism and humanism in most cases came later – in some cases in their fifties or sixties. Yet, there is no denying an underlying atheistic trajectory in much feminist oral narrative, one observable also in autobiography.[57]

The feminist perception of a Christian denial of personhood was best articulated by Tanya Long, whom we met earlier. Socially radicalized within Christianity in the 1960s and 1970s, she drifted from the church in the 1990s and came to humanism, leading her in interview to articulate very calmly a withering manifesto against the Christian churches' impact on women:

> It seems to me that the church has done more harm to women than just about any other institution. Now, I think there is an argument to be made the other way because if a person named Jesus ever did exist he probably was more aware of women and their rights as a person than anybody else in his society at that time. But it hasn't translated into the church by any stretch of the imagination. And I have a girlfriend who's Roman Catholic and basically we just don't talk about it because the fact that they're anti-abortion, anti-gay, anti-ordination of women just infuriates me when I think about it. And, as far as I'm concerned there's no rationalisation for that, because it's a denial of the full personhood of women. And so, yes, I would say that my involvement in feminism did contribute to my moving further and further away from any kind of organised religion ....[58]

Decisions were rarely easy. As a young daughter of an atheist in the Bible belt area of Texas in the 1970s, Leslie O'Hagan was humiliated at school by teachers asking each scholar in turn about their religious activities the previous Sunday; come Monday, she had nothing to report. In her narrative, the disempowerment of women was connected to this world of social alienation of the non-religious, and was being challenged by those like her mom, who, as a very strong feminist, taught women's courses at the community college on self-empowerment (even how to handle a chequebook), and fought for her daughter's right to be the first female student to take electrical and automotive classes.[59]

It is difficult to imagine modern feminism without atheism and atheism without feminism. Not every feminist is an atheist and not every atheist is a feminist, but very large numbers are in Europe and Canada. Not every feminist's atheism arose in family frenzy or in distress. Reflection, observation and reading were spoken of as revising women's thinking on religion and womanhood. On the one side, Sarah Flew from England, though subscribing to neither organized humanism nor feminism, spoke of how studying and reading in philosophy influenced her loss of belief in God; on the other side, Ena Sparks, after being widowed at 22 years old, travelled the world and started to think 'of religion as a power as opposed to a faith', especially over women as wielded both by the Catholic Church and Islam.[60] Moreover, some men came through the same route, speaking of feminism as the precursor to human rights emerging as the mark of late-twentieth-century atheist and humanist campaigning.[61] Few women I interviewed did not respond in positive tones about feminism. For the majority of those growing up in the 1960s, 1970s and 1980s, feminism was quite clearly rooted in their experiences. They speak of lives transformed by the advent of educational opportunities that were denied to their mothers, of jobs and careers gained through increasing gender equalization of opportunity and of their sense of personhood. They take it for granted that their lives and that of their sisters have been revolutionized by the dismantling of patriarchy in work, family and everyday life. They take the human rights of equality for all living beings as a given, and generally react with huge positivity to the subject of feminism.

The New Age and 'absolutely no god thing'

One of the gendered dimensions of religiosity since the middle of the twentieth century has been the influence of the New Age religions. Though much of this was rooted in Theosophy, to which Annie Besant was attracted in 1889 to supplement rather than substitute for her secularism, a new religious atmosphere after 1960 emphasized seeking, spirituality, mysticism and 'the god within'. The New Age was a strongly female-supported phenomenon, and many of my respondents – now humanists and most atheists – traversed it on a long road from conventional religious faith to unbelief. As Doug Owram has written of Canada in the 1960s, the religious overtone of the decade was 'dabbling' and not redemptive conversionism, as was emphasized in the 1950s.[62] The outcomes of this religious experimentation were diverse manifestations of New Age spiritualities which have been identified as clearly a characteristic more common amongst young women than young men.[63] This has been widely viewed in religious studies as one element of people's impulse for authenticity in their religious experience.[64] Less frequently has it been noted that the impulse was in a lot of cases to remain unsatisfied within the religious sphere, and led women to locate a road towards agnosticism or atheism, often via feminism. In this way, the New Age attracted many, but retained few, making it a major route to the secularization of the individual.

West coast North America – from California to British Columbia – was the centre of New Age spiritual searching from the 1960s onwards.

New religious movements mushroomed there as nowhere else. Stark and Bainbridge showed that, by 1978, new religious cults were concentrated in California, but, tellingly, they also showed that within the United States and Canada such cults and movements tended to be strongest where irreligion was rife.[65] And I found this legacy amongst my interviewees and also how this was a staging post for many on the atheist trail.

Vancouver was one Canadian centre of sixties liberalism, and Grace Daniels underwent a classic transition from Protestant worship in childhood to spiritual searching. Brought up by a mother who had experienced a harsh religious childhood in Seventh Day Adventism, Grace learnt about the way in which religion might subjugate a woman unkindly with bans on jewellery and self-adornment. 'I guess from the Seventh Day Adventist end of things, they were just very, very strict about what women wear. So like my cousins, they couldn't wear shorts, they couldn't [wear] jewellery.' For Grace, the attraction initially of Sufism was a sense of freedom and egalitarianism, which she later found outside of conventional faiths in humanism.[66] She spent time with a group of devotees of the Maharishi Mahesh Yogi and practised her mantra, but, coming to dislike that, she travelled to a camp in California to perform Sufi meditation with Pir Vilayat Khan. So, Grace found Sufism and meditation more attractive than the Christian church. She reported, 'I think too it came more from you personally, like you had that personal relationship, so it wasn't somebody telling you what it was like and sort of only through them that you got up to God. So it probably seemed more egalitarian.' Still interested in Eastern religions until she started her family, she then asked serious questions about the purpose of life. She described her progress 'as like a kid having these questions, "what is really going on here, like I don't get this?"' She detected 'corrupt things' in the New Age as in conventional religions, fostering questioning to 'figure out my life, figure out what's going on'. In the early 1980s, she decided to take her children for moral education to a Unitarian Universalist congregation, one which, at that time, was regarded as closely humanist and effectively secular in its doctrine, but it felt to her 'rather churchy' and, even though she wasn't an atheist at that point, she felt 'an imposter' there. Her breakthrough really came in taking a university psychology course relating to consciousness,[67] including religious consciousness and experience, and this led Grace to a wider understanding of impulses to religious experience, and at the course's end led her to say to herself: 'No, I don't believe anymore.' From this, she would develop her secular humanism.[68]

Such a route from conventional religion through New Age religious exploration was the template for several respondents. Tanya Long from Ontario left the United Church of Canada in her twenties and experimented with Buddhism, recalling that she was attracted by 'radiant emptiness' as an attractive phrase she heard there.[69] Occasionally, a route from faith via seeking to humanism might be slightly altered. One respondent noted how his daughter had been channelled in her youth into the Unitarian Universalists, but in adulthood developed a living by offering a telephone counselling service for 'Core Energetic Healing' grounded on 'personal growth and spiritual development' based in Arizona, which, with such a high concentration of alternative spiritual services, makes it what he described as 'the belly button' of the New Age.[70] Middlesex-born Liz Currie noted that there was a time when she would 'try anything' by way of religious experimentation, and her curiosity led her to a group in Cornwall. Like quite a few respondents, she remained attracted to visiting churches as a tourist; on holiday with a boyfriend in Spain, she explored many cathedrals, leading him to remark, 'what is it about you and churches?' She says, 'I'm not really a religious person … it's just the architecture that intrigues me.'[71] The sense of spirituality aroused the interest of some respondents despite a firm non-belief.

The movement into the New Age was often seen later by respondents as the repercussion of the indoctrination in the original mainline or conventional Christian religion in which they had been brought up. Julia Stuart from Dundee was slow to experience the characteristics of sixties counterculture, but she went through a succession of New Age gurus and cults, reading about them and sampling them, in characteristic 'seeking' mode: Lobsang Rampa (Buddhist), Erik von Daniken (advocate of Inca gods being visiting aliens), Aleister Crowley (occultist and magician), and those who used mescaline to open the mind. Whilst exploring these, Julia experienced a long disorganized period of her life, eventually moving back to Dundee 'trying to find the good folks without the religion', and discovering humanists were 'the first kind of group that I found [with] absolutely no god thing'.[72] The drive for the New Age exemplified much of the sixties' anti-establishment credentials. The process was not a clear-cut journey, but was often 'messy' in terms of choices, lifestyle, relationships and outcomes. Yet it tended throughout to deny deference, revoked traditional ecclesiastical trajectories to a conventional female self and, for a time at least, wistfully accepted spiritual reasons for putting flowers in your hair as one way of defining the autonomous woman.

The New Age not only conferred directly upon women new religious trajectories which might lead to humanism and atheism; it also facilitated intergenerational change. In Sterling Cooley's family, the religious counterculture of the Pacific West coast was an intermediate stage on the route from conventional churches to no religionism. His grandmother was a traditional Roman Catholic in post-war Los Angeles, and made her daughter dress up appropriately for Sunday service in the city in the 1950s and 1960s. But at the age of 16 the daughter rebelled, becoming what her son described as 'a spiritual hippy' of the 1960s, roaming up and down the West coast of the United States and Canada. Sterling describes her as being into Tarot card reading, palm reading and other sides to the New Age, what he called 'hippy spirituality'. But because of her experience with her own mother, she never tried to push her religious interests upon her son. 'So she made the decision to allow me to make my own decision really ... She never said "We're going to go to a hippy church or like a psychic fair or whatever."' First settling as a single mother in Oregon, she then moved to a new community where she allowed her son and daughter total religious freedom, from which Sterling's own atheism was to be fostered.[73]

Though the New Age was clearly influential as a means to discovering a route to humanism and atheism, many atheists and humanists have been very hostile to it. Ellen Ramsay from Canada described the gullibility of the sixties for New Age religion, watching out for 'what I now call spooky-ooky religions like the Hare Krishna and cult groups'. She speculated interestingly that 'they grew up in that time of secularism because there was more tolerance for anything that actually deviated from the mainstream'. But for her, they were just another group of brainwashers.[74] Another respondent from the Bay Area of San Francisco referred to the religious quality which adherents of organic foods or environmental concerns found in their movements:

> It's very comfortable ... [A] lot of people in this area have substituted a lot of New Age religious ideas for traditional religious ideas, which means they're not as dogmatic, but they still really like that true belief ... [T]hey oppose anything that isn't totally from nature, which for them is another way of saying from God ... They just wanna believe.[75]

Despite much academic recounting of the New Age fostering the view that spirituality is the new religion,[76] 'spirituality' is a term with profoundly confused discourses. 'Spirituality' and 'spiritual' are terms much referred to – 156 times in the transcripts of my interviews with 77 no-religionist interviewees. The narrative about spirituality is that its ownership is at best contested and, at one extreme of argument, the domain of those without religion. Indeed, for many humanists and atheists, spirituality describes the emotive state of being *when devoid of religion*. For others it is *the sovereignty of reason*. This last point was made most succinctly to me by Jeanne Willig in Cambridge, Massachusetts. A member of the Boston Ethical Society, Jeanne claims the term without fuss or the interviewer's prodding: 'I think I am a spiritual person. I think spirituality really has nothing to do with organised religion, because I think organised religion is about power.'[77] She then relates her position to the deist anti-Trinitarian founders of the United States, claiming a patriotic context for her position. This does demonstrate the democratic claim to 'spirituality' as being free from ecclesiastical control or manipulation – a claim made by those with and without a faith alike.

But the term 'spirituality' goes further and deeper than this in the domain of people who live their lives as if there is no god. Gillian Stewart explained to me, 'I do believe in the human spirit in the sense of we have a collective consciousness and that we are linked through that, but it's not a spirit that continues to live or exist after we die.' She acknowledged that the word is very emotive amongst her humanist-celebrant colleagues and that some people struggle with it and say, 'well, we can't say that in our ceremonies, we can't talk about the human spirit'. But for her it's about the context, about someone being here in spirit: 'They're here in your hearts and in your memories, they're not here floating about in some ether out there.'[78] By far the largest proportion of references to spirituality comes from female respondents – like Tanya Long, who told me how a phrase from Buddhism, 'radiant emptiness', suggested to her that 'there was still an awe about life and still a sense of the meaningfulness of life without there having to be any godly component to that'.[79] Furthermore, spirituality has a growing currency that transcends the world of religionism and that of humanism. For humanist organizers in the United Kingdom, spirituality is the new context for chaplaincy in the National Health Service, with 'spiritual care' an agreed term to denote the activity of chaplains of religious and non-religious backgrounds alike.[80] Two of my interviewees were actively engaged in the discussions and negotiations at governmental level to redefine chaplaincy work in hospitals and care institutions, and in the drawing up of policies and publications to accompany the changes.[81] In this process of negotiation between religionists and non-religionists, there is an acknowledgement of both shared conceptions of the spiritual and division of perception. This may not be a fully rehearsed philosophical narrative that defines the consensual and divisive elements of spirituality, and may not require to be. Yet, humanists are quite clear that this is not merely an administrative convenience to gain bureaucratic entry to the world of chaplaincy services. It is an acknowledgement of a common modality concerning the human condition, one with a shared ownership by the atheist and the theist alike.

Flying through the air

Women's de-conversion took diverse forms. One was described by an interviewee as seemingly painless despite being near fatal. Ruth Majors became an evangelical Christian at the age of 11, and went through university undertaking various missionary and charitable endeavours at home and abroad. But in her mid-twenties she developed doubt about her evangelical Christian faith, in part focused on disquiet after experiencing evangelical missionaries' treatment of non-Christian cultures in the Far East. Finally, she experienced clarity during a motoring accident whilst on furlough in England, when riding in a car that overturned. Though nobody was hurt, she recalled this as her 'turning point', reporting, 'as we were flying through the air [laughter] I can remember thinking "I don't believe in life after death" and imagining this policeman announcing to my mother that we were all dead [still laughing]. And I think, I do think that from that moment on I felt I was living a hypocritical life by still going to church'.[82]

Accompanying her change of faith position, Ruth developed an academic career as a feminist scholar – her fear of flying, if you will, undermined by flying through the air.[83] This is a case that shows that, no matter the trigger, a Western woman's change of faith position in the last half of the twentieth century was often entwined with change to the female self.

Western femininity in the post-war decades embarked on a remarkably quick transformation. It became one in which individualism and questioning of religion were invariably necessary preludes to modern feminism and life-changing careers and family structures. Though a Christian feminist movement did emerge in the late 1970s, breaking the mould of a femininity that had placed early domesticity and motherhood ahead of life fulfilment – Betty Friedan's 'problem with no name' – became interlinked for my female respondents with renegotiating their place in the world of organized religion and religious belief. And for them this sometimes meant blazing rows in family and personal life, often intensely traumatic grief or personal tragedy, and a remapping of the woman's individual self and her world. Female humanists, secularists and atheists have privileged me with their narratives of ordeals and suffering which, they told me, shaped who they became, gave them new definition and granted them an enhanced place in the world.

For the modern cultural theorist, one of the remarkable features of this corpus of intense testimony must be how the transformation was initiated by so many of my narrators without a template to follow. With no public discourse available for women losing religion, the composure about their life stories was more difficult to achieve in the 1960s and 1970s than it is now. Yet, even now, there is no well-known template available for women – no female Bertrand Russell or Richard Dawkins comes to mind in public culture, prefigured and full of social approval. The term 'feminism' becomes critical here: it is a name available to describe the walk to autonomy back in the 1960s. But, to be clear, feminist literature of the 1960s and 1970s rarely described the atheist woman; my respondents each, one by one, recrafted for themselves a new womanhood, having to not just shape but *name* what they experienced. Michel Foucault was likely wrong in the 1960s, at the very time when this was happening, to write that discourse changes in 'the anonymity of a murmur'.[84] The testimony of woman humanists and atheists would suggest otherwise. Discourse changes when individuals, brave and courageous, undertake it themselves, usually alone in hostile or sceptical family circles. They created the model for the humanist woman, the atheist woman, the secularist woman.

The change is narrated by the sixties generation of women as strongly family centred. This is paradoxical. Family is related as the origins of many of their gruelling problems in adapting to an acceptable modernity. Yet, they return to it again and again to recount their story. The paradox is actually quite logical. Family is where the renegotiation of the new humanist and atheist woman of the late twentieth century had to take place; it set the launch pad for new family structures, career opportunities and female liberation – including widening sexual experience, later marriage and first-births, a plunging birth rate and increasing cohabitation and singlehood.[85] The reformulated versions of family demonstrate that the new woman without religion redefined but did not neglect her family. Indeed, there remain unresolved tensions here. The modern Western atheist family is a work in progress, as a woman's journey to a life without god is accompanied by a thoroughgoing transformation of the female self.

Only a few of the women I interviewed prioritized reason, reading and education in their narratives. We encountered earlier Sarah Flew and Carolyn Nalbandian, who each spoke of reading philosophy extensively on the way to atheism and humanism. Another example was Kirsten Bulmer, who, after being a sceptical child about religion, met and married an atheist and started to read widely:

> he was the first atheist that I'd met and at that point I still thought it's a bad word you can't say that, you know, and I said you should describe yourself as agnostic, and he was like 'No absolutely not, these are the reasons why I believe this or don't believe.' And he introduced me to all the great freethinkers – Dawkins, Hitchens, Harris – and I just consumed them all. I thought finally, this fits with my viewpoint, although I didn't know that before then, but it just felt absolutely right to me and that's certainly where I've been since.[86]

When respondents had failed to mention any of these authors, I asked about them. I asked about the influence of reading in their journey from religion, and a few more did speak of its importance. But if reading was a low priority for most, reason was widely referred to. Lorraine Hardie in Vancouver pointed to the developing of the inquisitive and questioning mind from tender years of childhood, asking her mother at the age of four how she could distinguish dreams from not dreams, on to god's failure to help her in the midst of depression at the age of 11. Her questioning, jarring in a family where the parents were 'pretty authoritarian', impacted a Christian faith that was soon to dissolve.[87]

Perhaps the starkest scientific rationale for humanism that I encountered came from the humanist author and sociologist Pat Duffy Hutcheon, a woman who grew up with a freethinking father who set her on a course of non-belief, to be challenged by an abusive husband and disappointing academic sexism. Though her account of her non-religion is set in a very stark and lengthy story of suffering, yet her justification for humanism is set in a scientific context:

> Right from the beginning in sociology, I was humanist. I was very interested in the scientific, being scientific rather than as Marxist and all the other ideologies that entered into the social sciences. And so the scientific aspect was always very important to me all my life, and

to me that's what humanism is about – it's looking at the world in a scientific way. My approach to evolution is like Dawkins'. I see the whole world evolving always and the human species was just one of the many species evolving. A cultural evolution going on. The culture is part of the environment just as the physical is, and it is the feedback from the environment that alters the biological evolution. And at the same time of course the cultural evolution is being altered always by feedback around it, and there is a three-way feedback among these. And so that if you understand evolution, and I see humanism is based on evolution very much, and so that's what makes it scientific. And you can't really understand evolution and believe in it without being a scientist and being scientific in your approach to everything. I never was a dualist – that is two different worlds, the world of the spirit and mind and whatever, and then the physical world. I don't think that is the world; it's all one. In one of my books, *Leaving the Cave*, I trace this evolution of various religious beliefs, and then the evolution beyond that to a belief in the way the world works. It's really all about the way the world works. I used to say to my students, 'why' isn't the question to ask, it's 'how come?' You know the good old farm question, how come? How did this come around?[88]

Pat Duffy Hutcheon opposed anything, from religion to Marxism, that became a belief system. For this reason, she never 'taught' humanism to her students, not wanting it to be seen as a prepackaged, totalizing alternative to religion. 'We have to start with, like a sort of an axiom, that knowledge is not absolute. It depends on evidence and has to follow the evidence – alters as the evidence that is available to the human mind changes.'[89] If, with great difficulty, she had broken free from the embraces of one totalizing thought system that had engulfed women for centuries, she wasn't about to promote another.

CHAPTER SIX

Men, Reason and Radicalism

Absences and silences

Men's accounts of losing religion are rather different from those of women. True, there are points where the characteristics are shared, and these will be signposted. But for the men of the sixties generation, the styles of narrative, the contextualization of losing religion, the ideological frameworks and the identified triggers to loss tend each to differ in frequency of occurrence.

Exploration of the linkage between loss of religion and masculinity is novel. Scholars have explored the history of secularist movements, small in numbers and comprising mostly men, which emerged from eighteenth-century rationalism and peaked in their impact in the Victorian and Edwardian periods.[1] Admittedly, Victorian religionists were preoccupied with the lapsing of men from religious practice, and considerable energy was expended on ways to reclaim to observance the careless, the lapsed and the 'home heathens', largely by tackling the diverting temptations of drink, gambling and womanizing.[2] But permanent desertion of Christianity has rarely been studied. Religious historians have until recent times tended to assume the impermanence of religious disaffection.[3] Nor has the distinctively gendered nature of the *losing* of religion been the focus of historical research. However, studies of masculinity have looked at important characteristics and emotions which could help understand the way men narrate transiting from religiosity to no religionism. At the forefront of this analysis, reason, rationality, science, reading and education have been commonly recognized as a group of related features in men's narratives. Psychological studies of masculinity point to its fragility in Western societies, signalled by a suggestion of a 'breakdown in rationality' in which, in recent decades, a rising willingness to express emotions, followed by gradual articulation of an apparently non-rational position, has led to a blending of emotional and rational selves. This trend in psychology reveals an apparently deeply engrained assumption that a man's embrace of rationality is a necessary bulwark to masculinity, and that a loss of this tempts crisis in the sense of manhood.[4] Indeed, academics analysing both contemporary and historical culture seem to associate a linkage between men with reason and rationality as a normative state. Critical scholars from various backgrounds have taken issue with the implicit acceptance of the relationship between rationality and masculinity, and the paucity of wider gendered approaches to reason.[5] However, a feminist scholar some twenty years ago noted how, in a non-Western postcolonial Pakistani context, modernist rationalism and science shared with religious fundamentalism 'an extremist, masculine, lopsided view of human nature' – a critique of religious criticism that might not be wholly alien in the West.[6] Indeed, Tim Whitmarsh has recently observed how the original Ancient Greek imagining of the *atheos*, the atheist, may have been as 'a powerful, masculine vanquisher of the gods'.[7] This may have instigated a very long heritage associating atheism with masculine power, though, in historical studies, the links with rationality have rarely been scrutinized critically.[8] Rather tentatively, Connell has suggested that the equivalence of masculinity with rationality is not always a 'given' in modern society, being challenged in the workplace and elsewhere; he notes the variations between working- and middle-class conceptions of rationality.[9] But analysis of the cultural construction of masculinity has been underdeveloped, leaving a gap in academic thinking about the link between gendered versions of rationality and losing religion.[10] The present project does not have the space to systematically develop these themes, but it does throw up some suggestive findings.

Losing religion in the West since 1960 has had very different consequences for a man than it has had for a woman. Nothing like the new autonomous self of the Western woman has emerged for men – no comprehensive remodelling of the working and sexual life, and of self-identity accompanied by the angst, uncertainty and familial distress felt by many women. Compared to the way femininity has been remade, masculinity has been merely modified but is largely unscathed. True, there have been consequences for men's relationships with women, and the demographic impacts upon women have had repercussions upon the work–life balance for men (in regard to shared child-rearing and cultural change). But the narratives of lives lived in the West in the past sixty years are highly gendered, and this has been as evident in this project as in oral history archives. Women talked engagingly about the relationship between their careers and family experiences as a lived as much as an ideological feminism, accompanied in very many cases by growing alienation from church, faith and god. Broadly, the men I interviewed did not have an equivalent family-based, career-changing story to tell.

This has immediate consequences in distinguishing male from female oral history. Male narratives contain distinctive absences and silences: the absence of conflict over gender roles, the lower intensity of self-doubt and, characteristically, silence on the linkage between family and a new religion-free identity. In the testimony that follows, we will rarely find the sinewy familial scuffle as a new religion-free identity emerges, or an equivalent to the woman's wrestling with a disappearing conventional femininity. In their life stories, men don't talk about their families as much, or worry over how to handle relationships, or bring up the bearing of religion upon these. They don't see the question of religion wrapped up with a larger self; it is packaged as a neater issue of reflection, reason and function. They have different objects of focus, seemingly more straightforward and perhaps predictable, and the traumas they experience tend to have been – certainly in the second half of the twentieth century – rather different from women's. And perhaps most strikingly, if women of the mid-twentieth century lacked a template for how to talk about losing religion, this was a rarer problem for men, who had access to a well-rehearsed storyline of male atheism.

Even if the Greek model is long forgotten in modern public culture, the very nature of atheism and humanism has a heritage of being considered masculine and a man's domain. Alicja Stettin, a respondent from Toronto, explained how a surprising distinction between the two channelled her intellectual and religious views: 'I think I'm probably more of an atheist than a humanist. It seems the humanist movement is very taken over by men, you know, I don't like that part of it. So I think I'm more an atheist than a humanist most likely ... And of the history about humanism that I've read, you know, it's not very partial to women.'[11] As I entered meetings of humanist, secularist and atheist organizations in Britain, the United States and Canada, the dominance of men was quite marked across the board, and offers something of a contrast to Christian congregations, which are dominated by women.[12] Men's role in philosophy, then in nineteenth-century secularist and atheistical organizations, belonged to a wider male culture of social mobilization in intellectual confrontation, public-speaking and debate.[13] This tradition lingers. Though women were counted amongst national leaders of secularism and atheism in both the nineteenth and twentieth centuries,[14] the patriarchal ethos of organized secularism remains, and this is manifest in the narratives of male loss of religion.

Reason – the male prerogative?

Men place the power of reason and intellect central to their accounts of their journey from faith. They discuss in depth the roles of their mind, their education and scientific-based learning in transiting from religion to no religion. Many talk about mental anguish and inner turmoil experienced during escape from theology or religious irrationality, or social suffering during escape from communities rendered dysfunctional by theocracy or sectarianism. Male narratives focus upon a reconstruction of the mind,

Table 6.1 The natural world in oral history narratives

Rank order of terms	No. of cases	No. of cases by men
Earth	32	16
Planet(s)/planetary/planetarium	24	24
Universe*	21	18
Moon	15	15
Stars*	11	11
Sky	10	8
Cosmos	5	5
Pale blue dot/spot**	2	2

Note: The interviewer's usage is discounted. Excludes written testimony.
*In astronomical or natural world sense.
**A term of astronomer Carl Sagan, variously remembered.

where they tell of personal struggles against unreason and injustice. But much less than for a woman, it rarely changed their whole being – their lifestyle, occupational destiny, parenthood decisions or decisions on breaking relationships. Their de-conversion is a story told as if it was an account of a task they had to complete – a project within their lives.

Science and the natural world are two touchstones in many male narratives. Table 6.1 shows a list of terms and their frequency of occurrence in the aggregated interview testimonies for this project. Some of these are fleeting references, and some are metaphorical rather than scientific, but the usage is dominated by men: of the 119 references checked for gender usage, 98 (or 82 per cent) were made by men (when men only comprised 62 per cent of the interviewees). Likewise, the language of science and analysis features prominently in my conversations with male interviewees – the words 'science', 'scientific' and 'scientifically' featured 319 times in the testimony, 'world' 422 times, 'evidence' 53 times.

Some men made lengthy reference to science in their answers, talking especially of recent advances. Harish Mehra from Birmingham, England, a graduate in science, told me, 'We have sent the Apollo [spacecraft] to moon and beyond, now to Mars, and then informed there are so many stars, millions and millions of them, so where does that so-called God live, where is it?'[15] Allusions to the sky and the stars dotted testimony. But for a few respondents, they constructed comprehensive explanations of loss of religion based on their experience of the natural universe. One who did this was Robin Russell, who we encountered in Chapter 3, where he described his loss of god at the age of 12 as 'a purely, as I recall it, intellectual decision', but one informed by the sense of awe he felt on looking at the stars and galaxies visible in the Saskatchewan night sky.[16] Here there is a linkage between reason and emotion. In descriptions of the power of the cosmos and stars to induce a rationality that overcomes religion, there is also citation of emotion – sometimes of 'awe' and 'beauty' (terms which appeared in the aggregated testimony seven and nine times, respectively), but more often implicitly in the narration. As we noted in the previous chapter, spirituality also appears in relation to the natural world.

The power of reason to dislodge religion came faster for the younger men I interviewed. Khalid Sohail, born in Pakistan in 1952 but now resident in Canada, spoke of how he started science classes in his early teens: 'I experienced a conflict between teachings of religion based on divine revelations and logical thinking of science.' But then he went into years of conflict between his studies in psychiatric medicine and those in the Quran, for a period becoming what he described as a fundamentalist before becoming an atheist in his twenties.[17] For an older respondent like David Fowler, born in 1947, the infusion of reason was slow. Having experienced what he regarded as abuse in a fundamentalist Sunday school, then attending a more liberal school until 13 and later being a poor attender for a number of years, he started to attend confirmation classes (in what became the United Church of Canada) when he was 17 years old. It is here that he recalled his first rational doubts as developing. The minister taking the confirmation class was the first to instigate uncertainty, asserting that access to heaven was only via acceptance of Jesus Christ: 'That's the first time I questioned it. I didn't question it seriously because he was an authoritarian figure to me, but I thought to myself, can that be true?'[18] (David kept going to church for some years, in large part to meet girls; indeed, it was in church service that he met his wife at the age of 18.) In the West Midlands of England, John Edwards, a year older than David, had been a member of the British Antarctic Survey, becoming an expert on the limited flora of the continent. His study at home was covered in posters and materials relating to this, and his testimony was clear. His route from faith was slow, a transition that was underway from the Baptist church during his teens and years at university, but in his fifties, after approaching a leading British humanist, he adopted that term for himself.[19] From Copenhagen in Denmark, Kai Kristensen, born in 1933, explained how his scientific mentor also guided him to humanism. In his youth, Kai was influenced by a fundamentalist paternal grandfather, by a general Sunday school upbringing and by a mother who became more conservative in her Christianity as she got older. But emigrating in 1948 with his parents to the United States, he entered CalTech at about the age of 18 and fell under the influence of the leading chemist and humanist Linus Pauling. In a lengthy exposition to me on science, Kai cited this as the background to him losing religion:

I also totally discarded my old religion because it just didn't make any sense and I remember my reaction when we had a lecture from an emeritus Nobel Prize winner physicist who invoked religion, and I thought, 'he has got a wall down his brain'. Now, my mother was, I never told her because she didn't want to hear anything nasty, she didn't want to hear anything but good, and if you couldn't say something good then you don't say anything, that was kind of her philosophy.

As a result of Pauling's example, Kai decided to study medicine and went on to become a pathologist, but he became more estranged from his mother.[20] He said, 'It was the rationality of science that basically excluded religion without me specifically reading much in the way of philosophy until I sort of retired and had more time to read then. But I found out that reading philosophy is --- I get exasperated with the argumentation [laughs], it's obvious.'[21] A similar lengthy transition took place for Alex Colias, born in Michigan in an evangelical household, who was an active Christian into his twenties when his doubts started, but then were sustained in what became a decades-long shift towards humanism. He recounts it as not triggered by science but 'my own process of doubt in the faith I believed in', and 'strictly an internal matter, so much more on the reflection side'.[22] Here, it is a lifelong process of drift through an unarticulated atheism fostered by science for some, for others by personal intellectual advancement.

Younger respondents narrate much quicker resolution of their doubt, with scientists and engineers displaying quite precise, articulate and categorical scientific foundations for their atheism. One such was Justin Trottier from Quebec, born in 1982, who studied astronomy at the University of Toronto; as a student, he became involved in removing religious ritual from graduation ceremonies. Was it scientific proof and conception of the world, the universe, which has driven him to a quite considered view of being a non-religious world?

> Yeah, I think, you know, the methodology of science to me is the most important thing. It's not really just the facts but more the way you approach knowledge, and I think that it is a beautiful system which doesn't always work, as it is used by people. But the idea of evidence, falsification, fallibility among other things, accountability, that's the best system we have developed. It's similar to the system that informs our political democracies in fact. That's one thing I find people don't really, really appreciate is the connection between the scientific method and the democratic method, so to me that's at the root of a lot of the knowledge we have obtained. And I think that's beautiful, and that's what I am committed to educating people about.[23]

This was the same expression of beauty with atheism as from older scientists, but in the context of the late twentieth century with a much faster transition from the world of religion.

One characteristic of some respondents was to narrate a cross-over between thinking theologically and thinking rationally about the route from faith to unbelief. It was not always the case that reason was in a straight contest over a blind faith, but that doubt arises within the theology, and it is there that reason is applied, internally if you will, to the problems of belief. Terry Martin was educated in a Dominican school, where ordinary teaching was conducted by nuns who gave a daily faith diet: 'the theology was there in a very simple basic sense of piety and telling the children how to behave and, you know, the catechism and so on'. But the Dominicans were 'educated, highly articulate priests and they were also English priests to a great extent, they were not Irish priests', and they came to the school on weekly visits. They provided an intensely intellectual perspective, one which nurtured Terry and left a lasting impression, so that despite his loss of religion and belief at the age of 15 he has kept in touch with members of the order; he notes that 'the Dominican concept of heaven that you go to in the afterlife is a wonderful eternal seminar that the Dominican order is focussed on'. Terry's intellectual development began in arguing about the existence of god and sin, but the nuns would have none of it and he was belted (corporal punishment). But one particular priest monk, a history teacher, would sometimes have what he described as 'gentle' conversation with him: 'He once said to me: "Terry," he said "I want you to think about this. There is no God and Mary is His mother."' This comment just before he left school stuck with Terry, and years later, with reading Wittgenstein, 'it clicked what he was getting at, but the fact that he seemed to focus on me for that was perhaps a little bit of respect or intuition about how I would eventually develop'.[24] This was an important encouragement to Terry in intellectual endeavour, one drawing him away from theological thinking to philosophical and secular thought.

In the following case, the impetus to bringing the individual out from faith was a religious book. Frank O'Hara was born in 1926 in a strongly Catholic family in Ontario. He reports of his teenage years: 'I was a very faithful altar boy. For I guess some years I went to mass pretty well every day, like seven days a week. And also on the weekends we'd go to Benediction in the evening cause I was serving on the altar most of the time. And so unquestioning.' In his later teens he was questioning some things, but not seriously. After naval service, he went jointly to a Catholic college and to the University of Toronto, and happened to take three courses on psychology, two at the Catholic college and one at the university, and taught with conflicting content at each institution. This 'really got me thinking about some things' though he 'was still thoroughly indoctrinated'. After marriage to a nominal Lutheran, his three children were baptized at his mother's insistence, but reading voraciously in the early 1950s turned him from being a Catholic to being 'nothing', with an intellectual fascination for Buddhism and 'the

idea that you could have a religion without a god'. 'I was very conscious
of the fact that I was breaking away from everything that I had been raised
to believe.'[25] Becoming a humanist in his later decades, Frank exemplifies
being launched on a route from faith not by reason or science as by religious
history rooted in theology.

This can be taken a step further. There are limits to the role of reason
in the narratives of male losers of religion. A few of my respondents had
a very intense religious faith. Tim Unsworth, born 1954 in Bolton in
Lancashire and educated at a boarding school in Carlisle, had a deep faith
for the first three decades of his life, though he only briefly considered
entering the priesthood. 'I would say I had a relationship with God, I
spoke to God, yes. It was, it was something that really I didn't question.'
He lived in a Catholic hall of residence at the University of Manchester,
and, looking back, Tim sees himself as highly institutionalized, both at
university and at church – when he moved to London, he went to Mass
seven days a week. God intruded into his every decision in life; in opening
an envelope which might tell him of gaining a new job, he felt, ' "Thy will
be done Lord." I remember this feeling as I opened this envelope you know,
"Thy will be done." Yea, very, very religious. A true believer.' The hints of
religious change came for Tim during preparation for his wedding at age
29, but he remained a Catholic in marriage and had two children. It was
on the eve of the baptism of his second child, when large numbers of his
family were travelling long distances to attend, that he had a crisis of faith.
After that he moved gradually but decisively to become 'obsessively' and
'intensely' atheistic. He recalls only one further major turning point: when
a conversation with a religious friend led him to drop the idea of angels
and the devil. 'So I think my approach to atheism was the realisation of the
implausibility of spirits, I think. So I still had the idea of God the creator,
I couldn't give up that, but I eventually got rid of that. I suppose I don't
remember doing a great deal of soul searching on the subject.' He describes
himself as gradually leaving 'the religious framework', and discovering
that 'other people aren't talking about it': 'I think it's a gradual thing,
realisation that actually most people aren't all that bothered. You know
the business of adult life, you know getting married, buying houses, house
insurance etc., etc., mortgages, all the paraphernalia, it's just that actually
religion isn't an element to it.' Tim's was not a damascene moment of de-
conversion. 'When did I become a full blown atheist? I don't remember
ever thinking, "Good heavens I am an atheist!" It was very gradual, it was
definitely gradual.'[26]

So, secular reason is not always the foundation for male narratives of
losing religion. Sometimes, it is highly charged emotional anguish, partly
conducted within the thinking of faith. There is a step for those who
experience intense religious feeling to tackle within their faith, before
contemplating the wider reasoning or reading of a secular, scientific

discourse. One group, one might speculate, that felt the intensity of religious thought would be those in the ministry who contemplated leaving their faith for a life without god.

Leaving the priesthood

I interviewed nine men who were Christian clergy or training for the ministry when they abandoned their church and, in most cases, their faith entirely. Religious doubt has long been claimed as one of the characteristics of being a Christian clergyman. Victorian clerical biography and autobiography made the doubts of pious men the very central feature of the clerical life, with the struggles invariably overcome – sometimes repeatedly – to make the minister and priest closer to understanding the struggles of others.[27] But as Timothy Larsen has shown, some Victorian doubters were prone to returning to faith.[28] Indeed, leaving was a comparatively rare phenomenon, and seems to have remained so until the mid-twentieth century. It is at that juncture that doubts turned into permanent abandonment of church and faith with much greater demographic frequency.

David Lambourn's journey from belief in any supernatural being started from within the Anglican priesthood. In the mid-1960s he became priest in charge of a London parish where, though his work with young people was well regarded, he encountered opposition from parents to the liberal way he framed the Christian training of their children. As David reported, 'this tension just got too much for me, and eventually, one day, I simply walked out of the Mass and drove to a Thames-side pub and I don't know what happened in the church, but this, it was this tension, I just couldn't cope with it'.[29] Matters grew worse, with his radical views instigating a massive personal crisis for David, involving loss of his parish, his respect for the church and much of his faith, as well as schism from his family. He eventually resigned in 1970, and found himself being ecclesiastically ostracized. This slow estrangement from the Anglican Church led him into more secular youth work and to university research into teaching. Stressing throughout his narrative the need for 'coherence', David described his faith position:

I have no problem about the religion of science; for all my life it has never seemed to me to be an issue about religion and science, there might be a Church and science problem, but not a faith and science problem. I am entirely comfortable with that. I have no belief in any supernatural being; my understanding of the Old Testament's stories, I'm entirely comfortable with that as well, it seems to me that if I were not a Christian I would certainly be a Jew, by choice, because I think I understand the way, in their history, that they developed.[30]

Eschewing the label 'Christian', David said this of Christ: 'But I see him as a friend and colleague so to speak, not as a god, so I'm not a member of the church for this reason, because that's a requirement. I would love to have known him [chuckling].'[31] For some observers, especially those who may have lost their religion more concretely and resolutely, David Lambourn represents in some ways an ambiguous stance on religion and faith. He became associated in the 1990s with the Sea of Faith network (SOFN) inspired by Don Cupitt, and holds discussion meetings with humanists as well as those within the 'Sea' movement; in 2013 he was the membership secretary of SOFN.[32] But the ambiguity is centred in a 'doubt' which is seen by Sea of Faith and others as central to a new theologically liberal position on religion outside of the churches.

This permanency of doubt is the basis of a religious-humanist position. A slightly different narrative, but with some similarity of character regarding doubt, came from Bill Kennedy in Ontario, who spent fifteen years in the Jesuits, starting training at the age of 17 and leaving at the age of 32. He had been thinking about what he described as 'the colour of life' since he was a little boy, the youngest in a family of eight, but when I suggested to him that he left his change of mind until quite late, he only responded, 'I'm a slow eater, a slow talker and I guess I'm a slow learner.' It was after coming out of the Jesuits that his loss of religion crystallized. The Jesuits had cultivated his taste for hard thinking, and he found ordinary parish sermons 'boring un-intellectual pap'. It was this that led to him losing interest in going to church.

> I didn't have any reasoning toward silliness or superstition or any of the stuff that I hear coming from other humanists who have come to humanism in a different way. I simply lost my taste for the Catholic thing. Some of them will say I decided at age 12 that this was all nonsense, I reasoned my way through it [laughs]. I didn't.

After leaving, he was led more strongly to what he saw as his first love – philosophy – and commenced study for a master's degree and a doctorate on Descartes.[33] This was a period when he didn't belong to anything, but was consumed by intellectual learning. One of the reasons he gave for leaving the church shortly after he quit training was 'unintellectual sermons'; he wanted better 'conversation companions', studied philosophy and psychoanalytic theory, and found in these deep resonance with an absence of religion and a humanist outlook. He told me,

> So my trip from altar boy to humanist --- Calling myself an atheist doesn't matter. I don't care if I'm an atheist or not, it isn't important. To simply stop thinking about something up there and an afterlife isn't important. I mean it doesn't matter if it's named, that's what I'm trying to say. So the trip is not very religious. And as I look back on that, I think maybe I wanted to please

and connect rather than worship. Even as a Jesuit what engaged me was the intellectual challenges. And even though I did all the ritual meditation and masses and things that they do, I prayed but I never heard an answer. And as I look back on it I think it doesn't matter. It was just something I was trying.[34]

His was an intensely intellectual and hugely prolonged process – his trip from altar boy to humanist, as he put it. The intellectual issue of atheism was unresolvable, leaving a doubt, but one that could be laid aside. For Bill, the humanism was paramount.

If doubt lay at the heart of David Fowler's and Bill Kennedy's accounts, for others doubt in the sense of an intellectual reasoning was a major instigator for losing religion and discarding doubt. Conrad Hadland was Presiding Minister in the Jehovah's Witnesses in the remote north of British Columbia. After seven years leading a congregation, he had doubts: 'I wasn't believing in what I was doing anymore, I didn't feel. I felt uncomfortable.' He initially thought he wanted out. But though by now married, he was concerned because all his friends were Jehovah's Witnesses; a social isolation beckoned if he left, especially given that he would be subjected to 'shunning'. So, he decided to 'get my faith back' by becoming a missionary to South America. In the public library he happened upon Will and Ariel Durant's history series, *The Story of Civilisation*, and in one of his books, *Caesar and Christ*, Conrad reported thus:

> I remember looking up that book and going to the chapter called Christ, and it started off 'Did Christ exist or did Christ exist?' Five or six pages afterwards he probably did, but you did pro and con reasons for thinking that which struck me as an interesting way to look at things, to look for the pro and con of things.

The novelty of this form of dialectical argument started him off. Then, he was lent a psychology textbook by a friend, and this furthered his interest in knowledge and science. Next, on his door-to-door work, he met a man who argued with him over a cup of coffee, developing further his interest in intellectual dispute. He then befriended a Pentecostal minister, and each met in a kindly way, trying to show the other the error of his ways. In the midst of this, Conrad read another book – William Sargant's *Battle for the Mind*, which discussed brainwashing and mind control, and this fascinated him.[35] Still unsettled, he and his wife signed up to become missionaries in Bolivia, but, whilst waiting in Burnaby to fly out, he took three evening classes which further developed his reasoning and curious mind. Out in Bolivia, he read more books from a library and became more aware of public affairs through reading *Time* magazine. This was his trigger point: he was asked to deliver a reading from 2 Samuel 28, where it was said that God sent a pestilence to kill 80,000 Israelites.

And that blew my mind. All of a sudden the whole house of cards came crashing down because, you know it was just waiting for something like that to trip me over. And I thought: 'I couldn't believe in a God like that, I couldn't worship, I couldn't honour, you know the, that was, that was *evil* you know, it was not right.'

This plunged him into hours of distress, where, caught in limbo in Bolivia, he recalled three articles he had previously read in a book in Vancouver – articles by Bertrand Russell, one on the Unitarians and one by a humanist. This was the tipping point: 'And then I decided I am going to get out of here.' In haste, he and his wife travelled on a lengthy bus trip through South, Central and North America, arriving in Vancouver, where he looked in the phone book for a Unitarian church. 'So the first Sunday we were back we went down to the Unitarian Church of Vancouver, and I didn't understand half of what the minister was saying but it sounded incredibly interesting and fascinating and that's how my soldiering with the Unitarians started.'[36] And he became first a Unitarian minister, then an organizer of BC Humanists. Conrad's narrative is lengthy, detailed and a travelogue through the Americas – a spiritual journey in a geographical dimension. His account places rationality and evidence at the heart of the change. Having discarded one religion, he became fanatical for evidence to guide him: 'I am interested in where I came from, what I am here for, where I am going and I want evidence, for as much evidence as I can for those beliefs.' He also became focussed on his own potential, especially for argument and debate, which he finds enthralling. He calls himself atheist: 'I am not trying to make an issue out of it, but I just feel it's a waste of time believing nonsense basically. Life is too short for me and I am somewhat blunt to people.'[37]

If Conrad had a moment of clarity instigating immediate departure from clerical office, Art Mielke's journey from faith to agnosticism was one of the most circuitous I encountered. The son of an American Presbyterianism minister, from the mid-1960s he was on a track to join him in clerical bands despite absorbing 'uncomfortable' lessons from philosophy class at college – which he described as 'a huge part of the formation of "me" and my life at the time and intellectually, emotionally, in terms of dealing with authority figures'. Despite or even because of such questioning, he continued on to Yale Divinity School, where, amongst other studies over three years, he trained as a psychiatric hospital chaplain and as an intern pastor in Plattsburg. He was still moving towards Presbyterian ordination, but a short and confused spell as a theology student at Oxford University set him on a different tack. He joined first the merchant navy on the Great Lakes and then became a truck driver – an occupation he undertook off and on for the next twenty-five years. This was something that exhilarated him for its opening of a door onto working-class work experience. He commented, 'I probably still thought of myself as an elitist, but [one] who was kind of wearing camouflage.' But in the midst of decades on the trucks, he undertook a doctorate – on Christians, feminists and the culture of pornography. In this long journey from his teens to his fifties, his faith shifted, but in ways perhaps only really evident in retrospect. One point he remembers was at age 28, when, after assisting his father in worship with an Old Testament reading, a family member asked him if he believed 'that stuff', to which he recalls pausing and replying 'No'. This was 'no crisis faith or dark night of the soul', Art explains, it was just an offhand question that prompted him to reflect for a moment and to realize he didn't take the Bible literally. He had already 'worked through' fear of God's punishment, his training in psychiatric hospital and in psychology giving him insight into his emotions. He describes the journey: 'So, somewhere on the other side of that, this kind of wearing away of my Christian identity was happening, but I've never really sat and tried to plot the stages on the way.' In later years, having quit the church and joined the Freedom from Religion Foundation, he took to study of Christianity and psychotherapy, taught clinical psychology subjects, but still entered religious debate by taking work leave to engage with theologians. Describing himself as 'a cultural Christian' and agnostic, he presents paradoxes of pigeonholing. 'The stuff has been sort of slow, and what has built over time is that kind of fiendish pleasure in reading the work of the New Atheists, and I'm getting way too much satisfaction out of that stuff.' But he also seems to enjoy divinity schools: 'So the theme is still there, the ideas, but I don't describe myself as a religious person – at all.'[38]

The last example presents a different context again. Dick Hewetson was born in Chicago but brought up from the age of 7 in Minneapolis, and found himself on an inexorable track through Episcopal school and seminary to the priesthood despite entertaining suppressed doubts about faith. His religious doubt united with concerns about his sexuality, producing a feisty combination of anguish:

> All through seminary I had a really tough time because an awful lot of it didn't make a lot of sense to me. But by this time, you know, I had realised that most people in this country were Christians and all that kinda thing, and there was something wrong with me if I wasn't getting it. So I tried really hard and I prayed and, you know, they told me it's okay to doubt, and that's very healthy and all this stuff. So I went through the whole process, became a priest, served churches in small communities in Minnesota and Wisconsin, and in 1967 I had one of my terrible depression episodes and the bishop sent me to a psychiatrist and I told the psychiatrist that I was quite sure I was homosexual, and that was bothering me. And he convinced me that I wasn't [laughs].[39]

After intense worry over many years about faith and sexuality, eventually in the early 1970s Dick left the priesthood and came out as a gay man. Even then, reconstructing his life took a period of time, and eventually led him to relocate to San Francisco. In the process, his emergence as an atheist became a key component of his identity with family and friends, and his attendance at atheist conferences and events contributed a special measure of intellectual verve and campaigning action.

Reading

The power of reason amongst children from the age of 7 years onwards is quite impressive from testimony. By the age of 16 and 17 years, many young atheists had found 'advanced' reading in school or public libraries. Robin Wood from Worthing in Sussex was 17 in 1958, when, after two years of drifting around evangelical organizations like the Crusaders' Union, he was drawn by the lure of girls in dancing classes and for cinema-going on Sundays rather than going to religious services. But at the same time, he found new arguments. First, at the age of 16 his dad lent him Winwood Reade's *The Martyrdom of Man* (1872), which made a deep impression on him as an alternative narrative of human society and evolution. And then, perhaps a year later, somebody in the school library put him on to Friedrich Nietzsche. And what so impressed him was that the story he was being told in the Crusaders, the Scripture Union and school RE lessons was being contradicted by an alternative point of view from books – the books impressing as a powerful reasoning and evidential base.[40]

The power of books is testified to by many male respondents. At the age of 28 in the late 1950s, Frank Brown attended an 'eye-opener' of a university course on religion where he first encountered Bertrand Russell, Carlos Castaneda, Descartes, Spinoza, Tillich and many others, and, after coming to humanism in his late forties, reported reading as a key element. At the interview, he supplied me with a typed-up bibliography of the twenty most significant humanist books in his life.[41] Ian Caughlan's journey as a young man from faith to humanism in the 2010s involved reading Descartes and philosophy, a classic journey: 'I went from this kind of agnostic, questioning kind of phase into a really existentialist phase. I really brooded on absurdity and the meaninglessness of a world without God. It was a big loss, God had been a very big part of my life. And I felt a gap there, a hole. So it was a big deal.'[42] Larry Hicok, brought up in Oregon in the 1950s and 1960s, had emerged at age 12 as an atheist in a contest over prayers at school, and, rather shunned by his schoolmates for this, became in his own words a bookworm, and not emerging socially until after high school graduation and going onto college.[43] Anders Östberg attributed reading from 10–11 years of age with developing his settled atheism by the age of 15 years. On coming to Scotland and discovering a society with stronger residual religious influence in various aspects of life, he found that reading in Richard Dawkins and others helped to make him what he calls 'a much more active atheist' – joining a humanist organization, campaigning on atheist issues and becoming in the late 2000s chairman of the Humanist Society of Scotland.[44]

Conrad Hadland told me in Vancouver, 'I know a lot of very decent and very smart bright people disagree with me and you know that for sure, but that's life. So I am probably more, more a Dawkins kind of believer in many ways, you know, and to some extent I think Dawkins has given me the courage to be more forthright in my statements.'[45] This is a common way in which the leading print authors of atheism and humanism are referred to by my respondents. Books affirm people, and in particular men, in their avowal of atheism, giving arguments, examples and courage to express themselves. Many of my respondents did not fully agree with the tenor of Dawkins' style, but they found in him a scientist leader who inspired them. A few other writers did likewise. Paul Bulmer recalled his transition to affirmed atheism developing in middle age through reading A.C. Grayling's column in *The Guardian* newspaper: 'every time I read it, I just thought that guy is speaking with, you know, with my mind'. From this, Paul became a voracious reader of Bertrand Russell, Richard Dawkins, Christopher Hitchens and Sam Harris.[46] These authors are cited by a majority of male respondents, and, significantly, by a greater proportion than women. They find the reading exhilarating, full of a certainty that gives explanation for their own positions. They also find some of the reading very difficult. One respondent found Steve Jones hard, commenting, 'well, God's sake, that is so complex'.[47] There appears to be a need for some men to encounter intellectual struggle in their loss of religion, but an encounter from which they emerge convinced of the rightness of their journey.

Peter Barton described with vigour and detail his intensive and long-term religious 'seeking' through wide-ranging reading. He left boarding school an atheist (and endured the anger of his father in the mid-1930s for proclaiming his position), but on return from war service in India and Burma, he married a woman whose parents were strongly committed Theosophists. As a first-year medical student, religion intimidated and intrigued, and he embarked on a ten-year quest to ascertain 'whether there *could* be a GOD as the creator of the universe, who was also as claimed (at least by the Anglican Church) to be a *loving* God'. This search led him in the 1950s through encounters with his local Baptist church, and a succession of Eastern 'gurus' – in order, Gudjieff, Muhammad Subuh Sumohadiwidjojo (the Subud movement), Maharishi Mahesh Yogi and Sant Thakar Singh. This ended with reading philosophical literature, starting with Socrates and Plato, and resulted in him emerging at the age of 40 'a convinced atheist, on the grounds that no believers or cults could provide any *evidence* in support of their claims'. From there to the age of 88 he remained interested in scientific explanations as to why humans invent religions, but dismayed at 'apparently otherwise, intelligent people' converting to religion: 'In this respect I count myself to be placebo deficient!'[48] This interest in religions was presented by men as mostly a learned searching but, like Barton, might involve New Age seeking. So it was also for Martin Vallik in Estonia, who noted a surge of interest in Buddhism and Eastern religions in Tallinn after the fall of communism in 1991 – despite Estonia having the lowest level of god-belief in the world.[49]

Reading features almost uniformly in the account of men losing religion. Reading is reported often as instrumental in furthering a move from religion that is already under way by offering an intellectual articulation of an existing doubt or feeling. Sometimes, other people perceived that a respondent had become atheist before the respondent knew where their scepticism might be heading. In the mid-twentieth century, the available readings for rationalists were considerably less accessible and numerous than they were to become with New Atheism in the early twenty-first century. In mid-century, apart from the philosophers (Bertrand Russell and A.J. Ayer were the most prominent) and the less well-known works of some humanists (such as Margaret Knight), the most famous writings were those of Joseph McCabe (1867–1955), an Englishman who left the Catholic priesthood at the age of 29 to become the most prolific publicist for rationalism, writing hundreds of books.[50] In the mid-1960s in his early teens, Alistair McBay recalled that the minister who took religious education classes at his school found it difficult to handle the questions from the class and became quite upset. One day, Alistair told me,

> I got a call at the school and [he] said, 'McBay come here, I've got something for you', and it was a little blue book by a man called Joseph McCabe. And he said, 'You might---with your attitude', or 'With your leanings, or something, you might enjoy this,' and I've still got, not that original copy but I've got some of McCabe's stuff now, and I thought looking back at that now, that was quite interesting that he did that.

Though it was to take some years before Alistair became a debater, controversialist and eventually vice president for the National Secular Society, he said that 'once I started reading McCabe and then getting into some other things, then the die was cast'.[51]

Reading invariably led some men to joining organizations. Ken Matthews, for example, described how once he had taken to reading Dawkins, Hitchens and others, he joined the Royal Philosophical Society of Glasgow (RPSG), 'where I really became, I then became an atheist. I just did: I [asked] why am I hanging on to this? Because it is a fear'. Meetings at the RPSG opened up a series of philosophical and scientific affirmations of a world without a god.[52]

Deserting dysfunction

Some narrators rationalize their loss of faith by their recoil from religious bigotry and sectarianism. This frequently starts with discussing their upbringing in a culture of youth organizations which were segregated in their structure. Those respondents raised in Northern Ireland, to a person, refer to the sectarian divide as the landscape upon which faith was first moulded and then broken, and each had to escape the province for their journey towards atheism and humanism. But dysfunction extended further.

Kathleen Dillon was raised in a Presbyterian family in Belfast in the 1930s and 1940s, but though her father was a religious believer and she went to church occasionally, she described her upbringing as not overtly religious: 'if somebody asked me you know, what are you, I would have said Presbyterian, but I never went to church, which is typical of Northern Ireland'. But her family knew no Catholics other than a cleaning woman, and all her friends were Protestants, and it was only after emigrating with a woman friend to Canada in 1958 that she left a religiously defined community.[53] Likewise, in Northern Ireland James Machin was raised in a family with only modest religious habits, but he felt the social divisions acutely: 'it was very separate, you know, so it was like an apartheid. Sure we had the people working but you never socialised, all the socialising was with our different Protestant people'.[54] Ivan Middleton and his wife decided to leave Northern Ireland in 1969, when, on his first appointment as a newly qualified social worker, his new boss 'had me into his office and closed the door and said: "That's great," he said, "You are a protestant....There is twelve of us and there is only eleven of them".'[55] This was the cue for the couple leaving the province for Scotland, and for Ivan to become later in the century the leader of the humanist movement there. But Northern Ireland's divide had its shadow in Scotland as a result of large-scale immigration in the nineteenth century. Glasgow was sharply divided between Protestants and Catholics, and Kenneth Matthews recalled that 'if you are brought up in Glasgow, if you are a Jew you are a Protestant Jew or a Catholic Jew, there is no sitting on the fence Jews and --- Yes there was always sectarianism'. He grew up submerged in the popular Protestant culture – going every 12th of July to see the Orange Order Walk, as well as to Sunday school and Boys' Brigade. He noted wryly that 'we had, as everybody in the West of Scotland has, a religion no matter whether you have no religion'.[56]

The level of social dysfunctionality generated by religion varies by culture and country. Rationalists and atheists from India pinpoint the caste system as a product of religion. Harish Mehra commented about Hindus in England:

[O]ur people, they have only wasted their time worshipping something that doesn't exist, and they have wasted so much time. And the cultural bit, most of the cultural values, they are based on superstition and by the religious people. I strongly believe that the cultural values actually are guided by the religious ethics of any country. For example, in Hinduism the caste system is dividing people and is more harmful than the racism in the Western world. And that is dictated by the religious scriptures, so the values of the society are dictated by the religions, either its Christianity or its Islam or Hinduism or Sikhism, and those religions actually are dividing people and that's why I shun them, I don't need them.

Though he says that the caste system has not had a direct impact on the rationalist movement at all, it is the case that 'the majority of the people who have joined the rationalist movement in this country and also back in India, they come from the so called lower caste'. This is because what he calls 'the rationalist people' are much more active in promoting and seeking human rights – for women, the disabled and concerning sexual orientation. He concluded that the caste system 'is a cancer to the society, it is worse than racism, and the religion actually has dictated that'.[57]

Khushi Ram spoke to me eloquently and passionately about Indian Partition in 1947: 'I have seen the Partition, even before Partition, the communal riots between the Hindus and Muslims especially. Too bad, just sheer madness.' Khushi noted the way in which people's names revealed their religion, and how in the subcontinent it is impossible to hold a name like Mohammad and *not* be a Muslim, or Ram and *not* be a Hindu. But Khushi went further to note also how religions stratified society – Hinduism being the essential underpinning to the caste system which he so deplored. 'Nobody can live without religion', he says, because of this naming and positioning in society. For 'almost 99.9% of people', he goes on, 'some sort of religion has to be there for them, at least for their what is called crucial stages of their life'. For births, marriages and funerals, and for the bad things in life, he says, 'we try to catch on to something and God is the handy thing you know, then even when we cry we say, "Oh God!", like that, or when we are happy then we would like to thank somebody who has turned all things nice to us'. He notes that in times of crisis, the value of a 'simple hypothesis of God is probably not that bad'. What is bad, he says, is the superstructure of institutional religion.[58]

The irrationality of dispute between religions and churches was cited often as causing respondents' disdain. In the 1940s and 1950s, Nigel Bruce witnessed diverse dysfunctionalities of religion whilst serving as a diplomat for the British Foreign Office in first the Middle East, where he could see what organized religion did to divide humans between different gods and make 'one god' so impossible, and then in Africa, where in around 1960 he had a 'peak experience'[59] in what was then Tanganyika.

In this he came to see four strands in ethics: intellectual, emotional, aesthetic and moral integrity. He returned from Africa with the idea that ethics could replace religion, and became deeply involved in the 1960s in humanist writing, activism and philanthropy.[60] Ethics and morality were discussed in depth by four respondents, from different perspectives, and we shall return to this issue in the last chapter. But what was shared by them was a view of this domain as a rationale for humanism in the modern world.

Trauma

Noting the adage 'there are no atheists in fox-holes', a Canadian writer, Pierre Berton, wrote in 1966 that, 'of all the nonsense uttered by the pious during World War II, this one sentence was…surely the most inanc'. He reported that all those friends who entered fox holes as atheists emerged as atheists. He concluded, 'The churches offended many of us during the war by subtly encouraging that phrase: it suggested that men could be (and perhaps should be) blackmailed into a form of religion by the imminence of death.'[61]

The testimony of those raised in the first half of the twentieth century raises the distinctive role of military service, and more particularly combat, in disaffecting men from religion. One of my respondents, Ellen Ramsay, noted that her parents had both grown up in households with weak religious atmospheres, but each separately became more religious with the start of the Second World War and became confirmed in the Anglican Church.[62] Many historians have written about the influence of the two wars on sustaining, though less raising, religiosity, both amongst combat troops and those on the home front.[63] But the evidence of my atheist respondents is that war could be a trigger in the opposite direction.

The starkest testimony came from Nigel Bruce. The emotional and the rational seem closely entwined in his religion loss. Brought up in a liberal Anglican household in the 1920s and 1930s, he experienced a moment of intense and traumatic revelation at the bloody tank battle of Caen after the British military landing on D-Day in June 1944. There, he was overcome with the unreason of the war:

> And then of course came the attack, when we attacked from Normandy to Caen with pretty disastrous results really, and a number of my friends were killed and I saw, the padre came into action you know, and blessed them all. This was a terrible time and, this made me feel that there wasn't a God, there couldn't be a God, this was absolutely ridiculous, and here [were] we God lovers being killed by other God lovers, it made no sense

at all. So I think it was in the midst of the battle that I said, 'Oh fuck you God!' [laughs] – quite angry, quite angry. The other impressive thing at that time was when night time came, one officer was left on guard beneath the night sky, while the others took their rest, and when there were clear skies the effect of the stars above on this sleeping battle field was somehow very, very moving and, I developed a feeling that the universe was something that should influence one's life, that one should see oneself as a mere animal living under this, this gorgeous universe. So I had quite a sort of emotional feeling towards human life as animal life at that time.

In the midst of this it was the emotion of war bereavement as well as an aesthetic connection with the natural world that thrust the logic forcefully to his mind: 'I mean, there happened to be wonderful skies that time, and I think several of us, it was always the junior officers that were left on at night, the senior officers went to their beds, but several of my friends were very, very moved by this experience.'[64]

There were, of course, varied religious reactions to combat in that and other wars. Some had their faith affirmed, some found new religious experience and some had temporary loss of religion.[65] But it is also clear that the reaction of members of some Western armed forces changed significantly in the mid- to later twentieth century. In Glasgow, Frank Brown had attended Sunday school followed by sporadic churchgoing, but recalls largely losing contact with organized religion on being conscripted for service during the Korean War in the early 1950s.[66] In 2006, the senior padre in the British armed forces noted that his department was 'struggling for coherence'. He wrote thus: 'Britain's rapid secularisation since the 1960s, combined with encroaching professionalism and fiscal accountability, has left chaplains lacking sure legitimacy within a culture that no longer deems Christian discourse normative… Civil society has largely embraced secular liberalism, marginalising religion in the public space.'[67] Something of the geography of this transition emerged from the account given me by Peter Scales, who served twenty-one years as an officer in the Royal Canadian Air Force (RCAF), initially in acting as a navigator, and then as an intelligence officer. He noted with great certainty that combat experience in the 1980s did not change faith:

[N]one of my soldiers, or the soldiers that I had worked with who had gone into combat, ever spoke about it changing their faith, in part because I don't think they had faith when they went over…. [I]t's not miracles and it's not God who helps you in times of trouble, it's your training and your gear, and your buddies, and if your training, your gear and your buddies are okay then you have got luck…. There is no supernatural force that's going to come down and put a shield over you that would be bullet proof. Your helmet is the bulletproof part.[68]

There was great admiration in general for military chaplaincy services. Peter Scales noted that Canadian military chaplains were very useful in fixing problems for personnel; they were able to talk equally to generals and enlisted men. But, he said, 'They didn't get their theology into it very often'. Yet, each one was expected to undertake the last rites of a dying or dead man in the field irrespective of his religion, and had a special book which gave them instructions accordingly. Speaking of himself, Peter Scales discovered humanism in a typical manner; whilst a RCAF officer, he read an article in a copy of the *Mensa Canada Register*, to which he subscribed, describing humanism; 'and I went, "that's me"'. He continued, 'All this time of monkeying around with all different definitions of what I may or may not be. And I changed my dog tags. I went into the administration people and said: "I want to take United Church off my dog tags and put Humanist". And they didn't have Humanist, so they put atheist.'[69] This trend towards predominantly secular military personnel seems well established in many Western nations, though the US military seems to have resisted this trend with accounts of a strong, popular religious culture.

Not all of my respondents had the same immediate reaction to military service. Iain Mathieson was in the British army during the Second World War, when, with the Seaforth Highlanders, he saw considerable action – what could readily be described as trauma – in Burma and afterwards with the Dutch in Indonesia. He then spent five years with the Parachute Regiment 'territorials' (reservists) in the 1950s. In neither was his attachment to the Church of Scotland formally upset. What did change Iain was the cot death of his daughter in 1959. 'After a cot death', he told me, 'are you testing God, see if he'll do it again?' This brought retrospective re-evaluation of his war years:

> It had been in the back of my mind, just questioning it. Not only in my own personal life but in the world as a whole. Having seen the Bengal Famine, having seen all of these things, at that time. Okay, you were picking up dead bodies as if they were wood, in Calcutta, one saw that famine in India. And all of these things were happening when I was young, and they were going somewhere back into my memory. And probably as I got older, I suppose, yeah.

In his eighties, the death of his wife brought his loss of god into sharper focus, and he became a humanist.[70]

Other non-combat forms of trauma were extremely rare amongst my male respondents. One man reported at great length on the tortuous years he had spent under a cloud of suspicion of sexual abuse, and the religious belief framework of the adult complainant and of the psychiatric specialists who initially believed the child and failed to challenge the authenticity of the abuse memories. He garnered the support of his wife, friends and his Christian congregation, and, when the case was abandoned, he gave evidence to advise legislators on ways to change the handling of abuse cases. In the end, after many years and major readjustments to his life, he had found succour in humanism. 'I had to stand up on my own hind legs and fight this demon all by myself. And that was the darkness of my life. And there's nothing sad about my unbelief. I'm happier today as a committed atheist than I ever was as a doubting and disillusioned Christian.'[71] This case is complex, revealing the paradox the respondent felt: the failure of supposedly scientific professions to come to his aid to expose the power of belief, whilst irrationality and fantasy undermined the humanity of social institutions like churches and legal authorities.

In terms of losing religion, while female trauma reported to me was strongly rooted in a series of distinctive fields (in grief, female subordination, relationships, lack of autonomy and abuse), that for men was strongly intellectual. It tended to be introspective. Alex Colias wrote me thus: 'It was a slow brick-by-brick process, and I started to display some self-abusive but liberating behavior: music & alcohol stuff. I was very confused for several years.'[72] Male respondents characteristically gave stronger voice to intellectualization of their trauma, through reading or self-analysis, or in their justification of loss of religion as an outcome of their distress. Though rarer in type, men's distressful experiences in losing religion may not have been felt to be less severe than it was for women.

Being an atheist man

Kenneth Matthews from Glasgow spent most of his life as an agnostic. An electrical engineer, he became a senior marketing executive for photocopiers, and in this religion was not an important part of his life. He had become alienated from the church in his mid-teens, but he felt able in his early thirties to join the Masonic Order with not too many scruples: 'So if you take it that way, religion was never an important part of my life before, it was there, it was always that I had questions but it was never an gnawing thing at me as to where it really was so.' It was after he retired at the age of 56, with more time and freedom, that he became more interested in the issue. Having sought out the company of fellow non-believers, in his sixties he came to the view that he was an atheist and a humanist. He speaks of this transition from 'still having a dream' as an agnostic to not having one:

> The agnostic part of it is nice to have if my mother dies, my father dies, any of my kids die, they are away to a nice wee farm somewhere and all nice sunshine and playing music and they are all wealthy. It's a lovely way --- it's *marvellous* to have that in your head. But if you are really going to study Darwinism, if you are really going to look at what life is

all about and look at wee places in heaven and floating about, you realise you are kidding yourself on.

The change came at a literary book event in Glasgow's main library when the chair of the meeting asked the audience,

> 'Before we start this meeting, people who believe in God put their hands up.' It was only about six, and this was in the main library reading room, there must have been around four-five hundred at it, and only six put their hands up. And you know at that point there and then I suddenly felt I am in church. I was in a --- I was in a church for atheists, and I suddenly felt as if I wasn't the only one.

After a few more years, he joined the Humanist Society of Scotland, and he reported that he felt finally to have come out, rather like a gay man, and found the company of likeminded people. 'And I now know who I am, which is a bit late in life, but at least I have got there eventually.'[73]

In a sense, there has been no inherent contradiction between masculinity and being an atheist. We have seen how there could be significant issues concerning a woman's femininity until late in the twentieth century if she contemplated coming out as an atheist, and there was little acceptable tradition to emulate. But from the 'original' *atheos* of Greek antiquity, there has been a long tradition of male agnostics and atheists whose oratory and bravery in speaking, and occasionally in suffering arrest, imprisonment and, like Socrates, death for denying a god or gods, to which men can point. If abjuring silence, the woman atheist risked her respectability and being vilified by family, press and public; contrastingly, the man atheist might become a hero of intellect or science, and be admired for his vigour in debate and public speaking. By the mid-twentieth century, normative codes of masculinity were not totally in conflict with being devoid of God.

Indeed, men beset by doubts, renegotiating their faith and toying with dispensing with god entirely, have had, in many circumstances, the benefit of masculinity on their side. A man holding a minority or controversial view might gain respect for integrity and pluck, for the gall of intellectual challenge to 'bible-thumpers', especially if argued from science and philosophy. Whilst Annie Besant and Margaret Knight were castigated by many, Robert Ingersoll in the United States, Bertrand Russell in Britain and Pierre Berton in Canada were revered and admired, even by those otherwise opposed to their faithlessness. Being a radical, even being a little of a rascal, was not unconducive to manhood and stature. It is no accident that, in the 1950s, 1960s and 1970s, a dozen of my male interviewees combined their harbouring of religious doubt with varieties of radical political insurgency: in the American civil rights movement, opposition to the Vietnam War, Canadian left-wing political activism, in Marxism and Trotskyism, the Campaign for Nuclear

Disarmament and through campaigning for embryonic environmental causes like Greenpeace and a variety of anti-poverty movements. Converting from Catholicism to Marxism, Terry Martin said he changed in one evening from 'a Dominican veneer of religious discussion to full-blooded dialectical materialism – nothing compares with that moment'.[74] Paradoxes abounded in their voyages. The civil rights movement was intertwined with African American churches and the charismatic leadership of a Christian minister, the Reverend Dr Martin Luther King, and yet from this movement atheist impulses grew. An African American humanist I interviewed emerged from the era of the civil rights movement, Black Power and the Nation of Islam. One of my white interviewees was radicalized in the mid-1960s by marching in Illinois with a man of the cloth under the banner of an end to segregation. Another white man, a radio journalist and humanist, told me that he stood in Washington on the platform behind King whilst he stirred the world with his 'I have a dream' speech, and said he was also 'the last white boy' to see Malcolm X alive, interviewed by him on a street in Harlem before he was assassinated. The exposure of these exponents to radical religious movements in the sixties was a stage in their journeys from faith. Subjection to absurd racism could have the same effect. One young Scottish engineer working in the United States was jarred by being told by a white work colleague, a religious man, to refrain from using an office water cooler reserved for 'coloreds', and thus he committed for civil rights and non-religionism. Another told me he lay in the road in London's Whitehall, outside 10 Downing Street, beside atheist Bertrand Russell in the CND Committee of 100 'sit down' – with Russell oblivious to my interviewee's role as a Trotskyite 'entryist' agitator for world revolution. All of these incidents took place in the heady long 1960s, when radicalisms overlapped and suborned one another to different agendas. The causes had different successes. But, uniting my respondents over the long term was to be their converging destinies as atheists and humanists.

My male respondents spoke, many of them, of these sixties radicalisms as energizing. Some women I spoke to also referred to them, but overall women spoke less of these causes and more of feminism and gender equality. Most white men did not share, or could not share, the redefining nature of feminism upon women's autonomy and their comprehensively altered lives in the last forty years of the twentieth century. The position of ethnic minority men and women, however, could be different.

CHAPTER SEVEN

Atheism and Ethnicity

It is striking just how racially imbalanced humanists and atheists are, especially amongst the sixties' generation. The organizer of the Washington DC Atheists commented in a report to his members that he was pleased when there were six months with consecutive attendance by one or more African Americans.[1] In my visit to humanist and atheist groups in North America and the United Kingdom, white faces accounted for easily 98 per cent of all attenders. Dave Kong, organizer of the American Atheists chapter in San Francisco, made the point to me that it was as hard for an African American to come out as an atheist as it was to come out as a gay person.[2]

The way in which religion is lost, and atheism and humanism gained, is sharply shaped by race and ethnicity. This is partly demonstrable in numbers, but more acutely in terms of cultures. Looking at numbers first, persons of colour have tended to have higher rates of churchgoing than whites. In the United States in 2014, 61 per cent of black Protestants claimed to attend church 'almost every week' or weekly, compared to only 50 per cent of white Protestants (though some data have suggested churchgoing rates amongst teenage blacks are lower than for teenage whites).[3] In England and Wales in 2011, white people accounted for 86 per cent of the population but 93 per cent of those of no religion, with the racial divergence increased over the previous decade.[4] The white dominance seems starker amongst members of humanist, secularist and atheist groups; though one survey in 2014 found 89 per cent of members of the British Humanist Association to be 'white British'[5] (i.e. about the same as in the general population), attendance at humanist meetings in the United Kingdom suggests fewer than one in ten, perhaps one in twenty, are non-white.[6] This will be borne out in this chapter as we see how some ethnic and religious traditions generate ultra-low levels of secularism, with corresponding effects upon the isolated individuals who forsake the faith customs of their family and community.

Unsurprisingly, it is the cultural context that plays a determining part in differences between peoples of colour and whites. Culture moulds the individual's experience of leaving a religious background, the nature of the difficulties and the form of the leaving, and, not least, the reaction of family and friends. But the cultural context of the leaving also fashions the character of the non-religious position at which the individual arrives. For the nature of the atheism that emerges is very different. Moreover, the nature of the narratives produced differs considerably. Of course, race is not the only factor here. There are major national differences, so that the African American experience in the United States differs from the Afro-Caribbean experience in the United Kingdom. Indeed, the nature of the groups being explored in this chapter varies. Most of the categories here have been minority groups in Western nations, resulting from migration either recently or over a longer period, whilst, for whites, theirs has been a majority experience in which their race has been domiciled in a nation for the whole of recorded history or, as in the case of whites in North and South America, since they became the majority through conquest. This immediately makes for different experiences for losing religion. For example, the circumstances of white peoples are demographically different from non-white groups in that the former are in the majority in nearly all Western nations whilst the latter are in the minority. In a similar vein, most Western nations are founded on majority Christian heritages, whilst some of the minority groups are non-Christian. Yet, we are also considering here minority groups which are racially different but religiously the same, and some whose ethnicity is mainly white but religiously different. The consequence is that religious-ethnic minorities present a range of circumstances – cultural and demographic – in which those losing religion have felt distinctive experiences of their journeys towards atheism and humanism.

It is important to note that the categories explored in this chapter imply clear separation between ethnic and religious groups, which of course does not reflect the reality of mixed race dominance in the Western world, and the significant degree of crossover experiences between the categories. Some groups are not wholly racially defined – 'Muslim' and 'Jew', for instance, are terms which can each cover a variety of self-reporting racial identities. Moreover, racial differences and similarities are not absolutes, but exist on complex spectra of skin colour and facial features, for example, often loosely referred to as 'mixed race'. This chapter acknowledges these intricate factors in studying race and ethnicity, but eschews the difficulties to concentrate on the secularizing dimensions – how ethnic and religious differences affect the experiences of losing religion and journeying towards living life as if there is no god. Lastly, and requiring much emphasis, the racial profiling of religious losers cannot emasculate the individual experiences of all people of all ethnicities in travelling towards atheism. In every case, the individual remains an agent, no matter the background. There is individual choice.

But that choice is circumscribed by various factors that tend, in practice, to make the experience of non-Christian and non-white groups in the West different from that of white atheists from former Christian backgrounds. Being a minority non-Christian and non-white group makes for special circumstances – including of difference, of isolation socially or politically, of racism and religious sectarian feeling, and of a community under stress from discrimination and hostility from at least part of the majority white population. In this context, faith becomes a source of identity when there may be a danger of a community's sublimation beneath a majority culture.[7] Again, a contrast between a minority faith and the majority faith in a Western nation may be exaggerated if the majority of people have been losing their faith fast. Where secularization is diminishing the social significance of religion, the members of minority racial-faith groups may find the sense of difference swollen, heightening the sensation of discrimination, and making secularization – including the rise of atheism – seem to some to be a threat and instigate deep anxiety. As one Muslim respondent told me, he found his leaving of Islam 'painful', 'traumatic' and full of 'grief'. He asked himself: 'What were my values? What other models were out there?' He reported that he struggled to find Muslims to speak to. 'I went through stages, redefining what a Muslim was.'

The African American

There is a significant literature on the problematic honour that black secular atheism must pay to the African American churches for their pioneering role in black consciousness. Works of postcolonial theory, notably by Frantz Fanon, wrestle with the conflict between a pacifying Christian religion perceived as foisted upon African slaves by Western colonialism and capitalism, and the identity forged in the distinctive black Christian churches of the plantations and since. Fanon wrote that 'the good and merciful God cannot be black: He is a white man with bright pink cheeks'.[8] Fanon writes of the pre-existing meaning, culturally inescapable for the black man, that is 'waiting for me' and 'waiting for that turn of history' when the pillars of the world will be shaken.[9] On this same theme, Michael Lackey has written recently of the African American atheist dilemma that 'genuine atheism' takes time to gain traction, for the culture to eliminate God from its consciousness, even when there is an apparent absence of the God concept.[10] So, there is a quandary for black freedom. In the testimony that follows, we see how the narrative is intimately structured around its reality, not the classroom theory. Religion has shaped identity, fostered resistance and illuminated the road to freedom, but is regarded by some at the same time as an ideological enslavement. This is the African American atheist dilemma.

Ernest Parker was born in Washington DC in 1949, and his testimony revealed the strength of African American religious culture upon his life. He demonstrated the inescapable presence of the religious heritage of the black community within the consciousness and identity of the individual black secular humanist in North America. Whilst Ernest's father never went to church when his children were young (though he became a churchgoer in his seventies), Ernest's mother was a firm Baptist during his early years, singing in the gospel choir at their church. On moving to a new part of DC when he was about seven or eight, his mother was drawn to the Jehovah's Witnesses, taking Ernest with her on her first night (a night he recalled in detail, including getting lost on strange streets, almost leading to abandonment of the journey). A strong connection was readily set up with the church, involving him in two-hour midweek Bible Studies sessions and a two-hour Sunday meeting, with additional time needed to study for those. And on top of that was the minimum of ten hours per month given over to knocking on people's doors, the duty of each Jehovah's Witness. He soon was admitted to the Theocratic Ministry School, where he learned public speaking, how to study the Bible and how to discuss it with people. At the age of 8 or 9 he gave his first talk, on the Book of Job. From that very first sermon, he recalled his doubts:

> The guy that was in charge of the Ministry School said that I didn't convincingly discuss God's righteousness. And I just didn't feel it, I didn't feel that God had righteousness, even though he restored all of Job's possessions. He got a new family, wife and all that, but, what about the kids that innocently died? You know, what happens to them? What is their life worth?

Such doubt, at so young an age, was surprisingly widespread in interview recollection amongst those, of all ethnicities, destined at a young age for ministry training.[11]

Ernest had more and more questions, and when his mother stopped leading his bedtime prayers he said to himself: 'Well, this is cool, now I can talk to God!' But in a witty aside, resonant again of doubt, he added that 'I just could not get over the feeling that I was talking to myself'. Still, giving up the practice of his church was not an option, and he became deeply entangled in the congregation's work and was baptized at about age 12. Eventually at 15 he became the Ministry School servant, teaching other people. Despite this leadership role, he developed more doubt about the church. Stark in his mind was an incident in which he and a male friend were abducted at gunpoint and raped, but even though the perpetrator was caught and imprisoned, he was criticized by the church for not resisting unto death. But still, he remained, leading the congregation, and when he reached 18 or 19 he started to dress in the fashion of the sixties – tailored bell bottoms with wide lapels and stripes, and an afro hair style. This led to a congregational complaint to the Watchtower Society headquarters, but though no action followed, the incident grated with Ernest.

From his late teens, Ernest was employed most of his working life for the Federal Housing Authority, first as a mail clerk, then as a data processer and latterly moving into management analysis, where he became involved in the housing field in Bill Clinton's 'Reinventing Government' initiative. In the Jehovah's Witnesses, his early work in the civil service caused some friction, coming to a head when he had to miss meetings because of his shift pattern. The elders came and, in a disturbing scene with his mother, told him he 'wasn't in good standing with the congregation', and ordered him to leave his mother's house where he might be a bad influence upon her. His mother, torn by her own place in the church, supported Ernest and his right to stay in her home. But a month later he left and found his own apartment, rooming with another ex-Jehovah's Witness; when elders called, they found marijuana being consumed, and, after rejecting Bible instruction, he was, in 1976 at the age of 25, finally 'disfellowshipped', or excommunicated.[12]

From there he started studying other faiths. 'It was hard for me to look at other religions as having any more, as being any more true.' He went through them:

> With the Witnesses, it was a bit like a big trash bin – the Baptists are in there, the Catholics are in there. I had some friends who were into Buddhism and other religions, and I always had this feeling in the back of my mind that at one time it's possible that there was some truth. And you know, maybe if you go back in time or something like that, and studying and looking at these things, that eventually you can find it. But I eventually reached a conclusion that either they're all right or they're all wrong. And there's no evidence that any of them are right. So they must be all wrong. And that was the day that it occurred to me that there was probably no god.

He was particularly put off by the claims of each religion, especially the Witnesses, to be 'the true religion'. He tried meditation with Bhagwan Shree Rajneesh, but could not abide the test of devotion and obedience.[13] He tried Mormonism, but 'couldn't get past their racial thing'. He attended one Pentecostal-style religious service in support of a friend's child, but he and the mother and child fled when the preacher targeted him to come down to be 'saved'; talking about it later, 'nobody was feeling inclined to re-examine our decision to not be in a religion'.

By these accumulative strokes, Ernest became progressively more confirmed in a position of no religion. He was alienated by 'these folks, they were going at it full throttle emotional' to persuade and sustain faith in the African American community. 'There was no appeal to logic or reason', no asking 'do you feel the loss of religion in your life?' Ernest said, 'They's just going full out with the music and the singin' and the dancin' and you know,

"save your soul from hell" and all of that stuff.' For almost thirty years, he
stood apart from religion, but without adopting a named identity:

> Like most African American non-believers, we think we're the only one.
> There are so few of us, the influence of the church in our community
> is so pervasive, that we think: 'I'm the only one that feels this way, or
> thinks this way'. And uhm, quite frankly, until recently there's been little
> or no [secular humanist] outreach into the African American community,
> because the assumption has been that all black people are religious.[14]

Ernest recalled being at a humanists' conference in DC in 2009 and a man
coming up to him to ask if he was Norm Allen, a well-known black humanist
speaker and author: 'And I said "No". And he said: "Wow, I told them I was
looking for Norm Allen[15] and they said you can't miss him, he's the only
black guy here." And then all of a sudden there was two!'

Ernest Parker spoke with vigour on the context for ethnic minority
unbelief – about the slave heritage, the segregation, discrimination, the
denial of civil rights and justice under the law. And he spoke of being 'dirt
poor', and the division between the black and white poor. He conversed
eloquently on the resistance of the black churches to fighting for equality,
disparaging the discourse of '"You gotta wait for the time for the Lord
to take action for you." Even though today the Black Church takes a lot
of credit for the Civil Rights Movement, that's a load of crap.' The black
churches, Ernest explained, excused doing nothing:

> The sheer *gall* of their assertions! Every year during the Martin Luther
> King birthday celebrations, there's all this clappin' and singin' and
> carryin' on. But what people don't understand is, yeah they went to the
> churches, because that was the only place you could go! White people
> wouldn't let you have any of the halls or anything around it. If you were
> outside, the Klan was going to come after you. Even the churches weren't
> safe, they bombed them. But that was the only meeting place that the
> black community had. It wasn't necessarily that the churches supported
> it, but where else were you gonna go?[16]

In around 2000, Ernest picked up a pamphlet on the Washington Metro
about humanism. He joined a slow-growing group of African American
humanists, affiliated to the Centre for Inquiry, where he became the
organizer of the first conference of African American Humanists and
Atheists, attracting seventy people from across the United States, and, in the
decade since, the movement has grown and become organized.

The humanism he supports is deeply inflected with race issues. At
length he described the continued struggle for racial equality. Non-belief
is inextricably linked for him in the race issue – with Christianity a device
of, first, white-imposed and, then, self-imposed black subordination. He is

aggrieved that, in his words, 'the churches have hijacked Black history', so he was a strong advocate of the African Americans for Humanism when, on the last Sunday in February 2011, they created the 'Day of Solidarity for Black Non-believers' as part of the Black History Month. Since then, though still modest in scale, the Day of Solidarity has been extending its influence and celebration across the United States and internationally.[17]

There is a conundrum at the heart of African American atheism. Reflecting this, Ernest worries about how the black non-believers should deal with black churches. The latter are so important to black identity, and have been so central to civil rights movements and to the cultural resistance to white supremacy, that it is unimaginable for black humanists to attack them. Ernest's extended family are still in one church or another – some of them, he said, were 'so religious', one in a 'weird church'. Organized religion is still at the forefront of his life and mind. His testimony was inflected throughout with references to the Bible, to Bible stories and the rhetorical style of the black preacher – gained (he says after my recorder has stopped) while working for the Jehovah's Witnesses. He has a familiarity with Bible stories, and is in a position to argue from a very informed position. Towards the end of my interview with him he explained how he had gone to Christmas dinner with a close relative and their family, and when he had been asked if he went to church, he explained that he was a non-believer. And when they warned of the danger of him going to hell, he replied,

> Nobody in the Bible who has been dead and brought back to life, and there's several instances of this in the Bible in the New Testament and the Old Testament, and nobody thought to ask them what it was like to be dead. In fact, I think the Book of Mark, where Jesus was raised from the tomb, and in Mark it talks about all the tombstones opened and all these people that were there got up and walked, nobody ran up to them and said, 'Homey, what was it like? Did ya see god? Did you see the devil? Did you burn --- what happened?' But you got all of this speculation about heaven and hell and fire and brimstone and all of that, I'm not worried about that. I'm worried about what's going to happen to me today, tomorrow and the next day, what happens to people now. Whatever's gonna happen to me after I die is going to happen, and I don't think going to church is going to change that. So I'm expecting to come back for Christmas dinner this year and I don't expect to get asked that question! [laughing][18]

Here is a confirmed African American humanist who has spent most of his adult life outside of church and faith, yet is drawn by the culture of his family and his fellow blacks to constantly confront belief issues. He has a familiarity with it, understands its temperament and sensibilities, and above all understands its history. And it is very difficult for him to ignore the role of the black church in African Americans' struggles for identity, for cultural freedom, for an end to segregation and for civil rights and equality. He must remain living within this cultural framework. This is the paradox for minority cultures. It is common in African American narratives of atheism and humanism, probably a pervasive presence.[19] But, as we shall see, amongst ethnic minorities whose religion is also a minority faith which marks out the group, the severity of the isolation of the non-believer can be even greater.

Ernest Parker regarded himself as one of the oldest active African American humanists in the United States. There is a generational gap, Ernest noted, with the bulk of humanists under 30 years and few over 50. Certainly, he saw his commitment and experience as emblematic of a movement that is small, though growing fast, but one that, in his testimony, will need to negotiate the difficult homage it has to owe – and cannot neglect to pay – to black churches for their history of civil rights resistance, anti-segregation struggle and modelling of African American identity. The dilemma is exigent, the negotiation seemingly irresolvable for the African American community of non-believers at large, certainly in the short term. But for individual black humanists and atheists, it is one that has to be confronted.

The Jews

The negotiation has long since been accomplished by secular Jewry, probably the most mature, intellectually sustained and distinctively ethnic-related atheism in the West. By the late nineteenth century, there was already a developed community and intelligentsia of secular Jews in Eastern Europe, which, when scattered by the pogroms, established the tradition in new contexts in the West. One form of this, common to many places, was that of secularist labour organizations and socialist thought. This helps to explain why this tradition was already mature in the early twentieth century. For this reason, many Jews felt that they were raised in what was often described as either Jewish secularism or a relaxed agnostic religiosity.

One of my interviewees, Ernest Poser (1921–2012), wrote in a book chapter in 1999 that 'it makes sense to speak of Jewish but not of Catholic, Islamic, or Hindu secular humanists'. The last three of these, he explained, 'refer primarily to religious belief systems and are therefore incompatible with a secular worldview. Only the term Jewish carries both a religious and/ or ethno-cultural connotation.'[20] This distinctive combination of race and religion in the term 'Jewish' carries with it also the distinctive possibility of separation, so that racial identity may survive the religious. This theme tends to dominate Jewish atheist and humanist testimony.

Ernest was the first in his family to develop into first a freethinker then a humanist, and fostered his father's interest in humanism too. Born in Vienna, Ernest and his parents moved to Leipzig, making up a family in which the

Jewish religion was lightly practiced, and there his father built his house at the non-Jewish end of town. He described his mother as 'totally liberal in the sense of having no particular interest of any sort in matters religious', and turned later in her life 'I might say anti-religious': not anti-Jewish, but against the concept of religion, saying, 'How would anybody know anything about God? What is important is how to deal with your fellow human being.'[21] His father was different, coming from a quasi-Orthodox Jewish background, shedding the orthodox part of that but clinging to what Ernest described as 'the ethnic cultural aspect of Judaism', having a great interest in Judaic and Jewish history. When his father's parents came to visit, the family went through the motions of offering a quasi-kosher kind of household – with ham sandwiches disappearing for a while. Ernest's father allowed him to stop attending a Hebrew class at six years old, marking the end of his formal exposure to religion. In Ernest's view, this followed the track of high Jewish assimilation in Germany, where, compared to the *shtetl* communities of the east they had fled, they were able to enter the professions, and they advanced the process through allowing their children to be even better assimilated by not practicing their religion. So Ernest saw himself as part of this process – one he noted that was proved to be disastrous after 1930.[22]

Having in his own words effectively rejected the religious aspect of Judaism, Ernest became 'in a funny sort of way' engrossed in issues of religion, God and the afterlife. With his family's emigration from Germany to England in 1933, he became intellectually conflicted, noting that his rejection of the religious aspect of Judaism was not possible as 'all of Judaism is religious'.[23] Yet, when he came across publications of the Rationalist Press Association (now the Rationalist Association), he described having 'an epiphany', finding it represented his views exactly; when he took out a subscription to a freethought magazine his copies ended up on his father's bedside table, who described them as 'fascinating stuff' and 'very worthwhile' (though his father reverted to Jewish reading when he was dying, wanting something more 'traditional').[24] Ernest grew into the humanist movement, notably after he married and settled in Montreal and later Vancouver, in both cities becoming a leading light in local humanist groups, promoting conflict resolution and educational opportunities free from religious belief.

Running parallel to his infusion with humanist ideas and humanistic ideals, Ernest explained that he became increasingly aware of his Jewish identity during the era of the Third Reich and the refugee years he experienced mostly in England. He wrote the following in an essay:

> For me, however, being Jewish derived not so much from *feeling* as from *knowing*. I cannot say that I ever *felt* Jewish, but I certainly knew that I was. More importantly, I assumed rightly or wrongly that others perceived me as being Jewish. And this assumption is at the root of my Jewish identity. It is the basis of a kinship I feel with a beleaguered

people seen by others as being 'different.' And because being 'different' is historically associated with persecution, it makes some of us loath to be Jewish, but also afraid of denying it, lest we lose the support of our hereditary tribesmen.[25]

The tribe, he explained, was a 'common stock…acting under a central authority', a central authority for 'Jewish tribesmen' being the religion of Judaism. Ernest felt he denied and rebelled against that authority when, at the age of 17, he joined the British-based Rationalist Press Association. But he denied that this makes him 'a non-Jew'. And he asks, 'What then is left of my Jewishness? Is it the culture, ethnicity, nationality, or all three of these?' Not being a Zionist or a nationalist of any stripe, he saw neither as being his tie to Jewishness. Though seeing the value of a Jewish homeland, but deploring the internal religious strife and rigid territoriality going with it, he wrote, 'That leaves culture and ethnicity as possible explanations of that "pintyele yid"[26] still lurking within me. I see these components as representing Jewish nurture and nature respectively.' The culture he found in arts, science, Jewish humour, 'gefilte fisch' (an Ashkenazi Jewish fish dish) and a yearning for learning, a Jewish culture rich in philosophy and inquiry, of inquiry especially into the mind to which he dedicated his academic life in clinical psychology.[27] Surrounding this was a culture of liberalism, of modernity and human rights, of a woman's right to choose and an end to human conflict.

Most of the Jewish humanists I interviewed had strong liberal and educational credentials. Born in Oakland, California, in 1967, Moses Klein reported that he didn't think very much about religion, but carried a liberal Judaism lightly:

> MK   I guess I had a sense of, you know, being of the Jewish religion as one of the things that defined us. It distinguished us from most of my peers. Never lived in a Jewish neighbourhood. Never went to a predominantly Jewish school, there were usually a few other students who would be taking the high holidays off. And I guess in elementary school every year when Christmas came around and all the decorations came up, the teachers would usually ask me and one or two other Jewish students in the class to do a presentation explaining about Hanukkah. So it was always something that I was pigeonholed into very early. I didn't really feel a tension, you know, a lot of my friends were either Christian or atheist. I didn't really feel that was an issue between us in any way.
>
> CB   Did you have a settled view on religion when you were young?
>
> MK   Not really. I don't think I thought that much about it. I mean, we went to services occasionally and I think at the time I liked that.[28]

Moses felt that he was probably agnostic at that time, and, if asked if he believed in God, over many years would have given a range of answers from 'maybe' to 'probably not'. His was a measured ambivalence, a contentment with a human-invented or metaphorical God. Like Ernest Poser, though reversing the parental religious origins, Moses' family background involved an element of Orthodox Judaism on his mother's side, even if she became active in a Reconstructionist movement which emphasized evolving Jewish civilization and modernity, with a liberal and 'fairly humanistic approach to religion'. Meanwhile, his father was a completely secular Jew from a home that was mostly 'nationalistically Jewish'. Moses reported: 'They had a very strong sense of who their people were: a very strong loyalty, often insular, toward their people.'[29] He described how he was left with a sense that 'I belonged to a group; it was part of my life, but it was not a dominant part of my life because I was never part of a social circle beyond the family that was defined through Judaism'. His grandmother in Rhode Island spoke a great deal of Judaism to him, but he visited only infrequently. Having had a bar mitzvah, it was at university that it really occurred to him that this religion didn't mean much to him:

> I think [in] in my first year there, I had a revelation one day in the dining hall that I had been for months been very scrupulously planning my menu choices. If I was eating meat I would make sure I didn't have a creamy dressing on my salad. And it suddenly dawned on me that [there] seemed absolutely no point to this. And right then and there I decided I wasn't keeping kosher anymore.

He reported that he 'didn't think of it so much as an act of rebellion; it's just that once [I] was on my own, I started making my own choices where I had just previously had assumptions'.[30]

Secular Jews and Jewish humanists have a familiarity and place in Jewish culture. They have a tradition stretching back at least to the nineteenth century, and a sophisticated scholarship tradition well rooted in the intellectual world of the twentieth century. There are societies which embrace secular Jewry, and there is also, as already noted, a rich Jewish vocabulary of terms about them.[31] For all that Jewish atheists might appear to be at odds with Jewish religion, there is still a place in the wider Jewish culture in which their intellectual tradition is revered and marked as Jewry's contribution to the modern world. This means that there is a distinctive character to the Jew's loss of religion. For Jewish humanists and atheists, the leaving of the religion is a negotiation, a careful recalibration to accommodate the atheism with Jewish identity and culture. This has been a familiar, well-trodden path, even for Ernest Poser in the 1920s and 1930s. This is not to belittle the sense of inner struggle and contemplation, but it is noteworthy that, on both an intellectual and social level, the Jewish secular humanist has a cultural envelope within which to undertake the negotiation. When Moses Klein spoke at length to me about the death of his sister from cancer in 2005, he recounted the tradition of being in a house of mourning where members of the Jewish community come to console the family members, and cited his own sense of distance from some of those people who visited who were 'really trying to come to grips with God wanting Elka with Her [*sic*] so early, and, you know, they were trying to reconcile it with a sense of a just and benevolent order to the world'. By contrast, Moses said he 'wasn't trying to attach any moral significance to cancer. As far as I'm concerned it's a completely amoral agent. I was trying to come to grips with the fact that Elka was no more. Not in this world, not in another world'. He referred to the twice daily prayers at the time of bereavement, and how he found these alienating, and decided to leave the house to drive his sister's friend, also a secular humanist, to the airport – when, by convention, community friends should have done this for him. This departure from custom enabled him for a period to mourn in a different, humanist way within the greater Jewish tradition, and Moses sensed that his mother recognized his need for this. There is in this account, told in considerable detail, clear signs of the tension for the secularist within the Jewish religious tradition (in this case of bereavement). But at the same time, there is tender negotiation, a tethering of the religious non-believer to the wider Jewish identity, and latitude – a give and take – within which the non-believer may function.[32]

So, Jewishness and a secular humanistic identity can be accommodated, even within a religious tradition, like any other, that has a strong conservative orthodox wing which is given to censure of the unbeliever. There is room for the individual to bargain and manoeuvre, to work out ways of being a humanist with Jewish tradition and have a separate political and ethical framework within which to pursue with fellow nonbelievers the just causes that he or she is compelled to uphold. There are some exceptions to this. There remain areas where the tensions between believing and non-believing Jews could be at their greatest, especially over Zionism, which Ernest Poser opposed very strongly; of course many Jews are also opposed to Zionism, so this was not necessarily a line of demarcation between believer and non-believer.

In another dimension for secular Jews, the break from Jewish identity might be firmer, but leave various forms of legacy. Here are three diverse examples. After attending synagogue and temple school with his father around the ages of 4 to 6, Harris Sussman broke with Jewish faith and society in New York at the age of 8 in about 1952 when his father died and his mother remarried a man in a Unitarian ceremony, and didn't see the inside of a religious building again, emerging as a humanist in adulthood. His mother's family had been Russian Jews, and she spent a Junior Year Abroad in the Soviet Union in 1936 from a very liberal American college; he found that the Russian side of his family had had little knowledge of religious ritual, only the identity. Meanwhile, Harris' wife came from a family of mixed Jewish and Russian origins. Harris quoted a comedian who remarked that 'I am not a Jew, I am Jewish', and added, 'So, I live in this kind of untethered world which is true for a lot of American secular Jews, so called cultural Jews.'[33] In a different vein, on leaving Germany for England as a teenager in the 1930s, Jutta Cahn (1925–2014) decided first to join the Church of England, and was confirmed, but her freethinking impulses led her quickly to lose respect for religion, and she abandoned all organized religion as she trained in the late 1940s and 1950s as a doctor.[34] In a third example of the quick religious break, Justin Trottier (born 1982), Jewish on his mother's side, attended a Jewish Saturday school for three years, and took bar mitzvah at age 13 – 'done because it's just what you do when you are Jewish', and because his grandfather would have 'flipped' if he hadn't. Looking back on this, Justin rationalized that this was part of family identity, and that he spoke at the ceremony without knowing what he was saying; his 'maftir portion' from the Torah was transcribed phonetically for him to recite in Hebrew, 'but I had no clue of what I was saying at any point, which really rubbed me the wrong way because I like to be in control, I like to know what am I saying, and why I am saying it'. In his narrative, this is followed immediately by his recounting how he gained control through going to secondary school and starting to read in scientists like Carl Sagan and Richard Dawkins.[35] In these ways, various degrees of legacy remain.

But some became secularized Jews, not by a break, but by prolonged drift from the religious faith. Jeanne Willig was born in London 1931, but already her mother didn't eat kosher all the time, and she recalled at the age of 6 or 7 being offended by her father telling her mother in Yiddish not to let her daughter play with a non-Jewish child; Jeanne told me that she should have become a humanist right there and then. As a wartime evacuee to Cornwall, she was mostly with Christian families and children, but on returning to London, she still mixed with Jews on a social basis, yet dated non-Jewish men and had non-Jewish friends. In this manner, she dropped in and out of Jewish culture. She felt that Jewry was about 'kin' and little else: 'I was not brought up with any philosophical understanding of Judaism, it was all the rights, keeping up the rights. There was not the religion really.' Emigrating to the United States in 1957, she met and married a Jewish man, and he too wasn't religious, though his family was, and when they had a son in 1966 the question arose of circumcision; she insisted it wasn't the rabbi but a surgeon who performed it, satisfying his family, but indicating to me and herself that a line had been crossed. Her son and daughter learned something of Jewish culture, but she became a Buddhist, and Jeanne joined the Workmen's Circle, a left-leaning non-religious Jewish organization that fights for social justice. In this way, she, like other secular Jews, straddled the identity but not the religion. She said to me, 'I am this old Jew.'[36]

For the Jewish humanist and atheist, there seems in this process of negotiating a position within Jewish culture less possibility of rancour with family than for those in other ethnic-religious minority groups. Compromise, flexibility and accommodation pervade the secular Jew's testimony. Alison Bowes, in her study of an atheist Israeli kibbutz, argued that the culture of unbelief involves a constant testing of atheism in an environment – indeed, in a state – founded on religion, involving reinterpretation of religious ritual and reuse of Jewish religious symbols and language, and resulting in constant ambiguities. But their community of unbelievers survived and replenished with new members.[37] Both in Israel and the wider diaspora, there is a general, though perhaps not a universal, acceptance that the Jew who leaves his or her religion is still a Jew, is still 'loyal', if that is the right word, to Jewish culture and to the Jewishness within. Though one Israel-based historian has written that 'I wish to resign and cease considering myself a Jew',[38] compared to the African American humanist or atheist there is no recognized ideology attending non-belief that posits the Jewish religion to be part of the enslavement of the ethnic group. There is acceptance that the religion has upheld identity and group defence and resistance to persecution, especially in the never-diminishing shadow of the Holocaust. In this regard, there is little sense of the individual non-believing Jew being traitorous. There is an accommodation which sustains the wholeness of Jewishness whilst freedom is grasped by the humanist and atheist to not believe. Bar mitzvah is taken as a badge of ethnic identity, not for all as a symbol of religiosity.

The Muslim

In his interview with me, Hakim (a pseudonym) pointed out that there is no recognized term 'secular Muslim'. He told me that 'unlike the Jewish community or the Jewish culture, where you can be racially and ethnically a Jew, and you could be a staunch atheist Jew or a secular Jew, this is an alien concept to Islam, you are not a Muslim through, well officially you are not a Muslim through birth. You should be a Muslim through your faith'.[39] Hakim's story, and that of two other former Muslims, was very different to that of all the other eighty-two I heard. Hakim's route from Islam was highly charged by the faith and culture from which he was emerging. However, he was not just leaving his faith. At the same time, he left his family, his community, heterosexuality and his job. In the midst of distress, he feared retribution.

Hakim was born and raised in the Middle East in the 1960s in a Sunni Muslim family and later came to live in England. He started by describing how, while growing up in the Middle East, he did not have religious education as such, but was immersed through language in Islam: 'If you wanted to do something you would say God willing or Insha'Allah, and a lot of the expressions of "I wish this happened", you would say "oh I am grateful to God for something happening". The word Allah would feature in everyday language, wishes, and fears.' This was initially a liberal religious background, but religion grew more important for him. Just before puberty a Muslim boy encouraged him to pray.

> And so that's when the interest in religion started to develop, just before puberty. And also there was a sense that what was happening between Israel and Arabs in the area but you couldn't trust any of the superpowers, and that the general sentiment was to rely on God, because he is the one who controls everything. So I think from that sort of age there was this sense that the only one you could trust is God. And that no matter what people plan, it's not up to them as to what happens: fate, God's control over fate.

His values – honesty, truth, justice and a mounting disquiet with materialism – developed around this growing sense of faith: 'I felt I had to be interested in religion in order to live a principled existence.' At a school in England in the 1980s, the few Muslims bonded around prayers and faith, and then at 16–17 years of age he started attending the local mosque, coming across various Muslim groups, the first being Tableeghi-Jamaat, which encouraged living a simple virtuous life and preaching about heaven and hell. He came across a large community of Palestinians who focused more on political and military ways for Muslims to right the wrongs imposed by the West through colonialism and the Cold War. Hakim said, 'So Islam was not just about praying, but Islam was about living each aspect of your life in a way God would be pleased with, in other words not just rituals and worship, but also your politics, and that you could not be ruled by anyone who obeyed anything other than Islamic rule.'

At university in Britain he studied science, drawing him to the fundamentalist approach which verified every source of doctrine, and that led in his faith to the Salafi way of thinking (sometimes associated with Wahhabism), regarded by some as disparaging, in which theological argument was based on evidence and strict following of fundamentals, in a way like science. Towards the end of his university degree, he became part of a group that wanted regime change in the Middle East, not just through military jihadi, but a scientific-like system based on the message used by the Prophet Muhammad and by all previous prophets, involving grassroots change based on a regular study circle. From this group, the suggestion emerged that it was important for 'a full Muslim' to be wed, and so he soon married a Muslim woman.

Hakim then went through a tortuous period of questioning his sexuality, which predated his marriage, but he thought gay encounters were a test of faith. Yet once married, he sought out contact with gay men, but still considered himself a Muslim. He was quite involved with the mosque, attending study circles and giving talks, and even took on a teaching role and gave Friday sermons to university mosques, and was receiving many requests to speak. But at the same time, over a number of years of marriage, he entered a profession and all the while prayed to avoid men. But gradually, he met gay men socially, and heard their stories of everyday life, and bit by bit he started to see himself as homosexual:

> I started seeing myself more as a gay man, and that actually the plights and concerns of gay men were no different than anyone else's. And then I started sort of questioning God in the sense of, sort of asking Him what sort of plan could He have to deliberately and knowingly put urges within me which He then decreed were wrong. Why should I have this affliction and others not? I could not understand either the compassion or the justice of that type of game. And so I eventually sort of accepted myself, and said 'well it's not for other people to judge me, it's okay for me to be gay, and God will, He knows what he is doing and I have done enough good deeds to counter balance anything else'. And so I had given myself a dispensation to be gay and act on it, and to deal with my guilt. So I sort of washed my own guilt away, so to speak.

From this point, different things started to happen in tandem. The Bosnian war exposed not just the charitable effort of Muslims but also some of the fraudulent work of those making money: it exposed Muslims as being like other peoples – some were good; some were bad. He felt guilty for his wife's lack of his companionship, but resolved to leave the marriage. And his work as a lecturer around mosques was troubling him. He decided, 'I had to make a clean break, as it were, and run away almost.'

So, he almost seemed to disappear from the company of his Muslim friends, and eventually they stopped phoning him. Hakim had not at that point come out as a gay man, but it petrified him that he would be threatened with violence: 'I was very afraid of it being known in the bigger community, in the Islamic community, that I was gay. So yes, there was that fear.' He also wanted to conceal his sexuality to spare his wife the shame and taunting that might follow. In any event, he divorced and came out fully on the gay scene and, for separate reasons, also lost his job. Through the gay dance scene, he got into trance music and explored New Age Buddhism. He also met other gay Muslims, those who really wanted to be openly gay and also definitely be Muslim. He felt it was 'quite a live experience for me to be Muslim rather than just a routine or just repetitive Muslim' and found interest in the intellectual activity of different schools of Islamic thought. But through this, he found Islam was not an answer to all his concerns. He met with people with different perspectives on religion and sexuality, and read about secularist and theosophist Annie Besant and the match stick girls and her contribution to Indian secularism.[40] After many years of reading about and exploring different religions, Hakim came across a humanist stall at a Gay Pride event: 'They did a questionnaire: "Are you a Humanist?" So you went through a few of the questions. And I started thinking, "Yeah, actually that seems to make sense.”’ The questionnaire prompted him that he was undecided on the existence of God. Through this, Hakim eventually found a gay humanist group, steering himself to finally reassess his religious position in a series of intellectual steps constructed both for his own transition and for that of others amongst family and friends who were seeking to understand how he had changed.

Hakim was incredibly thoughtful and reflective in his interview. He has had to dwell on the very possibility of being a secular Muslim when this combination essentially has not existed in his cultural background.

> I’d become quite fundamentalist, and I defined Islam by strict criteria. If you were to ask me questions about, ‘Do you believe there is such a thing as secular Islam?’, I would put my fundamentalist head on, and say to you: ‘No, it is impossible to have secular Islam, because Islam is explicit about saying that God is the source of all your life including how you wash, how you govern, how you wage war, in that your mission is to ensure that living according to God’s wishes is something that you should enforce upon all God’s creation.’ That would be my jihadist mission to ensure that that’s what happened, and if people were unhappy as a result of my impact, their happiness didn’t matter, because God’s happiness and God’s contentment was my only parameter, and that’s how I should be living my life. So that would be my sort of fundamentalist response to any question of merging, or keeping Islam on the margins, and keeping it relevant to our everyday lives. I would quite proudly sort of dismiss you [out of] hand if the issue had arisen.

In his intellectual and personal transformation, moving on from that position has been a complex exercise for Hakim. It has been a transition replete with doubt and apprehension, fear and guilt, heady exploration and confusion.[41]

For a Muslim, losing faith in the West remains almost as hard as it is in the mainly Muslim nations of the Middle East or South East Asia. Even those with the greatest bravado or intellectual strength find it difficult to sustain a steady determination to prevail in an open way. Another young humanist and atheist, a former Muslim, I spoke with in Britain referred to himself as having swung from being an ardent Muslim believing in jihad to an ardent atheist with commitment enough to join and participate in the meetings of a major secularist organization. But, after initially volunteering keenly to be interviewed for this project, he later withdrew. Fear of retribution from family and community is high, and this shapes both the character of leaving the religion and the nature of the non-religious life that is subsequently forged. Although former British Christians who, in the late nineteenth and early twentieth century, wished to surrender their religion might have found it difficult to come out as atheists, the intensity of the feared retribution is much greater for the Muslim – being not merely socially alienating or threatening a livelihood but also potentially deadly. There is bravery about participating in a project such as this. Hakim told me at length his reasons:

> I wanted my comment to be part of the recording if it's possible. I am keen for my journey to be shared, and for that to add insight. There are two elements that make me apprehensive: the amount of taboos that I have breached, both in Middle Eastern culture, Islamic religion, societal norms as far as sexual practice, that are all mentioned in the interview, when I am dealing with the culture that doesn't just deal intellectually disapprovingly with those matters but can often deal physically, and violently with those issues. That can be a disincentive for any one person to identify themselves…There is no sense of shame about my journey. Actually, I am very proud of myself for having been willing, at each time I have moved from the comfort and protection of one set of thinking and beliefs with its accompanying friends and networks, I have been proud of the fact that I have been able to, well, run the risk of losing relationships and infrastructure, and move into new territory where I might have to rebuild new network of friends and co-believers, if, that's a laden term, but people who share my views.

The Hindus

The Hindu route to losing religion seems to be different again, with some distinctive characteristics. I have interviewed four humanists and secularists who were all born in India, of whom three were resident in Western nations. There are shared features to the triggers to losing religion, to the routes towards atheism and to the quality of the self-identity they ascribe to their post-religion state. Interestingly, they each started the process of moving away from Hinduism whilst still in India, so that it was not initially their personal contact with the West that started the process. However, their views and their humanistic steadfastness progressed whilst in the West. Behind all four accounts of no religionism is a uniform resolve concerning education, science or social science and rationality. Their confident and assertive narratives thus share a recognition of the influence of largely Western-style, mostly colonial-era, education. There is strength of purpose propelling them that emanates from the time of the British Raj.

As we have seen already, those seeking to escape religion are in some cultural contexts escaping from other things too. In Khushi Ram's case in India in the 1970s and 1980s, he reported that his priority was to escape the caste system, as he had been born to the lowest, labouring caste – 'untouchables' (or *Dalits*). To do this, he perceived the need to get out from his religion. He started to study religions, and struck upon the Baha'i and its doctrine of progressive revelation (where God sends a succession of prophets, and is continuing to do so) as an antidote to the Hindu faith, which sustained the rigidity of his caste. Though the Baha'i gave him some ideas, his education prevented him from accepting it:

> By that time there was too much of brain here, so I had to look up at religion critically, and I thought all are humbugs, just don't bother. But I had no set philosophy like humanistic ideas, I was a freelancer, just, you know, a free thinker. And so when I was with the State Bank of India for six years I had to move from city to city, and I would go to book stalls, and then I happened to read something about Bertrand Russell, and so that's how I got an idea that there is another world too.[42]

He emigrated to Canada in 1986, and when he arrived he started to read widely in library material. His first book was Bertrand Russell's *A History of Western Philosophy* (1945). One day he saw an advertisement in a train for the Humanist Society of Canada, attended their meeting and 'never looked back'.

The link between religion and inequality was a driving force for Khushi Ram's loss of religion. In the Indian diaspora, Hinduism was seen as underpinning caste inequality. B.R. Ambedkar, a leading Indian intellectual, and himself from the lowest untouchable caste, was influential in arguing that Indians should get out of Hinduism and move to Buddhism to escape their lot.[43] Khushi notes that the caste system survives amongst Hindus in Canada, preventing mixing of people of different positions. Khushi Ram turned to Buddhism for this escape from caste: 'No honour in that religion, come out and embrace Buddhism. So I needed a religion, so I formally went over to Buddhism.' He regarded himself as humanist and Buddhist:[44]

> It is only for the sake, for this reason, that it tallies with humanism. Humanism is my first preference, if anything goes against humanism, I just throw it. But almost, I would say 90% of it, scientific ideas, humanism, evolution, all this tallies with what Buddha said. According to me, my interpretation, there may be orthodox people indulging in what is reincarnation and rebirth. Because I feel that Buddha did not teach all those things, they are later additions by people who went over to Buddhism through Hinduism and carried these ideas, and this is too big a hypothesis to be given up unless you know how science works, the cause and effects. Although Buddha gave the cause and effect very clearly, nothing happens without a cause and there is no God, there is no soul. If these two things are missing, how can you build up any superstructure. So I believe in Lord Buddha's teachings as interpreted by Dr. Ambedkar and that's the end of it. He is there. You won't find any photograph of any God or religion or anything, just---he is my friend, he is Lord Buddha.[45]

So, Khushi saw no incongruity in holding to both Russell's humanism, to science, reason and evolution, and, at the same time, Buddhism shorn of what he perceived as the later additions of reincarnation. He held on to Buddhism so much that Khushi had a statue of the Buddha in the corner of the lounge of his house as I interviewed him. In this way, Khushi Ram's account of his journey from religion straddled an escape from the injustice of the caste system to the viability of an alternative American-style Buddhism requiring no belief in God and Western reason in the mould of Russell's logical positivism.

For those born in Hindu communities, the leaving of religion can be difficult, but the rationalism evident in Khushi Ram's testimony in Canada is found amongst each of my respondents. Interviewed in Birmingham in England, Harish Mehra was very proud of how he developed a rationalist and humanist outlook. He explained thus:

> I think at that time, because I was born and brought up in a small village and had my higher education in the near town which was about 7–8 miles from my home where I used to go to, for my university study which is D.A.V College Jallunder, which is quite well known. The whole atmosphere is religious and you are conditioned right from the beginning and you don't question that, I think I started questioning when I read one book which is called *Hints for Self Culture* by one of the intellectuals, Indian intellectuals which name is Lala Har Dayal who got Ph.D. from here from Oxford University, and I think his book *Hints for Self Culture* was written in 1935. And he was a rationalist and he was revolutionary and that book actually transformed me and made me to question, particularly my views on religion, and I started questioning my father. I said, 'What is this, can you explain to me?', and he actually he couldn't explain to me.[46]

In this way, he explained the significance of a scientific rationalism and Marxist intellectualism, rendered through higher education in India, upon his journey from the religiosity of his family. His parents and siblings were more religious and religiously observant than he, especially one sister whom he described as 'very religious'. For a long time, his changed outlook in the 1950s was criticized by his family, and though this has diminished with the decades, still into the 2010s his non-belief in God is not free from trouble. Yet, despite the familial friction, he was very proud of his championing of reason within the Hindu community, especially in Britain, where he developed an important role in an organization to promote rationalism amongst Asians in the United Kingdom.[47] He spoke of how his higher education and employment in British local government 'actually gave me more power over the other members of my family, that they could not question me'. Also, his work as a journalist and author, writing ten books on social work and racism, and having his books used in degree teaching in India, together with some media exposure on radio and television, means 'they actually do not criticise me now'. And yet, he says that his relatives 'do feel that something must go wrong to him because he does not believe in God'.[48] As with Khushi Ram in Canada, Harish looked upon the Buddha as not believing in God at all, and that his role is not to promote a supernaturalism. Like Ram, too, he read Bertrand Russell's *Why I Am Not a Christian?* on coming to Britain, and cites this as influential upon him. 'I think personally that it is proud to be an atheist, proud to be rationalist and proud to be a humanist. And also the mind is very open and very flexible to grasp the knowledge from different aspects of life from anywhere to enrich my knowledge.'[49]

In all my oral history testimonies, the power of education and rationality is nowhere so proudly summoned up in narrative as explanation and justification as in the Hindu journey to atheism. As with Khushi Ram and Harish Mehra, so Gian Thind, a retired aircraft maintenance engineer, told me that to turn back the power of religion and supernatural belief in Hindu culture, 'to upset the whole thing', as he put it, 'you got to have good education'. Yet, he recounted how he was aghast at meeting a highly educated man who was strongly religious, telling him, 'Look, you are PhD. What's the matter with you? Can you think, why don't you think? Why do you go, you follow a guy who had no education at all? That's 300 years ago..., they were scared of the thunderstorm, they thought that's God...All kind of nonsense they believe in.' I told him, 'Which you don't believe in now. But why do you believe in God too?'[50]

This unswerving logic infuses the Hindu atheists and humanists I interviewed, with science its powerhouse. In the fourth interview, Narendra Nayak recounted being raised in an Indian household with symbols of multiple gods – the Christian god, Krishna and Rama. To be without a god was unthinkable: 'I don't think I have seen an atheist. I think the first atheist I saw was myself.' Nayak was born at the opposite end of the social scale to Khushi Ram, to the 'cream of the caste' Brahmins, born to be pampered by everybody else. Caste got carried into the religious system, but it was his father, who ran a chemist's shop, who turned him at about the age of 12 against religion and against god. After testing god in prayer, he was persuaded that no god existed. This ended family religious rituals for him and set him on a road to science education in chemistry, then to leading a major rationalist society in India, and active campaigning against the pernicious effects of religion and dishonest money-making preachers upon credulous and vulnerable peasants.[51]

If the four interviews are to be taken as culturally revealing, they demonstrate the distinctive emphasis amongst Indian atheists on education and rationalism. In the three places they lived – Vancouver in Canada, Birmingham in England and in India – each interviewee stressed the role of the educated and the science-minded to combat the outrageous folly of putative swamis and gurus who fooled the gullible by tricks and sleight of hand. It produced a distinctive and uniform vigour to their testimonies, a mission to educate their families and communities and, as it was reported to me, if necessary to inform the police of religious fraud being perpetrated. Yet at the same time, two of my interviewees were quite nonchalant about having devotional statuary in their homes, sitting in the corner of the room as we spoke. Though, as some authorities suggest, India is the most religious country in the world, there remains a willingness to negotiate rationalism into the culture of its Hindu diaspora.[52]

The whites

Secularization and the rise of atheism is an overwhelmingly white affair. Why is this?

Before approaching this question, a number of observations are important. First, white experience of losing religion is not uniform. In the genesis, pace and outcomes of religious decline, there are major national differences amongst the majority white nations in the West. There are huge differences in the nature of the process between the ecclesiastical backgrounds of those who experience loss of religion. And most importantly, there are major differences between individuals who instigate and react differently to losing their religion; there is individual agency, character, temperament and resolve involved. As can be seen from this book, where seventy of the eighty-five respondents were white and Christian in their cultural backgrounds, there are huge differences in their experiences.

Yet, there are generalizations to be made. Those who are without religion and are drawn to atheism come from a variety of ecclesiastical Christian backgrounds, but a disproportionate number tend to come from a liberal church milieu – notably from the Church of England, the Lutheran and the liberal Presbyterian churches, and also from liberal elements of Roman Catholicism.[53] This is hardly surprising since those without religion tend to be of liberal dispositions, certainly on political issues of the day (such as gay rights, women's rights and dignity in dying), and tend to vote for more liberal, radical or left-wing political parties. This applies even to those coming from less liberal ecclesiastical backgrounds. For instance, two former Jehovah's Witnesses I interviewed, and those who experienced evangelical or Pentecostal churches, tended to have finally eschewed those in part because they found their own liberal dispositions to be incongruent with attachment to more conservative religions. Some interviewees were inside evangelical or conservative religious traditions which were, in hindsight, plain mistakes for them to have joined.

For all ethnic groups, losing religion is something which, in the main, belongs to the domain of the liberal, the radical or the left-winger. This has been marked in the past amongst white people who lose religion, but is tending to change with growing right-wing atheism in Europe, making it a cross-political phenomenon. But in the United States and Canada, right-wing politics retain an association with a religious-based conservative culture. I noted in Chapter 2 how patriotism is a feature of the testimonies of those with a religion, appearing in both oral and autobiographical testimony a great deal, especially in the United States. What is interesting is that this patriotism is also to be found amongst those who have moved from traditional churches and religions to non-religious positions. The anti-establishment credentials of sixties' disaffection from organized religion are not necessarily still the case. Still, in American presidential elections since the 1980s, religious 'nones' have risen to be a major voting constituency (rising from 5 per cent in 1980 to 16 per cent in 2012), and those nones increasingly voted for Democratic presidential candidates (41 per cent in 1980, 73 per cent in 2012).[54] In this regard, nations with white liberal traditions have been the most advanced in secularization. Liberalism is spreading in terms of morality on a range of issues – an issue we return to in the next chapter.

It's not for me to judge humanism

On 7 October 2009 in Vancouver, I interviewed five humanists in one day. They represented the multifaith melange of humanism and of Canadian society as a whole. The five I interviewed comprised two Indian-born former Hindu men, one German-born ethnic female Jew, one Austrian-born ethnic male Jew and a white former Protestant woman raised in British Columbia. In the previous two days, I had interviewed a further seven from Christian backgrounds. I discussed the religious legacy upon humanists with the last I interviewed, Ernest Poser, raised in Vienna and Leipzig in the 1920s and early 1930s. He said to me, 'I want to ask whether you think that those humanists, liberally interpreted, who arrive at that position but retain a part of their tradition of origin are really humanists in the strict sense of the word?'[55] Ernest was an intellectual, a former university professor with immense learning in Jewish culture, religion and humanist thought. I felt he was asking me a question about the genuineness of humanism when influenced by the religious baggage of a person's upbringing, and as a cultural historian researching the roots and identity of atheists and humanists, I resisted (and still resist) the notion of there being a central 'test' of a person's religious or non-religious position. The identity lies in the self-expression, not in an outsider's test which, in any event, will in itself be both highly debated and largely impossible to apply to the bulk of those who live their lives as if there is no god.

CB (in my reply to Ernest)   In some ways I regard that as a separate issue. What was being put to me today was that Buddhism is not necessarily the starting point. It's Hinduism and Sikhism as a starting point that, if you come from South East Asian Buddhism, is the route to secularism.

And by Buddhism we're talking about an Americanised version, not a Sri Lankan, not an Indian or Burmese version, that there is now in Western society. In USA, Canada, Western Europe, there is a different version of Buddhism which is popular and it is that which is part of the process of moving from Hinduism/Sikhism to humanism.

EP Right, I can see that. But when you get to the end point, one might expect that most of the travellers who have taken that journey will have shed at least the mainstream of their tradition. Now we have an example in Western society. I grant you that as soon as you go outside of that it gets a little dicey, because Buddhism is to some extent a way of life…But as you say, we have here in this area, Western Canada, a lot of humanists who came by humanism through Unitarianism and they are even as members of the humanist organisation at all stages of the transformation process and there are some who go to both places. I mean, they could go to humanist meetings and the Unitarian church faithfully every Sunday, because both groups tend to meet on Sunday.

CB Yep. These are difficult areas which I'm not sure there's a single answer to the question you posed to me…the arrival point: is it really humanism? I'm not sure first of all as a professional historian whether it is for me to set a litmus test as to what is and is not true humanism. It will be for me to record and explain different versions of it. But it's not for me to set, as a professional historian, to set a test…But even Khushi Ram this morning said that --- I asked him his definition – he said 'no transcendent God'. And that seems to be one core and he's able to say, as many are, that Buddhism does not necessarily need a transcendent God. The Buddha was a prophet about our lives. Now, that's not for me to disagree with. That's how he's rightly or wrongly interpreted.[56]

This chapter has, to an extent, been about the negotiation of atheism within – in reality, *into* – religious and ethnic cultures, and partly about the fear of coercion upon atheists in certain minority religious and ethnic groups. The negotiating of atheism into a religious and ethnic culture is the first step to making non-belief socially acceptable and widely open to individuals. The process of negotiation is most intense and perhaps difficult where the ethnic group is a minority, the defences are up and the hackles easily raised to any perceived threat to the integrity and cultural survival of groups, perhaps especially when they are parts of diasporas. For white majority societies infused with growing liberalism in the later part of the twentieth century, atheism has been able to take root in the form of hard-fought principle, but also in the form of rising and wide-scale indifference to religion. It is when the fighting stops over defending religious culture *against* this negotiation of atheism into it that living without a god becomes second nature and an alternative normal.

CHAPTER EIGHT

The Humanist Condition

After religion

Audiences of Christians can be incredulous when presented with evidence of the high moral standards of atheists. Examples of philanthropic endeavour, the caring and supportive roles they take in hospices and bereavement counselling, and the work they proudly devote to the conduct of funerals, marriage celebrancy and chaplaincy can meet with sceptical guffaws. There is a resolute conviction amongst some pastors, priests and church laity that only religious faith can produce social good. Of course, some atheist values are opposed by nearly all churches, and these tend, in the round, to distinguish the moral cosmos of the non-believer – notably full gay rights and assisted suicide. This cosmos has been under construction through individuals making decisions which, with surprising speed, have been, or are in the process of being, adopted in most Western nations. With a few exceptions, most religious traditions have fought these developments tooth and nail. There is no agreed common name for this new moral cosmos. The most appropriate name is probably humanism.

Where does humanism come from? A conventional explanation is that it is traced through the history of philosophy in which intellectual elites generated, disseminated and bequeathed humanist thought from as early as Greek antiquity, through Christian humanism, the Enlightenment and late modern secular moralists.[1] Another line of scholarship, that on the history of freethinking and atheism, has placed emphasis upon the intellectual deviancy and heroic activism of a very small minority.[2] But what narrative do we turn to when humanists claim they are not intellectuals and did not find a new conception of human rights and morality from reading books or listening to humanist speakers? What if they say the ideas of morality were already there, within them, before they thought atheism or humanism were possible? How then do we account for the humanism in the Western world? If they are not finding a discursive humanism in wider culture upon which to draw, are they finding it within? This, an argument introduced by Michael Roper, raises the prospect that we should pay more attention to the role of individuals in cultural change.[3] This chapter pursues the idea that humanism is a moral position that emerges from people without widespread intellectualizing or exposure to the humanist movement. Since 1945 a huge proportion of the Western population has seemingly, at different points, started to passively nurture an indifference to religionism. Within that indifference, humanist values have come to dominate Western moral culture.

All my humanist respondents told me, without exception, that they were 'humanists' before they discovered the term. Humanism was neither a philosophy nor an ideology that they had learned or read about and then adopted. There was no act of conversion, no training or induction which turned them into humanists. Only one respondent mentioned attending a humanist-movement course, though the impact on his values seems to have been restricted. During the period of indifference to religion, which I explored in detail in Chapter 4, and sometimes before that when many were still notionally attached to a religion, they had developed concepts and principles to turn them from a religious mould into something they came later to recognize could be called humanism. Respondents consequently say that a humanist condition precedes being a self-conscious humanist. They made plain very vigorously in interview that they had been a humanist already, usually for some considerable time. An implication of this is that the humanist condition has been quite widespread in Western society, indeed very common during the key decades, the 1950s to 1990s, represented by the people I have interviewed. It suggests, further, the possibility that humanism is a condition that many in Western society have held but few may have realized.

In this final chapter, I will explore both the humanist condition preceding discovery of being a humanist and the humanism with which the individual came to identify and, inspired by a compelling moral imperative, to *perform*, relating to a world to which they believe they have much to offer. Those I interviewed spoke with force about the identities, values and the activism into which they were led. Their values were in nearly all cases well crafted and fully formed before they lost religion, though they rarely attributed the values *in toto* to their religious background. Much more frequently, they attributed the genesis of their journey between the 1950s and the 1990s away from religion to the realization that those values which they held were inconsistent with their church or faith. By this means, we can explore – in order – the nature of the moral values of the humanist condition, and the coming upon humanism as the ideological and philosophical consolidation of after-religion morality.

The hesitant atheist

Before we come to the humanist condition, it is important to step sideways for a moment, if you will, to describe the narrating qualities of my respondents. Because there are features in the way they spoke to me that cast light on the transition from indifference to religion to commitment as a humanist.

Oral historians are accustomed to encountering a variety of speech characteristics in interviewees. One set of features that is much discussed is that of disrupted speech. This may comprise intense incidence of hesitancy, unfinished sentences, harrumphs (clearing of the throat), verbal tics and rapid change of direction in topic – all accompanied by occasional loudness of voice and occasional quietness of voice, and shifting body postures. These signal that a lack of sureness in narration has taken grasp of the speaker. Oral historians have written at length of the circumstances that produce this, and most often it is associated with the recounting of what are called crisis or trauma narratives. The trauma includes what might be regarded as extreme circumstances, including those narrating experiences of the Nazi Holocaust, and child and domestic abuse. By contrast, it is taken as more 'normal' to encounter a greater sureness of narration, a composure, with diminished hesitance and associated symptoms, amongst those recounting less upsetting memories and with a greater confidence that they have a composed story to tell.[4]

Interestingly, I found a rather different position. Let me start with the laughter. My transcribers were asked to note [laughs] in the transcriptions they produced. Examination of the transcription compendium (COT) reveals laughter occurred 662 times and chuckles 56 times – an average of almost 9 times per respondent; other sounds were infrequent, occurring fewer than 5 times each. To analyse this feature, I would say first that the intersubjectivity between me and my respondents was far from frolicsome; jokes were rare, my demeanour verging on the serious. Though space prevents a close analysis here, it is clear that the causes of the laughter were the respondents' memories of themselves in early life – recollection of their own religious gullibility, over-devotion to churchgoing and innocence of their former religious view. The laughter punctuates the testimonies, often nervously in recall of a naivety, perhaps even being duped. Those who spoke of being brainwashed were less likely to laugh, but those who spoke of experiencing distress or trauma still laughed at themselves. By contrast, the narration of trauma was really rather clear, with stories the narrators had in many cases told many times; there was a conviction and certainty of direction, a fierce determination to complete the story, though sometimes still accompanied by outward signs of distress. Most interviews, ones with an absence of trauma narration, contained a period of calm contemplation of their religious lives, almost a placidity, and including tender laughter as if the topic they are discussing deserved to be handled gently. There is a *general* hesitancy, a reaching out for a manner of exposition, an uncertainty over how to speak about the early days of their struggles with faith and doubt – the questioning phase, sometimes in childhood – a hesitance which, amongst women, related often to the realm of family (as the domain, perhaps, in which they felt they should speak about the construction of their identity) and amongst men showed indecision over the manner of narration. The consequence in interview was the production of quite a lot of broken speech – unfinished phrases and sentences, in some an intensification of verbal tics. My understanding of what was happening is this. Those with traumatic backgrounds to or exits from religion were the most familiar with their own story, with the greater self-rehearsal and understanding, having sometimes written it down or narrated it to others. Those for whom my interview was the earliest comprehensive narration of losing religion generated more hesitance, especially about long periods of indifference. Middling indifference had left a legacy in indecisive speech, and uncertainty of why this was. Laughter helped to express this – their past vulnerabilities, victimhood and survival. Some spoke of how hard it was to lose religion. This was especially the case for people from high-religious societies: from those raised in the American Bible belt or introspective religious groups across the Western world. Those coming out of the Jehovah's Witnesses referred to their desperate intellectual grasping for evidential judgement and their fear of 'shunning'; those from Roman Catholic backgrounds, again notably women, spoke about their 'relentless guilt' (a word that appeared thirty times in the interview testimonies); and Protestants from Northern Ireland, and some from Scotland, spoke of the problematic release from demanding levels of godly observance. Khushi Ram described how hard it was to lose religion whilst a member of the Hindu community.

> You know it is very difficult for children to be non-observing religion, if their parents are observing it; it is tough. Actually for example, when my [grandmother] died, after two or three days I asked the younger [grandchild], he was plus five at that time…, in the hospital itself when she was dead and when we were coming home, I separated him just for the sake of curiosity. I said, 'Boy, now where is your grandma? What happened to her?' He said, 'She is dead'. I said, 'What, what do you mean by this?' I was trying to be funny with him. He said, 'You don't know, she was motionless, we were trying to speak to her, she did not respond, so she is dead. That's all, that's gone'. And after five or six days, I again asked that guy, small one, I said: 'Now Boy, do you remember still your grandma?' He said, 'Yeah'. 'But where is she?' And he told me: 'She is in heaven.'

Despite his tempting with reason and evidence, and though not forcing them, some of his grandchildren failed to follow his own atheistic views. Khushi went on:

> You require a lot [of] intelligence and you require a lot of courage, two things, to be humanist. To declare that I don't believe in God in a society where everybody believes in God, they simply throw you out. And human beings being social in nature, he would like to be a part of them, and so willy-nilly says 'okay, I am with you'.[5]

The social impetus to be a part of one's society can make it difficult to forge a non-religious identity.

A corollary is the victimization of the unbeliever. We have seen how many recount this in childhood, formulating it as the cause of their loss of religion. But adulthood can bring discrimination. Ellen Ramsay from British Columbia felt that she experienced unfairness at work in the 1980s and 1990s from Christian staff, resulting from a general fear of atheism: 'It still seems to be unacceptable to be an atheist. The word scares people. I went around with an atheist t-shirt on and I went through a district of Vancouver and a woman grabbed her children and pulled them away from me on the street as if I was the devil incarnate.'[6] Not many respondents spoke directly of the psychological impact of losing religion, but one who did was John Manuel, who came at the age of 60 to realize that his lifelong attachment to the Church was not based on a rational foundation. He reported his transition over fifteen years as an acceptance of a position he had evidently long held, but had not realized, likening his loss

> to a wide corridor, that I moved from one side of the corridor to the other side of the corridor. It wasn't like stepping over a line or something like that. And there was a corridor that led me to the other side, and once I reached the wall on the other side as it were, I reached through you know, the nearest opening and I was away.[7]

John was the only respondent to offer such a metaphor, though a few spoke of the task becoming easier in the 2000s than before. Lorraine Hardie explained how for many decades she described herself as an agnostic because she 'had not been that comfortable' with stating her atheist position; but in later years she became 'much more comfortable', a change she attributed to media discussion of Richard Dawkins and Christopher Hitchens: 'it's getting easier and easier to state your position'.[8]

With diminishing hesitancy, there are a variety of monikers to adopt. Academics cannot agree on a single satisfactory term: *unaffiliated, non-adherents, apostates, godless, nones, non-religionists* or *no-religionists*. These are terms rarely adopted by the non-religious, who prefer one or more of atheist, agnostic, humanist, secularist, freethinker, bright. Each of these refers to separate aspects of being non religious, and some are open to multiple meanings. Table 1.1 on page 14 provides a count of the terms used in my interviews, demonstrating how humanism was by far the identity most spoken of, followed by atheism and agnosticism. Humanist attracted implicit and explicit support and identification. One respondent said that being a humanist provided a point of reference, a set of agreed ideas in the movement, with which he could feel secure; however, one leading member of the movement had left in the early 1980s declaring himself a freethinker, wishing to be free of scripted principles entirely.[9]

Yet it is the multiple usage of terms by non-believers that is most marked. This multiplicity leads to their simultaneous use by many I have interviewed. Justin Trottier from Quebec became a scientist, studying astronomy at the University of Toronto, emerging in his twenties as a leading figure in North American atheism, and Canadian director of the Center for Inquiry. Science has defined his life and work. I asked him whether he described himself as an atheist, agnostic or what?

> I think all those are appropriate. I've used them all on different occasions. I guess I am an agnostic about, you know the epistemology of the God question, but from a practical point of view I am an atheist. I live my life as if there is no God. I am also a humanist when it comes to my sort of ethical world view, so all of those terms would fit me.[10]

This multiple identity within no religionism is very common. Moses Klein described himself in very similar terms:

> If you ask me am I an atheist, the answer is yes. If you ask me am I an agnostic, the answer is yes. If you ask me, how do I define my worldview, my stance on the questions that are often traditionally addressed by religion, I would see myself as a humanist or a secular humanist, sometimes as a freethinker.[11]

Multiple terms identify different aspects of being without religion and God. My respondents were very precise and sophisticated about this, and certainly not being in any way confused. Several preferred to call themselves agnostic because of its greater scientific underpinning – with atheist being founded forlornly on trying to disprove a negative. Ron McLaren told me, 'I never actually became atheist. I'm an agnostic. For reasons of evidence. You can't prove one or the other.'[12] With that precision, though, comes an emotive attachment to it. There emerges in the second decade of the twenty-first century a joy to atheism, rarely remarked upon. Coming through long-term distress over the concept of hell, Maria Berger's emergence in her thirties into first agnosticism and then atheism gave great pleasure: 'I call myself an atheist now. Most atheists don't want to be called atheists anymore nowadays, but for me it give me this great feeling of life. It gives my life an aspect that I never had before. I mean, it has a lot to do with hedonism as well and I love the expression.'[13] Cecil Bannister gives a similar account of the fulfilment that losing religion has done for him:

I get the emails periodically about, you know the difference and it makes me, it's made me so much aware, and then trying to label yourself, without the baggage, the atheist who is in people's mind. And you know what I found fantastic is when people ask, 'you are a believer', I say 'yeah I am a believer', and they say, 'well what do you believe in?' and I say, 'well I believe that there is no God', you know. So yeah, I have beliefs and it's not that an atheist does not have beliefs, you know what I mean, it just removes that. I am only saying that only to accommodate the people that cannot accept that people don't have beliefs, you know. I am perfectly happy being an atheist.[14]

In a similar vein, John Manuel told me that 'there's nothing sad about my unbelief. I'm happier today as a committed atheist than I ever was as a doubting and disillusioned Christian'.[15] For some there is a frequent elision between the self-descriptors 'agnostic' and 'atheist'. Agnostic is often chosen as a politer, less aggressive or assertive posture, one which might cause less rankling in social company. But it causes confusion in some hearers who take agnostic to be a weaker position, one which reveals somebody who is undecided, one hedging his or her bets over the existence of God. Robin Russell reported,

I used to call myself an agnostic and I stopped because of the reaction I would get from religious people; it's like, 'Oh well you believe that it's possible.' And then I --- Well no, I need to put the nuance in there. 99.9 to the millionth per cent probability there are no sky fairies. So just that tiniest possibility that there are says you're agnostic, and it's stupid to be an atheist claiming, you know, when you can't know. But on the other hand if you just say you're an atheist, then if they're interested enough you can give that nuance to them. But it gets rid of the nonsense that people still seem to cling to that: 'Well, you know, you're 50/50 you know.' No I'm not 50/50. I'm gonna run my life entirely on the basis that there are no sky fairies. No, there are atheists in foxholes, you know – all these aphorisms that are nonsense, you just try to deal with.[16]

So for some, the selection of a term of self-description is a moveable feast, and the movement is one not necessarily determined by any philosophic, scientific or belief change, merely an assertion of determination not to be misunderstood. For David Fowler, there was no great pressure to have a label from his teens, and even in his mid-thirties he was uncertain: 'I would have probably called myself an agnostic then, and even with my own wife, we didn't talk a lot about these things but I think we both, I know we both agreed that we probably were atheist, but we didn't use that term, so we very closely agreed on how we viewed things.'[17] For Kirsten Bulmer, 'atheist' became in part a term to provoke: 'I used to be really uncomfortable with the term atheist, but now I'm an out and proud atheist, I'm proud of that, yes … Humanist gives, tells you a little bit more about me cause it tells you more about my morals and all the rest of it. So yeah, I'm comfortable with both of those.'[18] Not everyone I interviewed accepted 'humanist' as a term of identity; a handful acknowledged the term without prejudice, though one – a secularist – specifically said it did not apply to him. Notwithstanding this, the qualities which the vast bulk of my respondents claimed to themselves were seen by them as humanist.

The hesitant atheist in some ways does not entirely lose the aura of hesitancy, much as he or she might wish to. Terminological profusion can make it difficult for outsiders to appreciate the resolve of the atheist community as a whole, and not just the minority seemingly castigated by religionists and some scholars as 'militant atheists'.[19] Yet, as I said earlier in the book, being label-less applies to most who live their lives as if there is no god, and must be regarded as one feature of the atheist identity – and certainly for the indifferent who have no terms to draw upon. Yet, being label-less is not being value-less.

Finding the humanist condition

The idea that a humanistic culture has been displacing Western Christianity is one that has gained traction recently amongst some Christian scholars. Charles Taylor built a benevolent 'exclusive humanism' into his model of the 'secular age' arising in the nineteenth century – a humanism based on altruistic duty, unhinged from any reward in an afterlife, that loosened Christian belief and practice in Europe and elsewhere. Taylor sources this humanism to an unwitting Christianity, which, as he noted, went into deep crisis from 1945.[20] But two things he doesn't contemplate: first, that humanism emerges from humans, often children, who, one by one, find much of Christian ethics and the churches morally unacceptable; and second, that atheism becomes core to the humanism – what in the United States tends to be called 'secular humanism'.

The rise of humanistic values is most associated with Western culture in the period since 1960. The legal framework was the notion of human rights which emerged from the Second World War and which became crucial to the formation of the United Nations and especially to European law. But that was only a framework, and required the wider social acceptance of secularized values which emerged mainly after 1960. One was the gay revolution, starting with decriminalization in some nations in the 1960s, followed by criminalization of homophobic hate crimes, and on to the advent of gay (or equal) marriage from 1989. The last of these is now, in the 2010s, legalized in at least nineteen jurisdictions in Western Europe and North America, with only one (Italy) not having national legislation at the time of writing. Recent scholarship in religious history has made much of liberal Christian roles in decriminalization.[21] But less acknowledged has been the fact that the churches and conservative Christians have also been the main opponents, usually far more numerous than the liberals. Furthermore, as Kelly Kollman demonstrates, the spread of same-sex unions arose not through intergovernmental policy agreement nor church policy change, but through a rapid and widespread convergence based, notwithstanding varied timings associated with national domestic conceptions of the nuclear family, on new moral positions associated with declining religiosity.[22] The change in public opinion has been dramatic and in defiance of the majority of churches. Support for gay marriage rose amongst Americans from 35 per cent in 2001 to 55 per cent in 2015, and support for assisted suicide rose from 51 per cent in 2013 to 68 per cent in 2015.[23] In Britain, in 2015, 82 per cent supported assisted dying legislation, and 68 per cent supported same-sex marriage (even 68 per cent in highly conservative Northern Ireland).[24] Kollman's proposition of a correlation between secularization and same-sex unions seems incontrovertibly extendable to medically assisted suicide (and likely also to abortion and wider social approval of sexual freedoms). The rise of nones, of people without religious affiliation, and disbelief in god, seems undeniably linked to the flourishing of new moralities.

But the humanist condition is considerably wider than merely tolerance of gay marriage and assisted suicide. It is a web of moral change amongst Western people, dominated by those who have lost religion. At root, it is founded on doubt about god, scripture, religious authority and religion (in the sense of hierarchical ecclesiastical command), though this doubt can develop into different qualities and social outcomes which we, as historians, find in historical sources: religious indifference or apathy, scoffing, protest, dissent, blasphemy and on to outright agnosticism and atheism.[25] It is also based on the separation of morality from either godly authority or spirituality, with a basic tolerance towards belief and unbelief, and a receptivity to materialistic understandings of the world and of the human condition. These are the driving impulses of the humanist condition.

Amongst the testimonies of those who had spent years in indifference before declaring for humanism was to be found a moral framework embedded in a series of values. This can be seen in part in Table 8.1, where some of the variety of key terms can be discerned. Respondents uniformly said they held these values before discovering humanism or coming out as humanists. The source of these values was not in the individual respondent's adoption of a formal humanist identity, but lay in the individual himself or herself. Losing religion changed few values because the discovery of the loss of faith affirmed the rest of their lives. Take Mary Wallace. When asked about changes in values, she reported,

Table 8.1 Leading 'outside' reference terms used by respondents

Terms used in interviews with 77 respondents: Rank order of usage	Incidence of use
Gay/gay rights	183/16
Rights/human rights/right to choose/abortion	171/39/9/111
Moral/morality/morals	161/40/18
Science/scientific	148/80
Ethical/ethics	86/50
Feminist/feminism	38/34
Euthanasia/assisted suicide	38/30
Socialist/socialism	34/14
Democratic/Republican	22/6
Golden rule	16
Charity/charitable	15/12

No change whatsoever [in] everything I always did believe in, in terms of gay sexuality being absolutely fine, sex before marriage being absolutely fine, to being a pacifist, a feminist, a socialist, everything I did believe in in terms of core values. I mean, I was brought up very strictly, and manners, honesty, respect, I suppose, were the three biggies. And all of those things continue through my life, so I don't think humanism has affected my morality. I think that was all set in my childhood and teenage years, perhaps became more kind of developed, but nothing major changed. My humanism just sort of fit like a comfy old hat. When I found it, it was like 'Oh that's what I am then [laughs], I'm a humanist'. So it didn't actually change anything, I can't think of anything that it changed, no. It just fit with what I already believed, I could --- I found a kind of label for myself.[26]

This is a widespread sentiment. In Wales, Cerys Davies told me, 'I know now that I have been a humanist from about nine years of age.' Though she did not know the word until her mid-thirties, she reported science as instilling in her an appreciation of the 'naturalistic' way of looking upon things. 'My Humanism has been a spontaneous part of me from childhood', she said. Looking back, she understood now that she had been living as a humanist without supernaturalism, but, like nearly all the others, did not have a word for it until very many years later.[27] Likewise, Ron McLaren from Scotland said that 'for the first thirty-five/forty years of my humanist view I didn't know that's what it was called'. He reported,

I discovered there was a thing called humanism from sitting in the dentist surgery, waiting to have a tooth out or something, and reading this little article in the *Scottish Field* magazine. Humanism. It gave an address, PO box number I think and why not join and be freethinking or something like that? And I wrote away from that and you know here we are twelve years later.[28]

Again, this narrative is common. After twenty years of religious indifference, Frank Brown from British Columbia encountered humanism 'by the simple act of picking up a humanist magazine in our local library'.[29] Joan Gibson told me, 'I discovered I was a humanist and thought I was sort of on my own.'[30] The way in which the respondents described their emergence into formal humanism precludes a role for a discourse they were emulating: they invariably read materials after discovering the term, leaving their individual stories as experience-rooted narratives.

The values of the humanist condition may be described as falling under six headings. With one or two exceptions, each was close to being an axiomatic belief amongst my respondents. The first is that of what is referred to by several respondents as 'the golden rule' of doing unto others as you would have them do unto you. This guiding principle, one predating Christianity, was seen to have, by its general application, the ability to define the moral condition of being human and thereby undergirds most principles of the humanist movement and philosophy. Second was the right of every person to have not merely freedom of religion but freedom from religion, and the consequent separation of church and state. A third strand was the rights of women, notably birth control (including free access to it, education and writing about it). Fourth were sexual freedoms – the freedom of men and women to have sexual relations without marriage, and for homosexual relations to be free from censure and having equality before the law including in marriage and divorce. Fifth, there was the whole gamut of modern equality issues, starting for a number of my respondents in their experience of racial discrimination and segregation in the mid-twentieth century, which energized humanist approaches to racial equality. And sixth, there is the rapidly emerging right in Western nations to medically assisted suicide – to dignity in dying. In each of these six strands, the opposition has been consistently the churches, despite the support of some liberal churchpeople.

From these six values of the humanist condition developed two impulses which characterized the behaviour of those I interviewed: the impulses, first, to action in caring and, second, to campaigning for human rights. The impulses developed usually during the periods of indifference to religion, within an identified humanist condition, which then led them to organized humanism within which the impulses characteristically grew stronger, notably in relation to campaigning activism. But in a few cases, it produced a desire for caring which could not be satisfied within the humanist movement, and instigated private activism. The six value headings were traced by my humanist respondents to their years before joining humanist organizations and becoming activists. These were values they took to be 'natural' in a moral society. They didn't claim any special divine-like status for these; they weren't revelations born out of damascene conversion, but the base morality of what they took to be human. Respondents often took *caring* as the defining value. When asked, one Scottish humanist man told me that the most important quality was 'being humanitarian and caring about people. Equality'.[31] This linkage of caring with equality was common amongst both men and women.

In terms of both philosophical beliefs and moral standpoints, no interviewee contradicted the notion that becoming a humanist was a process of becoming aware of what they already were, of realization of their self. Moses Klein, though diffident as a Jew in his youth, discovered at university at Yale that he was humanist: 'in some sense on an intellectual level I'd always been a secular humanist, so that I was identifying with it as a movement only starting in university. But that you know the ethical worldview I think was really quite in keeping with what I had before then'.[32] This *intellectual* understanding of humanism was important for some, and indeed is seen by a few as a necessary element of the humanist condition and the movement that follows. For Terry Martin, who described himself to me as 'a Marxist Humanist', it required what Foucault called 'a panoptic gaze' as to what was going on around, to anticipate and to plan for humanist campaigns.[33] Yet, the vast majority spoke to me of not being intellectuals; the women especially said they didn't read much about humanism, but instead spoke of the charity work they undertook. Gillian Stewart from Fife gave me a typical account: 'I'm not a big reader, I have to say. I'm not a big intellectual. I'm a bit lazy when it comes to things like that, but I guess I know how I feel and that's enough for me … But after our son died I went to work.' She then explained how she started to work in a children's hospice, and after eight years undertook training in counselling, considered becoming a funeral director, but instead became a humanist and then a humanist celebrant.[34] This was very common in testimony – women's sentiment to deny intellectualism. Humanism was a moral condition into which they grew naturally, and which guided their actions above all else.

Respondents describe with relish the moment of discovery of humanism. In California, Alex Colias distinguished his own agency from that of humanism:

> Thinking made me arrive at humanism … My lack of belief has changed my life in many ways, but I don't know that I would describe humanism as the active agent of change. I mean, it's not like I learned about humanism somehow and went 'Hey – I really like that! I think it's right, so that's what I'll believe.' … I wouldn't say humanism did anything to me – ever. For me it's just a thinking-thing & that's that. So yes, my attitudes towards everything you mention have completely changed, but not because of humanism.[35]

Ronald Brown from Glasgow, having drifted from organized religion for decades, discovered a humanist group by accident after retirement: 'I became a member as their thoughts were mine also.'[36] John Edwards in the English West Midlands drifted from organized religion and belief in God between 14 and 18 years of age. But it was when he was in his early forties that he had a breakthrough moment. He went to the humanist funeral of a fellow teacher around 1990: 'I suddenly [went], as a lot of people, "crikey I didn't know people believed this stuff".' As a result, John looked up the telephone directory and found the number for a leading British humanist, Harry Stopes-Roe.[37] 'So I phoned him and he said, "Oh yes, it's always good to find out while you are alive [chuckling], just not find out you're a humanist when you're about to die!"'[38] John called himself a humanist from that point on, attending meetings and becoming a local organizer of a humanist group.

This breakthrough moment was widely replicated amongst my respondents, founded upon hearing the values within them expounded in a concept and a name. Kenneth Matthews from East Kilbride in the West of Scotland placed the emergence of his humanism as the result of life. He states, 'So what brought me to where I am today is just been general life and crossing off bits that are really ---. It was the "university of life"[39] – as he put it, the university of hard knocks as one other man put it. The way he tells it is to resort to a succession of stories, incidents from his life, ranging through his work, social activity and his children's lives.' Moses Klein told me that two shaping causes for his humanism were green politics, working for a period as a canvasser for an environmental organization, and CND: 'On an intellectual level I'd always been a secular humanist so that was identifying with it as a movement only start[ed] in university. But that, you, the ethical worldview I think was really quite in keeping with what I had before then.'[40] Robin Wood expressed this need for an intellectual system, and found it in joining the British Humanist Association (BHA) at the age of 24 in 1964: 'It gave me a philosophy.'[41] Quite a number of my respondents paid due acknowledgement to the churches they left behind as one of the sources of their philosophy or moral values, one or two being drawn to visit churches at home and abroad in fascination with the architecture and ambience. Bill Kennedy felt very kindly towards the Catholicism he left:

> I liked the ceremonies, I still do. I have a fond memory of all that ceremonious stuff. It's not tinged with any sort of resentment or disdain or --- It's comforting it's like comfort food even though I'm an atheist now. So my attitude toward religions is tolerant and understanding. Getting together with a lot of people who are friendly and accepting is a good feeling.[42]

But this did not dull the feeling of making sure the distinctive humanist appeal was heard. As Moses Klein told me, 'as secular humanists we need to be visible, you know. We need to be recognised a part of the diversity of the society. We cannot count on religious people to speak up for us'.[43]

When and how the humanist condition, in all its moral constituents, was formed will take a different type of history project to study. But the individuals' claims to pre-forming humanism require explanation. Though this is clearly a speculative case, the humanist condition may well have had an existence across the religious periods of human history. It has a persistence grounded in a moral outlook that has existed outside or beside religious faith, fostered by doubt and humans' relentless leanings towards rationalism, materialism and also justice. Scholarship is starting to make the evidence-supported case that religious scepticism and atheism existed in antiquity, the Middle Ages and early modern societies.[44] Further, this scholarship is clear that a culture of atheism was not allowed to exist as either discourse or sub-culture in the medieval and early modern periods; the historian Susan Reynolds has discounted any significant link between scepticism and organized heresy or dissent: 'One Montaillou woman, when inquisitors asked whence she got her doubts about hell and the resurrection, said that she got them from no one: she thought of them for herself.'[45] Keith Thomas, in his recent study of early-modern fulfilment, is sceptical about the reach of churchly authority and the extent of popular submission to the afterlife: 'In practice most of the population implicitly took a more secular view: they cherished life for its own sake, not merely as a preliminary to some future state.'[46] In this way, we see the individualism of humanism at its very origins in the isolated individual. Scepticism may well have been a source for heresy, but what is now in the non-religious movement throughout the world called skepticism seems to have been a fairly universal root for tolerance of belief and unbelief. In this endurance of tolerance, further research may come to discern more detail of the humanist condition – ideas of goodness, fulfilment and tolerance coming from within human experience, not from authority, supernaturalism or prefigured cultural discourses. Reason alone may construct humanism.

Becoming atheist with a heart

When the religiously indifferent come to commit to the atheist or humanist movement, their values follow them. If you ask humanists, atheists, skeptics and secularists how to define their values, humanists are by far the least formulaic; on the one hand they are the most strained to find a vocabulary, on the other hand the most genuine when they find it. From Scotland, when asked if she could define her humanism for me, Mary Wallace told me,

> Yeah, yeah --- just good without god covers it beautifully for me. I just think that, for me, it's about living a moral, ethical life, living life by a code that says there are principles that we should all adhere to about, treating

each other well and with respect and consideration about equality, and that if we all do that, we can do that without recourse to any religion whatsoever. I'm not at all anti-religious. I've got lots of friends who have quite firm religious beliefs and I'm totally respectful of that and actually that's one thing that I feel very strongly about that I know colleagues who have come at their humanism from a rather more negative angle, don't share – that they rather enjoy the religious bashing stuff and the anti-religious element. I don't. For me humanism isn't about that. Humanism is about saying we should all respect each other regardless of what our differing beliefs are. Doesn't matter a toss to me if somebody else wants to believe in God, that's absolutely fine, I'm completely respectful of that because I don't, that's fine. Not a problem for me, so that's, I suppose, a bit of a long-winded way of saying it. But that's what my humanism's about.[47]

These sentiments encapsulate pretty much what nearly all my respondents told me. Humanists tell of the one life we live, that this isn't a rehearsal, and the need to make the best of it.[48] They speak of humanism as giving a framework by which to understand the complex things they already hold to: Robin Wood told me, 'Instead of being anti-religion, it gave me a positive thought. This is atheism with a heart. It says this world is all there is, this is what we know – all we know – about this, make it a better place.'[49] Those of my respondents who joined humanist groups reported very positive emotions. Julia Stuart said, 'I am glad I joined them. I am much happier being an atheist, knowing about the humanists…Humanists are good folks without the religion.'[50] Humanists almost to a man and woman declared a commitment to common values noted previously. One woman, having experienced the loss of her son and working in a children's hospice, placed euthanasia as a vital humanist cause.[51] They all spoke with enthusiasm for the blossoming of their values, and savoured the opportunity to show that care and activism lay at the heart of the humanist movement.

The positive emotions extend to gaining comfort from the fellowship found in the movement. Joyce Murphy, born in Bradford in Yorkshire in 1934, emigrated to Western Canada in 1956, and, like many who journey from Christianity in the United States and Canada, was led to the Unitarian Universalist Church:

So I really, really felt this was something I wanted to explore, but I also because I had just come to the country and was very --- I mean these people were very good to me…I wanted to be a joiner at church, not because they were such nice people. So I succeeded because when I came to Vancouver and then thought, now I am ready to join the Church, they were completely surprised, they never even thought that I was in the least bit interested in it. So for me, it became a discussion, if you like, on what happens to us after death. But nothing, I shouldn't say *nothing* else, but it wasn't that important. What we have here, what we do with each other is how we, how I feel that we govern our lives now.[52]

Joyce moved quite quickly into an organization reflecting her humanistic outlook. But many waited many years and even decades. The world into which those who lost religion moved in the middle to late twentieth century may have shown doubt and uncertainty, perhaps for decades, perhaps permanently, over faith, god and the afterlife. But they showed little doubt over their moral world.

The absence of dogma and scripture was much mentioned in testimony. Humanism struck both Ian and Sheralee Hayes-Fry as something open and flexible, and brought them to a positive view of how well it fitted their wedding vows: 'It gave us the freedom to, I don't know, ultimately to set our own agenda…We just had the absolute freedom to write the script within our own moral outlook.' Building in the equality in their relationship into their marriage ceremony, almost as human rights, was the aim: 'It was going into a marriage where there would be balance and equal commitment.' They wanted to avoid shallow, ritualized and formulaic vows with no meaning for the couple: 'we have been to so many weddings where the people mouthed the script with no thought or commitment'.[53] On the other hand, about half of my respondents spoke of humanism as a firm, seasoned and reasoned belief system. Using key phrases demonstrating this, John Manuel told me how he turned to this firmness of belief in his sixties:

> Humanism to me is the acceptance of the fact that people and only people can and do make a difference. That's a definition that I've kind of developed myself from my own comfort that humanism places people, human beings as the focus of my dependence. Through people --- And I used to say you know as a Christian that God lives through people. That God does nothing by himself. Look about you [at] the randomness of storms and floods. And 'oh God saved my house'. Well, yeah, but what about your 10,000 neighbours who lost theirs? Was that the same God? Or do you recognise the difference you know? I never really accepted that God could do anything except through the will and commitment of people. So as a Christian I felt that all along. And that's very humanist. It's very much humanist based.[54]

Such strength of claim and commitment was held by a minority of respondents, albeit a significant minority. But identifying the false claims of religions was a fairly common theme.

Commitment led to action. One of the important areas for humanists has been the working out of practical humanist ethics. Frank O'Hara spoke eloquently of the loss of his Catholic faith in his twenties, but described in his late eighties how he had developed his own personal philosophy which for many decades had driven him in charitable work. He told me,

I have had ongoing interest in what you might say philosophical things. Morality and so on…I have evolved to the point now where my attitude is a very personal one that is such that in a sentence I feel that it's up to me to do what little I can and little it is in the world; it's what little I can on a day-to-day basis. So that for example I've done a number of websites for non-profit organisations for free. As well as my volunteering for years with CESO [Canadian Executive Service Organization].[55] And I just volunteered a couple days ago to work with another volunteer organisation whose object is to help non-profit organisations with whatever their needs are like money-raising or in my case it would be might be website development or it might be marketing cause that's my background.

This led Frank to years of overseas volunteering in many countries – including in China, Albania and the Caribbean. He helped a humanist organization for a period, managing their website for free and attending their meetings. He recalled being quizzed by a woman who led a musical group to which he belonged when a young adult, and she asked if he believed in God. And he recalled replying thus:

I don't have answers for everything. I don't know how the universe started or what preceded the universe or anything like that. Well, I've looked for the answers and I can't find them and so because I can't find them doesn't mean I'm gonna accept some answer or other. And so that's my position as far as religion is concerned. As far as morality is concerned as I told her I said I haven't seen any great indication that the people who are more moral are religious. Quite the contrary.[56]

He went on: 'So my morality right now is to, on a day to day basis, do what I can. I don't have any long range plans. When you're 83 years of age you don't ever think too far into the future [laughs]. As a matter of fact my concern is how long can I do it.' In 2011 he was decorated with the Ontario Senior's Achievement Award for his charitable work with CESO, and the following year the Queen's Diamond Jubilee Award.[57]

Between the 1940s and 1970s, Nigel Bruce pursued humanist ethics specifically in relation to children's rights. Bruce became involved in assisting the process that drafted the development of the UN Charter on Children's Rights, his particular concern being that a child should have the right to know who its parents were. Then in Edinburgh in 1964 and 1967, he co-founded two homes for boys with behavioural problems, which for fifteen years were funded by British humanists and took children sent both by parents and by the local social work authority. From this Bruce became involved in the foundation in Scotland of Children's Panels, which removed younger children from the criminal court system and created a more effective and humane atmosphere in which children could be dealt with. Together with his pamphlet writing on humanism and frequent letters in newspapers, Nigel Bruce became the leading figure in the movement in Scotland, leading the project to erect the first statue to David Hume in Edinburgh, and earning him the sobriquet 'Mr Humanism'.[58]

Becoming a humanist led to the desire in respondents to make a tangible difference. This difference started with trying to make people understand how good is humanism. A major element in the work of humanists from the 1960s, 1970s and 1980s was becoming involved in ecumenical exchange with churches and religious groups to explain humanism – attending meetings in churches to explain what humanists believe, that humanists don't try to convert you, and discussing Darwin, science and the evidential problems with scripture.[59] I found quite strong opposition to attempted conversion. Kai Kristensen in San Francisco said that 'I don't believe that's part of humanism, and that's where I kind of disagree with some of the atheists who are much more activist'.[60] Amongst my interviewees, there were many who were campaigners for secularist causes, such as against ecclesiastical privilege in the law. But moral activism called most to action. Robert Sanford from Portland, Oregon, a leading member of the humanist group in that city, told me quite vigorously that 'my vision, my sense of what we should be spending our time doing, is not sitting in meetings but being out doing public service, and we should have [on] our humanist or atheist or agnostic or whatever the hell shirt you want to wear'.[61] This might include action directed against irrationality, religious fraud and, for some, homeopathy. In Ottawa, David Fowler recalled as a chemistry teacher demonstrating to his class the principles of homeopathic dilution, whilst at least one of my UK interviewees joined with skeptics in a wider '10:23 campaign' from 2009 which included well-publicized purchases and deliberate overconsumption of homeopathic remedies at pharmacies.[62] Such campaigns have attracted mostly a younger generation of activists, those born after about 1980, and fewer of the older humanists and atheists who were the mainstay of my project interviewees seemed to be involved. Indeed, one mature American humanist told me that he saw the participant in such action as being 'a fundamentalist secularist' and was not to his taste.[63] Fear of religious fundamentalism was rife amongst respondents, and this led many to be chary of atheist fundamentalism in themselves.[64]

For the older generation of humanists, there was a distinct agenda of action, split between the caring and campaigning. Caring is being extended by the development of humanist chaplaincy on both sides of the Atlantic. I interviewed one postgraduate trainee humanist chaplain at Harvard University,[65] whilst in Britain Terry Martin and Ron McLaren decided in the late 1990s to get involved in spiritual care policy on behalf of humanists in the National Health Service in Scotland. Terry told me that he felt that his 'post-retirement mature humanism is a reflection of this public engagement', and that if he hadn't done the public stuff, 'I think my humanism would be very narrow, insular, sect-like humanism, and I would probably just be a secularist and no more'.[66] One important item of caring was humanist weddings and funerals. Becoming a celebrant or officiant was a popular direction for those who entered the movement in the 1980s and 1990s, many attracted by the funeral side. One pioneer in Scotland, Robin Wood, who had conducted the first humanist wedding in 1982, later decided to give up on the weddings and concentrate on funerals. It was here, he felt strongly, that great caring for bereaved families and friends was possible, and was much more exemplary of humanist principles than conducting weddings. Accentuating this outlook has been the widely held humanist view of the poor quality of the care provided by many religious celebrants before and at funerals. He told me, 'I think funerals are practical humanism…you're helping people at a time when they're under stress. They don't know what to do and you can help them.' When I spoke to him in 2009, he was conducting eighty funerals a year.[67] Robin's view was not shared by all humanist celebrants and officiants. The marriage ceremony was regarded by some as an event of the greatest possible joy, and it was in the humanist innovation of allowing couples within a non-religious framework to plan their own ceremony with readings, song and even drama, culminating in vows of their own composition, which endowed a ceremony with depth of personal investment and meaning. I interviewed ten celebrants and officiants from England, Scotland and Canada. One told me that 'we're touching a nerve with people, no question. People want something that is personal, that doesn't bring God into it, but that is reflective of them as a family or as a couple that really concentrates on them as individuals'.[68]

Equal marriage – that including lesbians and gay men, transgender and bisexual and queer-identified people – has been available from humanists as 'non-legal' weddings since the 1990s and 'legal' weddings in mainland Britain since 2014. Only two significant churches have been campaigning for gay marriage – the Society of Friends (Quakers) and the Unitarian Universalists – and it is instructive that many of the latter also count themselves as within the humanist community, whilst I have interviewed two humanists who were brought up in the Quakers. Joyce Murphy, officiant in the Unitarian Universalist community in Victoria in British Columbia, spoke to me of how gay marriage had been one of the cornerstones of the moral and civil rights campaigned for her group in Canada.[69] The campaign for equal marriage has energized atheist sector organizations, but it has also quite clearly shown humanism to be the closest life philosophy to the outlook of the vast majority of citizens in Western nations. In effect, the battle for equal marriage has popularized atheism as a moral position, and the one that has led the transition from a religious-based moral universe. It has crystallized cultural perceptions of key modern rights in the West: the right to equal marriage for all couples irrespective of sexual orientation, the right to be free from state sanction of sexual practices between consenting adults and the right to be free from religious monopoly of ceremonial weddings. Where it has taken off in popularity, notably in Scotland and Norway, the humanist wedding has become, alongside the humanist funeral, an advertisement for the movement as a whole, spreading basic ideas and impressions concerning Humanist self-expression and human rights.[70] This has not led to mass membership, though. In part this might be down to our time being a generation of 'non-joiners'. But in larger part, it symbolizes the way in which having a moral position is seen as not requiring membership and affiliation in the manner traditionally advocated by the churches. The average Westerner no longer sees her or his morality as a commodity requiring existential valorizing and the imprimatur of external authority.

Those who stress their identity as secularist or atheist tend to emphasize a rights-based agenda. Unifying the movement across national boundaries, it has been a struggle that has emerged from the individual sacrifices of those with religious doubt across at least a thousand years of European history. In the United States, respondents were unequivocally focussed on defence of the first amendment to the constitution which separates church from state. The paradox of the United States has been that, notwithstanding the eighteenth-century origins of modern atheism, religious freedom and separation of church and state, the mid-twentieth century is widely regarded in the atheist community as creating a surge of religious involvement in public affairs which has not entirely yet been spent. They point to features as diverse as the appearance of 'God' on the dollar bill in 1957, the intrusion of God in 'The Star Spangled Banner' and the resulting rise of singing praise to God in the American classroom. American atheists I interviewed cited one or both of Robert Ingersoll, the nineteenth-century American agnostic and claimed atheist, whose debating skills were much vaunted in his time and still revered as a patriot, and Madalyn Murray O'Hair, founder and leader of American Atheists from the 1960s till her death in the 1990s.[71] These are the inspirers of American atheist and secularist action. Larry Hicok from Oregon described his coming to atheism at high school where he tackled the principal over the holding of religious worship at the start of the school day; having got the backing of the Portland branch of the American Civil Liberties Union, he confronted the principal and won the suspension of the worship.[72] Dave Kong, the California Chapter Director of American Atheists, started out as an anti-religious band leader in 1978 leading an atheist rock band called Sin, writing a song, 'Damn the Preacher', which became their Bible-burning theme tune. He denied that his work had become a mission. He said it was not 'an evangelistic fever'.[73] He noted, too, the remarkable successes possible at local level in the United States, recalling how his organization gave support to Mayor Ralph Appezzato of the small island town of Alameda outside of San Francisco who, in 2002, gained 95 per cent local support to successfully end religious invocations at the opening of town council meetings.[74] Atheist campaigning can work in the United States; indeed, it has the apparent ability at community level to achieve success not matched – despite human rights legislation of the 2010s – in Britain. More broadly, American atheists and humanists gain kudos by having a distinctively strong patriotic and community-affirming concept of loss of religion, one they celebrate with exuberance.

Men's activism seems stronger than women's, but it is largely different. Men are more likely than women to be in the greater atheist movement confronting the privileged power of religion in civil society. A few expressed quite clearly their anti-religion standpoint. Tim Unsworth from south-west England said that he didn't really want to hold discussions about atheism with other atheists because there was little to talk about and it didn't interest him – certainly not in a philosophical sense. He said, 'I am anti-religion, I am particularly anti-Christian, and particularly anti-Catholic, I am opposed to the Catholic Church.' Men will be more willing to describe themselves as 'militant atheists', as wanting to attack religion and notably the churches that they have left. Church policies – such as birth control and abortion in the Catholic Church, and opposition to assisted dying by most if not all churches – become issues of concern for atheists. Recalling his own experience, Tim says, 'the only way you can get people to believe nonsense is to dominate them, to make them feel small, and to assert power over them, to make them see this'.[75] A not uncommon term from respondents who were former religionists, and who considered themselves in some way victims or survivors of their church, is that a religion is 'abuse' – a term used sixteen times in my testimony – when forced upon young minds in church and schools.

For the majority of my female respondents, such anti-religious activism was much more muted. Gillian Stewart told me, 'One thing I struggle with still is the anti-religion thing, you know. That for me [is] definitely not what humanism's about.'[76] My encounters demonstrated that far more men than women are active organizers. The conduct and planning of meetings, the type of meetings (invariably the visiting-speaker model, focussed on campaigning or philosophical issues) and committee work tend to be male-led. Indeed, for fifty years the humanist movement as a whole has been dominated by men. A survey from 1964 showed the 1,236 members of the British Humanist Association to be 73 per cent male, 77 per cent middle-class, 59 per cent over the age of 40 and 40 per cent from London and south-east England. On the face of it, little had changed by 2011, when another survey by Michael Engelke showed the 12,000 BHA members to be 69 per cent male, 72 per cent having a university degree and nearly 89 per cent self-describing as 'white British'.[77] A sampling study of the BHA published in 2014 indicated that males had dropped to 65 per cent, 82 per cent were over 40 and more than 80 per cent had higher education.[78] Though the movement is small, female participation and leadership in secularist and atheist campaigns seems to be rising on both sides of the Atlantic. With female 'nones' almost equal in number to male ones in Britain and Canada, and moving upward in the United States, the present trend suggests increasing feminization of the 'nones' who feed the humanist movement.[79]

The transition generation

Respondents became very reflective towards the end of their interviews. Many were deeply affected by losing religion and coming, often after many decades, to a self-recognition as a humanist. For Dennis Duncan, the way he narrated his loss of religion fitted within a wider narrative of childhood trauma and adulthood success. From age 8 to 14 he narrated in detail the succession of humiliations he felt in the Catholic Church in both Scotland and Canada. But after false starts over several years, he found his vocation as a chemical engineer, accompanied by being happily married and raising a family. The loss of religion he timed precisely to his unhappiness as a child; his drift towards atheism and humanism coincided with the culmination of a successful career. He noted, 'You can be an atheist and a humanist and sit in your own armchair and do nothing else and be quite happy with your own thoughts. Takes a little bit of effort to go out and try to do something worthwhile with it, but then --- oh yeah, there is a very broad range in humanism.'[80]

The respondents upon whom this project has been based represent a particular generation. They were born mostly between 1920 and 1965, a 45-year age cohort composed of those who described in their testimonies quite distinct realms of engagement with religion – as children, losing religion and belief in god often between 7 and 16 years of age, and then, characteristically, a long indifference to religion through to their forties, fifties and sixties. Despite their alienation from god and religion in youth, their years as young adults, from about 1955 through to 1985, were turbulent and testing, with moral and political arguments, and movements like civil rights, CND, feminism, socialism and Marxism. Ron Kerr's narrative involved many twists and turns as he moved from Arbroath to America and back again, joining civil rights marches and being a Marxist. After telling his story in detail, he reflected:

> The life I was leading, I didn't have any real belief system in anything for a long time, and I think a part of dealing with that was going through this business of being a Communist, and then just looking for something, some way of life and belief system that would suit me. Unfortunately [I] didn't find it till I was about sixty.

Education was the thing, he says, that saved him from many personal pitfalls: 'I could have finished up, probably been a down-and-out or something.' Humanism was the other part of the formula too, seeming to soften his belief system after the radical struggles of mid-century.[81]

This was the generation that was important to the progress of secularization in the West. It was during their losing of religion triggered in the 1960s and 1970s that Christendom, the cultural dominance of society, collapsed in most of Western Europe. It was the generation that had the hard struggle to negotiate their way out of religious culture, belief and family constriction. On one level, narrating secularity was hard; there was scant language, discourse, heritage or common memory of atheism upon which to draw, thus explaining, perhaps, David Nash's finding that Christian narratives survived surprisingly well in Britain, even when secularizing rapidly in the third quarter of the twentieth century.[82] On another level, for some losers of religion this was arduous, at times distressing, and they make clear in retrospect that their cultural transition was long delayed for want of an atheistical cultural paradigm at that time. The generations that followed them – Generation X and Generation Y, call them what you will – did not have the same problems of delay, of indifference and doubt. The young I have interviewed, born since 1975, came out readily as non-believers in their teens, notably at university and college in the 1990s and 2000s, kindling a mushrooming of humanist and skeptics' groups and a burgeoning public atheism across the Western world in the 2010s.

So the respondents most focussed upon in this book made up a unique transition generation that crafted ways to leave religion in late modernity, moulding a moral landscape founded on human rights and respect for the individual. What made this generation so important? Other studies will be necessary to decide if childhood atheism, which I featured in Chapter 3, was a new or very old part of human experience. But personal testimony offers compelling evidence that gender shapes loss of religion quite extensively, and it was the feminist impulses – not of high theory so much as of lived experiences of education and career change – that made a real difference to the post-sixties generation of women. If men's narratives of losing religion were strongly founded in traditional intellectual struggles, involving theology, reason and civil rights, women's were founded on the lived feminism they created for themselves between the 1950s and 1990s. We saw how these women defied the cultural constraints and religious discourses to craft a new female self. The women of the long sixties generation I interviewed were the first *en masse* to confront religion, to find ways of losing it, to not base their ideal femininity upon it and to seek new demographic outcomes to their lives with new patterns for careers and families. We saw the way in which women, far more than men, placed their journeys from religion in the context of family. This bears out the argument of my previous book that, in terms of quantitative demography in Canada, Ireland, the United Kingdom and the United States, women's experience of the family was central to the rapid secularization that took off in the Western world in the 1960s.[83] Lynn Abrams, in her own oral history study of Britain, concludes that, for women growing up in the post-war decades, the religious narrative was becoming irrelevant as a way to make sense of a life. She goes on:

> rather, they acknowledged that there was such a narrative – one that would have been framed by issues of respectability, outward presentation, social convention, and the face one presents to the public – but that it belonged to their mothers' generation. When the daughters were asked questions about religion their answers referred to their parents' and sometimes their grandparents' generation and their own girlhoods.[84]

The process that vented rudely upon the West from the 1960s has been a markedly female one. The statistical evidence and the personal narratives of women who have lost religion allow us to observe the collapse of discursive Christianity in the wider cultural re-constructions of the age.

The outcome of secularization revealed in this book is a positive story of the human discovery of a new moral cosmos. It is, so far, a distinctly Western one, sown in seeds evident amongst my older respondents in the 1930s and the 1940s, but then spilling out from a mainly European heartland from the 1960s and 1970s. The cosmos was linked to the changing demographics of Western people, and to the discovery for many individuals that a life without god was eminently possible, even in the unlikeliest of places. In 1962, Ivan Middleton saw an advertisement in his local newspaper, the *Belfast Telegraph*, for a local Humanist Society meeting. Knowing of no other escape from the way that religion governed everything in sectarian-divided Northern Ireland, this young man went along out of curiosity. Recalling it almost fifty years later, he told me, 'It was really, it was like Eureka or something, because I suddenly find all these adults who couldn't care less about religion.'[85] This was the beginning of the awakening of his humanist condition.

Atheist / humanist need each other
Tower of Babel

NOTES

Chapter 1

1   Acknowledgement of this definition of atheism is to be found in James M. Nelson, *Psychology, Religion and Spirituality* (New York: Springer, 2009), p. 13.

2   Tim Whitmarsh, *Battling the Gods: Atheism in the Ancient World* (New York: Alfred A Knopf, 2015); John H. Arnold, *Belief and Unbelief in Medieval Europe* (London: Bloomsbury Academic, 2005).

3   Hugh McLeod, *The Religious Crisis of the 1960s* (Oxford: Oxford University Press, 2007), p. 1. McLeod and I both draw upon Marwick for the concept of the long sixties. Arthur Marwick, *The Sixties: Social and Cultural Transformation in Britain, France, Italy and the United States, 1958–74* (Oxford: Oxford University Press, 1998).

4   This worldwide slogan of the humanist and atheist movements started in 2010.

5   Frank O'Hara, born 1926 Silver Center, Ontario, COT, p. 445; Maria Berger (pseud.), born 1976 Switzerland COT, p. 773; Conrad Hadland, CWT, p. 9.

6   This is the sum of occurrences in my Compendium of Oral Testimony (COT) and my separate Compendium of Written Testimony (CWT). Each is explained later in this chapter.

7   Charles Taylor, *A Secular Age* (Cambridge, MA: Belknap, 2007); Callum G. Brown, 'The necessity of atheism: making sense of secularisation', *Journal of Religious History* forthcoming.

8   Grace Davie, *Religion in Britain since 1945: Believing without Belonging* (Oxford: Blackwell, 1994); idem, *Religion in Modern Europe: A Memory Mutates* (Oxford: Oxford University Press, 2000); Wade Clark Roof, *A Generation of Seekers: The Spiritual Journeys of the Baby Boom Generation* (San Francisco, CA: Harper, 1993); idem, *Spiritual Marketplace: Baby Boomers and the Remaking of American Religion* (Princeton, NJ: Princeton University Press, 1999).

9   Andrew Greeley, 'Unsecular Europe: the persistence of religion', in Detlef Pollack and Daniel V.A. Olson (eds), *The Role of Religion in Modern Societies* (New York: Routledge, 2008), pp. 141–61; José Casanova, 'The religious situation in Europe', in Hans Joas and Klaus Wiegandt (eds), *Secularization and the World Religions* (Liverpool: Liverpool University Press, 2009), pp. 206–28; Peter Berger, Grace Davie and Effie Fokas, *Religious America, Secular Europe? A Theme and Variations* (Farnham: Ashgate, 2008).

10   The poor management argument is heard from (some) church managers, and is best expressed by Robin Gill concerning late Victorian 'overchurching' which erected too many buildings with small congregations, undermining

morale and triggering non-churchgoing; Robin Gill, *The 'Empty Church' Revisited* (Aldershot: Ashgate, 2003).

11　For example, see Jane Garnett et al. (eds.), *Redefining Christian Britain: Post 1945 Perspectives* (London: SCM Press, 2006). See also Callum G. Brown, 'Christian Britain – redefined or misdefined?', *The Expository Times* vol. 119 (2008), pp. 541–2; Jeremy Morris, 'Secularization and religious experience: arguments in the historiography of modern British religion', *Historical Journal* vol. 55 (2012), pp. 195–219; J.C.D. Clark, 'Secularization and modernization: the failure of a "grand narrative"', *Historical Journal* vol. 55 (2012), pp. 161–94.

12　Bryan Wilson, *Religion in Secular Society* (Harmondsworth: Penguin, 1966).

13　Owen Chadwick, *The Secularisation of the European Mind in the Nineteenth Century* (Cambridge: Cambridge University Press, 1975); Talal Asad, *Formations of the Secular: Christianity, Islam, Modernity* (Stanford: Stanford University Press, 2003); Hugh McLeod, *Secularisation in Western Europe, 1848–1914* (Basingstoke: Macmillan, 2000).

14　Jeff Cox, 'Towards eliminating the concept of secularisation: a progress report', in C.G. Brown and M. Snape (eds), *Secularisation in the Christian World c.1750–c.2000 (Essays in Honour of Hugh McLeod)* (Farnham: Ashgate, 2010).

15　Stan Greenberg, 'I've seen America's future and it's not Republican', *The Guardian*, 5 November 2015.

16　Extreme examples are Christie Davies, *The Strange Death of Moral Britain* (n.p: Transaction, 2006); Gertrude Himmelfarb, *The De-moralization of Society: From Victorian Values to Modern Values* (London: IEA, 1995); idem, *One Nation, Two Cultures: A Searching Examination of American Society in the Aftermath of Our Cultural Revolution* (New York: Vintage, 2001).

17　C. Kirk Hadaway and Penny Long Marler, 'How many Americans attend worship each week? An alternative approach to measurement', *Journal for the Scientific Study of Religion* vol. 44 (2005), pp. 307–322.

18　Callum Brown, *Religion and the Demographic Revolution: Women and Secularisation in Canada, Ireland, UK and USA since the 1960s* (London: Boydell, 2012), pp. 106–7; Dr. Sarah Wilkins-Laflamme, *Report: religion in Canada* (2014) at http://www.ceetum.umontreal.ca/documents/capsules/2014/wilk-en-2014.pdf (accessed 14 August 2015).

19　Brown, *Religion and the Demographic Revolution*, pp. 114, 105–23; ONS, Census 2011, Table KS209EW Religion, local authorities in England and Wales at http://www.ons.gov.uk/ons/rel/census/2011-census/key-statistics-for-local-authorities-in-england-and-wales/index.html (accessed 30 December 2012).

20　Brown, *Religion and the Demographic Revolution*, p. 108; Gallup Poll for (2014) at http://www.gallup.com/poll/180347/three-quarters-americans-identify-christian.aspx (accessed 14 August 2015).

21　Association for Canadian Studies poll at http://news.nationalpost.com/holy-post/religion-not-important-to-most-canadians-although-majority-believe-in-god-poll (accessed 14 August 2015).

22　Callum G. Brown, *Religion and Society in Twentieth-Century Britain* (Harlow: Pearson Longman, 2006), p. 28.

23 Eurobarometer, *Social values, Science and Technology*, p. 9 at http://
ec.europa.eu/public_opinion/archives/ebs/ebs_225_report_en.pdf (accessed
18 October 2014).

24 Gallup poll, at http://www.gallup.com/poll/147887/americans-continue-
believe-god.aspx (accessed 14 August 2015).

25 Linda Woodhead, ' "No Religion" is the new religion', Press Release on
YouGov Poll (23 December 2013) at http://www.brin.ac.uk/news/2013/end-
of-year-round-up/ (accessed 18 October 2014). But she is seemingly moving
in a recent talk to emphasize the strength of god-belief, at http://www.britac.
ac.uk/events/2016/Why_no_religion_is_the_new_religion.cfm (accessed
27 April 2016).

26 Leading in 2015 to the Church of England's controversial Reform and
Renewal Programme, whose portal is accessed at https://churchofengland.org/
renewal-reform.aspx. *The Observer*, 22 November 2015, p. 20a.

27 Helen Boyd (pseud.), born England, COT p. 930.

28 I summarized this change for a significant part of the West in Callum G.
Brown, 'The people of no religion: the demographics of secularisation in the
English-speaking world since c.1900', *Archiv für Sozialgeschichte* vol. 51
(2011), pp. 37–61. See also the 2016 study that shows Scotland with
52 per cent of adults having no religion. www.scotcen.org.uk/media/1133114/
SSA-Religion_tables.pdf.

29 Data on this abounds. Examples are Michael Lipka, 'A closer look at
America's rapidly growing religious "nones" ', at pewresearch.org; and the
data summarized in Michael Shermer, 'Is God Dying? The decline of religion
and the rise of the "nones" ', *Scientific American*, 19 November 2013 (both
accessed 23 October 2015).

30 See for example Christopher Partridge, *The Re-enchantment of the West*, 2
volumes (London: Bloomsbury, 2005 and 2006); other present papers on this
theme, such as Rodney Stark, 'A Godless world? Signs of a global religious
revival', conference presentation, Baylor University, 5 May 2015.

31 See the attempt to quantify atheists in detail across the world in Ariela Keysar
and Juhem Navaro-Rivero, 'A world of atheism: global demographics', in
Stephen Bullivant and Michael Ruse (eds), *The Oxford Handbook of Atheism*
(Oxford: Oxford University Press, 2013), pp. 553–86. See also tabulated
summary estimates for the Americas (2000–14) at https://en.wikipedia.org/
wiki/Demographics_of_atheism#cite_ref-93 (accessed 20 December 2015).

32 Roof, *Generation of Seekers*; idem, *Spiritual Marketplace*.

33 See for example David G. Bromley (ed.), *Falling from the Faith: Causes and
Consequences of Religious Apostasy* (Newbury Park, CA: Sage, 1988); Ross
Douthat, *Bad Religion: How We Became a Nation of Heretics* (New York:
Free Press, 2012); William D. Hendricks, *Exit Interviews: Revealing Stories
of Why People Are Leaving the Church* (Chicago, IL: Moody Press, 1993);
Roger L. Dudley, *Why Our Teenagers Leave the Church: Personal Stories
from a 10-Year Study* (Hagerstown, MD: Review & Herald Publishing
Association, 2000), and Alex Robertson, *Lifestyle Survey* (Edinburgh: Church
of Scotland, 1987).

34 Much of the research concerning religious loss has used church recruits. This is
discussed in Chapter 3.

35 Robert D. Putnam, *Bowling Alone: The Collapse and Revival of American Community* (New York: Simon & Shuster, 2000).
36 Steve Bruce, 'Praying alone? Church-going in Britain and the Putnam thesis', *Journal of Contemporary Religion* vol. 17, no. 3 (2002), pp. 317–28.
37 Robert D. Putnam and David E. Campbell, *American Grace: How Religion Divided and Unites Us* (New York: Simon & Shuster, 2010).
38 One example is Timothy Larsen, *Crisis of Doubt: Honest Faith in Nineteenth-Century England* (Oxford: Oxford University Press, 2006). This trend in Christian scholarship in dealing with the sixties is examined in Brown, *Religion and the Demographic Revolution*, esp. pp. 29–70.
39 Most defection from religion to no religion is from the Roman Catholic and mainline Protestant denominations – the Church of England, the Church of Scotland, the United Church of Canada, the Anglican Church in Canada, the American Episcopal Church etc. The overall effect is *per capita* decline; for data on the United States, see the major report of the Pew Research Center, *America's Changing Religious Landscape* (May 2015) at http://www.pewforum.org/2015/05/12/americas-changing-religious-landscape/ (accessed 25 October 2015).
40 Reginald Bibby, *Unknown Gods: The Ongoing Story of Religion in Canada* (Toronto, ON: Stoddart, 1993), p. 158; idem, *Restless Gods: The Renaissance of Religion in Canada* (Toronto, ON: Stoddart, 2002), p. 41.
41 Rodney Stark, *What Americans Really Believe: New Findings from the Baylor Surveys of Religion* (Waco, TX: Baylor University Press, 2008), pp. 141–4.
42 Rodney Stark, Eva Hamberg and Alan S. Miller, 'Exploring spirituality and unchurched religions in America, Sweden, and Japan', *Journal of Contemporary Religion* vol. 20 (2005), pp. 3–23 at p. 20.
43 Chaeyoon Lim, Carol Ann MacGregor and Robert D. Putnam, 'Secular and luminal: heterogeneity among religious nones', *Journal for the Scientific Study of Religion* vol. 49 (2010), pp. 596–618 at p. 614. See also C. Kirk Hadaway and Wade Clark Roof, 'Those who stay religious "nones" and those who don't: a research note', *Journal for the Scientific Study of Religion* vol. 18 (1979), pp. 194–200; John Wilson and Darren E. Sherkat, 'Returning to the fold', *Journal for the Scientific Study of Religion* vol. 33 (1994), pp. 148–61.
44 This has seemed to be the approach of David Voas, who has driven much of the research on European fuzzy fidelity. David Voas, 'The rise and fall of fuzzy fidelity in Europe', *European Sociological Review* vol. 25 (2009), pp. 155–68; see also David Voas and Abby Day, *Recognizing Secular Christians: Toward an Unexcluded Middle in the Study of Religion* (2010) at http://www.thearda.com/rrh/papers/guidingpapers.asp (accessed 24 November 2014). See also his report on falling churchgoing for the Church of England, David Voas and Laura Watt, 'Numerical change in church attendance: national, local and individual factors' (2014) at http://www.churchgrowthresearch.org.uk/progress_findings_reports (accessed 20 December 2015).
45 Gareth Longden, 'A profile of the members of the British Humanist Association', *Science, Religion and Culture* vol. 2 (2015), pp. 86–95 at p. 87. *Statistics Canada, 2011 National Household Survey*, Statistics Canada Catalogue no. 99-010-X2011032. Americans are not asked this question in a government census.
46 Whitmarsh, *Battling the Gods*, pp. 120–4.

47 Leslie Stephen, *An Agnostic's Apology and Other Essays* (London: Smith, Elder and Co., 1893), p.1.

48 See for example Merlin B. Brinkerhoff and Marlene M. Mackie, 'Casting off the bonds of organized religion: a religious-careers approach to the study of apostasy', *Review of Religious Research* vol. 34 (1993) pp. 235–58; Joseph O. Baker and Buster G. Smith, 'The Nones: social characteristics of the religiously unaffiliated', *Social Forces* vol. 87, no. 3 (2009), pp. 1251–63; and Joseph O. Baker and Buster G. Smith, 'None too simple: examining issues of religious nonbelief and nonbelonging in the United States', *Journal for the Social Scientific Study of Religion* vol. 48 (2009), pp. 719–33.

49 See Chapter 3.

50 Notable here is Gordon Lynch, *Losing My Religion? Moving on from Evangelical Faith* (London: Darton, Longman and Todd, 2003).

51 Such as Norm R. Allen Jr. (ed.), *The Black Humanist Experience: An Alternative to Religion* (Amherst, MA: Prometheus, 2003); and Russell Blackford and Udo Schüklenk (eds), *50 Voices of Disbelief: Why We Are Atheists* (Chichester: Wiley-Blackwell, 2009).

52 See the useful discussion in Jaber F Gubrium et al. (eds), *Sage Handbook of Interview Research: The Complexity of the Craft*, Second Edition (London: Sage, 2012), pp. 27–44.

53 Lynn Abrams, *Oral History Theory* (London: Routledge, 2010).

54 For example, see Christian Smith, *Soul Searching: The Religious and Spiritual Lives of American Teenagers* (Oxford: Oxford University Press, 2005).

55 These ideas pervade Hendricks' oral history study of twenty-four leavers, in which his analysis of one individual, 'Robert', includes asking, 'is he just an obstinate child of God?'; Hendricks, *Exit Interviews*, pp. 61, 248–9.

56 Natalie Zemon Davies, *Trickster Travels: The Search for Leo Africanus* (London: Faber & Faber, 2006); idem, *Women on the Margins: Three Seventeenth-Century Lives* (Cambridge, MA: Harvard University Press, 1995), pp. 126–8.

57 Peter Coleman, Daniela Koleva and Joanna Bornat (eds), *Aging Ritual and Social Change: Comparing the Secular and Religious in Eastern and Western Europe* (Farnham: Ashgate, 2013).

58 Alister Hardy, *The Spiritual Nature of Man* (Oxford: Clarendon Press, 1979); Nelson, *Psychology, Religion and Spirituality*, pp. 285–7. Nelson suggests *inter alia* that Stalinist purges were primarily atheists murdering Christians; ibid., p. 427.

59 Bob Altemeyer, 'The decline of organized religion in Western civilization', *International Journal for the Psychology of Religion* vol. 14 (2004), pp. 77–89; Tatjana Schnell, 'Dimensions of Secularity (DoS): an open inventory to measure facets of secular identities', *International Journal for the Psychology of Religion* vol. 25 (2015), pp. 272–92.

60 Luke W. Galen, 'Atheism, wellbeing, and the wager: why not believing in God (with others) is good for you', *Science, Religion and Culture* vol. 2 (2015), pp. 54–69. Luke W. Galen and J. Kloet, 'Mental well-being in the religious and the non-religious: evidence for a curvilinear relationship', *Mental Health, Religion, & Culture* vol. 14 (2011), pp. 673–89.

61 Luke W. Galen, M. Sharp and A. McNulty, 'The role of nonreligious group factors versus religious belief in the prediction of prosociality', *Social*

Indicators Research vol. 122 (2015), pp. 411–32; Luke W. Galen, 'Does religious belief promote prosociality?: A critical examination', *Psychological Bulletin* vol. 138 (2012), pp. 876–906.

62   Matthew Engelke, 'The coffin question: death and materiality in humanist funerals', *Material Religion* vol. 11 (2015), pp. 26–49; idem, 'Humanist ceremonies: the case of non-religious funerals in England', in Andrew Copson and A.C. Grayling (eds), *The Wiley Blackwell Handbook on Humanism* (Oxford: Wiley, 2015); idem, 'Christianity and the anthropology of secular humanism', *Current Anthropology* vol. 55, no. S10 (2014): S292–S301.

63   The project was ethically approved first in 2009 by the University of Dundee, then in 2013 by the University of Glasgow to which I had transferred.

64   The website is still in existence to demonstrate the method; it is at http://www.gla.ac.uk/schools/humanities/staff/callumbrown/modernhumanismasocialandculturalhistory/#d.en.287899 (accessed 27 April 2016).

65   MeetUp is an online community networking system, widely used by American and Canadian atheist, humanist and secularist groups on a local basis. It is less well used by similar groups in Europe.

66   On an Olympus LC-10 and an LC-5.

67   Interviewees dislike the infelicities of unrehearsed speech being presented in transcription as error-like. I regard it as ethically necessary for this transition from speech to the page to avoid imparting a sense of humiliation.

68   Quoted in Callum G. Brown, *Postmodernism for Historians* (London: Longman Pearson, 2005), p. 136.

69   Callum G. Brown, 'How Anglicans lose religion: an oral history of becoming secular', in Abby Day (ed.), *Contemporary Issues in the Worldwide Anglican Communion: Powers and Pieties* (Farnham: Ashgate, 2016).

70   Brown, *Postmodernism*.

Chapter 2

1   For three varied examples, try Carole Garibaldi Rogers, *Poverty, Chastity, and Change: Lives of Contemporary American Nuns* (Woodbridge, CT: Twayne, 1996); Claudia Lauper Bushman and Caroline Kline, *Mormon Women Have Their Say: Essays from the Claremont Oral History Collection* (Draper, UT: Greg Kofford Books, 2013); Felipe Honojosa, *Latino Mennonites: Civil Rights, Faith and Evangelical Culture* (Baltimore, MD: John Hopkins University Press, 2014).

2   Hugh McLeod, 'New perspectives in Victorian working-class religion: the oral evidence', *Oral History Journal* vol. 14 (1986); Sarah Williams, *Religious Belief and Popular Culture in Southwark, c.1880–1939* (Oxford, Oxford University Press, 1999); Callum Brown, *The Death of Christian Britain: Understanding Secularisation 1800–2000*, Second Edition (London: Routledge, 2009).

3   Penny Summerfield, *Reconstructing Women's Wartime Lives: Discourse and Subjectivity in Oral Histories of the Second World War* (Manchester, NH: Manchester University Press, 1998), p. 15.

4   Michael Roper, 'Slipping out of view: subjectivity and emotion in gender history', *History Workshop Journal* no. 59 (2005), pp. 57–72.

5   Brown, *Death of Christian Britain*, pp. 11–15, 170–86.

6   Kevin J. Christiano, *Religious Diversity and Social Change: American Cities, 1890–1906* (Cambridge: Cambridge University Press, 1987), pp. 49–50.

7   Thomas, Anne Moreau Oral History Interview, 2 May 2008, by Sandra Stewart Holyoak and Jessica Ondusko, transcript, pp. 11–12, Rutgers Oral History Archives. All the interview transcripts cited below from this collection are at http://oralhistory.rutgers.edu/alphabetical-index/156-t (accessed 25 September 2015).

8   On Catholic–Protestant antagonisms, see Robert Wuthnow, *The Restructuring of American Religion: Society and Faith since World War II* (Princeton, NJ: Princeton University Press, 1988), pp. 71–99.

9   Monica Strack (born 1905), interviewed 2002 by Michael Pierce and Charles Nabholz, Arkansas Memories Project, transcript, p. 28, The David and Barbara Pryor Center for Arkansas Oral and Visual History, University of Arkansas. All the interview transcripts cited below from this collection are at http://pryorcenter.uark.edu/arkansasmemories.php (accessed 25 September 2015).

10   Mrs B2 (born 1907, Bannockburn, Scotland), Stirling Women's Oral History Archive, compendium compiled by Alison Giles and Anne Bailey (eds), *Scottish Women's Oral History* (Stirling, Smith Art Galley and Museum, 2004), p. 602.

11   Annie Snow, born 1885 Hinckley, transcript. Interviewers: Mr H. A. Beavin and Mr D. J. Wood (1984) at www.oralhistory.co.uk (accessed 26 June 2015).

12   Mrs W1, born 1913, Stirling, Stirling Women's Oral History Archive, Compendium, p. 1176.

13   On this paradox, and oral history recollection of special Sunday meals, see Callum G. Brown, 'Spectacle, restraint and the twentieth-century Sabbath wars: the "everyday" Scottish Sunday', in L. Abrams and C.G. Brown (eds), *A History of Everyday Life in Twentieth-century Scotland* (Edinburgh: Edinburgh University Press, 2010), pp. 153–80.

14   Jim Clark (1922–2007), former sheriff of Dallas County, interviewed by Jim Reeston, 1976, at Fort Payne, Alabama, B-0015, in the Southern Oral History Program Collection #4007, Southern Historical Collection, Wilson Library, University of North Carolina at Chapel Hill, p. 4. All the interview transcripts cited below from this collection are at http://sohp.org/oral-history-interviews/ (accessed 27 April 2016).

15   Interviewee 142, transcript, p. 19. P. Thompson and T. Lummis, *Family Life and Work Experience before 1918, 1870–1973* [data collection], Seventh Edition (UK Data Service, 2009). SN (2000) at http://dx.doi.org/10.5255/ UKDA-SN-2000-1 (accessed 27 April 2016).

16   For example, the 'Religion and Politics in North Carolina' project at the Southern Oral History Program of University of North Carolina at Chapel Hill at http://dc.lib.unc.edu/cdm/project/collection/sohp/ (accessed 27 April 2016).

17   The interviewer went on to pose a question about grace at mealtimes. Jim Blair (born 1935) interviewed 2008 by Scott Lunsford, transcript, pp. 22, 24, Arkansas Memories Project, The David and Barbara Pryor Center for Arkansas Oral and Visual History, University of Arkansas.

18   Thomas Bradley, 1917–1998, born Calvert, Texas, interviewed by Bernard Galm 1978, unpaginated transcript UCLA Oral History Research Center. Details of his life are at http://www.mayortombradley.com/biography (accessed

27 April 2016). All the interview transcripts cited below from this archive are at http://oralhistory.library.ucla.edu (accessed 27 April 2016).

19   This affair is analysed in Callum G. Brown, 'Best not to take it too far: how the British cut religion down to size', *Open Democracy*, 8 March 2006, at https://www.opendemocracy.net/globalization-aboutfaith/britain_religion_3335.jsp (accessed 25 June 2015).

20   Busch, Mary Lou Norton, Oral History Interview, 17 August 2007, by Shaun Illingworth, Matthew Lawrence and Jessica Thomson Illingworth, transcript, pp. 6, 36–7, 39, Rutgers Oral History Archives.

21   McLeod, *The Religious Crisis of the 1960s*, pp. 41–5, 141–60; Holger Nehring, '"The Long, Long Night Is Over." The Campaign for Nuclear Disarmament, "Generation" and the politics of religion (1957–1964)', in Jane Garenett (eds), *Redefining Christian Britain: Post 1945 Perspectives* (London: SCM Press, 2007), pp. 138–47.

22   Robinson, Mary, Oral History Interview, 28 October 1994, by G. Kurt Piehler, Linda Lasko and Bruce Chadwick, transcript, Rutgers Oral History Archives.

23   Bell, Bertha, Oral History Interview, 23 June 2005, by Sandra Stewart Holyoak and Susan Yousif, transcript, Rutgers Oral History Archives.

24   Griffin, Marie, Oral History Interview, 16 March 1996, by Kathleen Plunkett, transcript, pp. 8, 54, Rutgers Oral History Archives.

25   Moncrief, Ruth Sheeler, Oral History Interview, 5 October 2007, by Sandra Stewart Holyoak, Sabeenah Arshad and Hanne Ala-Rami, transcript, pp. 5, 27–8, Rutgers Oral History Archives.

26   Hugh McLeod, *Religion and the People of Western Europe 1789–1989* (Oxford: Oxford University Press, 1997), pp.132–5; Brown, *Religion and the Demographic Revolution*, pp. 71–126.

27   Brown, *Death of Christian Britain*, pp. 35–114.

28   Jim Blair (born 1935), interviewed 2008 by Scott Lunsford, transcript, pp. 23, 28, Arkansas Memories Project, The David and Barbara Pryor Center for Arkansas Oral and Visual History, University of Arkansas.

29   Anon., *Lewis, Land of Revival: The Story of the 1949–52 Lewis Revival as Told By the Islanders*, Audio cassette (Belfast: Ambassador Productions Ltd, 1983); and Richard Sykes, 'Popular religion in decline: a study from the black country', *Journal of Ecclesiastical History* vol. 56 (2005), pp. 287–307.

30   Interviewee 142, transcript, p. 19. Thompson and Lummis, *Family Life and Work Experience before 1918, 1870–1973*. Walker's testimony is discussed in detail in *The Death of Christian Britain*, pp. 118–22.

31   Archibald, Alice Jennings (DOB unknown, but c.1904), oral history interview, 14 March 1997, by G. Kurt Piehler and Eve Snyder, transcript, pp. 3–4, 7, 15–16, 22, 33, Rutgers Oral History Archives.

32   Revd Naomi Craig, interviewed by Ashley Johnson, 1998, transcript, np., The Whole World Was Watching: An Oral History of 1968, Rhode Island, South Kingstown High School and Brown University's Scholarly Technology Group. All the interview transcripts cited below from this collection are at http://cds.library.brown.edu/projects/1968/ (accessed 25 September 2015).

33   McLeod, Bruce, Oral History Interview, 22 March 2011, by Sandra Stewart Holyoak and David Ley, transcript, pp. 5, 8, Rutgers Oral History Archives.

34 Alexander, II, Walter G., Oral History Interview, 6 November 2009, by Sandra Stewart Holyoak and Catherine Dzendzera, transcript, p. 15, Rutgers Oral History Archives.

35 Pinsdorf, Marion K., Oral History Interview, 26 July 2011, by Shaun Illingworth, transcript, pp. 1–2, 5, Rutgers Oral History Archives.

36 Birmingham Black Oral History Project, testimony quoted in Callum G. Brown, *Religion and Society in Twentieth-Century Britain* (Harlow: Pearson Longman, 2006), pp. 212–4.

37 Katherine Acey, interview, Voices of Feminism Oral History Project, Sophia Smith Collection, Smith College, Northampton, MA 01063, Tape 1, p. 4. All the interview transcripts cited below from this collection are at http://www.smith.edu/libraries/libs/ssc/vof/vof-intro.html (accessed 25 September 2015).

38 Ibid., p. 10.

39 Ibid., p. 7.

40 Ibid.

41 Ibid., p. 18.

42 Ibid., p. 21.

43 Ibid.

44 Ibid., p. 22.

45 Ibid., p. 34.

46 Callum G. Brown, 'Women and religion in Britain: the autobiographical view of the fifties and sixties', in C.G. Brown and M. Snape (eds), *Secularisation in the Christian World c.1750–c.2000 (Essays in Honour of Hugh McLeod)* (Farnham: Ashgate, 2010), pp.159–73; idem, 'Gendering secularisation: locating women in the transformation of British Christianity in the 1960s' in I. Katznelson and G. Stedman Jones (eds), *Religion and the Political Imagination* (Cambridge: Cambridge University Press, 2010), pp. 275–94.

47 Sara Gould, interview by Kelly Anderson, transcript of video recording, 16 November 2006, Voices of Feminism Oral History Project, Sophia Smith Collection, Smith College, Northampton, MA 01063, p. 52.

48 Dolores Alexander, interview by Kelly Anderson, transcript of video recording, 20 March 2004, Voices of Feminism Oral History Project, Sophia Smith Collection, Northampton, MA 01063.

49 Dorothy Allison, interview by Kelly Anderson, transcript of video recording, 19 November 2007, Voices of Feminism Oral History Project, Sophia Smith Collection, Northampton, MA 01063, pp. 15, 71, 74, 92.

50 The standard Catholic Church school catechism used in the United States from the 1880s to the 1960s, and regarded as strict and 'old school'.

51 Virginia Apuzzo, interview by Kelly Anderson, transcript of video recording, 2 June 2004, Voices of Feminism Oral History Project, Sophia Smith Collection, Northampton, MA 01063, p. 20.

52 Ibid., p. 23.

53 Dázon Dixon Diallo, interview by Loretta Ross, transcript of video recording, 4 April 2009, Voices of Feminism Oral History Project, Sophia Smith Collection, Northampton, MA 01063.

54 Ibid., p. 37.

55 Kristin Aune, 'Much less religious, a little more spiritual: the religious and spiritual views of third-wave feminists in the UK', *Feminist Review* vol. 97

(2011), pp. 32–55; idem., 'Evangelical Christianity and Women's Changing Lives', *European Journal of Women's Studies* vol. 15 (2008), pp. 277–94, at p. 288.

56   Regina Jones, born 1942 Los Angeles, interviewed by Alex Cline 2012, unpaginated transcript, UCLA Oral History Research Center. Regina was the wife of Ken Jones (1938–93), the first African American weeknight TV news anchor in Los Angeles who covered the Watts Riots and other major events of the sixties, and together they published *SOUL* magazine (1966–82) covering black music and affairs.

57   Anonymous female respondent, interviewed by Michaela Bell, 1998, The Whole World Was Watching: An Oral History of 1968, Rhode Island at http://cds. library.brown.edu/projects/1968/narrators/default.htm (accessed 27 April 2016).

58   Ibid.

59   Ibid.

60   Ibid.

61   Brown, *Religion and the Demographic Revolution*, esp. pp. 141–63, 172–266.

62   An insightful Christian academic form of this narrative is Ronald B. Flowers, *Religion in Strange Times: The 1960s and 1970s* (Macon, GA: Mercer University Press, 1984).

63   McLeod, *Religious Crisis*, pp. 246–55.

64   Jim Blair (born 1935), interviewed 2008 by Scott Lunsford, transcript, pp. 29–30, 156, Arkansas Memories Project, The David and Barbara Pryor Center for Arkansas Oral and Visual History, University of Arkansas.

65   Only one secularist is reported amongst sixty interviewees in a recent international oral history project: Peter Coleman, Daniela Koleva and Joanna Bornat (eds), *Aging, Ritual and Social Change: Comparing the Secular and Religious in Eastern and Western Europe* (Farnham: Ashgate, 2013).

66   Null, Miriam, Oral History Interview, 23 August 2006, by Shaun Illingworth and Jonathan Wolitz, transcript, p. 43, Rutgers Oral History Archives.

67   Male narratives of questioning religion were evident in the Black Birmingham Oral History Project archive, University of Birmingham Special Collections.

68   Hugh McLeod, 'New perspectives on Victorian working-class religion: the oral evidence', *Oral History Journal* vol. 14 (1986), p. 33.

69   Brown, 'The People of No Religion', pp. 37–61.

70   Mike Beebe (born 1946), interviewed 2008 by Scott Lunsford, transcript, pp. 28–9, 55, 65, Arkansas Memories Project, The David and Barbara Pryor Center for Arkansas Oral and Visual History, University of Arkansas.

71   Roper, 'Slipping out of view'.

72   Quoted in Brown, *Death of Christian Britain*, p. 183.

73   David Nash, *Christian Ideals in British Culture: Stories of Belief in the Twentieth Century* (Basingstoke: Palgrave Macmillan, 2013), p. 17.

74   Penny Edgell, Joseph Gerteis and Douglas Hartmann, 'Atheists as "Other": moral boundaries and cultural membership in American society', *American Sociological Review* vol. 71 (2006), pp. 211–34.

Chapter 3

1   David Pollock, born 1942, London, COT, p. 1046.

2   Paul M. Cooey, 'Neither seen nor heard: the absent child in the study of religion', *Journal of Childhood and Religion* vol. 1 (2010), pp. 1–31 at pp. 1–3.

3   William James, *The Varieties of Religious Experience; A Study of Human Nature* (London: Longmans Green & Co, 1902); James Fowler, *Stages of Faith: The Psychology of Human Development and the Quest for Meaning* (San Francisco: Harper & Row, 1981), esp. pp. 119–98.

4   See for instance Eugene C. Roehlkepatain et al. (eds), *The Handbook of Spiritual Development in Childhood and Adolescence* (London: Sage, 2006).

5   Most key works tend to use normative religious concepts; D.M. Wulff, *Psychology of Religion: Classic and Contemporary Views* (New York: Wiley, 1991).

6   For example in Hendricks, *Exit Interviews*; Christian Smith et al., *Lost in Transition: The Dark Side of Emerging Adulthood* (Oxford: Oxford University Press, 2011), pp. 11–13.

7   One study found its interviewees were predominantly in their thirties or forties when they left; Alan Jamieson, *A Churchless Faith: Faith Journeys beyond the Churches* (London: SPCK, 2002), p. 143.

8   James C. Conroy et al., *Does Religious Education Work? A Multi-dimensional Investigation* (London: Bloomsbury, 2013).

9   Khushi Ram, born 1921 Punjab, COT, p. 351.

10   Much of psychology research on religious loss has used church recruits. Amongst studies of children, see William K. Kay and Leslie J. Francis, *Drift from the Churches: Attitudes Toward Christianity during Childhood and Adolescence* (Cardiff: University of Wales Press, 1996); Leslie J. Francis and Y.J. Katz (eds), *Joining and Leaving Religion: Jewish and Christian Perspectives* (Leominster: Gracewing, 2000); and Leslie J. Francis and Philip Richter, *Gone for Good? Child-leaving and Returning in the 21st Century* (London: Epworth Press, 2007).

11   The development of these scales is outlined in Jeff Astley, Leslie J. Francis and Mandy Robbins, 'Assessing attitude towards religion: the Astley–Francis Scale of attitude towards theistic faith', *British Journal of Religious Education* vol. 34, no. 2 (2012), pp. 183–93.

12   Julia Stuart, born 1952 Dundee, COT, p. 687.

13   Dale McGowan, *Parenting beyond Belief: On Raising Ethical, Caring Kids without Religion*; Deborah Mitchell, *Growing Up Godless: A Parent's Guide to Raising Kids without Religion*, Sterling Ethos (2014) at http://raisingkidswithoutreligion.net (accessed 27 April 2016); Secular Earth on Facebook.

14   In earlier research I noted how respondents cited the dramatic childhood appeal of standing up to be saved 'several times a week' at evangelical services; Callum G. Brown and Jayne D. Stephenson, '"Sprouting Wings"? Working-class women and religion in Scotland c.1890–c.1950', in E. Breitenbach and E. Gordon (eds), *Out of Bounds: Women in Scottish Society 1800–1945* (Edinburgh: Edinburgh University Press, 1992), pp. 95–120.

15   Robert Sanford, born 1941 Seattle, WA, COT, p. 860; Leslie O'Hagan (fem.), born 1961 Palo Alto, CA, COT, p. 898.

16   Ann Auchterlonic, born 1942 Dundee, Scotland, COT, p. 815.

17   Ibid., p. 817.

18   Maria Berger (pseud.), COT, pp. 766–7.

19   Moses Klein, born 1967 Oakland, CA, COT, p. 503.

20   Harris Sussman, born 1944 New York City, COT, p. 969.

21   Claudine Raulier, born Liege, Belgium, 1923, COT, pp. 624–6.

22 Ann Auchterlonie, COT, pp. 817–8.
23 Robin Wood, born 1941 Worthing, Sussex, COT, p. 144–5.
24 Pat Duffy Hutcheon, 1926–2010, born Alberta, COT, p. 414.
25 Kathleen Dillon, born 1934 Belfast, COT, p. 313.
26 So small was the proportion that until 1961 'nones' were added to the 'not stated' in the presentation of census reports. See the discussion of this issue in Brown, *Religion and the Demographic Revolution*, pp. 113–5.
27 James Machin (pseud.), 1931–2012, born County Armagh, Northern Ireland, COT, p. 316.
28 Conrad Hadland, born 1935 Prince Rupert, BC, COT, p. 271.
29 Mary Wallace, born 1960 Northwich, Cheshire, COT, p. 12.
30 See for example Baker and Smith, 'None too simple'.
31 The Church of Sweden was disestablished in 2000; Frank Cranmer, 'The Church of Sweden and the unravelling of establishment', *Ecclesiastical Law Journal* vol. 5 (2000), pp. 417–30.
32 Anders Östberg, born 1979 Växjö, Sweden, COT, pp. 649–50.
33 Ibid., pp. 649–51.
34 Veronica Wikman, born 1965 Arboga, Sweden, COT, p. 1069.
35 Grant Hill, born 1979 Dundee, COT, p. 935.
36 Brown, *The Death of Christian Britain*, pp. 116–7, 181–5.
37 Kenneth Matthews, born 1947 Glasgow, COT, p. 608.
38 David Lambourn, born 1937 London, COT, pp. 720–5.
39 David subsequently left the ministry and came to a complex attitude to Christianity and humanism.
40 Joan Gibson, born 1943 Cheltenham, COT, pp. 72, 76.
41 Ruth Majors (pseud.), born 1941 London, interviewed by Lynn Abrams.
42 Lorraine Hardie, born 1939 Vancouver, COT, p. 293.
43 James Machin (pseud.), COT, pp. 303–4.
44 Dave Kong, born 1962 Iowa, COT, p. 186; Dick Hewetson, born 1930 Harvey, Illinois, COT, p. 226; David Fowler, born 1947 Welland, Ontario, COT, p. 563.
45 Grace Daniels, born 1958 Vancouver, COT, pp. 320–3.
46 Mary Wallace, COT, p. 13.
47 Dick Hewetson, COT, p. 227.
48 Ernest Parker, born 1949 Washington, DC, COT, pp. 1087–9.
49 Conrad Hadland, COT, p. 258.
50 Dick Hewetson, COT, p. 228.
51 Gillian Stewart, born 1960 Malaysia, p. 88.
52 David Lord, born 1942 Colliers Wood, London, COT, p. 633.
53 Ibid., p. 636.
54 Alicja Stettin (pseud.), born 1947 Eastern Europe, COT, pp. 521–2.
55 Terry Martin, born 1941 London, COT, p. 43.
56 Robert Sanford, COT, p. 852–3.
57 Robin Russell, born 1955 Yorkton, Saskatchewan, COT, pp. 550–2.
58 Ibid., pp. 550–1.
59 Kirsten Bulmer, born 1975 Livingston, Scotland, COT, pp. 595–6.
60 Nanendra Nayak, born 1951 Mangalore, India, COT, pp. 945–6.
61 Ellen Ross, born 1957 Vancouver, COT, p. 397.
62 Dave Kong, COT, p. 186–7.

63   An offensive American term to describe somebody regarded as prone to making mistakes or having bad luck. *Encarta* online.

64   Dennis Duncan, born 1929 Edinburgh, Scotland, COT, pp. 335–6.

65   Kai Kristensen, born 1933 Thisted, Denmark, COT, pp. 245–6.

66   Larry Hicok, born 1949 Albany, Oregon, COT, pp. 166–8.

67   James Machin (pseud.), COT, p. 305.

68   Santa Claus was referred to thirteen times in the testimonies.

69   Terry Martin, COT, pp. 30–9.

70   Grant Hill, COT, pp. 934–6.

71   Jutta Cahn (Poser), 1925–2014, born Berlin, COT, pp. 388–9.

72   Cerys Davies (pseud.), born 1939 Wales, CWT, pp. 43–6.

73   Peter Barton, 1921–2010, born London, written testimony p. 2. For Peter's obituary, see *British Journal of Oral and Maxillofacial Surgery* vol. 48 (2010), pp. 566–7.

74   Alistair McBay, born 1954 in Dunfermline, Scotland, COT, p. 799.

75   Gillian Stewart, COT, p. 87.

76   Bill Kennedy, born 1930 Winnipeg, COT, p. 537.

77   Robin Wood, COT, p. 137.

Chapter 4

1   Recent works that emphasize the proclaimed death of god in their narration of the rise of atheism include: From social history, Laura Schwartz, *Infidel Feminism: Secularism, Religion and Women's Emancipation 1830–1914* (Manchester: Manchester University Press, 2013). From sociology, Phil Zuckerman, *Society without God: What the Least Religious Nations Can Tell Us About Contentment* (New York: New York University Press, 2010). From history of philosophy, Taylor, *A Secular Age*; and Peter Watson, *The Age of Nothing: How We Have Sought to Live since the Death of God* (London: Weidenfeld & Nicolson, 2014).

2   Described in James M. Nelson, *Psychology, Religion and Spirituality* (New York: Springer, 2009), p. 286.

3   Prestigious organizations like the Pew Foundation and the *Guardian* newspaper repeat this claim; http://www.pewforum.org/2008/06/19/global-anglicanism-at-a-crossroads/; *The Guardian*, 27 September 2015, p.1a. Kevin Ward, *A History of Global Anglicanism* (Cambridge: Cambridge University Press, 2006), p. 1. Under 2 million is a more accurate statistic.

4   Quoted in Michael Lackey, *African American Atheists and Political Liberation: A Study of the Sociocultural Dynamics of Faith* (Gainesville: University Press of Florida, 2007), p. 50.

5   John Edwards, born 1946 Liverpool, COT, p. 756.

6   I first discussed this in Brown, *The Death of Christian Britain*.

7   Stephen Parker, *Faith on the Home Front: Aspects of Church Life and Popular Religion in Birmingham 1939–1945* (Bern: Peter Lang, 2005), p. 29.

8   Susan Wiltshire, 'Spirit of our age: dimensions of religiosity among Scottish youth', unpublished PhD thesis, University of Edinburgh, 2001.

9   Lynch, *Losing My Religion?*, pp. 32–3.

10 David Lord, born 1942 London, COT, p. 636.

11 Anders Östberg, born 1979 Växjö, Sweden, COT, p. 649.

12 Pew Forum in 2012 reported thirty-two nations with laws against blasphemy and twenty against apostasy. http://www.pewforum.org/2012/11/21/laws-penalizing-blasphemy-apostasy-and-defamation-of-religion-are-widespread/.

13 David Nash, *Blasphemy in Modern Britain: 1789 to the Present* (Aldershot: Ashgate, 1999); and idem, *Blasphemy in the Christian World: A History* (Oxford: Oxford University Press, 2007).

14 Michael Graham, *The Blasphemies of Thomas Aikenhead: Boundaries of Belief on the Eve of the Enlightenment* (Edinburgh: Edinburgh University Press, 2008).

15 Nash, *Blasphemy in Modern Britain*, pp. 197–202.

16 Robin Wood, COT, p. 159.

17 David Fowler, COT, pp. 567–8.

18 Pierre Berton, *The Comfortable Pew: A Critical Look at Christianity and the Religious Establishment in the New Age* (Toronto: McLelland & Stewart, 1965), pp. 69, 75.

19 Harris Sussman, COT, p. 970.

20 Amongst other things, Durr's wife Virginia was accused of receiving cabinet papers from Eleanor Roosevelt, who was allegedly passing them to a Communist spy ring. Virginia employed Rosa Parks as a part-time seamstress, and on her 1955 arrest in the Montgomery segregated buses issue, Clifford Durr legally represented Parks. Durr interviewed by Candace Waid and Allen Tullos, 29 December 1974, Southern Oral History Program, University of North Carolina at Chapel Hill, pp. 30–70, http://sohp.org/oral-history-interviews/. See also Hollinger F. Barnard (ed.), *Outside the Magic Circle: The Autobiography of Virginia Foster Durr* (Tuscaloosa: University of Alabama Press, 1990).

21 Callum G Brown, '"The Unholy Mrs Knight" and the BBC: secular humanism and the threat to the Christian nation, c.1945–1960', *English Historical Review* vol. 127 (2012), pp. 345–76.

22 S. Pixer, 'The oyster and the shadow', in Liz Heron (ed.), *Truth, Dare or Promise: Girls Growing Up in the Fifties* (London: Virago, 1985), p. 85.

23 Peter Scales, born 1963 Burns Lake, BC, COT, p. 811.

24 Edgell, Gerteis and Hartmann, 'Atheists as "Other"'.

25 Martin Vallik, born 1970 Tallinn, Estonia, COT, pp. 1012, 1017–8.

26 Ann Auchterlonie, COT, pp. 821–4.

27 Cecil Bannister, born 1949 Santiago, Chile, COT, p. 918.

28 Sterling Cooley, born 1988 Ashland, Oregon, COT, p. 219.

29 Lorraine Hardie, COT, p. 294.

30 Paul Bulmer, born 1956 Halifax, West Yorkshire, COT, p. 586.

31 David Lord, COT, p. 636.

32 Ron McLaren, COT, p. 58.

33 Frank Brown (pseud.), born 1930 Glasgow, written testimony, p. 1.

34 Frank O'Hara, COT, p. 446.

35 Gillian Ferris, born 1977 Dundee, COT, p. 849.

36 Mary Wallace, COT, p. 15.

37 Alistair McBay, COT, p. 800.

38 Ena Sparks (pseud.), born 1954 Trenton, Ontario, COT, p. 436.

39 Pat Duffy Hutcheon, COT, p. 423.
40 John Manuel, born 1940 Liverpool, COT, p. 486.
41 Ibid., p. 487.
42 Kris Kristensen, COT, p. 248.
43 Larry Hicok, COT, p. 176.
44 Dick Hewetson, COT, p. 237.
45 Lackey, *African American Atheists*, p. 50.
46 Jouffroy quoted in James, *The Varieties of Religious Experience*, p. 176.
47 Dennis Duncan, COT, pp. 338–40.
48 Sheralee Hayes-Fry, born Rochford, Essex, 1964, COT, p. 699.
49 Ibid., p. 700.
50 Ibid.
51 Ian Hayes-Fry, born 1963 Rochford, Essex, COT, pp. 711, 714.
52 John and Kirsten Bulmer from Edinburgh.
53 Alistair McBay, COT, p. 803.
54 Peter Scales, born 1963 Burns Lake, BC, COT, pp. 880–1, 887.
55 Kenneth Matthews, COT, p. 616.
56 Ann Auchterlonie, COT, p. 833.
57 Brown, *Religion and the Demographic Revolution*, pp. 233–44.

Chapter 5

1 For example, T.C. Smout, 'Born again at Cambuslang: new evidence on popular religion and literacy in eighteenth-century Scotland', *Past and Present* no. 97 (1982), pp. 114–27; Clive Field, 'Adam and Eve: gender in the English Free Church constituency', *Journal of Ecclesiastical History* vol. 44 (1993), pp. 63–79.
2 Brown, *Religion and the Demographic Revolution*, pp. 120–1.
3 Ibid., p. 121.
4 For which see Brown, 'Gendering secularisation', pp. 275–94; and idem, 'Women and religion in Britain'.
5 Calculated from data in *Church Statistics 2009/10*, p. 50, online at http://www.churchofengland.org/media/1333106/2009churchstatistics.pdf (accessed 30 November 2012).
6 See especially Brown, *The Death of Christian Britain*.
7 Brown, 'The People of No Religion'.
8 Interviews need to be one to one in quiet locations. I used outdoors on two occasions, but the recording quality was not ideal.
9 Abrams, *Oral History Theory*, pp. 119–21.
10 Alessandro Portelli, 'Oral history as genre', in M. Chamberlain and P. Thompson (eds), *Narrative and Genre: Contexts and Types of Communication* (London: Routledge, 2004), pp. 23–45; Jennifer Coates, *Men Talk: Stories in the Making of Masculinities* (Oxford: Wiley-Blackwell, 2003).
11 For which see Callum G. Brown, 'Unfettering religion: women and the family chain in the late twentieth century', in John Doran, Charlotte Methuen and Alexandra Walsham (eds), *Religion and the Household. Studies in Church History vol. 50* (Woodbridge: Boydell Press, 2014), pp. 469–91; and idem,

'Men losing faith: the making of modern no-religionism in the UK 1939–2010', in Lucy Dulap and Sue Morgan (eds), *Men, Masculinities and Religious Change in Britain since 1900* (Basingstoke: Palgrave, 2013), pp. 301–25.

12   Schwartz, *Infidel Feminism*, p. 23.
13   Danièle Hervieu-Léger, *Religion as a Chain of Memory* (Cambridge: Polity Press, 2000), pp. 133–4.
14   See my description of Ron Lesthaeghe's work in Brown, *Religion and the Demographic Revolution*, pp. 8–12.
15   Ibid., passim.
16   Aune, 'Evangelical Christianity and Women's Changing Lives'.
17   Lynn Abrams, 'Mothers and daughters: negotiating the discourse on the "good woman" in 1950s and 1960s Britain', in Nancy Christie and Michael Gauvreau (eds), *The Sixties and Beyond: Dechristianization as History in Britain, Canada, the United States and Western Europe, 1945–2000* (Toronto: Toronto University Press, 2013), pp. 60–82 at p. 80.
18   Kristina Minister, 'A feminist frame for the oral history interview', in Sherna Berger Gluck and Daphne Patai (eds), *Women's Words: The Feminist Practice of Oral History* (New York: Routledge, 1991), pp. 27–41; Portelli as discussed in Abrams, *Oral History Theory*, p. 28.
19   Kristin M. Langellier and Eric E. Peterson, *Storytelling in Daily Life: Performing Narrative* (Philadelphia: Temple University Press, 2004), pp. 108–9.
20   Abrams, *Oral History Theory*, esp. pp. 106–29.
21   Schwartz, *Infidel Feminism*, pp. 101–22.
22   Ibid., pp. 73–95.
23   Abrams, 'Mothers and daughters', pp. 60–82 at p. 80. Lynn Abrams, 'Liberating the female self: epiphanies, conflict and coherence in the life stories of post-war British women', *Social History* vol. 39 (2014), pp. 14–35.
24   See for example Mark Cave and Stephen M. Sloan (eds), *Listening on the Edge: Oral History in the Aftermath of Crisis* (Oxford: Oxford University Press, 2014); Alistair Thomson, 'Anzac memories revisited: trauma, memory and oral history', *Oral History Review* vol. 42 (2015), pp. 1–29; Kim Lacy Rogers et al. (eds), *Trauma and Life Stories* (London: Routledge, 2014).
25   Julia Stuart, COT, pp. 686–91.
26   Liz Currie, born 1945 Middlesex, COT, p. 838.
27   See the fabulous website run by Rose Bell. Based on her Masters research on mother and baby homes in England in the 1950s and 1960s, it includes both oral testimony and a bibliography. www.motherandbabyhomes.com (accessed 5 October 2015).
28   Annette Horton, born 1949 Plymouth, Devon, COT, p. 286.
29   Joan Gibson, COT, p. 75.
30   Maria Berger (pseud.), COT, pp. 766–73.
31   Alicja Stettin (pseud.), born 1947 Eastern Europe, COT, pp. 525–6.
32   Lynn Abrams, 'Mothers and daughters', pp. 60–82 at p. 79.
33   This theme is tackled in more detail in Brown, 'Unfettering religion'.
34   Gillian Stewart, born 1960 Malaysia, COT, p. 89.
35   Lynn Abrams, *The Making of Modern Woman 1789–1918* (London: Longman, 2002), pp. 17–41.
36   Jenny Daggers, *The British Christian Women's Movement: A Rehabilitation of Eve* (Aldershot: Ashgate, 2002).

37   Kathleen Berkeley, *The Women's Liberation Movement in America* (Westport, CT: Greenwood Press, 1999); Sarah Browne, *The Women's Liberation Movement in Scotland* (Manchester: Manchester University Press, 2014); Sheila Rowbotham, *The Past Is Before Us: Feminism in Action since the 1960s* (London: Pandora, 1989).

38   Joyce Murphy, born 1934 Bradford, COT, pp. 921–2.

39   Ibid., p. 923.

40   Sarah Browne, 'Women, religion and the turn to feminism: experiences of women's liberation activists in Britain in the seventies', in Michael Gauvreau and Nancy Christie (eds), *The Sixties and Beyond: Dechristianization in North America and Western Europe, 1945–2000* (Toronto: Toronto University Press, 2013), pp. 84–97 at p. 86.

41   Charlotte Linde, *Life Stories: The Creation of Coherence* (New York: Oxford University Press, 1993), p. 3. Abrams, 'Liberating the female self', p. 14.

42   Lorraine Lavoie, born 1944 Newport VT, COT, pp. 981–2.

43   Tanya Long, born 1944 Sudbury, Ontario, COT, p. 471.

44   Ibid., p. 476.

45   Ibid., p. 479.

46   Ibid., p. 478.

47   Ibid., p. 480.

48   Carolyn Steedman, *Landscape for a Good Woman: A Story of Two Women* (London: Virago, 1986).

49   Pat Duffy Hutcheon, COT, p. 415.

50   Earlier told in an autobiography: Pat Duffy Hutcheon, *Lonely Trail: The Life Journey of a Freethinker* (Ottawa: Aurora Humanist Books, 2009).

51   Carolyn Nalbandian, born 1934 Boston MA, COT, pp. 1002–8.

52   This is discussed in Brown, *Religion and the Demographic Revolution*, pp. 29–70; Brown, '"The Unholy Mrs Knight" and the BBC'.

53   Joan Gibson, COT, p. 67.

54   www.engender.org.uk/

55   Ellen Ramsay, born 1957 Vancouver, BC, COT, p. 399.

56   Ena Sparks (pseud.), COT, pp. 433–5.

57   See Brown, 'Women and religion', pp. 159–73.

58   Tanya Long, COT, p. 478.

59   Leslie O'Hagan (f), born 1961, Palo Alto, CA, COT, pp. 909–10.

60   Sarah Flew, born 1969 Truro, Cornwall, CWT, pp. 37–41; Ena Sparks (pseud.), COT, p. 434.

61   Nigel Bruce, born 1921 London, COT, p. 792.

62   Doug Owram, *Born at the Right Time: A History of the Baby Boom Generation* (Toronto: University of Toronto Press, 1997), p. 209.

63   Paul Heelas and Linda Woodhead, *The Spiritual Revolution: Why Religion Is Giving Way to Spirituality* (Oxford: Blackwell, 2004).

64   Taylor, *A Secular Age*, pp. 494–5.

65   Rodney Stark and William S. Bainbridge, 'Cults in America: a reconnaissance in space and time', in M.E. Harty (ed.), *Modern American Protestantism and Its World: 11: New and Intense Movements* (Munich: K.G. Saur, 1993), pp. 278–353; William S. Bainbridge and Rodney Stark (eds), 'Church and cult in Canada', *Canadian Journal of Sociology* vol. 4 (1982), pp. 351–66; David A. Nock, 'Cult, sect and church in Canada: a re-examination of Stark and

Bainbridge', *Canadian Review of Sociology and Anthropology* vol. 24 (1987), pp. 514–25.

66 Grace Daniels, COT, p. 323.

67 The course was taught by Barry Beyerstein (1947–2007), a skeptic and professor of psychology at Simon Fraser University in Vancouver, who researched brain mechanisms of perception, consciousness and the effects of drugs on cognition and emotion. http://en.wikipedia.org/wiki/Barry_Beyerstein (accessed 14 March 2015).

68 Grace Daniels, COT, p. 325.

69 Tanya Long, COT, p. 472.

70 Frank O'Hara, COT, p. 458.

71 Liz Currie, born 1945 Ealing, Middlesex, COT, p. 844.

72 Julia Stuart, COT, p. 693.

73 Sterling Cooley, born 1988 Ashland OR, COT, p. 205.

74 Ellen Ramsay, COT, p. 398.

75 Larry Hicok, born 1949 Albany, OR, COT, p. 169.

76 Heelas and Woodhead, *The Spiritual Revolution* has been influential in British Religious Studies in this regard.

77 Jeanne Willig, born 1931 London, COT, p. 961.

78 Gillian Stewart, COT, p. 93.

79 Tanya Long, COT, p. 472.

80 For 'spiritual caregivers' in the British NHS, see http://www.nhs-chaplaincy-spiritualcare.org.uk/ (accessed 5 October 2015).

81 The two were Terry Martin and Ron McLaren.

82 Ruth Majors (pseud.), born 1941 London, interviewed by Lynn Abrams.

83 A reference to Erica Jong, *Fear of Flying* (1973), a feminist novel on sexuality.

84 Michel Foucault, 'What is an author?' in P. Rabinow (ed.), *The Postmodern History Reader* (Harmondsworth: Penguin, 1984), pp. 118–20.

85 Which I previously studied at length in Brown, *Religion and the Demographic Revolution*.

86 Kirsten Bulmer, born Livingston, Scotland 1975, COT, p. 598.

87 Lorraine Hardie, born Vancouver, BC, 1939, COT, p. 299.

88 Pat Duffy Hutcheon, COT, pp. 425–6.

89 Ibid.

Chapter 6

1 Edward Royle, *Victorian Infidels. The Origins of the British Secularist Movement 1791–1866* (Manchester: Manchester University Press, 1974); idem, *Radicals, Secularists and Republicans: Popular Freethought in Britain 1866–1915* (Manchester: Manchester University Press, 1980); Nash, *Blasphemy in the Christian World*.

2 Discussed in Brown, *The Death of Christian Britain*, pp. 88–114.

3 For a study of impermanent desertion, see Timothy Larson, *Crisis of Doubt: Honest Faith in Nineteenth-Century England* (Oxford: Oxford University Press, 2006).

4 See Stephen Frosh, 'Screaming under the bridge: masculinity, rationality and psychotherapy', in J. Ussher (ed.), *Body Talk: the Material and Discursive*

Regulation of Sexuality, Madness and Reproduction (London: Routledge, 1997), pp. 70–84.

5   For example, two scholars refer to 'the embeddedness of the relationship between the concepts rationality and masculinity' in Western philosophical and sociological thought, and in management and organization theory; Anne Ross-Smith and Martin Kornberger, 'Gendered rationality? A genealogical exploration of the philosophical and sociological conceptions of rationality, masculinity and organization', *Gender, Work & Organization* vol. 11 (2004), pp. 280–305 at p. 296.

6   Durre S. Ahmed, *Masculinity, Rationality and Religion: A Feminist Perspective* (Lahore: ASR Publications, 1994), p. 76.

7   Tim Whitmarsh, *Battling the Gods: Atheism in the Ancient World* (New York: Alfred A Knopf, 2015), p. 124.

8   Vance noted how 'intuitive reason' rather than evidence led to belief in God during the conjunction of Victorian concepts of 'muscular Christianity' and 'rational religion'. Norman Vance, *Sinews of the Spirit: The Ideal of Christian Manliness in Victorian Literature and Religious Thought* (Cambridge: Cambridge University Press, 1985), p. 47.

9   R.W. Connell, *Masculinities*, Second edition (Berkeley: University of California Press, 2005), pp. 164–82.

10 For instance, in his studies of Scandinavia and the United States, Zuckerman does not raise such a series of connections; Phil Zuckerman, *Society without God: What the Least Religious Nations Tell Us about Contentment* (New York: New York University, 2008).

11 Alicja Stettin (pseud.), COT, p. 529.

12 Only the Ethical Society of Boston's Sunday morning meeting I attended in 2013 had a majority of women.

13 Brad Beavens, *Citizenship and Working-Class Culture, 1850–1945* (Manchester: Manchester University Press, 2005).

14 Women such as Annie Besant and Harriet Law in the nineteenth century and Madalyn Murray O'Hair and Barbara Smoker in the twentieth.

15 Harish Mehra, born 1951 Punjab, India, p. 751.

16 Robin Russell, born 1955 Yorktown, COT, p. 550.

17 Khalid Sohail, born 1952 Pakistan, CWT, p. 59.

18 David Fowler, COT, p. 566.

19 John Edwards, COT, p. 751.

20 Kai Kristensen, born 1933 Copenhagen, COT, p. 247. On Pauling's humanism, see Anthony Serafini, *Linus Pauling: A Man and His Science* (London: Simon & Schuster, 1989).

21 Kai Kristensen, COT, p. 252.

22 Alex Colias, born 1959 Coldwater, MI, CWT, pp. 26–9.

23 Justin Trottier, born 1982 Montreal, COT, pp. 463–4.

24 Terry Martin, COT, p. 33.

25 Frank O'Hara, COT, pp. 445–9.

26 Tim Unsworth, born 1956 Bolton, Lancashire, COT, pp. 661–7.

27 Brown, *The Death of Christian Britain: Understanding Secularisation 1800–2000*, pp. 98–105.

28 Larsen, *Crisis of Doubt.*

29 David Lambourn, born 1937 London, COT, pp. 720–36 at p. 727.

30 Ibid., p. 732.

31 Ibid., p. 735.
32 The Sea of Faith network holds to 'the continuing importance of religious thought, practice and the inspiration of sacred stories in our personal and cultural lives', but stresses 'the provisional nature of religious insight'. http://www.sofn.org.uk/pages/trustees.html accessed 4 October 2013.
33 Bill Kennedy, born 1930 Winnipeg, Manitoba, pp. 538–41.
34 Ibid., pp. 544–5.
35 Conrad Hadland, born 1935 Prince Rupert BC, COT, pp. 256–61.
36 Ibid., pp. 261–9.
37 Ibid., pp. 268–9.
38 Art Mielke, born 1949 Syracuse, New York, COT, pp. 1110–19.
39 Dick Hewetson, born 1930 Harvey IL, COT, p. 227.
40 Robin Wood, born 1941 Worthing, Sussex, pp. 137–8.
41 Frank Brown (pseud.), written testimony, pp. 1, 3–4.
42 Ian Caughlan, born 1988 Philadelphia, COT, p. 989.
43 Larry Hicok, COT, pp. 164–6.
44 Anders Östberg, Sweden, COT, p. 650.
45 Conrad Hadland, COT, pp. 268–9.
46 Paul Bulmer, born 1957 Halifax, West Yorkshire, COT, p. 587.
47 Kenneth Matthews, COT, p. 613.
48 Peter Barton, written testimony, pp. 2–3.
49 Martin Vallik, COT, p. 1013.
50 Nicolas Walter, 'McCabe, Joseph Martin (1867–1955)', *Oxford Dictionary of National Biography* (Oxford University Press, 2004); online edn, October 2009, http://www.oxforddnb.com/view/article/34674 (accessed 16 October 2012).
51 Alistair McBay, born 1954 Dunfermline, Scotland, COT, p. 800.
52 Ken Matthews, COT, p. 614.
53 Kathleen Dillon, born Belfast 1934, COT, pp. 313–4.
54 James Machin (pseud.), 1931–2012, COT, p. 304.
55 Ivan Middleton, born 1942 Holywood, County Down, COT, p. 110.
56 Kenneth Matthews, COT, p. 604.
57 Harish Mehra, COT, p. 748.
58 Khushi Ram, COT, pp. 354–5.
59 Defined by Abraham Maslow in an influential work of the early 1950s.
60 Nigel Bruce, COT, p. 784.
61 Berton, *The Comfortable Pew*, pp. 22–3. For an analysis of this influential book, see Nancy Christie, '"Belief crucified upon a rooftop antenna": Pierre Berton, *The Comfortable Pew*, and Dechristianization', in Nancy Christie and Michael Gauvreau (eds), *The Sixties and Beyond: Dechristianization in North America and Western Europe, 1945–2000* (Toronto: University of Toronto Press, 2013), pp. 321–50.
62 Ellen Ramsay, born 1957 Vancouver BC, COT, pp. 397–7.
63 See Stephen Parker, *Faith on the Home Front: Aspects of Church Life and Popular Religion in Birmingham 1939–1945* (Oxford: Peter Lang, 2006); and Michael Snape, *God and the British Soldier: Religion and the British Army in the First and Second World Wars* (London: Routledge, 2005).
64 Nigel Bruce, COT, p. 781.
65 Including a soldier interviewed by one of my students, Bernard, who lost God at the Battle of Salerno in September 1943, then slowly regained

a churchgoing habit in peacetime. Interviewed by Fleur Webb, 2010. Cited with permission.

66 Frank Brown (pseud.), written testimony, p. 1.
67 Andrew Totten, 'Coherent chaplaincy', *Journal of the Royal Army Chaplains' Department* vol. 45 (2006), p. 6.
68 Peter Scales, COT, p. 882.
69 Ibid., pp. 882–3.
70 Iain Mathieson, COT, p. 1124.
71 This respondent requested his testimony on this matter to be presented anonymously.
72 Alex Colias, CWT, pp. 27–8.
73 Kenneth Matthews, COT, pp. 614–16.
74 Terry Martin, supplementary written response, p. 2.

Chapter 7

1 Email circular to members of the Washington DC Atheists MeetUp Group, 20 June 2014.
2 Dave Kong, COT, p. 203.
3 Figures given at http://www.gallup.com/poll/180347/three-quarters-americans-identify-christian.aspx?utm_source=CATEGORY_RELIGIOUS_BELIEFS_AND_PRACTICES&utm_medium=topic&utm_campaign=tiles (accessed 23 June 2015). Data on teenage churchgoing in Smith, *Soul Searching*, pp. 274–5, 279.
4 Data at http://www.ons.gov.uk/ons/rel/census/2011-census/key-statistics-for-local-authorities-in-england-and-wales/rpt-ethnicity.html, and at http://www.ons.gov.uk/ons/rel/census/2011-census/detailed-characteristics-for-local-authorities-in-england-and-wales/sty-religion.html (accessed 23 June 2015).
5 Engelke, 'The coffin question', pp. 26–49 at p. 32.
6 I have attended or spoken at around twenty humanist, ethical society, atheist, skeptics' and secularist meetings in Scotland, England, Canada and the United States during 2009–15, and non-white faces were rare.
7 This was what has been called by sociologists the 'ethnic defence'; see Steve Bruce, *Firm in the Faith* (London: Gower, 1984).
8 Frantz Fanon, *Black Skin, White Masks* (orig., 1952; London: Pluto Press, 1986), p. 51.
9 Ibid., p. 134.
10 Lackey, *African American Atheists and Political Liberation*, p. 50. See also Liam McLaughlin, 'Is it harder to "come out" as an atheist if you're black?', *New Statesman*, 7 August 2013.
11 Ernest Parker,, COT, pp. 1087–8.
12 Ibid., pp. 1090–1.
13 On Rajneesh, see Paul Heelas, *The New Age Movement: Religion, Culture and Society in the Age of Postmodernity* (Oxford: Wiley-Blackwell, 1996), pp. 22, 40, 68, 72, 77, 95–6.
14 Ernest Parker, COT, p. 1095.
15 Norm R. Allen Jr. (born 1957) was the founder in 1989 of African Americans for Humanism and has been an active organizer and an author on this issue

ever since. At http://www.blackpast.org/aah/allen-norman-robert-jr-1957 (accessed 23 June 2015).

16 Ernest Parker, COT, p. 1098.

17 Use a search engine to find the Facebook page and website for this.

18 Ernest Parker, COT, pp. 1107–8.

19 Observable in the autobiography of a leading African American humanist, Anthony B. Pinn, *Writing God's Obituary: How a Good Methodist Became a Better Atheist* (Amherst, NY: Prometheus Books, 2014).

20 Ernest Poser, 'On being a Jewish "Geschmattet"', in David Ibry (ed.), *Exodus to Humanism: Jewish Identity Without Religion* (Amherst, NY: Prometheus, 1999), pp. 95–103 at p. 101. 'Geschmattet' is a Jew who converts out and is described as a worthless piece of cloth.

21 Ernest Poser, born 1921 Vienna, Austria, COT, pp. 365–6.

22 Ibid., p. 367.

23 Ibid., p. 368.

24 Ibid., p. 373.

25 Ernest Poser, 'On being a Jewish "Geschmattet"', p. 100.

26 The indestructibly Jewish part within every Jew.

27 Ernest Poser, 'On being a Jewish "Geschmattet"', pp. 100–1.

28 Moses Klein, COT, pp. 502–3.

29 Ibid., p. 502.

30 Ibid., p, 504.

31 Such as the Society for Humanistic Judaism, the International Institute for Secular Humanistic Judaism and the International Federation for Secular & Humanistic Judaism.

32 Moses Klein, COT, pp. 511–13.

33 Harris Sussman, COT, pp. 970–3.

34 Jutta Cahn, born 1925 Berlin, COT, p. 388.

35 Justin Trottier, born 1982 Montreal, COT, p. 463.

36 Jeanne Willig, pp. 958–64 at https://circle.org/who-we-are/our-values/ (accessed 21 June 2015).

37 Alison M. Bowes, 'Atheism in a religious society: the culture of unbelief in an Israeli kibbutz', in J. Davis (ed.), *Religious Organization and Religious Experience* (London, Academic Press, 1982), pp. 33–49.

38 Shlomo Sand, *How I Stopped Being a Jew* (London: Verso, 2014), p. 99.

39 Hakim (pseud.), born 1960s in the Middle East. His testimony is anonymized and withheld from the oral history compendium.

40 Annie Besant (1847–1943) was a British socialist, feminist, secularist, birth-control campaigner and Theosophist, with a varied career including support of the London matchgirls' strike of 1888 and a period of residence in India.

41 Public discussion of loss of faith amongst British Muslims is reflected in Andrew Anthony, 'Losing their religion', *The Observer New Review*, 17 May 2015, pp. 18–20.

42 Khushi Ram, born 1923 Punjab, India, COT, p. 351.

43 B.R. Ambedkar (1891–1956) is credited with persuading hundreds of thousands of *Dalits* to transfer to Theravada Buddhism.

44 Khushi Ram, COT, p. 352.

45 Ibid.

46 Harish Mehra, COT, p. 738.

47 The Asian Rationalist Society Britain.
48 Harish Mehra, COT, p. 739.
49 Ibid, pp. 739–42.
50 Gian S. Thind, born late 1940s India, COT, p. 356.
51 Narendra Nayak, born 1951 Mangalore, India, COT, pp. 944–7. See an entry for him at https://en.wikipedia.org/wiki/Narendra_Nayak (accessed 23 June 2015). Four psychologists experimented with atheists daring God: Marjaana Lindeman et al., 'Atheists become emotionally aroused when daring God to do terrible things', *International Journal for the Psychology of Religion* vol. 24 (2014), pp. 124–32.
52 Karen Armstrong, 'The sacred facts of life', *The Guardian*, 15 November 2003 at http://www.theguardian.com/world/2003/nov/15/usa.health (accessed 23 June 2015).
53 I examined some of this in Brown, How Anglicans lose religion', pp. 245–66.
54 Juhem Navarro-Rivera, 'The evolution of the religiously unaffiliated vote, 1980–2008' at http://publicreligion.org/2012/10/the-evolution-of-the-religiously-unaffiliated-vote-1980-2008/#.Vh_kI7tdEiF (accessed 15 October 2015).
55 Ernest Poser, COT, p. 371.
56 Ibid., pp. 371–3.

Chapter 8

1 Humanist intellectuals have always tended to emphasize this. For example, Margaret Knight (ed.), *Humanist Anthology: From Confucius to Bertrand Russell* (London: Rationalist Press Association/Barrie & Rockcliff, 1961); Watson, *The Age of Nothing*.
2 In addition to works already cited, see Bryan F. Le Beau, *The Atheist: Madalyn Murray O'Hair* (New York: New York University Press, 2003).
3 Roper, 'Slipping out of view', pp. 57–72.
4 Lynn Abrams, *Oral History Theory*, Second Edition (London: Routledge, 2016), p. 183.
5 Boy is a pseudonym. Khushi Ram, born 1923 Punjab, India, COT, pp. 353–5.
6 Ellen Ramsay, born 1957 Vancouver, COT, pp. 410–1.
7 John Manuel, COT, p. 487.
8 Lorraine Hardie, COT, p. 301.
9 Cited by Ivan Middleton, born 1942 Holywood, Northern Ireland, p. 107 et seq. The former humanist is referred to by Robin Wood, COT, p. 148.
10 Justin Trottier, COT, pp. 461–4.
11 Moses Klein, CA, p. 517.
12 Ron McLaren, born 1940 Dundee, COT, p. 55.
13 Maria Berger (pseud.), COT, p. 774.
14 Cecil Bannister, COT, p. 919.
15 John Manuel, born 1940 Liverpool, COT, p. 491.
16 Robin Russell, COT, p. 558.
17 David Fowler, COT, p. 571.
18 Kirsten Bulmer, COT, p. 599.

19 For example, in the editors' introduction in Coleman, Koleva and Bornat, *Aging Ritual and Social Change*, p. 6.

20 Taylor, *A Secular Age*, pp. 391–419, 473–504.

21 For example Mathew Grimley, 'Law, morality and secularization: the Church of England and the Wolfenden Report 1954–67', *Journal of Ecclesiastical History* vol. 60 (2009), pp. 725–41.

22 Kelly Kollman, *The Same-Sex Unions Revolution in Western Democracies: Internal Norms and Domestic Policy Change* (Manchester: Manchester University Press, 2013), pp. 1, 16, 87–95, 186.

23 US data are at http://www.pewforum.org/2015/07/29/graphics-slideshow-changing-attitudes-on-gay-marriage/; and http://www.gallup.com/poll/183425/support-doctor-assisted-suicide.aspx (both accessed 23 November 2015).

24 UK data are at http://www.dignityindying.org.uk/press-release/poll-assisted-dying/; and http://www.independent.co.uk/news/uk/home-news/poll-finds-overwhelming-support-for-gay-marriage-in-northern-ireland-despite-political-opposition-10370521.html (both accessed 23 November 2015).

25 Brown, 'The necessity of atheism'.

26 Mary Wallace, COT, p. 21.

27 Cerys Davies (pseud.), born 1939 Wales, CWT, pp. 43–7.

28 Ron McLaren, COT, p. 59.

29 Frank Brown (pseud.), written testimony, p. 1.

30 Joan Gibson, COT, p. 76.

31 Ron McLaren, COT, p. 55.

32 Moses Klein,, COT, p. 508.

33 Terry Martin, COT, pp. 47, 49.

34 Gillian Stewart, COT, p. 89.

35 Alex Colias, born 1959 Coldwater MI, CWT, pp. 26–30.

36 Ronald Brown, born 1940 Glasgow, COT, p. 1024.

37 Dr Harry Stopes-Roe (1924–2014), one-time chair of the BHA, was a philosopher and son of birth control pioneer Marie Stopes.

38 John Edwards, COT, p. 755.

39 Kenneth Matthews, COT, p. 607.

40 Miles Klein, born 1967 Oakland CA, COT, p. 508.

41 Robin Wood, COT, p. 142.

42 William Kennedy, born 1930 Winnipeg, Manitoba, COT, p. 537.

43 Moses Klein, COT, p. 507.

44 Arnold, *Belief and Unbelief in Medieval Europe*; Whitmarsh, *Battling the Gods*.

45 Susan Reynolds, 'Social mentalities and the case of medieval scepticism', *Transactions of the Royal Historical Society* vol. 1 (1991), pp. 21–41 at p. 36.

46 Keith Thomas, *Ends of Life: Roads to Fulfilment on Early Modern England* (Oxford: Oxford University Press, 2009), pp. 266–7.

47 Mary Wallace, COT, p. 19.

48 For instance Ivan Middleton, COT, p. 129.

49 Robin Wood, COT, p. 142.

50 Julia Stuart, COT, p. 694.

51 Gillian Stewart, COT, p. 103.

52 Joyce Murphy, COT, p. 922.

53 Ian Hayes Fry, born 1963 Rochford, Essex, COT, pp. 711–4.

54 John Manuel, COT, p. 587.

55 CESO was founded in 1967 as a domestic and international development charity putting volunteers into public and private organizations in support of business and people at http://www.ceso-saco.com/

56 Frank O'Hara, COT, pp. 448–50. To learn more about his life in his own words, see www.ohara.com/index.htm (last accessed 3 November 2015).

57 https://www.facebook.com/cesosaco/posts/320356898001193; www.ohara. com (accessed 3 May 2016).

58 Nigel Bruce and John Spencer, *Face to Face with Families: Report on the Children's Panel in Scotland* (Glasgow: Macdonald, 1976); idem, *The Challenge of Humanist Ethics* (n.d., n.p.). Ivan Middleton, COT, p. 116.

59 Robin Wood, COT, p. 161.

60 Kai Kristensen, COT, p. 249.

61 Robert Sanford, COT, p. 866.

62 David Fowler, COT, p. 573; Anders Östberg, COT, p. 656 at www.1023.org. uk (accessed 3 August 2015).

63 Harry Sussman, COT, p. 975.

64 Such as Grant Hill, COT, pp. 937–9.

65 Ian Caughlan, COT, pp. 988 et seq.

66 Terry Martin, COT, pp. 44–6.

67 Robin Wood, COT, pp. 150, 153–4.

68 Mary Wallace, COT, p. 26.

69 Joyce Murphy, COT, p. 929.

70 Humanist weddings were legalized in Norway in 2004 and in Scotland in 2005, and humanists led the campaigns for gay weddings – gained in 2007 and 2014, respectively.

71 These are mentioned by Larry Hicok, Dave Kong, Robin Wood, Sterling Cooley, Dick Hewetson and others at pp. 152, 155–6, 173, 176, 189, 190–5, 203–4, 212, 974, 1017–18.

72 Larry Hicok, COT, p. 164.

73 Dave Kong, COT, pp. 188–9, 191–2, 204.

74 Ibid., pp. 196–7. 'Alameda's "mayor for everyone"', *San Francisco Chronicle*, 22 September 2002.

75 Tim Unsworth, COT, p. 669.

76 Gillian Stewart, COT, p. 93.

77 Colin B. Campbell, 'Membership composition of the British Humanist Association', *The Sociological Review* vol. 3 (1965), pp. 327–37 at pp. 330–4. Engelke, 'The coffin question', pp. 26–49 at p. 32.

78 Longden, 'A profile of the members of the British Humanist Association', pp. 86–95.

79 Data from Brown, 'The people of no religion', p. 58

80 Dennis Duncan, COT, p. 345.

81 Ron Kerr, born 1940 Arbroath, COT, p. 683.

82 Nash, *Christian Ideals in British Culture*, esp. pp. 14–28, 184–92.

83 Brown, *Religion and the Demographic Revolution*, pp. 172–216.

84 Abrams, 'Mothers and daughters', pp. 60–82 at p. 79.

85 Ivan Middleton, COT, p. 109.

SOURCES

Original personal testimony

There were 85 respondents – born in: England (18), the United States (16), Canada (14), Scotland (14), India (4), Northern Ireland (3), Sweden (2), Estonia (2), Austria (1), Belgium (1), Chile (1), Denmark (1), Germany (1), Malaysia (1), Pakistan (1), Poland (1), Switzerland (1), Wales (1) and the Middle East (1).

Seventy-seven were interviewed by Callum Brown, 1 by Lynn Abrams and 7 contributed written testimony. Additionally, 4 interviewees also contributed written testimony. Interviews were conducted in Britain, the United States, Canada, France and Estonia between July 2009 and July 2015.

One interviewee refused to sign off on permission to use. One interview failed to record.

The interview testimonies were transcribed and collected in Compendium of Oral Testimony (COT) of 1,124 pages and 649,257 words. Written testimonies were collected in Compendium of Written Testimony (CWT). Footnotes refer to COT and CWT files.

The compendia and sound files will be deposited in Bishopsgate Archive, London, in 2017.

Oral history archive testimony (consulted for Chapter 2)

Those testimonies which are openly available online are indicated with an asterisk.

United States

- *Voices of Feminism Oral History Project, Sophia Smith Collection, Smith College, Northampton, MA: 61 transcripts.

- *Rutgers Oral History Archives, New Jersey: (a) African American history, 8 transcripts; (b) Women's history, 53 transcripts.

- *Southern Oral History Program, University of North Carolina (Chapel Hill); sample from 5,316 interviews, including: Series G, southern women, 92 interviews.

- *The Whole World Watching: An Oral History of 1968, Rhode Island, 31 transcripts.

- *Arkansas Memories Project, Pryor Centre, University of Arkansas, c.40 transcripts.

- *UCLA Center for Oral History Research, African Americans, 18 transcripts; Black Women Activists in LA, 3 transcripts; and Black music and musicians 4 transcripts.

United Kingdom

- Thompson-Vigne Edwardians oral history project, Qualidata, University of Essex, 499 transcripts. P. Thompson and T. Lummis, *Family Life and Work Experience Before 1918, 1870–1973* [data collection]. Seventh Edition (UK Data Service, 2009). SN: 2000, http://dx.doi.org/10.5255/UKDA-SN-2000-1

- Birmingham Black Oral History Collection, University of Birmingham Special Collections, 40 transcripts.

- Stirling Women's Oral History Archive, Smith Art Gallery and Museum, Stirling, 80 transcripts.

- *The David J Wood Collection of Oral History, at oral.history.co.uk, 24 transcripts.

Canada

- *Saskatchewan History and Folklore Society, 36 interviews.

Other oral history interviews

Clifford Durr interviewed by Candace Waid and Allen Tullos, 29 December 1974, Southern Oral History Program, University of North Carolina at Chapel Hill, http://sohp.org/oral-history-interviews/

Primary text sources

'Alameda's "mayor for everyone"', *San Francisco Chronicle*, 22 September 2002.
Nigel Bruce, *The Challenge of Humanist Ethics* (n.p.: n.d.).
Nigel Bruce and John Spencer, *Face to Face with Families: Report on the Children's Panel in Scotland* (Glasgow: Macdonald, 1976).

Secondary sources

Lynn Abrams, *The Making of Modern Woman 1789–1918* (London: Longman, 2002).
Lynn Abrams, *Oral History Theory*, Second Edition (London: Routledge, 2016).

Lynn Abrams, 'Mothers and daughters: negotiating the discourse on the "good woman" in 1950s and 1960s Britain', in Nancy Christie and Michael Gauvreau (eds), *The Sixties and Beyond: Dechristianization as History in Britain, Canada, the United States and Western Europe, 1945–2000* (Toronto, ON: Toronto University Press, 2013), pp. 60–82.

Lynn Abrams, 'Liberating the female self: epiphanies, conflict and coherence in the life stories of post-war British women', *Social History* vol. 39 (2014), pp. 14–35.

Norm R. Allen Jr. (ed.), *The Black Humanist Experience: An Alternative to Religion* (Amherst: Prometheus, 2003).

Bob Altemeyer, 'The decline of organized religion in Western civilization', *International Journal for the Psychology of Religion* vol. 14 (2004), pp. 77–89.

Anon, *Lewis, Land of Revival: The Story of the 1949–52 Lewis Revival as Told by the Islanders*, Audio Cassette (Belfast: Ambassador Productions Ltd, 1983).

Anon, 'Peter Barton, 1921–2010, obituary', *British Journal of Oral and Maxillofacial Surgery* vol. 48 (2010), pp. 566–567.

Talal Asad, *Formations of the Secular: Christianity, Islam, Modernity* (Redwood City, CA: Stanford University Press, 2003).

Karen Armstrong, 'The sacred facts of life', *The Guardian*, 15 November 2003, at http://www.theguardian.com/world/2003/nov/15/usa.health (accessed 23 June 2015).

Association for Canadian Studies poll, at http://news.nationalpost.com/holy-post/religion-not-important-to-most-canadians-although-majority-believe-in-god-poll (accessed 14 August 2015).

Jeff Astley, Leslie J. Francis and Mandy Robbins, 'Assessing attitude towards religion: the Astley–Francis Scale of attitude towards theistic faith', *British Journal of Religious Education* vol. 34, no. 2 (2012), pp. 183–193.

Kirsten Aune, 'Evangelical Christianity and women's changing lives', *European Journal of Women's Studies* vol. 15 (2008), pp. 277–294.

Kristin Aune, 'Much less religious, a little more spiritual: the religious and spiritual views of third-wave feminists in the UK', *Feminist Review* vol. 97 (2011), pp. 32–55.

William S. Bainbridge and Rodney Stark, 'Church and cult in Canada', *Canadian Journal of Sociology* vol. 4 (1982), pp. 351–366.

Joseph O. Baker and Buster G. Smith, 'The nones: social characteristics of the religiously unaffiliated', *Social Forces* vol. 87, no. 3 (2009a), pp. 1251–1263.

Joseph O. Baker and Buster G. Smith, 'None too simple: examining issues of religious nonbelief and nonbelonging in the United States', *Journal for the Social Scientific Study of Religion* vol. 48 (2009b), pp. 719–733.

Hollinger F. Barnard (ed.), *Outside the Magic Circle: The Autobiography of Virginia Foster Durr* (Tuscaloosa: University of Alabama Press, 1990).

Brad Beavens, *Citizenship and Working-Class Culture, 1850–1945* (Manchester: Manchester University Press, 2005).

Kathleen Berkeley, *The Women's Liberation Movement in America* (Westport, CT: Greenwood Press, 1999).

Pierre Berton, *The Comfortable Pew: A Critical Look at Christianity and the Religious Establishment in the New Age* (Toronto, ON: McLelland & Stewart, 1965).

Reginald Bibby, *Unknown Gods: The Ongoing Story of Religion in Canada* (Toronto, ON: Stoddart, 1993).

Reginald Bibby, *Restless Gods: The Renaissance of Religion in Canada* (Toronto, ON: Stoddart, 2002).

Russell Blackford and Udo Schüklenk (eds), *50 Voices of Disbelief: Why We Are Atheists* (Chichester: Wiley-Blackwell, 2009).

Alison M. Bowes, 'Atheism in a religious society: the culture of unbelief in an Israeli kibbutz', in J. Davis (ed.), *Religious Organization and Religious Experience* (London: Academic Press, 1982), pp. 33–49.

Merlin B. Brinkerhoff and Marlene M. Mackie, 'Casting off the bonds of organized religion: a religious-careers approach to the study of apostasy', *Review of Religious Research* vol. 34 (1993), pp. 235–258.

David G. Bromley (ed.), *Falling from the Faith: Causes and Consequences of Religious Apostasy* (Newbury Park, CA: Sage, 1988).

Callum G. Brown, *Postmodernism for Historians* (London: Longman Pearson, 2005).

Callum G. Brown, *Religion and Society in Twentieth-Century Britain* (Harlow: Pearson Longman, 2006).

Callum G. Brown, '"Best not to take it too far": how the British cut religion down to size', *Open Democracy*, 8 March 2006, at https://www.opendemocracy.net/globalization-aboutfaith/britain_religion_3335.jsp (accessed 25 June 2015).

Callum G. Brown, 'Christian Britain – redefined or misdefined?', *The Expository Times* vol. 119 (2008), pp. 541–542.

Callum G. Brown, *The Death of Christian Britain: Understanding Secularisation 1800–2000*. Second Edition (London: Routledge, 2009).

Callum G. Brown, 'Women and religion in Britain: the autobiographical view of the fifties and sixties', in C.G. Brown and M. Snape (eds), *Secularisation in the Christian World c.1750–c.2000 (Essays in Honour of Hugh McLeod)* (Farnham: Ashgate, 2010), pp.159–173.

Callum G. Brown, 'Spectacle, restraint and the twentieth-century Sabbath wars: the "everyday" Scottish Sunday', in L. Abrams and C.G. Brown (eds), *A History of Everyday Life in Twentieth-Century Scotland* (Edinburgh: Edinburgh University Press, 2010), pp. 153–180.

Callum G. Brown, 'Gendering secularisation: locating women in the transformation of British Christianity in the 1960s', in I. Katznelson and G. Stedman Jones (eds), *Religion and the Political Imagination* (Cambridge: Cambridge University Press, 2010), pp. 275–294.

Callum G. Brown, 'The people of no religion: the demographics of secularisation in the English-speaking world since c.1900', *Archiv für Sozialgeschichte* vol. 51 (2011), pp. 37–61.

Callum G. Brown, '"The Unholy Mrs Knight" and the BBC: secular humanism and the threat to the Christian nation, c.1945–1960', *English Historical Review* vol. 127 (2012), pp. 345–376.

Callum G. Brown, *Religion and the Demographic Revolution: Women and Secularisation in Canada, Ireland, UK and USA since the 1960s* (London: Boydell, 2012).

Callum G. Brown, 'Men losing faith: the making of modern no-religionism in the UK 1939–2010', in Lucy Dulap and Sue Morgan (eds), *Men, Masculinities and Religious Change in Britain since 1900* (Basingstoke: Palgrave, 2013), pp. 301–325.

Callum G. Brown, 'Unfettering religion: women and the family chain in the late twentieth century', in John Doran, Charlotte Methuen and Alexandra

Walsham (eds), *Religion and the Household. Studies in Church History vol. 50* (Woodbridge: Boydell Press, 2014), pp. 469–491.

Callum G. Brown, 'How Anglicans lose religion: an oral history of becoming secular', in Abby Day (ed.), *Contemporary Issues in the Worldwide Anglican Communion: Powers and Pieties* (Farnham: Ashgate, 2016).

Callum G. Brown, 'The necessity of atheism: making sense of secularisation', *Journal of Religious History* (forthcoming).

Callum G. Brown and Jayne D. Stephenson, ' "Sprouting Wings"? Working-class women and religion in Scotland c.1890–c.1950', in E. Breitenbach and E. Gordon (eds), *Out of Bounds: Women in Scottish Society 1800–1945* (Edinburgh: Edinburgh University Press, 1992), pp. 95–120.

Sarah Browne, 'Women, religion and the turn to feminism: experiences of women's liberation activists in Britain in the seventies', in Michael Gauvreau and Nancy Christie (eds), *The Sixties and Beyond: Dechristianization in North America and Western Europe, 1945–2000* (Toronto, ON: Toronto University Press, 2013), pp. 84–97.

Sarah Browne, *The Women's Liberation Movement in Scotland* (Manchester: Manchester University Press, 2014).

Steve Bruce, *Firm in the Faith* (London: Gower, 1984).

Steve Bruce, 'Praying alone? Church-going in Britain and the Putnam thesis', *Journal of Contemporary Religion* vol. 17, no. 3 (2002), pp. 317–328.

Claudia Lauper Bushman and Caroline Kline, *Mormon Women Have Their Say: Essays from the Claremont Oral History Collection* (Draper, UT: Greg Kofford Books, 2013).

Colin B. Campbell, 'Membership composition of the British Humanist Association', *The Sociological Review* vol. 3 (1965), pp. 327–337.

José Casanova, 'The religious situation in Europe', in Hans Joas and Klaus Wiegandt (eds), *Secularization and the World Religions* (Liverpool: Liverpool University Press, 2009), pp. 206–228.

Mark Cave and Stephen M. Sloan (eds), *Listening on the Edge: Oral History in the Aftermath of Crisis* (Oxford: Oxford University Press, 2014).

Owen Chadwick, *The Secularisation of the European Mind in the Nineteenth Century* (Cambridge: Cambridge University Press, 1975).

Kevin J. Christiano, *Religious Diversity and Social Change: American Cities, 1890–1906* (Cambridge: Cambridge University Press, 1987), pp. 49–50.

Nancy Christie, ' "Belief crucified upon a rooftop antenna": Pierre Berton, *The Comfortable Pew*, and Dechristianization', in Nancy Christie and Michael Gauvreau (eds), *The Sixties and Beyond: Dechristianization in North America and Western Europe, 1945–2000* (Toronto, ON: University of Toronto Press, 2013), pp. 321–350.

Church Statistics 2009/10, at http://www.churchofengland.org/media/1333106/200 9churchstatistics.pdf (accessed 30 November 2012).

J.C.D. Clark, 'Secularization and modernization: the failure of a "grand narrative" ', *Historical Journal* vol. 55 (2012), pp. 161–194.

Jennifer Coates, *Men Talk: Stories in the Making of Masculinities* (Oxford: Wiley-Blackwell, 2003).

Peter Coleman, Daniela Koleva and Joanna Bornat (eds), *Aging Ritual and Social Change: Comparing the Secular and Religious in Eastern and Western Europe* (Farnham: Ashgate, 2013).

R.W. Connell, *Masculinities*. Second Edition (Berkeley: University of California Press, 2005).

James C. Conroy, David Lundie, Robert A. Davis, Vivienne Baumfield, L. Philliup Barnes, Tony Gallagher, Kevin Lowden, Nicole Bourque and Karen Wennell, *Does Religious Education Work? A Multi-dimensional Investigation* (London: Bloomsbury, 2013).

Paul M. Cooey, 'Neither seen nor heard: the absent child in the study of religion', *Journal of Childhood and Religion* vol. 1 (2010), pp. 1–31.

Jeff Cox, 'Towards eliminating the concept of secularisation: a progress report', in C.G. Brown and M. Snape (eds), *Secularisation in the Christian World c.1750–c.2000 (Essays in Honour of Hugh McLeod)* (Farnham: Ashgate, 2010).

Frank Cranmer, 'The Church of Sweden and the unravelling of establishment', *Ecclesiastical Law Journal* vol. 5 (2000), pp. 417–430.

Jenny Daggers, *The British Christian Women's Movement: A Rehabilitation of Eve* (Aldershot: Ashgate, 2002).

Grace Davie, *Religion in Britain since 1945: Believing without Belonging* (Oxford: Blackwell, 1994).

Grace Davie, *Religion in Modern Europe: A Memory Mutates* (Oxford: Oxford University Press, 2000).

Christie Davies, *The Strange Death of Moral Britain* (n.p: Transaction, 2006).

Natalie Zemon Davies, *Women on the Margins: Three Seventeenth-Century Lives* (Cambridge, MA: Harvard University Press, 1995), pp. 126–128.

Natalie Zemon Davies, *Trickster Travels: The Search for Leo Africanus* (London: Faber & Faber, 2006).

Ross Douthat, *Bad Religion: How We Became a Nation of Heretics* (New York: Free Press, 2012).

Roger L. Dudley, *Why Our Teenagers Leave the Church: Personal Stories from a 10-year Study* (Hagerstown, MD: Review & Herald Publishing Association, 2000).

Penny Edgell, Joseph Gerteis and Douglas Hartmann, 'Atheists as "Other": moral boundaries and cultural membership in American society', *American Sociological Review* vol. 71 (2006), pp. 211–234.

Matthew Engelke, 'Christianity and the anthropology of secular humanism', *Current Anthropology* vol. 55, no. S10 (2014), pp. S292–S301.

Matthew Engelke, 'The coffin question: death and materiality in humanist funerals', *Material Religion* vol. 11 (2015a), pp. 26–49.

Matthew Engelke, 'Humanist ceremonies: The case of non-religious funerals in England', in Andrew Copson and A.C. Grayling (eds), *The Wiley Blackwell Handbook on Humanism* (Oxford: Wiley, 2015b).

Eurobarometer, *Social Values, Science and Technology*, p. 9, at http://ec.europa.eu/public_opinion/archives/ebs/ebs_225_report_en.pdf (accessed 18 October 2014).

Frantz Fanon, *Black Skin, White Masks* (orig., 1952, London: Pluto Press, 1986).

Clive Field, 'Adam and Eve: gender in the English Free Church constituency', *Journal of Ecclesiastical History* vol. 44 (1993), pp. 63–79.

Ronald B. Flowers, *Religion in Strange Times: The 1960s and 1970s* (Macon, GA: Mercer University Press, 1984).

Michel Foucault, 'What is an author?', in P. Rabinow (ed.), *The Postmodern History Reader* (Harmondsworth: Penguin, 1984), pp. 118–120.

James Fowler, *Stages of Faith: The Psychology of Human Development and the Quest for Meaning* (San Francisco: Harper & Row, 1981).

Leslie J. Francis and Y.J. Katz (eds), *Joining and Leaving Religion* (Leominister: Gracewing, 2000).

Leslie J. Francis and Philip Richter, *Gone for Good? Child-leaving and Returning in the 21st Century* (London: Epworth, 2007).

Stephen Frosh, 'Screaming under the bridge: masculinity, rationality and psychotherapy', in J. Ussher (ed.), *Body Talk: The Material and Discursive Regulation of Sexuality, Madness and Reproduction* (London: Routledge, 1997).

Luke W. Galen, 'Does religious belief promote prosociality? A critical examination', *Psychological Bulletin* vol. 138 (2012), pp. 876–906.

Luke W. Galen, 'Atheism, wellbeing, and the wager: why not believing in God (with others) is good for you', *Science, Religion and Culture* vol. 2 (2015), pp. 54–69.

Luke W. Galen and J. Kloet, 'Mental well-being in the religious and the non-religious: evidence for a curvilinear relationship', *Mental Health, Religion, & Culture* vol. 14 (2011), pp. 673–689.

Luke W. Galen, M. Sharp and A. McNulty, 'The role of nonreligious group factors versus religious belief in the prediction of prosociality', *Social Indicators Research* vol. 122 (2015), pp. 411–432.

Gallup Poll for 2014 at http://www.gallup.com/poll/180347/three-quarters-americans-identify-christian.aspx (accessed 14 August 2015).

Gallup poll, at http://www.gallup.com/poll/147887/americans-continue-believe-god.aspx (accessed 14 August 2015).

Jane Garnett et al. (eds), *Redefining Christian Britain: Post 1945 Perspectives* (London: SCM Press, 2006).

Robin Gill, *The 'Empty Church' Revisited* (Aldershot: Ashgate, 2003).

Michael Graham, *The Blasphemies of Thomas Aikenhead: Boundaries of Belief on the Eve of the Enlightenment* (Edinburgh: Edinburgh University Press, 2008).

Andrew Greeley, 'Unsecular Europe: the persistence of religion', in Detlef Pollack and Daniel V.A. Olson (eds), *The Role of Religion in Modern Societies* (New York: Routledge, 2008), pp. 141–161.

Stan Greenberg, 'I've seen America's future and it's not Republican', *The Guardian*, 5 November 2015.

Jaber F. Gubrium et al. (eds), *Sage Handbook of Interview Research: The Complexity of the Craft*. Second Edition (London: Sage, 2012), pp. 27–44.

C. Kirk Hadaway and Penny Long Marler, 'How many Americans attend worship each week? An alternative approach to measurement', *Journal for the Scientific Study of Religion* vol. 44 (2005), pp. 307–322.

C. Kirk Hadaway and Wade Clark Roof, 'Those who stay religious "nones" and those who don't: a research note', *Journal for the Scientific Study of Religion* vol. 18 (1979), pp. 194–200.

Alister Hardy, *The Spiritual Nature of Man* (Oxford: Clarendon Press, 1979).

Paul Heelas, *The New Age Movement: Religion, Culture and Society in the Age of Postmodernity* (Oxford: Wiley-Blackwell, 1996).

Paul Heelas and Linda Woodhead, *The Spiritual Revolution: Why Religion Is Giving Way to Spirituality* (Oxford: Blackwell, 2004).

William D. Hendricks, *Exit Interviews: Revealing Stories of Why People Are Leaving the Church* (Chicago, IL: Moody Press, 1993).

Danièle Hervieu-Léger, *Religion as a Chain of Memory* (Cambridge, Polity Press, 2000).

Gertrude Himmelfarb, *The De-moralization of Society: From Victorian Values to Modern Values* (London: IEA, 1995).

Gertrude Himmelfarb, *One Nation, Two Cultures: A Searching Examination of American Society in the Aftermath of Our Cultural Revolution* (New York: Vintage, 2001).

Felipe Honojosa, *Latino Mennonites: Civil Rights, Faith and Evangelical Culture* (Baltimore: John Hopkins University Press, 2014).

Pat Duffy Hutcheon, *Lonely Trail: The Life Journey of a Freethinker* (Ottawa, ON: Aurora Humanist Books, 2009).

William James, *The Varieties of Religious Experience: A Study of Human Nature* (London: Longmans Green & Co, 1902).

Alan Jamieson, *A Churchless Faith: Faith Journeys beyond the Churches* (London: SPCK, 2002).

William K. Kay and Leslie J. Francis, *Drift from the Churches: Attitudes toward Christianity during Childhood and Adolescence* (Cardiff: University of Wales Press, 1996).

Ariela Keysar and and Juhem Navaro-Rivero, 'A world of atheism: global demographics', in Stephen Bullivant and Michael Ruse (eds), *The Oxford Handbook of Atheism* (Oxford: Oxford University Press, 2013), pp. 553–586.

Margaret Knight (ed.), *Humanist Anthology: From Confucius to Bertrand Russell* (London: Rationalist Press Association/Barrie & Rockcliff, 1961).

Kelly Kollman, *The Same-Sex Unions Revolution in Western Democracies: Internal Norms and Domestic Policy Change* (Manchester: Manchester University Press, 2013).

Michael Lackey, *African American Atheists and Political Liberation: A Study of the Sociocultural Dynamics of Faith* (Gainesville: University Press of Florida, 2007).

Timothy Larson, *Crisis of Doubt: Honest Faith in Nineteenth-century England* (Oxford: Oxford University Press, 2009).

Chaeyoon Lim, Carol Ann MacGregor and Robert D. Putnam, 'Secular and luminal: heterogeneity among religious nones', *Journal for the Scientific Study of Religion* vol. 49 (2010), pp. 596–618.

Charlotte Linde, *Life Stories: The Creation of Coherence* (New York: Oxford University Press, 1993).

Michael Lipka, 'A closer look at America's rapidly growing religious "nones"' (May 2015) at pewresearch.org (accessed 22 November 2015).

Gareth Longden, 'A profile of the members of the British Humanist Association', *Science, Religion and Culture* vol. 2 (2015), pp. 86–95.

Gordon Lynch, *Losing My Religion? Moving on from Evangelical Faith* (London: Darton, Longman and Todd, 2003).

Dale McGowan (ed.), *Parenting beyond Belief: On Raising Ethical, Caring Kids without Religion* (n.p.: Amacon, 2007).

Liam McLaughlin, 'Is it harder to "come out" as an atheist if you're black?', *New Statesman*, 7 August 2013.

Hugh McLeod, 'New perspectives in Victorian working-class religion: the oral evidence', *Oral History* vol. 14 (1986), pp. 31–49.

Hugh McLeod (ed.), *European Religion in the Age of Great Cities 1830–1930* (London: Routledge, 1995).

Hugh McLeod, *Secularisation in Western Europe, 1848–1914* (Basingstoke: Macmillan, 2000).

Hugh McLeod, *The Religious Crisis of the 1960s* (Oxford: Oxford University Press, 2007).

Sarfraz Manzoor, 'Why Nazeem had to lead a double life', *The Guardian, Family*, 21 March 2015, pp. 1a–2c.

Arthur Marwick, *The Sixties: Social and Cultural Transformation in Britain, France, Italy and the United States, 1958–74* (Oxford: Oxford University Press, 1998).

Kristina Minister, 'A feminist frame for the oral history interview', in Sherna Berger Gluck and Daphne Patai (eds), *Women's Words: The Feminist Practice of Oral History* (New York: Routledge, 1991), pp. 27–41.

Deborah Mitchell, *Growing Up Godless: A Parent's Guide to Raising Kids without Religion* (New York: Sterling Ethos, 2014).

Jeremy Morris, 'Secularization and religious experience: arguments in the historiography of modern British religion', *Historical Journal* vol. 55 (2012), pp. 195–219.

David Nash, *Blasphemy in Modern Britain: 1789 to the Present* (Aldershot, Ashgate, 1999).

David Nash, *Blasphemy in the Christian World: A History* (Oxford: Oxford University Press, 2007).

David Nash, *Christian Ideals in British Culture: Stories of Belief in the Twentieth Century* (Basingstoke: Palgrave Macmillan, 2013).

Juhem Navarro-Rivera, 'The evolution of the religiously unaffiliated vote, 1980–2008' (2012) at http://publicreligion.org/2012/10/the-evolution-of-the-religiously-unaffiliated-vote-1980-2008/#.Vh_kI7tdEiF (accessed 15 October 2015).

Holger Nehring, '"The Long, Long Night is Over." The Campaign for Nuclear Disarmament, "Generation" and the politics of religion (1957–1964)', in Jane Garnett et al. (eds), *Redefining Christian Britain: Post 1945 Perspectives* (London: SCM Press, 2007), pp. 138–147.

David A. Nock, 'Cult, sect and church in Canada: a re-examination of Stark and Bainbridge', *Canadian Review of Sociology and Anthropology* vol. 24 (1987), pp. 514–525.

ONS, Census 2011 at http://www.ons.gov.uk/ons/rel/census/2011-census

Doug Owram, *Born at the Right Time: A History of the Baby Boom Generation* (Toronto, ON: University of Toronto Press, 1997).

Stephen Parker, *Faith on the Home Front: Aspects of Church Life and Popular Religion in Birmingham 1939–1945* (Bern: Peter Lang, 2005).

Christopher Partridge, *The Re-enchantment of the West*, 2 volumes (London: Bloomsbury, 2005 and 2006).

Pew Research Center, *America's Changing Religious Landscape* (Pew Research Center, May 2015) at http://www.pewforum.org/2015/05/12/americas-changing-religious-landscape/ (accessed 25 October 2015).

Anthony B. Pinn, *Writing God's Obituary: How a Good Methodist Became a Better Atheist* (Amherst, NY: Prometheus Books, 2014).

S. Pixer, 'The oyster and the shadow', in Liz Heron (ed.), *Truth, Dare or Promise: Girls Growing Up in the Fifties* (London: Virago, 1985).

Alessandro Portelli, 'Oral history as genre', in M. Chamberlain and P. Thompson (ed.), *Narrative and Genre: Contexts and Types of Communication* (London: Routledge, 2004).

Ernest Poser, 'On being a Jewish "Geschmattet"', in David Ibry (ed.), *Exodus to Humanism: Jewish Identity without Religion* (Amherst, NY: Prometheus, 1999), pp. 95–103.

Robert D. Putnam, *Bowling Alone: The Collapse and Revival of American Community* (New York: Simon & Shuster, 2000).

Robert D. Putnam and David E. Campbell, *American Grace: How Religion Divided and Unites Us* (New York: Simon & Shuster, 2010).

Susan Reynolds, 'Social mentalities and the case of medieval scepticism', *Transactions of the Royal Historical Society* vol. 1 (1991), pp. 21–41.

Alex Robertson, *Lifestyle Survey* (Edinburgh: Church of Scotland, 1987).

Eugene C. Roehlkepatain, Pamela Edstyne King, Linda Wagener and Peter L. Benson (eds), *The Handbook of Spiritual Development in Childhood and Adolescence* (London: Sage, 2006).

Carole Garibaldi Rogers, *Poverty, Chastity, and Change: Lives of Contemporary American Nuns* (Woodbridge, CT: Twayne, 1996).

Kim Lacy Rogers, Selma Leydesdorff and Graham Dawson (eds), *Trauma and Life Stories* (London: Routledge, 2014).

Wade Clark Roof, *A Generation of Seekers: The Spiritual Journeys of the Baby Boom Generation* (San Francisco, CA: Harper, 1993).

Wade Clark Roof, *Spiritual Marketplace: Baby Boomers and the Remaking of American Religion* (Princeton, NJ: Princeton University Press, 1999).

Michael Roper, 'Slipping out of view: subjectivity and emotion in gender history', *History Workshop Journal* vol. 59 (2005), pp. 57–72.

Anne Ross-Smith and Martin Kornberger, 'Gendered rationality? A genealogical exploration of the philosophical and sociological conceptions of rationality, masculinity and organization', *Gender, Work & Organization* vol. 11 (2004), pp. 280–305.

Sheila Rowbotham, *The Past Is before Us: Feminism in Action since the 1960s* (London: Pandora, 1989).

Edward Royle, *Victorian Infidels. The Origins of the British Secularist Movement 1791–1866* (Manchester: Manchester University Press, 1974).

Edward Royle, *Radicals, Secularists and Republicans: Popular Freethought in Britain 1866–1915* (Manchester: Manchester University Press, 1980).

Tatjana Schnell, 'Dimensions of Secularity (DoS): an open inventory to measure facets of secular identities', *International Journal for the Psychology of Religion* vol. 25 (2015), pp. 272–292.

Laura Schwartz, *Infidel Feminism: Secularism, Religion and Women's Emancipation 1830–1914* (Manchester: Manchester University Press, 2013).

Anthony Serafini, *Linus Pauling: A Man and His Science* (London: Simon & Schuster, 1989).

Michael Shermer, 'Is God dying? The decline of religion and the rise of the "nones"', *Scientific American* vol. 309 (19 November 2013).

Shlomo Sand, *How I Stopped Being a Jew* (London: Verso, 2014).

Christian Smith, *Soul Searching: The Religious and Spiritual Lives of American Teenagers* (Oxford: Oxford University Press, 2005).

Christian Smith, Karl Christoffersen, Hilary Davidson and Patricia Snell Herzog, *Lost in Transition: The Dark Side of Emerging Adulthood* (Oxford: Oxford University Press, 2011).

T.C. Smout, 'Born again at Cambuslang: new evidence on popular religion and literacy in eighteenth-century Scotland', *Past and Present* no. 97 (1982), pp. 114–127.

Michael Snape, *God and the British Soldier: Religion and the British Army in the First and Second World Wars* (London: Routledge, 2005).

Rodney Stark, *What Americans Really Believe: New Findings from the Baylor Surveys of Religion* (Waco, TX: Baylor University Press, 2008).

Rodney Stark and William S. Bainbridge, 'Cults in America: a reconnaissance in space and time', in M.E. Harty (ed.), *Modern American Protestantism and Its World: 11: New and Intense Movements* (Munich: K.G. Saur, 1993), pp. 278–353.

Rodney Stark, Eva Hamberg and Alan S. Miller, 'Exploring spirituality and unchurched religions in America, Sweden, and Japan', *Journal of Contemporary Religion* vol. 20 (2005), pp. 3–23.

Statistics Canada, 2011 National Household Survey, Statistics Canada Catalogue no. 99-010–X2011032.

Leslie Stephen, *An Agnostic's Apology and Other Essays* (London: Smith, Elder and Co., 1893).

Penny Summerfield, *Reconstructing Women's Wartime Lives: Discourse and Subjectivity in Oral Histories of the Second World War* (Manchester: Manchester University Press, 1998).

Richard Sykes, 'Popular religion in decline: a study from the black country', *Journal of Ecclesiastical History* vol. 56 (2005), pp. 287–307.

Charles Taylor, *A Secular Age* (Cambridge: Belknap, 2007).

Keith Thomas, *Ends of Life: Roads to Fulfilment on Early Modern England* (Oxford: Oxford University Press, 2009).

Alistair Thomson, 'Anzac memories revisited: trauma, memory and oral history', *Oral History Review* vol. 42 (2015), pp. 1–29.

Andrew Totten, 'Coherent chaplaincy', *Journal of the Royal Army Chaplains' Department* vol. 45 (2006).

Norman Vance, *Sinews of the Spirit: The Ideal of Christian Manliness in Victorian Literature and Religious Thought* (Cambridge: Cambridge University Press, 1985).

David Voas, 'The rise and fall of fuzzy fidelity in Europe', *European Sociological Review* vol. 25 (2009), pp. 155–168.

David Voas and Abby Day, *Recognizing Secular Christians: Toward an Unexcluded Middle in the Study of Religion* (2010) at http://www.thearda.com/rrh/papers/guidingpapers.asp (accessed 24 November 2014).

David Voas and Laura Watt, 'Numerical change in church attendance: national, local and individual factors' (2014) at http://www.churchgrowthresearch.org.uk/progress_findings_reports (accessed 20 December 2015).

Nicolas Walter, 'McCabe, Joseph Martin (1867–1955)', *Oxford Dictionary of National Biography* (Oxford University Press, 2004; online edn, October 2009) at http://www.oxforddnb.com.ezproxy.lib.gla.ac.uk/view/article/34674, (accessed 28 April 2016).

Kevin Ward, *A History of Global Anglicanism* (Cambridge: Cambridge University Press, 2006).

Peter Watson, *The Age of Nothing: How We Have Sought to Live since the Death of God* (London: Weidenfeld & Nicolson, 2014).

Tim Whitmarsh, *Battling the Gods: Atheism in the Ancient World* (New York: Alfred A Knopf, 2015).

Sarah Wilkins-Laflamme, *Report: Religion in Canada* (2014) at http://www.ceetum.umontreal.ca/documents/capsules/2014/wilk-en-2014.pdf

Sarah Williams, *Religious Belief and Popular Culture in Southwark, c.1880–1939* (Oxford: Oxford University Press, 1999).

Bryan Wilson, *Religion in Secular Society* (Harmondsworth: Penguin, 1966).

John Wilson and Darren E. Sherkat, 'Returning to the fold', *Journal for the Scientific Study of Religion* vol. 33(1994), pp. 148–161.

Linda Woodhead, '"No Religion" is the new religion', Press Release on YouGov Poll, 23 December 2013 at http://www.brin.ac.uk/news/2013/end-of-year-round-up/ (accessed 18 October 2014).

D.M. Wulff, *Psychology of Religion: Classic and Contemporary Views* (New York: Wiley, 1991).

Robert Wuthnow, *The Restructuring of American Religion: Society and Faith since World War II* (Princeton: Princeton University Press, 1988).

Phil Zuckerman, *Society without God: What the Least Religious Nations Can Tell about Contentment* (New York: New York University Press, 2008).

Phil Zuckerman, *Faith No More: Why People Reject Religion* (New York: Oxford University Press, 2012).

Phil Zuckerman, *Living the Secular Life: New Answers to Old Questions* (New York: Penguin, 2014).

Unpublished work

Susan Wiltshire, 'Spirit of our age: dimensions of religiosity among Scottish youth', unpublished PhD thesis, University of Edinburgh, 2001.

Websites (active at time of writing)

http://www.gla.ac.uk/schools/humanities/staff/callumbrown/modernhumanismasocialandculturalhistory/#d.en.287899.
www.engender.org.uk
http://www.nhs-chaplaincy-spiritualcare.org.uk/
www.motherandbabyhomes.com
http://raisingkidswithoutreligion.net;
Secular Earth on Facebook
http://en.wikipedia.org/wiki/Barry_Beyerstein
www.sofn.org.uk/
http://www.blackpast.org/aah/allen-norman-robert-jr-1957
https://circle.org/who-we-are/our-values/
https://en.wikipedia.org/wiki/Narendra_Nayak
www.ohara.com
https://www.facebook.com/cesosaco/posts/320356898001193
https://en.wikipedia.org/wiki/Demographics_of_atheism#cite_ref-93

INDEX

Note: In the index, 'resp.' indicates a respondent of the project; 'arch. resp.' indicates an archive respondent (from an existing oral history collection); 'pseud.' indicates a respondent who wished to be identified by a pseudonym. Locators with an 'n' indicate note numbers.